A HISTORY OF
THE CRUSADES

VOLUME I
THE FIRST CRUSADE
and the
Foundation of the Kingdom of Jerusalem

BY

STEVEN RUNCIMAN

CAMBRIDGE
UNIVERSITY PRESS

Published by the Press Syndicate of the University of Cambridge
The Pitt Building, Trumpington Street, Cambridge CB2 IRP
40 West 20th Street, New York, NY 10011-4211, USA
10 Stamford Road, Oakleigh, Victoria 3166, Australia

First published in hardback 1951
First published in paperback by Cambridge University Press 1987
Reprinted 1951, 1953, 1954, 1957, 1962, 1968, 1975,
1980, 1987, 1988, 1989, 1990, 1992

Printed in the United States of America

Library of Congress catalog card number: 75-10236

Volume I: ISBN 0-521-06161-X hardback
            ISBN 0-521-34770-X paperback
Volume II: ISBN 0-521-06162-8 hardback
            ISBN 0-521-34771-8 paperback
Volume III: ISBN 0-521-06163-6 hardback
            ISBN 0-521-34772-6 paperback
Set of three volumes: ISBN 0-521-20554-9 hardback
            ISBN 0-521-35997-X paperback

Paperback editions for sale in USA only

To
MY MOTHER

CONTENTS

Contents

LIST OF PLATES

frontispiece

A knight of the late eleventh century
(From a fresco at Tavant. Reproduced from *Les Fresques de Tavant* by permission of Les Editions du Chêne, Paris)

between pp. 178 and 179

LIST OF MAPS

PREFACE

This book is intended to be the first volume of three, to cover the history of the movement that we call the Crusades, from its birth in the eleventh century to its decline in the fourteenth, and of the states that it created in the Holy Land and in neighbouring countries. I hope in a second volume to give a history and description of the kingdom of Jerusalem and its relations with the peoples of the Near East, and of the Crusades of the twelfth century, and in a third a history of the kingdom of Acre and the later Crusades.

Whether we regard them as the most tremendous and most romantic of Christian adventures or as the last of the barbarian invasions, the Crusades form a central fact in medieval history. Before their inception the centre of our civilization was placed in Byzantium and in the lands of the Arab Caliphate. Before they faded out the hegemony in civilization had passed to western Europe. Out of this transference modern history was born; but to understand it we must understand not only the circumstances in western Europe that led to the Crusading impulse but, perhaps still more, the circumstances in the East that gave to the Crusaders their opportunity and shaped their progress and their withdrawal. Our glance must move from the Atlantic to Mongolia. To tell the story from the point of view of the Franks alone or of the Arabs alone or even of its chief victims, the Christians of the East, is to miss its significance. For, as Gibbon saw, it was the story of the World's Debate.

The whole story has not often been told in English; nor has there ever been in this country an active school of Crusading historiography. Gibbon's chapters in the *Decline and Fall* still, despite his prejudices and the date at which he wrote, well deserve study. More recently we have Sir Ernest Barker's brilliant summary of the movement, first published in the *Encyclopaedia Britannica*, and

W. B. Stevenson's short but admirable history of the Crusading kingdoms. But the British contribution consists mainly in learned articles, in the edition of oriental sources and in a few unscholarly histories. France and Germany have a larger and longer tradition. The great German histories of the Crusades begin with Wilken's, published early in the nineteenth century. Von Sybel's history, first published in 1841, is still of prime importance; and later in the century two fine scholars, Röhricht and Hagenmeyer, not only did invaluable work in the collection and criticism of source-material but themselves wrote comprehensive histories. Of recent years the German tradition has been maintained by Erdmann in his exhaustive study of the religious movements in the West that led to the Crusades. In France, the land from which the greater number of the Crusaders originally came, the interest of scholars was shown by the publication in the middle of the nineteenth century of the main sources, western, Greek and oriental, in the huge *Recueil des Historiens des Croisades*. Michaud's vast history had already appeared in the years following 1817. Later in the century Riant and his collaborators in the *Société de l'Orient Latin* produced much valuable work. In this century two distinguished French Byzantinists, Chalandon and Bréhier, turned their attention to the Crusades; and shortly before the war of 1939 M. Grousset produced his three-volume history of the Crusades, which, in the French tradition, combines wide learning with good writing and a touch of Gallic patriotism. Now, however, it is in the United States that the most active school of Crusading historians can be found, created by D. C. Munro, whose regrettably small literary output belied his importance as a teacher. The American historians have hitherto concentrated on detailed aspects, and none of them has yet attempted a full general history. But they have promised us a composite volume, in which some foreign scholars will join, to cover the whole range of Crusading history. I regret that it has not appeared in time for me to profit by it when writing this volume.

It may seem unwise for one British pen to compete with the massed typewriters of the United States. But in fact there is no

competition. A single author cannot speak with the high authority
of a panel of experts, but he may succeed in giving to his work an
integrated and even an epical quality that no composite volume
can achieve. Homer as well as Herodotus was a Father of History,
as Gibbon, the greatest of our historians, was aware; and it is
difficult, in spite of certain critics, to believe that Homer was a panel.
History-writing to-day has passed into an Alexandrian age, where
criticism has overpowered creation. Faced by the mountainous
heap of the minutiae of knowledge and awed by the watchful
severity of his colleagues, the modern historian too often takes
refuge in learned articles or narrowly specialized dissertations,
small fortresses that are easy to defend from attack. His work can
be of the highest value; but it is not an end in itself. I believe that
the supreme duty of the historian is to write history, that is to say,
to attempt to record in one sweeping sequence the greater events
and movements that have swayed the destinies of man. The writer
rash enough to make the attempt should not be criticized for his
ambition, however much he may deserve censure for the in-
adequacy of his equipment or the inanity of his results.

I give in my notes the authority for the statements that I make
and in my bibliography a list of the works that I have consulted.
To many of them my debt is enormous, even if I do not specifically
quote them in my notes. The friends who have given me helpful
criticism and advice are too numerous to be recorded by name.

A note is needed about the transliteration of names. Where
Christian names occur that have an accepted English form, such as
John or Godfrey or Raymond, it would be pedantic to use any
other form; and I have always tried to use the form most familiar
and therefore most acceptable to the average English reader. For
Greek words I have used the traditional Latin transliteration, which
alone allows for uniformity. Arabic names present a greater
difficulty. The dots and rough breathings enjoined by specialists
in Arabic make difficult reading. I have omitted them, but hope
that my system is nevertheless clear. In Armenian, where *k* and *g*,

and *b* and *p*, are alternatively correct according to the period or the locality of the word, I have kept to the more ancient equivalent. The French *de* presents a permanent problem. Except where it can be regarded as part of a definite surname, I have translated it.

In conclusion I should like to thank the Syndics and the Secretary of the Cambridge University Press for their unfailing kindness and help.

STEVEN RUNCIMAN

LONDON 1950

BOOK I

THE HOLY PLACES OF CHRISTENDOM

CHAPTER I

THE ABOMINATION OF DESOLATION

'When ye therefore shall see the abomination of desolation, spoken of by Daniel the prophet, stand in the holy place.' ST MATTHEW XXIV, 15

On a February day in the year A.D. 638 the Caliph Omar entered Jerusalem, riding upon a white camel. He was dressed in worn, filthy robes, and the army that followed him was rough and unkempt; but its discipline was perfect. At his side was the Patriarch Sophronius, as chief magistrate of the surrendered city. Omar rode straight to the site of the Temple of Solomon, whence his friend Mahomet had ascended into Heaven. Watching him stand there, the Patriarch remembered the words of Christ and murmured through his tears: 'Behold the abomination of desolation, spoken of by Daniel the prophet.'

Next, the Caliph asked to see the shrines of the Christians. The Patriarch took him to the Church of the Holy Sepulchre and showed him all that was there. While they were in the church the hour for Moslem prayer approached. The Caliph asked where he could spread out his prayer-rug. Sophronius begged him to stay where he was; but Omar went outside to the porch of the Martyrion, for fear, he said, lest his zealous followers might claim for Islam the place wherein he had prayed. And so indeed it was. The porch was taken over by the Moslems, but the church remained as it had been, the holiest sanctuary of Christendom.[1]

[1] Theophanes, ad ann. 6127, p. 333; Eutychius, *Annales*, col. 1099; Michael the Syrian, vol. II, pp. 425–6; Elias of Nisibin, p. 64. An excellent summary of the sources is given in Vincent and Abel, *Jérusalem Nouvelle*, vol. II, pp. 930–2.

3

This was according to the terms of the city's surrender. The Prophet himself had ordained that, while the heathen should be offered the choice of conversion or death, the People of the Book, the Christians and the Jews (with whom by courtesy he included the Zoroastrians) should be allowed to retain their places of worship and to use them without hindrance, but they might not add to their number, nor might they carry arms nor ride on horseback; and they must pay a special capitation tax, known as the *jizya*.[1] Sophronius cannot have hoped for better terms when he rode out on his ass under safe conduct to meet the Caliph on the Mount of Olives, refusing to hand over his city to anyone of lesser authority. Jerusalem had been beleaguered for over a year; and the Arabs, inexperienced in siege-warfare and ill equipped for it, were powerless against the newly repaired fortifications. But within the city provisions had run low; and there was no longer any hope of relief. The countryside was in the hands of the Arabs, and one by one the towns of Syria and Palestine had fallen to them. There was no Christian army left nearer than Egypt, except for the garrison holding out at Caesarea on the coast, protected by the imperial navy. All that Sophronius could obtain from the conqueror in addition to the usual terms was that the imperial officials in the city might retire in safety with their families and their portable possessions to the coast at Caesarea.

This was the Patriarch's last public achievement, the tragic climax to a long life spent in labour for the orthodoxy and unity of Christendom. Ever since the days of his youth, when he had travelled round the monasteries of the East with his friend, John Moschus, gathering for their *Spiritual Meadow* sayings and stories of the saints, to his later years, when the Emperor whose policy he opposed appointed him to the great see of Jerusalem, he had fought steadfastly against the heresies and nascent nationalism that he foresaw would dismember the Empire. But the 'honey-tongued defender of the Faith', as he was named, had preached and worked

[1] See the article 'Djizya' by Becker in the *Encyclopaedia of Islam*, and Browne, *The Eclipse of Christianity in Asia*, pp. 29–31.

in vain. The Arab conquest was proof of his failure; and a few weeks later he died of a broken heart.[1]

Indeed, no human agency could have stopped the disruptive movements in the eastern provinces of Rome. Throughout the history of the Roman Empire there had been a latent struggle between East and West. The West had won at Actium; but the East overcame its conquerors. Egypt and Syria were the richest and most populous provinces of the Empire. They contained its main centres of industry; their ships and caravans controlled the trade with the Orient; their culture, both spiritual and material, was far higher than that of the West, not only because of their long traditions but also because of the stimulus given by the proximity of Rome's only rival in civilization, the kingdom of Sassanid Persia. Inevitably the influence of the East grew greater; till at last the Emperor Constantine the Great adopted an eastern religion and moved his capital eastward, to Byzantium on the Bosphorus. In the next century, when the Empire, weakened by internal decay, had to face the onrush of the barbarians, the West perished, but the East survived, thanks largely to Constantine's policy. While barbarian kingdoms were established in Gaul, in Spain, in Africa, in distant Britain, and finally in Italy, the Roman Emperor ruled the eastern provinces from Constantinople. The government at Rome had seldom been popular in Syria and Egypt. The government at Constantinople was soon even more bitterly resented. To a large extent this was due to outside circumstances. The impoverishment of the West meant the loss of markets for the Syrian merchant and the Egyptian manufacturer. Constant wars with Persia interrupted the trade route that went across the desert to Antioch and the cities of the Lebanon; and a little later the fall of the Abyssinian empire and chaos in Arabia closed down the Red Sea routes controlled by the sailors of Egypt and the caravan-owners of Petra, Transjordan

---

[1] Σωφρόνιος δέ, ὁ μελίγλωσσος τῆς ἀληθείας πρόμαχος in Mansi, *Concilia, Nova Collectio*, vol. x, col. 607. It is now established that Sophronius the Patriarch and Sophronius the friend of Moschus are identical (see Usener, *Der Heilige Tychon*, pp. 85–104).

and southern Palestine. Constantinople was becoming the chief market of the Empire; and the far eastern trade, encouraged by the Emperor's diplomacy, sought a direct, more northerly route thither, across the steppes of central Asia. This was bitter to the citizens of Alexandria and Antioch, jealous already of the upstart city that threatened to overshadow them. It embittered the Syrians and Egyptians still more that the new governmental system was based on centralization. Local rights and autonomies were steadily curtailed; and the tax-collector was stricter and more exigent than in the old Roman days. Discontent gave new vigour to the nationalism of the East, which never slumbers for long.

The struggle broke out openly over matters of religion. The pagan emperors had been tolerant of local cults. Local gods could so easily be fitted into the Roman pantheon. Only obstinate monotheists, such as the Christians and the Jews, suffered an occasional bout of persecution. But the Christian emperors could not be so tolerant. Christianity is an exclusive religion; and they wished to use it as a unifying force to bind all their subjects to the government. Constantine, himself a little vague on matters of theology, had sought to unite the Church then torn by the Arian controversy. Half a century later Theodosius the Great made conformity part of the imperial programme. But conformity was not easily obtained. The East had taken avidly to Christianity. The Greeks had applied to its problems their taste for subtle disputation; to which the hellenized orientals added a fierce, passionate intensity that soon bred intolerance and hate. The main subject of their disputes was the nature of Christ, the central and most difficult question in all Christian theology. The argument was theological; but in those days even the man in the street took an interest in theological argument, which ranked in his eyes as a recreation only surpassed by the games at the circus. But there were other aspects as well. The average Syrian and Egyptian desired a simpler ceremonial than that of the Orthodox Church with all its pomp. Its luxury offended him in his growing poverty. Still more, he regarded its prelates and priests as the agents of the government at

Constantinople. His higher clergy were from jealousy easily persuaded into a like hostility. The Patriarchs of the ancient sees of Alexandria and Antioch were furious to find their upstart brother of Constantinople raised in precedence above them. It was inevitable that heresy should arise and should assume the form of a nationalistic and disruptive movement.

Arianism soon died out in the East, except in Abyssinia; but the heresies of the fifth century were more enduring. Early in the century, Nestorius, the Syrian-born Patriarch of Constantinople, promulgated a doctrine that overstressed the humanity of Christ. The theologians of the Antiochene school had always leaned in that direction; and Nestorius found many followers in northern Syria. His doctrine was denounced as heresy at the Oecumenical Council of Ephesus in 431; whereupon many Syrian congregations seceded. The Nestorians, proscribed in the Empire, made their headquarters in the territory of the king of Persia, in Mesopotamia. They soon turned their main attention to missionary work in the further East, in India, in Turkestan and even in China; but in the sixth and seventh centuries they still maintained churches in Syria and in Egypt, chiefly amongst merchants engaged in the far eastern trade.

The Nestorian controversy gave rise to another, still more bitter. The theologians of Alexandria, delighted at a double victory over Antiochene doctrines and a Patriarch of Constantinople, themselves overstepped the limits of orthodoxy in the opposite direction. They put forward a doctrine that seemed to imply a denial of Christ's humanity. This heresy is sometimes called Eutychianism after an obscure priest, Eutyches, who first suggested it. It is more usually known as Monophysitism. In 451 it was denounced by the fourth Oecumenical Council, meeting at Chalcedon; and the Monophysites in indignation broke off from the main body of Christendom, taking with them the majority of the Christians of Egypt and a number of congregations in Syria. The Armenian Church, whose delegates had arrived at Chalcedon too late for the discussions, refused to accept the Council's findings and ranged

7

themselves with the Monophysites. Later Emperors searched unceasingly for some conciliatory formula that would cover the breach and which, endorsed by an Oecumenical Council, could be accepted as a further precision of the true Faith. But two factors worked against them. The heretics did not particularly want to return to the fold, except on their own unacceptable terms; and the attitude of Rome and the western Church was steadfastly hostile to compromise. Pope Leo I, basing himself on the view that it was for the successor of Saint Peter and not for an Oecumenical Council to define the creed, and impatient of dialectical subtleties that he did not understand, issued a definitive statement of the correct opinion on the question. This statement, known in history as the *Tomus of Pope Leo*, though it ignored the delicacies of the argument, was accepted by the Council authorities at Chalcedon as a basis for their discussions, and its formula was embodied in their findings. Pope Leo's formula was clear-cut and crude, admitting of no gloss nor modification. Any compromise that would placate the heretics would involve its abandonment and in consequence a schism with Rome. This no emperor with interests and ambitions in Italy and the West could afford. Caught in this dilemma, the imperial government never evolved a consistent policy. It hovered between the persecution and the appeasement of the heretics; while they grew in strength in the provinces of the East, backed by the resurgent nationalism of the orientals.[1]

Besides the Monophysites and the Nestorians, there was another community in the eastern provinces that was constantly opposed to the imperial government, that of the Jews. There were Jews established in considerable numbers in all the great cities of the East. They were under certain civil disabilities; and occasionally

---

[1] The best account of the early history of the Nestorian and Monophysite churches is given in Vacant and Mangenot, *Dictionnaire de Théologie Catholique*, articles on 'Nestorius', by Amann, and 'Monophysitisme', by Jugie, and in the chapters by Bardy in vol. IV, and by Bréhier in vols. IV and V, of the *Histoire de l'Eglise*, ed. by Fliche and Martin.

they and their property would suffer damage in some riot. In return they seized every opportunity for doing harm to the Christians. Their financial resources and their widespread connections made them a potential danger to the government.[1]

During the sixth century the situation worsened. Justinian's wars in the West were long and costly. They embarrassed his religious policy, and they meant higher taxes and no compensating advantages for his eastern subjects. Syria suffered the worst; for in addition to her fiscal burden she underwent a series of cruel raids by Persian armies and a series of disastrous earthquakes. Only the heretics flourished. The Monophysites of Syria were organized into a powerful force by Jacob Baradaeus of Edessa, backed by the sympathy of the Empress Theodora. Their Church was henceforward usually known as the Jacobite. The Monophysites of Egypt, now called the Copts, included almost the whole native population. The Nestorians, safely entrenched beyond the Persian frontier and expanding rapidly eastward, consolidated their position within the Empire. Except in the cities of Palestine the Orthodox were a minority. They were named contemptuously the Melkites, the Emperor's men, with good reason, for their existence depended upon the power and prestige of the imperial administration.[2]

In 602 the centurion Phocas seized the imperial throne. His rule was savage and incompetent; and while Constantinople suffered a reign of terror, the provinces were given over to riots and civil war between the circus factions of the cities and between the rival religious sects. At Antioch the Jacobite and Nestorian Patriarchs openly held a joint council to discuss common action against the Orthodox. Phocas punished them by sending an army which slaughtered vast numbers of heretics, with the Jews gleefully giving

---

[1] For the arbitrary but not very oppressive imperial legislation against the Jews, see Bury, *Later Roman Empire* (A.D. 395–565), vol. II, p. 366, and Krauss, *Studien zur byzantinisch-jüdischen Geschichten*, pp. 1–36.

[2] See Bréhier, *op. cit.* vol. IV, pp. 489–93; Devreesse, *Le Patriarchat d'Antioche*, pp. 77–99.

their aid. Two years later the Jews themselves rose, and tortured and slew the Orthodox Patriarch of the city.[1]

In 610 Phocas was displaced by a young nobleman of Armenian descent, Heraclius, son of the governor of Africa. That same year King Chosroes II of Persia completed his preparations for the invasion and dismemberment of the Empire. The Persian war lasted for nineteen years. For twelve years the Empire was on the defensive, while one Persian army occupied Anatolia and another conquered Syria. Antioch fell in 611, Damascus in 613. In the spring of 614 the Persian general Shahrbaraz entered Palestine, pillaging the countryside and burning churches as he went. Only the Church of the Nativity at Bethlehem was spared, because of the mosaic over the door that depicted the Wise Men from the East in Persian costume. On 15 April he invested Jerusalem. The Patriarch Zacharias had been prepared to surrender the city to avoid bloodshed; but the Christian inhabitants refused to yield so tamely. On 5 May, with the help of Jews within the walls, the Persians forced their way into the city. There followed scenes of utter horror. With their churches and houses in flames around them, the Christians were indiscriminately massacred, some by the Persian soldiery and many more by the Jews. Sixty thousand were said to have perished and thirty-five thousand more were sold into slavery. The sacred relics of the city, the Holy Cross and the instruments of the Passion, had been hidden, but they were unearthed and were sent, together with the Patriarch, eastward as a gift to the Christian queen of Persia, the Nestorian Meryem. The devastation in and round the city was so vast that to this day the countryside has never fully recovered.[2]

[1] Theophanes, ad ann. 6101, p. 296; John of Nikiu, p. 166; Sebeos, pp. 113–14; Eutychius, *Annales*, col. 1084 (telling of riots in Tyre); *Chronicon Paschale*, p. 699 (attributing the murder of the Patriarch to rioting soldiers); Kulakovsky, 'Criticism of evidence in Theophanes' (in Russian), in *Vizantiiski Vremennik*, vol. XXI, pp. 1–14, and *History of Byzantium*, vol. III (in Russian), pp. 12–15, who collates the evidence and fixes the date.
[2] Antiochus the Stratege, pp. 9–15; Sebeos, pp. 130–1; *Anon. Guidi*, p. 3; *Chronicon Paschale*, pp. 704–5; Theophanes, ad ann. 6106, pp. 300–1. The

Three years later the Persians advanced into Egypt. Within a year they were its masters. Meanwhile, to the north, their armies had reached the Bosphorus.[1]

The fall of Jerusalem had been a terrible shock to Christendom. The part played by the Jews was never forgotten nor forgiven; and the war against the Persians assumed the nature of a holy war. When at last Heraclius was able, in 622, to take the offensive against the enemy, he solemnly dedicated himself and his army to God and set out as a Christian warrior fighting the powers of darkness. To subsequent generations he figured as the first of the Crusaders. William of Tyre, writing his history of the Crusades five centuries later, includes the story of the Persian war; and the old French translation of his book was known as the *Livre d'Eracles*.[2]

The Crusade was successful. After many vicissitudes, many moments of anxiety and despair, Heraclius at last defeated the Persians at Nineveh, in December 627. Early in 628 King Chosroes was murdered and his successor sued for peace; though it was not till 629 that the peace was established and the conquered provinces restored to the Empire. In August Heraclius celebrated his triumph in Constantinople. Next spring he journeyed south again, to receive back the Holy Cross and to carry it in pomp to Jerusalem.

It was a moving scene. Yet the Christians of the East had not fared badly under Persian rule. Chosroes had soon withdrawn his favour from the Jews and had even expelled them from Jerusalem. While his court favoured the Nestorians, he was, officially, equally benevolent towards the Monophysites and the Orthodox. Their churches were restored to them and rebuilt; and a council was held under his patronage at Ctesiphon, his capital, to discuss the reunion of the sects. The return of the imperial administration, once the

---

incident of the mosaics at Bethlehem is given in the letter of the eastern Patriarchs to Theophilus, in Migne, *Patrologia Graeco-Latina*, vol. xcv, cols. 380–1.

[1] For the history of the Persian war see Kulakovsky, *History of Byzantium*, vol. iii, pp. 33–49; Ostrogorsky, *Geschichte des byzantinischen Staates*, pp. 51–66; Bréhier, *op. cit.* pp. 79–101; Pernice, *L'Imperatore Eraclio*, pp. 58–179, *passim*.

[2] William of Tyre, i, 1–2, vol. i, pt. i, pp. 9–13. The full title of the old French translation is *L'Estoire de Eracles, Empereur, et la Conqueste de la Terre d'Outremer*.

first enthusiasm died down, was seen to benefit the Orthodox alone. Heraclius had inherited an empty treasury. He had only been able to finance his wars by a great loan from the Church. The booty taken from Persia was not enough to repay it. The Syrians and Egyptians found themselves once again obliged to pay high taxes and to see their money go to swell the coffers of the Orthodox hierarchy.[1]

Nor did Heraclius help matters by his religious policy. First, he took action against the Jews. He had not felt any animosity towards them; but, whilst he was actually staying with a hospitable Jew at Tiberias on his way to Jerusalem, he learnt full details of the part that they had played during the Persian invasions. Moved too, perhaps, by a vague prophecy that a circumcised race would ruin the Empire, he ordered the compulsory baptism of all Jews within the Empire, and he wrote to the kings of the West to urge them to follow suit. The order was impossible to execute; but it gave zealous Christians a fine opportunity for the massacring of the hated race. The only ultimate result was to make the Jews even more resentful of imperial rule.[2] Next, the Emperor plunged into the dangerous waters of Christian theology. The Patriarch Sergius of Constantinople, himself a Syrian Monophysite by birth, had gradually evolved a doctrine that, he thought, would reconcile Monophysites and Orthodox. Heraclius gave it his approval; and the new doctrine, known in history as Monoenergism, was promulgated throughout the Empire as soon as the Persian wars were over. But despite the advocacy of the Emperor and the Patriarch and the cautious approval of the Roman pontiff Honorius, it was universally unpopular. The Monophysite hierarchy rejected it at

---

[1] The Council of Ctesiphon is described in Sebeos, pp. 189–92, and *Anon. Guidi*, p. 20. The latter probably over-emphasizes the role of the Nestorians and their success.

[2] A full account, with references, is given in Bréhier, *op. cit.* pp. 108–11. Theophanes, ad ann. 6120, pp. 328–9 and Eutychius, col. 1089, are the main sources. The decree ordering the baptism of the Jews is recorded in Dölger, *Regesten*, no. 206, vol. I, p. 24. See also the *Doctrina Jacobi*, ed. by Bonwetsch, p. 88.

once. The majority of the Orthodox, led by the great mystic, Maximus the Confessor, in Constantinople, and by Sophronius in the East, found it equally unacceptable. Heraclius, with more en-thusiasm than tact, tried hard to force it on all his subjects. Apart from his courtiers and a few Armenians and Lebanese, known later as Maronites, it won no supporters. Heraclius later amended the doctrine; his *Ekthesis*, published in 638, advocated Monothe-letism equally fruitlessly. The whole episode, which was not finally cleared up till after the sixth Oecumenical Council in 680, merely added to the bitterness and confusion that were ruining the Christians of the East.[1]

When Heraclius was in Constantinople in 629, receiving con-gratulatory embassies from as far afield as France and India, it is said that there arrived for him a letter addressed by an Arabian chieftain, who announced himself as the Prophet of God and bade the Emperor join his faith. Similar letters were sent to the kings of Persia and Abyssinia and to the governor of Egypt. The story is probably apocryphal. It is unlikely that Heraclius had any idea as yet of the great events that were revolutionizing the Arabian peninsula. At the beginning of the seventh century Arabia was occupied by a number of unruly, independent tribes, some of them nomadic, some agricultural, and a few living in the merchant cities strung out along the caravan routes. It was an idolatrous country. Each district had its special idols; but the most sacred of all was the *kaabah* at Mecca, the leading merchant city. Idolatry was, however, on the wane; for Jewish, Christian and Zoroastrian missionaries had long been working in the country. The Zoroastrians had only been successful in the districts under Persian political influence, in the north-east and later in the south. The Jews had their colonies in many Arabian cities, notably in Medina, and had made a certain number of Arab converts. The Christians had achieved the most widespread results. Orthodox Christianity had its followers in Sinai and Petraea. The Nestorians, like the Zoroastrians, were to

[1] The best summary of Monoenergism and Monotheletism is given in Bréhier, *op. cit.* pp. 111–24, 160–200.

be found where there was Persian protection. But the Mono-physites had congregations down the great caravan routes as far as Yemen and the Hadramaut; while many important tribes on the edge of the desert, such as the Banū Ghassan and the Banū Taghlib, were wholly Monophysite. Arab merchants, frequently travelling to the cities of Syria and Palestine and Iraq, had many further occasions for studying the religions of the civilized world; while in Arabia itself there was an old tradition of monotheism, that of the *hanif*. At the same time there was in Arabia a need for expansion. The slender resources of the peninsula, grown slenderer since the destruction of the irrigation works of the Himyarites, were insufficient for the growing population. Throughout recorded history the desert populations had constantly overflowed into the cultivated lands around; and now the pressure was particularly strong.[1]

The peculiar and tremendous genius of Mahomet was exactly suited to these circumstances. He came from the holy city of Mecca, a poor relation of its great clan, the Qoraishites. He had travelled and seen the world, and he had studied its religions. In particular he was attracted by Monophysite Christianity; but the doctrine of the Trinity seemed to him inconsistent with the pure monotheism that he admired in the *hanif* tradition. The doctrine that he himself evolved, while it did not utterly reject Christianity, was an amended and simplified form far more easily acceptable to his people. His success as a religious leader was mainly due to his complete understanding of the Arabs. Though far the ablest of them he genuinely shared their feelings and their prejudices. In addition he possessed extraordinary political skill. This combination of qualities enabled him in ten years to build up out of nothing an empire that was ready to conquer the world. In 622, the year of the Hegira, his only following was his household and a small group of friends. In 632, when he died, he was lord of Arabia, and his armies were crossing the frontiers. The sudden rise of adventurers

[1] See Browne, *op. cit.* ch. I, and Lammens, *L'Arabie Occidentale avant l'Hegire*, *passim*.

is not uncommon in the East but their fall is usually equally sudden. Mahomet, however, left an enduring organization whose permanence was guaranteed by the Koran. This remarkable work, compiled by the Prophet as the Word of God, contains not only uplifting maxims and stories but also rules for the conduct of life and for the governance of an empire and a complete code of laws. It was simple enough to be accepted by his Arabian contemporaries and universal enough to suit the needs of the great dominion that his successors were to build. Indeed, the strength of Islam lay in its simplicity. There was one God in Heaven, one Commander of the Faithful to rule on earth, and one law, the Koran, by which he should rule. Unlike Christianity, which preached a peace that it never achieved, Islam unashamedly came with a sword.[1]

The sword struck at the provinces of the Roman Empire even during the lifetime of the Prophet, with some small and not very successful raids into Palestine. Under Mahomet's successor Abu Bakr, the policy of expansion became manifest. The conquest of Arabia was completed by the expulsion of the Persians from their dependency of Bahrein, while an Arab army crossed through Petraea along the trade route to the south Palestine coast, defeated the local governor, Sergius, somewhere near the Dead Sea, and advanced to Gaza which it captured after a short siege. The citizens were treated kindly, but the soldiers of the garrison became the first Christian martyrs to the sword of Islam.[2]

In 634 Abu Bakr was succeeded by Omar, who inherited likewise his determination to extend Moslem power. Meanwhile the Emperor Heraclius, who was still in northern Syria, realized that

[1] The fullest critical account of Mahomet and the rise of Islam is given in Caetani, *Annali dell' Islam*, vol. I. See also the article on 'Muhammed' by Buhl in the *Encyclopaedia of Islam*. For a discussion of the influence of the Monophysites on Islam, see Grégoire, 'Mahomet et le Monophysisme', in *Mélanges Charles Diehl*, vol. I, pp. 107–19.

[2] Theophanes, ad ann. 6123–4, pp. 335–6; 'Thomas the Priest' in *Corpus Scriptorum Christianorum Orientalium, Scriptores Syri*, vol. IV, p. 114; Michael the Syrian, vol. II, p. 413. The story of the martyrs of Gaza is given in *Passio LX Martyrum et Legenda Sancti Floriani*, ed. by Delehaye, in *Analecta Bollandiana*, vol. XXIII, pp. 289–307.

the Arab invasions must be taken seriously. He was short of man-power. The losses during the Persian war had been heavy. Since the end of the war he had disbanded many regiments for economy's sake; and there was no enthusiasm to join the army. All over his Empire there had fallen that atmosphere of lassitude and pessimism that so often after a long bitter war assails the victors no less than the conquered. Nevertheless he sent his brother Theodore at the head of the troops of the Syrian province to restore order in Palestine. Theodore met the two main Arab armies together at Gabatha, or Ajnadain, south-west of Jerusalem and was decisively defeated. The Arabs, secure in southern Palestine, next advanced up the trade route that went east of the Jordan to Damascus and the Orontes valley. Tiberias, Baalbek, and Homs fell into their hands without a struggle, and Damascus capitulated after a short siege in August 635. Heraclius was now seriously alarmed. With some difficulty he sent two armies southward. One was formed of Armenian levies, under the Armenian prince Vahan, and of a large number of Christian Arabs, headed by a sheikh of the Banū Ghassan. The other was commanded by Theodore Trithyrius and consisted of mixed troops. On the news of their approach the Moslems evacuated the Orontes valley and Damascus and retired towards the Jordan. Trithyrius caught up with them at Jabbia in the Hauran but was defeated. He managed, however, to hold a position on the river Yarmuk, just south-east of the Sea of Galilee, till Vahan's army could join him. There, on 20 August 636, in a blinding sandstorm the decisive battle was fought. The Christians had the larger army; but they were outmanoeuvred; and in the midst of the fighting the Ghassanid prince and twelve thousand Christian Arabs went over to the enemy. They were Monophysites and hated Heraclius; and their pay was many months overdue. The treason had been easy to arrange. It settled the issue. The Moslem victory was complete. Trithyrius and Vahan perished with almost all their men. Palestine and Syria lay open to the conquerors.[1]

[1] For the Battle of Ajnadain, Theophanes, ad ann. 6125, pp. 336–7; Sebeos, p. 165. Theophanes calls the site of the battle 'Gabitha'; Sebeos, whose

Heraclius was at Antioch when the news of the battle reached him. He was utterly despondent; it was the hand of God stretching out to punish him for his incestuous marriage with his niece Martina. He had neither the men nor the money to defend the province further. After a solemn service of intercession in the cathedral of Antioch he went down to the sea and took ship to Constantinople, crying bitterly as he left the shore: 'Farewell, a long farewell to Syria.'[1]

The Arabs quickly overran the country. The heretic Christians submitted to them without demur. The Jews gave them active help, serving as their guides. Only in the two great cities of Palestine, Caesarea and Jerusalem, was there organized opposition, and at the fortresses of Pella and Dara on the Persian frontier. At Jerusalem on the news of the Yarmuk Sophronius had repaired the defences of the city. Then, hearing that the enemy had reached Jericho, he collected together the holy relics of Christ and sent them by night down to the coast to be taken to Constantinople. They should not again fall into the hands of the infidel. Jerusalem withstood a siege of over a year. Caesarea and Dara held out till 639. But by then they were lonely outposts. The metropolis of the East, Antioch, had fallen the year before; and the whole country, from the isthmus of Suez to the Anatolian mountains, was in the hands of the Moslems.[2]

account is somewhat muddled, 'Rabboth-Moab'. For the battle of the Yarmuk, Theophanes, ad ann. 6126, pp. 337–8; Nicephorus, pp. 23–4; Michael the Syrian, vol. II, pp. 420–4; Sebeos, pp. 166–7; Eutychius, col. 1097. The Arab sources are summarized in Pernice, *op. cit.* pp. 279–81. See also *ibid.* p. 321 on the locality of the battle.

[1] The story of Heraclius's service of intercession and farewell is given in Michael the Syrian, vol. II, p. 424, who wrongly accuses him of having pillaged the Syrian towns of their treasures before he left. The tradition of his defeatism is repeated in Agapius, *Kitab al-Unvan*, p. 471, where he is said to have refused to fight against the will of God. According to Nicephorus, p. 23, Theodore ascribed the disasters to the Emperor's incestuous marriage with his niece.

[2] See Caetani, *op. cit.* vol. III, pp. 1119 ff. and de Goeje, *Mémoire sur la Conquête de la Syrie, passim*; Pernice, *op. cit.* pp. 267–89; Kulakovsky, *op. cit.* vol. III, pp. 152–6. The part played by the Jews is emphasized in all the original sources, especially Sebeos, pp. 173–4, and in the *Doctrina Jacobi*, pp. 86–8, written by a Jew of Constantinople who found himself at the time at Carthage.

They had meanwhile destroyed Rome's ancient rival, Persia. Their victory at Kadesiah in 637 gave them Iraq and a second victory next year at Nekhavend gave them the Iranian plateau. King Yazdegerd III, the last of the Sassanids, lingered on in Khorassan till 651. By then the Arabs had reached his eastern frontiers, on the Oxus and the Afghan hills.[1]

In December 639 the Moslem general 'Amr, with four thousand men, invaded Egypt. The administration of the province had been chaotic since the end of the Persian occupation; and the present governor, the Patriarch Cyrus of Alexandria, was both unwise and corrupt. He had been a convert from Nestorianism and was the Emperor's chief supporter in his Monothelete doctrines, which he determined to force on the unwilling Copts. So hated was his rule that 'Amr had no difficulty in finding allies amongst his subjects. Early in 640 'Amr entered the great frontier fortress of Pelusium, after a two months' siege. There he received reinforcements from the Caliph. Next he advanced on Babylon (Old Cairo), where the imperial garrison was concentrated. A battle at Heliopolis in August 640 forced the Romans to retire to the citadel of Babylon, which held out till April 641. Meanwhile the Arabs took over Upper Egypt. On the fall of Babylon, 'Amr marched through the Fayyum, its governor and garrison fleeing before him, to Alexandria. Cyrus had already been recalled to Constantinople on the justified suspicion of having entered into a treasonable pact with 'Amr. But Heraclius died in February, and his widow, the Empress-Regent Martina, was too insecure herself in Constantinople to defend Egypt. Cyrus was sent back to Egypt to make what terms he could. In November he went to 'Amr at Babylon and signed the capitulation of Alexandria. But meanwhile Martina had fallen and the new government repudiated Cyrus and his treaty. 'Amr had already broken his part in it by invading the Pentapolis and Tripolitania. It seemed, however, impossible to maintain Alexandria, with all the rest of Egypt now in Arab hands. The city

---

[1] Caetani, *op. cit.* vol. III, pp. 629 ff.; Christensen, *L'Iran sous les Sassanides*, pp. 494–503.

capitulated in November 642. But all hope was not yet lost. In 644 news came of 'Amr's disgrace and recall to Medina. A new army was sent by sea from Constantinople, which easily reoccupied Alexandria, early in 645, and which then marched on Fostat, the capital that 'Amr had founded near Babylon. 'Amr returned to Egypt and routed the imperial forces near Fostat. Their general, the Armenian Manuel, fell back on Alexandria. Struck by the utter indifference of the Christian population towards this attempt to recover the land for Christianity, he made no effort to defend the city but re-embarked for Constantinople. The Coptic Patriarch Benjamin restored Alexandria to the hands of 'Amr.[1]

Egypt was lost for ever. By the year 700 Roman Africa was in the hands of the Arabs. Eleven years later they occupied Spain. In the year 717 their empire stretched from the Pyrenees to central India and their warriors were hammering at the walls of Constantinople.

[1] Bréhier, *op. cit.* pp. 134-8, 152-5; Amélineau, 'La Conquête de l'Egypte par les Arabes' in the *Revue Historique*, vol. CXIX, pp. 275-301. The full account given in Butler's *The Arab Conquest of Egypt*, though out of date in places, is still useful.

CHAPTER II

THE REIGN OF ANTICHRIST

*'In our watching we have watched for a nation that
could not save us.'* LAMENTATIONS IV, 17

The Christians of the East accepted with a good grace the dominion
of their infidel masters. They could not well do otherwise. There
was small likelihood now that Byzantium would rise again, as in
the days of the Persians, to rescue the holy places. The Arabs,
wiser than the Persians, soon built a fleet, based on Alexandria,
that wrested from the Byzantines their most valuable asset, the
command of the seas. On land they were to retain the offensive
for nearly three centuries. It seemed pointless to hope for rescue
from the princes of Christendom.

Nor would such rescue have been welcomed by the heretic
sects. To them the change of rulers had brought relief and pleasure.
The Jacobite Patriarch of Antioch, Michael the Syrian, writing five
centuries later, in the days of the Latin kingdoms, reflected the old
tradition of his people when he told that 'the God of vengeance,
who alone is the Almighty... raised from the south the children
of Ishmael to deliver us by them from the hands of the Romans'.
This deliverance, he added, 'was no light advantage for us'.[1] The
Nestorians echoed these sentiments. 'The hearts of the Christians',
wrote an anonymous Nestorian chronicler, 'rejoiced at the domination of the Arabs—may God strengthen it and prosper it!'[2] The
Copts of Egypt were a little more critical; but their animosity was
directed more against the cruel conqueror 'Amr, and his treachery

[1] Michael the Syrian, vol. II, pp. 412–13 (Syriac text, p. 412).
[2] *Chronicle of Seert*, pt. II, § XCIV, in *Patrologia Orientalis*, vol. XIII,
p. 582.

and exactions, than against his people and religion.[1] Even the Orthodox, finding themselves spared the persecution that they had feared and paying taxes that, in spite of the *jizya* demanded from the Christians, were far lower than in Byzantine times, showed small inclination to question their destiny. A few mountain tribes, Mardaites of the Lebanon and the Taurus, still kept up the struggle; but they fought from lawlessness and pride rather than for the Faith.[2]

The effect of the Arab conquest was to fix the Churches of the East permanently in the positions in which they then stood. Unlike the Christian Empire, which attempted to enforce religious uniformity on all its citizens—an ideal never realized, for the Jews could neither be converted nor expelled—the Arabs, like the Persians before them, were prepared to accept religious minorities, provided that they were People of the Book. The Christians, together with the Zoroastrians and the Jews, became *dhimmis*, or protected peoples, whose freedom of worship was guaranteed by the payment of the *jizya*, which was first a capitation tax but soon was transformed into a tax paid in lieu of military service and to which a new land tax, the *kharaj*, was added. Each sect was treated as a *milet*, a semi-autonomous community within the state, each under its religious leader who was responsible for its good behaviour to the Caliph's government. Each was to retain those places of worship that it had possessed at the time of the Conquest, an arrangement that suited the Orthodox better than the heretic Christians, as Heraclius had recently restored many churches to their use. The last regulation was not strictly obeyed. The Moslems took over certain Christian churches, such as the great cathedral of St John at Damascus, and periodically destroyed many others; while a considerable number of churches and synagogues were continually built. Indeed, later Moslem jurists allowed the *dhimmis'* right to

[1] John of Nikiu, pp. 195, 200–1.
[2] Mardaite lawlessness in the time of the Caliph Moawiya is described by Theophanes, ad ann. 6169, p. 355. See also Sathas, *Bibliotheca Graeca Medii Aevi*, vol. II, pp. 45 ff.

erect buildings, so long as they were no higher than Moslem buildings and the sound of their bells and services were inaudible to Moslem ears. But there was no relaxation of the rule that the *dhimmis* should wear distinctive clothes and never ride on horseback; nor should they ever publicly offend against Moslem practices, nor attempt to convert Moslems, nor marry their women, nor speak slightingly of Islam; and they must remain loyal to the state.[1]

The *milet* system established a somewhat different conception of what was understood by nationality. Nationalism in the East had for many centuries past been based not on race, except in the case of the Jews, whose religious exclusiveness had kept their blood comparatively pure, but on cultural tradition and geographical position and economic interest. Now loyalty to a religion became the substitute for national loyalties. An Egyptian, for instance, would not regard himself as a citizen of Egypt but as a Moslem or as a Copt or as an Orthodox, as the case might be. It was his religion or his *milet* that commanded his allegiance. This gave to the Orthodox an advantage over the heretic sects. They were still known as the Melkites, the Emperor's men; and they considered themselves the Emperor's men. Cruel necessity might place them under the domination of the infidel, whose laws they were obliged to obey; but the Emperor was God's viceroy on earth and their true sovereign. Saint John Damascene, himself a civil servant at the Caliph's court, always addressed the Emperor, strongly though he disagreed with him on theology, as his lord and master, and referred to his employer merely as the Emir. The eastern Patriarchs, writing in the ninth century to the Emperor Theophilus to protest against his religious policy, used similar terms. The emperors accepted the responsibility. In all their wars and diplomatic dealings with the Caliphs, they kept in mind the welfare of the Orthodox beyond their frontiers. It was not a matter of administration. They

[1] *Encyclopaedia of Islam*, articles 'Djizya' by Becker and 'Kharadj' by Juynboll; Browne, *op. cit.* ch. v; Tritton, *The Caliphs and their non-Muslim Subjects*, ch. xv; Vincent and Abel, *op. cit.* vol. II, pp. 935–44.

could not interfere with the day-to-day government in Moslem lands; nor did the Patriarch of Constantinople have any jurisdiction over his eastern colleagues. It was an expression, sentimental but none the less powerful, of the continuance of the idea that Christendom was one and indivisible, and that the Emperor was the symbol of its unity.[1]

The heretic Churches had no such lay protector. They were entirely dependent on the goodwill of the Caliph; and their influence and their prestige suffered accordingly. Moreover their heresies had in origin been largely due to the desire of the orientals to simplify Christian creeds and practices. Islam, which was near enough to Christianity to be considered by many to be merely an advanced form of Christianity, and which now had the vast social advantage of being the faith of the new ruling class, was easily acceptable to many of them. There is no evidence to tell us how many converts were made from Christianity to Islam; but it is certain that the vast majority of these converts were drawn from the heretics and not from the Orthodox. Within a century of the Conquest, Syria, whose population had been predominantly heretic Christian, was a mainly Moslem country; but the numbers of the Orthodox had been very little reduced. In Egypt the Copts, owing to their wealth, lost ground less rapidly; but theirs was a losing battle. On the other hand, the continued existence of the heretics was ensured by the *milet* system, which by stabilizing their position made impossible any reunion of the Churches.

The growth of Islam in Syria and Palestine was not due to a sudden influx of Arabs from the desert. The conquerors' armies had not been very large. They had not provided much more than a military caste superimposed on the existing population. The racial composition of the inhabitants of the country was hardly changed. The townsmen and villagers, whether they accepted Islam or remained Christian, soon adopted the Arabic tongue for all general purposes; and we now loosely call their descendants

[1] See Runciman, 'The Byzantine "Protectorate" in the Holy Land', in *Byzantion*, vol. XVIII, pp. 207–15.

Arabs; but they were formed of a blend of many races, of the tribes that had dwelt in the land before ever Israel came out of Egypt, Amalekites or Jebusites or Moabites or Phoenicians, and of tribes like the Philistines that had been there almost as long, and of the Aramaeans that throughout recorded history had slowly and almost imperceptibly penetrated into the cultivated country, and of those Jews that, like the first apostles, had joined the Church of Christ. Only the practising Jews remained ethnologically distinct; and even their racial purity was slightly impaired. In Egypt the Hamitic stock was less mixed; but it had been swollen by intermarriage with immigrants from Syria and the deserts and the upper Nile and the coasts of the whole Mediterranean basin.

Arab immigration was inevitably at its thickest in the districts bordering on the desert and in the cities on the caravan routes that ran along its edge. The decline in the sea-trade of the Mediterranean, which followed on the Conquest, gave these cities, with their preponderantly Moslem population, a greater importance than that of the Hellenistic cities nearer to the coast. Alexandria was the only large port maintained by Arabs on the Mediterranean. There, and in the Hellenistic cities of Syria, Christians remained plentiful, probably outnumbering the Moslems. There was roughly the same difference in the Syrian countryside. The inland plains and valleys became increasingly Moslem; but between the Lebanon and the sea Christians of various sects prevailed. In Egypt the distinction was more between town and country. The *fellahin* were gradually converted to Islam, but the towns were largely Christian. In Palestine there was a more arbitrary division. While much of the countryside became Moslem, many villages clung to the older faith. Towns of special import to the Christians, such as Nazareth or Bethlehem, were almost exclusively Christian; and in Jerusalem itself, despite the Moslems' regard for it, the Christians remained in the majority. The Palestinian Christians were almost all of the Orthodox *milet*. In addition, there were important colonies of Jews at Jerusalem, and at several lesser towns, such as Safed and Tiberias. The chief Moslem city was the new administrative capital at Ramleh. The population of Syria, Palestine and Egypt remained grouped in this rough pattern for the next four centuries.[1]

The fifth of the Caliphs, Moawiya the Ommayad, had been governor of Syria; and after his accession in A.D. 660 he established his capital at Damascus. His descendants reigned there for nearly a century. It was a period of prosperity for Syria and Palestine. The Ommayad Caliphs were with few exceptions men of unusual ability and a broad-minded tolerance. The presence of their court in the province ensured its good government and a lively commercial activity; and they encouraged the culture that they found there. This was a Hellenistic-Christian culture, influenced by tastes and ideas that we associate with the name of Byzantium. Greek-speaking Christians were employed in the civil service. For many decades the state accounts were kept in Greek. Christian artists and craftsmen worked for the Caliphs. The Dome of the Rock at Jerusalem, completed for the Caliph Abdul-Malik in 691, is the supreme example of the rotunda-style of building in Byzantine architecture. Its mosaics, and the even lovelier mosaics set up in the courtyard of the Great Mosque of Damascus for his son, Walid I, are amongst the finest products of Byzantine art. How far they were the work of native artisans and how far they were helped by the technicians and material that Walid certainly imported from Byzantium is a matter of dispute. These mosaics carefully respected the Prophet's ban on the depiction of living creatures. But in their country palaces, discreetly removed from the eyes of disapproving *mullahs*—for instance, at the hunting-box of Kasr al-Amra, in the steppes beyond the Jordan—the Ommayads freely permitted frescoes depicting the human form, even in the nude. Their rule, indeed, brought no interruption to the

---

[1] For the structure of society in Palestine and Syria under the Caliphs, see Le Strange, *Palestine under the Moslems, passim*; Gaudefroy-Demombynes and Platonov, *Le Monde Musulman*, pp. 233–47; Browne, *op. cit.* ch. v; O'Leary, *How Greek Science passed to the Arabs*, pp. 135–9.

development of the Hellenistic culture of the near Orient; which now achieved its finest, but its final, flowering.[1]

The Christians had therefore no cause to regret the triumph of Islam. Despite an occasional brief bout of persecution and despite a few humiliating regulations, they were better off than they had been under the Christian Emperors. Order was better kept. Trade was good; and the taxes were far lower. Moreover, during the greater part of the eighth century the Christian Emperor was a heretic, an iconoclast, an oppressor of all the Orthodox that paid respect to holy images. Good Christians were happier under infidel rule.

But this happy period did not endure. The decline of the Ommayads and the civil wars that led to the establishment of the Abbasid Caliphs at Baghdad in 750 brought chaos to Syria and Palestine. Unscrupulous and uncontrolled local governors raised money by confiscating Christian churches which the Christians had then to redeem. There were waves of fanaticism, with persecutions and forced conversions.[2] The victory of the Abbasids restored order; but there was a difference. Baghdad was far away. There was less supervision of the provincial administration. Trade was still active along the caravan routes; but there was no great market to stimulate it locally. The Abbasids were stricter Moslems than the Ommayads. They were less tolerant of the Christians. Though they too were dependent on an older culture, it was not Hellenistic but Persian. Baghdad lay within the ancient territory of the Sassanid kingdom. Persians acquired the chief places in the government. Persian ideals in art and Persian habits of daily life were adopted. As with the Ommayads, Christian officials were

[1] For Ommayad civilization, see Diehl and Marçais, *Le Monde Oriental de 395 à 1081*, pp. 335–44, and Lammens, *Etudes sur le Siècle des Ommayades*. For its art, see Creswell, *Early Muslim Architecture*, especially ch. v, on mosaics, by M. van Berchem. For individual buildings, see Richmond, *The Dome of the Rock*, and the two volumes *Kuseir Amra*, published by the Kaiserliche Akademie der Wissenschaften of Vienna.

[2] Diehl and Marçais, *op. cit.* pp. 345–8; Gaudefroy-Demombynes and Platonov, *op. cit.* pp. 260–8.

employed. But these Christians were with few exceptions Nestorians, whose outlook was towards the East and not the West. The
Abbasid court had on the whole a greater interest in intellectual
matters than the Ommayad. The Nestorians were freely used to
translate philosophical and technical works from the ancient Greek;
and scientists and mathematicians were encouraged to come, even
from Byzantium, to teach at the schools of Baghdad. But this
interest was superficial. Abbasid civilization was fundamentally
unaffected by Greek thought, but followed, rather, the traditions
handed down from the kingdoms of Mesopotamia and Iran. It
was only in Spain, to which the Ommayads had fled for refuge,
that Hellenistic life lingered on in the Moslem world.

Nevertheless, the lot of the Christians under the Abbasids was
not unhappy. Moslem writers, such as al-Jahiz in the ninth century,
might make violent attacks on them; but that was because they
were too prosperous and were growing arrogant and heedless of
the regulations made against them.[1] The Patriarch of Jerusalem,
writing about the same time to his colleague of Constantinople,
says of the Moslem authorities that 'they are just and do us no
wrong nor show us any violence'.[2] Their justice and restraint were
often remarkable. When in the tenth century things were going
badly for the Arabs in their wars against Byzantium and Arab
mobs attacked the Christians in anger at their known sympathy
with the enemy, the Caliph always made restitution for the damage
done. His motive may have been fear of the renascent power of
the Emperor, who by then had Moslems within his dominions
whom he could persecute in revenge.[3] The Orthodox Churches,
with foreign powers backing them, had always maintained a

[1] Al-Jahiz, *Three Essays*, ed. by Finkel, p. 18. Labourt, *De Timotheo I,
Nestorianorum Patriarcha*, pp. 33–4, gives illustrations of the influence exercised
by the Nestorians at the Caliph's court.
[2] Letter of Theodosius of Jerusalem to Ignatius of Constantinople, in Mansi,
Concilia, vol. XVI, pp. 26–7.
[3] In 923 and 924 Moslem mobs destroyed Orthodox Christian churches in
Ramleh, Askelon, Caesarea and Damascus; whereupon the Caliph al-Muqtadir
helped the Christians to rebuild them (Eutychius, col. 1151).

favoured position. In the early tenth century the Nestorian Catholicus, Abraham III, during a dispute with the Orthodox Patriarch of Antioch, told the Grand Vizier that 'we Nestorians are the friends of the Arabs and pray for their victories', adding: 'Far be it from you to regard the Nestorians, who have no other king but the Arabs', in the same light as the Greeks, whose kings never cease to make war against the Arabs'.[1] But it was the gift of two thousand golden coins rather than his argument that enabled him to win his case. The only group of Christians against whom continual animosity was shown were the Christians of pure Arab descent, such as the Banū Ghassan or the Banū Tanūkh. Such of these tribesmen as refused to be forcibly converted to Islam were obliged to cross the frontier and seek refuge in Byzantium.[2]

The emigration of Christians into the Emperor's territory was continuous; nor did the Moslems take steps against it. There seems never to have been a sustained attempt to prevent the Christians within and without the Caliphate from keeping up close relations, even in times of war. During the greater part of the Abbasid period the Byzantine Emperor was not strong enough to do much for his co-religionists. The Arab failure before Constantinople in 718 had guaranteed the continuance of the Empire; but two centuries elapsed before Byzantium could seriously take the offensive against the Arabs. In the meantime the Orthodox of the East had discovered a new foreign friend. The growth of the Carolingian empire in the eighth century did not pass unnoticed in the East. When at the close of the century Charles the Great, soon to be crowned emperor at Rome, showed a particular interest in the welfare of the holy places, his attentions were very welcome. The Caliph Harun al-Rashid, glad to find an ally against Byzantium, gave him every encouragement to make foundations at Jerusalem and to send alms to its church. For a while Charles replaced the Byzantine Emperor as the monarch whose power was the safeguard

[1] Bar Hebraeus, quoted in Assemani, *Bibliotheca Orientalis*, vol. II, pp. 440–1.
[2] Balādhurī, Arabic text, p. 142, trans. by Hitti and Murgotten, pp. 208–9. See Nau, *Les Arabes Chrétiens de Mésopotamie et de Syrie*, pp. 106–11.

of the Orthodox in Palestine; and they repaid his charity by sending him honorific marks of their esteem. But the collapse of his empire under his descendants and the rebirth of Byzantium made this Frankish intervention shortlived and soon barely remembered, except for the hostels that Charles had built and the Latin services held in the Church of St Mary of the Latins, and the Latin nuns serving in the Holy Sepulchre. But in the West the episode was never forgotten. Legend and tradition exaggerated it. Charles was soon thought to have established a legal protectorate over the holy places, and even, in time, himself to have made the pilgrimage thither. To the Franks of later generations their right to rule in Jerusalem had been acknowledged and endorsed.[1]

The eastern Christians were more nearly interested in the renascence of Byzantine power. In the early ninth century the Empire had still been on the defensive. Sicily and Crete were lost to the Moslems; and almost every year saw some great Arab raid into the heart of Asia Minor. In the middle of the century, largely owing to the prudent economies of the Empress-Regent Theodora, the Byzantine navy was reorganized and re-equipped. Thanks to its strength, Byzantine dominion over southern Italy and Dalmatia was soon reaffirmed. Early in the tenth century the Abbasid Caliphate began rapidly to decline. Local dynasties arose, of which the chief were the Hamdanids of Mosul and Aleppo and the Ikshids of Egypt. The former were fine fighters and fervent Moslems, and for a time formed a bulwark against Byzantine aggression. But they could not stop the decay of Moslem power. Rather, they added to it by encouraging civil wars. In the course of these civil wars the Ikshids won control of Palestine and southern Syria. The Byzantines were quick to take advantage of the situation. Their offensive was cautious at first; but by 945, in spite of the prowess of the Hamdanid prince, Saif ad-Daula, their general, John Curcuas, had won for the Empire towns and districts in upper Mesopotamia

[1] See Runciman, 'Charlemagne and Palestine', in *English Historical Review*, vol. L, pp. 606 ff.

that had not seen a Christian army for three centuries.[1] After 960, when the great soldier, Nicephorus Phoças, took command of the imperial army, things moved faster. In 961 Nicephorus recaptured Crete. In 962 he campaigned on the Cilician frontier and took Anazarbus and Marash (Germanicia) thus isolating Moslem Cilicia. In 963 Nicephorus was engaged at home, planning the *coup d'état* that brought him, with the help of the army and the Empress-Regent, to the throne. In 964 he returned to the East. In 965 he completed the conquest of Cilicia; and an expedition sent to Cyprus re-established absolute Byzantine control of the island. In 966 he campaigned on the middle Euphrates, to cut communications between Aleppo and Mosul.[2] The whole Christian East was aroused and saw deliverance at hand. The Patriarch John of Jerusalem wrote to him, urging him to hasten down to Palestine. But such treason proved for once too much for the patience of the Moslems. John was arrested and burnt at the stake by the furious population.[3]

John's hopes were premature. In 967 and 968 Nicephorus was busy on his northern frontier. But in 969 he led his army southward again, right into the heart of Syria. He marched up the Orontes valley, capturing and sacking, one after the other, the great towns of Shaizar, Hama and Homs, and crossing to the coast to the suburbs of Tripoli. He then returned northward, leaving Tortosa, Jabala and Lattakieh in flames behind him, while his lieutenants besieged Antioch and Aleppo. The ancient metropolis of Antioch was taken in October. Aleppo surrendered at the end of the year.

Antioch, where the Christians probably outnumbered the Moslems, was absorbed into the Empire; and it seems that the Moslems were obliged to emigrate from its territory. Aleppo, which was almost entirely a Moslem city, became a vassal state.

[1] Vasiliev, *Byzantium and the Arabs* (in Russian), vol. II, pp. 229–37; Runciman, *The Emperor Romanus Lecapenus*, pp. 135–50.

[2] Schlumberger, *Un Empereur Byzantin, Nicéphore Phocas*, chs. VIII and X.

[3] Yachya of Antioch, in *P. O.* vol. XVIII, pp. 799–802. The date is discussed in Rosen, *Emperor Basil the Bulgar-slayer* (in Russian), p. 351.

The treaty made with its ruler carefully delineated the frontier between the new imperial province and the tributary towns. The ruler of Aleppo was to be nominated by the Emperor. The vassal state was to pay heavy taxes, from which the Christians were to be exempt, directly to the imperial treasury. Special privileges and protection was to be given to imperial merchants and caravans. These humiliating terms seemed to foreshadow the end of Moslem power in Syria.[1]

Before Aleppo had fallen the Emperor was murdered in Constantinople by his Empress and her lover, his cousin John Tzimisces. Nicephorus was a grim, unlovable man. Despite his victories, he had been hated at Constantinople for his financial exactions and corruption and his bitter quarrel with the Church. John, who was already known as a brilliant general, succeeded without difficulty to the throne, and made his peace with the Church by throwing over his imperial paramour. But a war with Bulgaria kept him busy in Europe for the next four years. Meanwhile there was a revival in Islam, led by the Fatimid dynasty, which established itself in Egypt and southern Syria, and in 971 even attempted the recapture of Antioch. In 974 John could turn his attention to the East. That autumn he descended into eastern Mesopotamia, capturing Nisibin and reducing Mosul to vassalage, and even contemplating a sudden march on Baghdad. But he realized that the Fatimites were more dangerous enemies than their Abbasid rivals, and next spring he advanced into Syria. Following the route of Nicephorus, six years before, he swept up the Orontes valley, past Homs, which submitted without a blow, and Baalbek, which he took by force, right into Damascus, which promised him tribute and a humble alliance. Thence he went on into Galilee, to Tiberias and to Nazareth, and down to the coast at Caesarea. Envoys from Jerusalem came to him to beg him to spare them the horrors of a sack. But he did not feel able to advance to the Holy City itself with the towns of the Phoenician coast untaken behind him. He retired northward, overpowering them one by one, with

[1] Schlumberger, *op. cit.* ch. xIV.

the exception of the fortress-port of Tripoli. Winter was coming on, and the Emperor was obliged to postpone his efforts for a season. On his way back to Antioch he captured and garrisoned the two great castles of the Nosairi Mountains, Barzuya and Sahyun. Then he returned to Constantinople. But his campaign was never resumed. Quite suddenly, in January 976, he died.[1]

These wars had made the Christian Empire once more the great power in the East. With the prospect of the deliverance of the Christians of the East in sight, they had, moreover, reached the status of religious wars. Hitherto, wars against the Moslem had been wars regularly waged for the defence of the Empire and had been, so to speak, taken for granted as a part of daily life. Though now and then Christian captives might be given the choice of apostasy or death by some fanatical Moslem victor and their martyrdom would be duly remembered and honoured, such cases were rare. To public opinion in Byzantium there was no greater merit in dying in battle for the protection of the Empire against the infidel Arab than against the Christian Bulgar; nor did the Church make any distinction. But both Nicephorus and John declared that the struggle was now for the glory of Christendom, for the rescue of the holy places and for the destruction of Islam. Already when an Emperor celebrated a triumph over the Saracens the choirs sang: 'Glory be to God, Who has conquered the Saracens.'[2] Nicephorus emphasized that his wars were Christian wars, partly, perhaps, in an attempt to counteract his bad relations with the Church. He failed to induce the Patriarch to support a decree announcing that soldiers dying on the eastern front died as martyrs; for to the eastern Church even the exigencies of war did not entirely excuse the act of murder.[3] But in his insulting

[1] Schlumberger, *L'Epopée Byzantine*, vol. I, ch. IV.
[2] Constantine Porphyrogennetus, *De Ceremoniis* (Bonn ed.), vol. I, pp. 332–3, ed. by Vogt, vol. II, pp. 135–6. The acclamations were probably first used for Michael III's triumph over the Saracens in 863. See Bury, 'The Ceremonial Book of Constantine Porphyrogennetos', in *E.H.R.* vol. XXII, p. 434.
[3] Zonaras, vol. III, p. 506.

manifesto to the Caliph that he sent before starting on his campaign of 964, he saw himself as the Christian champion, and even threatened to march on Mecca, to establish there the throne of Christ.[1] John Tzimisces used the same language. In his letter describing his campaign of 974, written to the king of Armenia, 'our desire', he says, 'was to free the Holy Sepulchre from the outrages of the Moslems'. He tells how he spared the cities of Galilee from being pillaged, because of their part in the history of the Christian faith; and mentioning his check before Tripoli he adds that but for it he would have gone to the Holy City of Jerusalem and prayed in the sacred places.[2]

The Arabs had always been readier to envisage war as a religious matter; but even they had grown slack. Now, frightened by the Christians, they tried to revive their fervour. In 974 riots in Baghdad forced the Caliph, who personally had not been sorry to see the Fatimids defeated, to proclaim a holy war, a *jihad*.[3]

It had seemed that at last the Holy Land would be restored to Christian rule. But the Orthodox of Palestine waited in vain. John's successor, the legitimate Basil II, great warrior though he became, was never given the opportunity to continue the southern advance. Civil wars followed by a long war against the Bulgarians demanded all his attention. Only twice could he visit Syria, to restore Byzantine suzerainty over Aleppo in 995, and to march down the coast as far as Tripoli in 999. In 1001 he decided that it would be useless to make further conquest. A ten years' truce was made with the Fatimid Caliph; and the peace thus inaugurated was not seriously broken for more than half a century. The frontier between the empires was fixed to run from the coast between Banyas and Tortosa to the Orontes just south of Caesarea-Shaizar. Aleppo officially remained within the Byzantine sphere of

---

[1] Schlumberger, *Un Empereur Byzantin*, pp. 427–30, quoting from an Arabic manuscript at Vienne.

[2] Matthew of Edessa, pp. 13–20.

[3] Miskawaihi, *The Experiences of the Nations*, in Amedroz and Margoliouth, *The Eclipse of the Abbasid Caliphate*, vol. II, pp. 303–5 (Arabic text) and vol. v, pp. 326–8 (English trans.).

influence; but the Mirdasite dynasty established there in 1023 soon obtained independence in fact. In 1030 its Emir severely defeated a Byzantine army. But the loss of Aleppo was counterbalanced next year by the incorporation of Edessa into the Byzantine Empire.[1]

The peace suited both the Empire and the Fatimids; for both were disquieted by the revival of the Baghdad Caliphate under Turkish adventurers from central Asia. The Fatimid monarch, accepted by the Shia Moslems as the true Caliph, could not afford any strengthening of Abbasid claims; while Byzantium considered her eastern frontier more vulnerable than her southern. Fear of the Turks led Basil II first to annex the provinces of Armenia that lay nearest to the Empire and then to take over the south-easternmost district of the country, the principality of Vaspurakan. His successors continued his policy. In 1045 the king of Ani, the chief ruler in Armenia, ceded his lands to the Emperor. In 1064 the last independent Armenian state, the principality of Kars, was absorbed into imperial territory.[2]

The annexation of Armenia was dictated by military considerations. Experience had taught that no reliance could be placed on the Armenian princes. Though they were Christians and had nothing to gain from a Moslem conquest, they were heretics, and as heretics they hated the Orthodox more passionately than any Moslem oppressor. In spite of continued trade and cultural relations, and in spite of the many Armenians who migrated into the Empire and reached its highest offices, the animosity never died down. But from the valleys of Armenia it was easy, as past border-

---

[1] Basil's activities in Syria are described from the Arabic sources (Kemal ad-Din, Ibn al-Athir and Abu'l Mahāsin) in Rosen, *op. cit.* pp. 239–66, 309–11. In 987–8 Basil had sent ambassadors to Cairo who provided money for the upkeep of the Holy Sepulchre at Jerusalem (*ibid.* pp. 202–5, quoting a text from a MS. of Abu'l Mahāsin.). For the frontier see discussions in Honigmann, *Die Ostgrenze des byzantinischen Reiches*, pp. 106–8, 134 ff., also his article 'Shaizar' in the *Encyclopaedia of Islam*. Shaizar was still administered by the bishop in the Emperor's name up to 1081 (Michael the Syrian, vol. II, p. 178).

[2] A full summary, with references, of Armenian history at this period is given in Grousset, *Histoire de l'Arménie*, pp. 531 ff. See below, p. 61.

warfare had shown, to penetrate into the heart of Asia Minor. The military authorities would have been foolish to allow such a danger-spot to remain out of their control. Politically the annexation was less wise. The Armenians resented Byzantine rule. Though Byzantine garrisons might man the frontier, within the frontier there was a large and discontented population whose disloyalty was potentially dangerous and who now, no longer anchored by allegiance to a local prince, began to wander about spreading lawlessness within the Empire. Wiser statesmen, less obsessed than the soldier-emperors of Byzantium by the military point of view, would have hesitated to create an Armenian question to destroy the uniformity of the Empire and to add a discordant minority to its subjects.

Northern Syria had passed to the rule of the Christians; but the Christians of southern Syria and Palestine found the dominion of the Fatimids easy to bear. They suffered only one short period of persecution, when the Caliph Hakim, the son of a Christian mother and brought up largely by Christians, suddenly reacted against his early influences. For ten years, from 1004 to 1014, despite the re-monstrances of the Emperor, he passed ordinances against the Christians; he began to confiscate Church property, then to burn crosses and to order little mosques to be built on church roofs, and finally to burn the churches themselves. In 1009 he ordered the destruction of the Church of the Holy Sepulchre itself, on the ground that the annual miracle of the holy fire, celebrated there on the eve of Easter, must certainly be an impious forgery. By 1014 some thirty thousand churches had been burnt or pillaged, and many Christians had outwardly adopted Islam to save their lives. Similar measures were taken against the Jews. But it should be noted that the Moslems were equally liable to arbitrary persecution by the head of their faith; who continued all the time to employ Christian ministers. In 1013, as a concession to the Emperor, Christians were allowed to emigrate into Byzantine territory. The persecution only stopped when Hakim became convinced that he himself was divine. This divinity was publicly proclaimed in 1016 by his friend Darazi. As the Moslems were more deeply shocked by this behaviour of their leading co-religionist than the non-Moslems could be, Hakim began to favour the Christians and the Jews, while he struck at the Moslems themselves by forbidding the Ramadan fast and the pilgrimage to Mecca. In 1017 full liberty of conscience was given to the Christians and the Jews. Soon some six thousand of the recent apostates returned to the Christian fold. In 1020 the Churches had their confiscated property restored to them, including the materials taken from their ruined buildings. At the same time the regulation demanding distinctive dress was abolished. But by now the fury of the Moslems was aroused against the Caliph, who had substituted his own name for that of Allah in the mosque services. Darazi fled to the Lebanon, to found there the sect that is called the Druzes, after his name. Hakim himself disappeared in 1021. He was probably murdered by his ambitious sister, Sitt al-Mulk; but his fate remained and still remains a mystery. The Druzes believe that in due course he will come again.[1]

After his death Palestine was held for a while by the Emir of Aleppo, Salih ibn Mirdas; but the Fatimid rule was fully restored in 1029. In 1027 a treaty had already been signed permitting the Emperor Constantine VIII to undertake the restoration of the Church of the Holy Sepulchre, and allowing the remaining apostates to return unpenalized to Christianity. The treaty was renewed in 1036; but the actual work of rebuilding the church was only carried out some ten years later, by the Emperor Constantine IX. To supervise the work imperial officials voyaged freely to Jerusalem; where to the disgust of Moslem citizens and travellers the Christians seemed to be in complete control.[2] So many Byzantines

---

[1] See the article 'Hakim' by Graefe in the *Encyclopaedia of Islam*, also Browne, *op. cit.* pp. 60–2.

[2] William of Tyre, vol. I, pt. 1, pp. 391–3; Schlumberger, *L'Epopée Byzantine*, vol. III, pp. 23, 131, 203–4; Riant, *Donation de Hugues, Marquis de Toscane*, p. 157; Mukaddasi, *Description of Syria*, trans. by Le Strange, p. 37. Mukaddasi tells us (p. 77) that in Syria and Palestine the scribes and physicians were almost all Christians, while the tanners, dyers and bankers were Jews.

were to be seen in its streets that the rumour arose amongst the Moslems that the Emperor himself had made the journey.[1] There was a prosperous colony of Amalfitan merchants protected by the Caliph but also protesting the vassaldom of their Italian home-city to the Emperor, in order to share in the privileges shown to his subjects.[2] Fear of Byzantine power kept the Christians safe. The Persian traveller, Nasir-i-Khusrau, who visited Tripoli in 1047, describes the number of Greek merchant ships to be seen in the harbour there and the fear of the inhabitants of an attack by the Byzantine navy.[3]

In the middle of the eleventh century the lot of the Christians in Palestine had seldom been so pleasant. The Moslem authorities were lenient; the Emperor was watchful of their interests. Trade was prospering and increasing with the Christian countries overseas. And never before had Jerusalem enjoyed so plentifully the sympathy and the wealth that were brought to it by pilgrims from the West.

[1] Nasir-i-Khusrau, *Diary of a Journey through Syria and Palestine*, trans. by Le Strange, p. 59.

[2] William of Tyre, vol. I, 2, pp. 822–6; Aimé, *Chronicon*, p. 320.

[3] Nasir-i-Khusrau, *op. cit.* pp. 6–7; Mukaddasi, *op. cit.* pp. 3–4, writing about the year 985, says that in Syria 'the people live ever in terror of the Byzantines... for their frontiers are continuously ravaged and their fortresses are again and again destroyed'.

CHAPTER III

THE PILGRIMS OF CHRIST

'Our feet shall stand within thy gates, O Jerusalem.'   PSALMS CXXII, 2

The desire to be a pilgrim is deeply rooted in human nature. To stand where those that we reverence once stood, to see the very sites where they were born and toiled and died, gives us a feeling of mystical contact with them and is a practical expression of our homage. And if the great men of the world have their shrines to which their admirers come from afar, still more do men flock eagerly to those places where, they believe, the Divine has sanctified the earth.

In the earliest days of Christianity pilgrimages were rare. Early Christian thought tended to emphasize the godhead and the universality of Christ rather than the manhood; and the Roman authorities did not encourage a voyage to Palestine. Jerusalem itself, destroyed by Titus, lay in ruins till Hadrian rebuilt it as the Roman city of Aelia. But the Christians remembered the setting of the drama of Christ's life. Their respect for the site of Calvary was such that Hadrian deliberately erected there a temple to Venus Capitolina. By the third century the cave at Bethlehem where Christ was born was well known to them; and Christians would journey thither and to the Mount of Olives, to the Garden of Gethsemane and to the place of the Ascension. A visit to such holy spots for the purpose of prayer and of acquiring spiritual merit was already a part of Christian practice.[1]

---

[1] Jerome, *Epistolae* XLVI, 9, *M.P.L.* vol. XXII, col. 489, refers to early pilgrimages to Palestine. The first pilgrim whose name we know was a bishop of Caesarea in Asia Minor in the early third century, called Fermilian (Jerome, *De Viris Illustribus*, *M.P.L.* vol. XXIII, cols. 665–6). Later in the third century we know of a Cappadocian bishop, Alexander, who visited Palestine (Eusebius,

With the triumph of the Cross the practice grew. The Emperor Constantine was glad to give strength to the religion that he had chosen. His mother, the Empress Helena, most exalted and most successful of the world's great archaeologists, set out to Palestine, to uncover Calvary and to find all the relics of the Passion. The Emperor endorsed her discovery by building there a church, which through all its vicissitudes has remained the chief sanctuary of Christendom, the Church of the Holy Sepulchre.[1]

At once a stream of pilgrims began to flow to the scene of Helena's labours. We cannot tell their numbers; for most of them left no record of their journey. But already in 333, before her excavations were finished, a traveller who wrote of his voyage came all the way from Bordeaux to Palestine.[2] Soon afterwards we find the description of a tour made by an indefatigable lady known sometimes as Aetheria and sometimes as Saint Silvia of Aquitaine.[3] Towards the close of the century one of the great Fathers of Latin Christendom, Saint Jerome, settled in Palestine and drew after him the circle of rich and fashionable women that had sat at his feet in Italy. In his cell at Bethlehem he received a constant procession of travellers who came to pay him their respects after viewing the holy places.[4] Saint Augustine, most spiritual of

Historia Ecclesiastica, pp. 185-6). Origen (*In Joannem* VI, 29, *M.P.G.* vol. XIV, col. 269) talks of the desire of Christians to 'search after the footsteps of Christ'.

[1] Eusebius, *Vita Constantini*, chs. XXV-XL, given in *Palestine Pilgrims' Text Society*, vol. I.

[2] The *Itinerary of the Bordeaux Pilgrim* is published in the *P.P.T.S.* vol. I, in a trans. by A. Stewart.

[3] The pilgrimage of Aetheria is published in an English trans. by J. H. Bernard in the *P.P.T.S.* vol. I, under the name of *The Pilgrimage of Saint Silvia of Aquitaine*, with whom the editor identifies her, almost certainly incorrectly.

[4] The letter of Paula and Eustochion to Marcella, describing the life led in Palestine in Saint Jerome's circle, is published among Saint Jerome's letters as no XLVI (cols. 483 ff. in *M.P.L.* vol. XXII). Jerome himself, in letter no. XLVII, 2 (*ibid.* col. 493) recommends a visit to the holy places to his friend Desiderius; and he himself explains that his visit to Palestine enables him to understand the scriptures better (*Liber Paralipumenon*, preface, in *M.P.L.* vol. XXVIII, cols. 1325-6). But in his disgruntled moments, as in his letter LVIII, 2, to Paulinus of Nola (*ibid.* vol. XXII, col. 580) he thought nothing was missed by a failure to visit Jerusalem.

the western Fathers, considered pilgrimages to be irrelevant and even dangerous and the Greek Fathers tended to agree with him;[1] but Saint Jerome, though he did not maintain that actual residence in Jerusalem was of any spiritual value, asserted that it was an act of faith to pray where the feet of Christ had stood.[2] His view was more popular than Augustine's. Pilgrimages multiplied, encouraged by the authorities. By the beginning of the next century there were said to be already two hundred monasteries and hospices in or around Jerusalem, built to receive pilgrims, and almost all under the patronage of the Emperor.[3]

The mid-fifth century saw the height of this early taste for Jerusalem. The Empress Eudocia, born the daughter of a pagan philosopher at Athens, settled there after an unhappy life at court; and many pious members of the Byzantine aristocracy came in her train. In the intervals of writing hymns she patronized the growing fashion for collecting relics; and she laid the foundation of the great collection at Constantinople by sending there the portrait of Our Lady painted by Saint Luke.[4]

Her example was followed by pilgrims from the West as well as from Constantinople. From immemorial ages the material luxuries of the world came from the East. Now religious luxuries too went westward. Christianity was at first an eastern religion. The majority of the early Christian saints and martyrs had been easterners. There was a spreading tendency to venerate the saints. Authorities such as Prudentius and Ennodius taught that divine succour could be found at their graves and that their bodies should

[1] Saint Augustine, letter LXXVIII, 3, in *M.P.L.* vol. XXXIII, cols. 268-9, *Contra Faustum* XX, 21, *ibid.* vol. XLII, cols. 384-5. Saint Gregory of Nyssa disapproves strongly of pilgrimage (letter no. II in *M.P.G.* vol. XLVI, col. 1009). Saint John Chrysostom is almost equally disapproving (*Ad Populum Antiochenum* V, 2, in *M.P.G.* vol. XLIX, col. 69), but elsewhere he wishes that his duties allowed him to be a pilgrim (*In Ephesianos* VIII, 2, *ibid.* vol. LXII, col.57).

[2] See p. 38 n. 1.

[3] Couret, *La Palestine sous les Empereurs grecs*, p. 212.

[4] See Bury, *Later Roman Empire* (A.D. 395-565), vol. I, pp. 225-31. See Nicephorus Callistus, *Historia Ecclesiastica*, in *M.P.G.* vol. CXLVI, col. 1061, for Eudocia's relic-hunting.

be able to work miracles.[1] Men and women would now travel far to see a holy relic. Still more, they would try to acquire one, to take it home and to set it in their local sanctuary. The chief relics remained in the East, those of Christ at Jerusalem till they were moved to Constantinople, and those of the saints for the most part at their native places. But minor relics began to penetrate to the West, brought by some lucky pilgrim or some enterprising merchant, or sent as a gift to some potentate. Soon there followed small portions of major relics, then major relics in their entirety. All this helped to draw the attention of the West to the East. The citizens of Langres, proud possessors of a finger of Saint Mamas, would inevitably wish to visit Caesarea in Cappadocia where the saint had lived.[2] The nuns of Chamalières, with the bones of Thecla in their chapel, would take a personal interest in her birthplace at Isaurian Seleucia.[3] When a lady of Maurienne brought back from her travels the thumb of Saint John the Baptist, her friends were all inspired to journey out to see his body at Samaria and his head at Damascus.[4] Whole embassies would be sent in the hope of securing some such treasure, maybe even a phial of the Holy Blood or a fragment of the true Cross itself. Churches were built in the West called after eastern saints or after the Holy Sepulchre; and often a portion of their revenues was set aside to be sent to the holy places from which they took their names.

This interconnection was helped by the commerce that was still kept up round the coasts of the Mediterranean. It was slowly

[1] Prudentius, *Peristephanon* VI, pp. 132, 135; Ennodius, *Libellum pro Synodo*, p. 315. Saint Ambrose believed firmly in the virtue of relics, and was himself inspired to discover some (letter XXII in *M.P.L.* vol. XVI, cols. 1019 ff.). Saint Victricius, in his *Liber de Laude Sanctorum*, asserts that relics have a virtue and a grace (*M.P.L.* vol. XX, cols. 453-4.) Saint Basil, on the other hand, liked to be absolutely certain about their authenticity. See his letter to Saint Ambrose about the body of a bishop of Milan, letter nþ. CXCVII in *M.P.G.* vol. XXXII, cols. 109-13.
[2] *Historia Translationum Sancti Mamantis vel Mammetis*, in *Acta Sanctorum*, 17 August, vol. III, pp. 441-3.
[3] Mabillon, *Annales Ordinis Sancti Benedicti*, vol. I, p. 481.
[4] Gregory of Tours, *De Gloria Martyrum*, in *M.P.L.* vol. LXXI, cols. 719-20. See Delehaye, *Les Origines du Culte des Martyres*, p. 99.

declining, owing to the growing impoverishment of the West; and at times it was interrupted, as when the Vandal pirates in the mid-fifth century made the seas no longer safe for unarmed traders; and discontent and heresy in the East added further difficulties. But there are many itineraries written in the sixth century by western pilgrims who had travelled eastward in Greek or Syrian merchant ships; and the merchants themselves carried religious news and gossip as well as passengers and merchandise. Thanks to the travellers and the traders, the historian Gregory of Tours was well informed on Oriental affairs. There exists the record of a conversation between Saint Symeon Stylites and a Syrian merchant who saw him on his pillar near Aleppo, in which Saint Symeon asked for news of Saint Geneviève of Paris and sent her a personal message.[1] In spite of the religious and political quarrels of the higher authorities, the relations between eastern and western Christians remained very cordial and close.

With the Arab conquests this era came to an end. Syrian merchants no longer came to the coasts of France and Italy, bringing their wares and their news. There were pirates again in the Mediterranean. The Moslem rulers of Palestine were suspicious of Christian travellers from abroad. The journey was expensive and difficult; and there was little wealth left in western Christendom. But intercourse was not entirely broken off. Western Christians still thought of the eastern holy places with sympathy and longing. When, in 682, Pope Martin I was accused of friendly dealings with the Moslems, he explained that his motive was to seek permission to send alms to Jerusalem.[2] In 670 the Frankish bishop Arculf set out for the East and managed to make a complete tour of Egypt, Syria and Palestine, and to return through Constantinople; but the journey took several years, and he met with many hardships.[3] We know the names of other pilgrims of the time, such as Vulphy

[1] *Vita Genovefae Virginis Parisiensis*, p. 226.
[2] Martin I, letter to Theodore, in *M.P.L.* vol. LXXXVII, cols. 199–200.
[3] Arculf's narrative, written by Adamnan, is given in the *P.P.T.S.* vol. III, trans. by J. R. Macpherson.

of Rue in Picardy, or Bercaire of Montier-en-Der in Burgundy and his friend Waimer.[1] But their stories showed that only rough and enterprising men could hope to reach Jerusalem. No women seem to have ventured on the pilgrimage.

During the eighth century the number of pilgrims increased. Some even came from England; of whom the most famous was Willibald, who died in 781 as Bishop of Eichstadt in Bavaria. In his youth he had gone to Palestine, leaving Rome in 722 and only returning there, after many disagreeable adventures, in 729.[2] Towards the end of the century there seems to have been an attempt to organize pilgrimages, under the patronage of Charles the Great. Charles had restored order and some prosperity to the West and had established good relations with the Caliph Harun al-Rashid. The hostels that were erected by his help in the Holy Land show that in his time many pilgrims must have reached Jerusalem, and women amongst them. Nuns from Christian Spain were sent to serve at the Holy Sepulchre.[3] But this activity was shortlived. The Carolingian empire declined. Moslem pirates reappeared in the eastern Mediterranean; Norse pirates came in from the West. When Bernard the Wise, from Brittany, visited Palestine in 870, he found Charles's establishments still in working order, but empty and beginning to decay. Bernard had only been able to make the journey by obtaining a passport from the Moslem authorities then governing Bari, in southern Italy; and even this passport did not enable him to land at Alexandria.[4]

The great age of pilgrimage begins with the tenth century. The Arabs lost their last pirate-nests in Italy and southern France in the course of the century; and Crete was taken from them in 961. Already by then the Byzantine navy had been for some time

---

[1] *De Sancto Wlphlagio*, in *Aa. Ss.* 7 June, June, vol. II, pp. 30–1.

[2] Willibald's *Hodoeporicon*, trans. by Brownlow, is given in the *P.P.T.S.* vol. III.

[3] 'Commemoratorium de Casis Dei vel Monasteriis', in Tobler and Molinier, *Itinera Hierosolymitana*, vol. I, p. 303.

[4] The *Itinerary of Bernard the Wise*, trans. by J. H. Bernard, is given in the *P.P.T.S.* vol. III.

sufficiently in command of the seas for maritime commerce in the Mediterranean to have fully revived. Greek and Italian merchant ships sailed freely between the ports of Italy and the Empire and were beginning, with the goodwill of the Moslem authorities, to open up trade with Syria and Egypt. It was easy for a pilgrim to secure a passage direct from Venice or from Bari to Tripoli or Alexandria; though most travellers preferred to call in at Constantinople to see its great collections of relics and then to proceed by sea or by the land route, which recent Byzantine military successes had now made secure. In Palestine itself the Moslem authorities, whether Abbasid, Ikshid or Fatimid, seldom caused difficulties, but, rather, welcomed the travellers for the wealth that they brought into the province.

The improvement in the conditions of pilgrimage had its effect on western religious thought. It is doubtful at what age pilgrimages were first ordered as canonical penances. Early medieval *poenitentialia* all recommend a pilgrimage, but usually without giving a specified goal. But the belief was growing that certain holy places possessed a definite spiritual virtue which affected those that visited them and could even grant indulgences from sin. Thus the pilgrim knew that not only would he be able to pay reverence to the earthly remains and surroundings of God and His saints and so enter into mystical contact with them but he might also obtain God's pardon for his wickedness. From the tenth century onwards four shrines in particular were held to have this power, those of Saint James at Compostella in Spain and of Saint Michael at Monte Gargano in Italy, the many sacred sites at Rome, and, above all, the holy places in Palestine. To all of these access was now far easier, owing to the retreat or the goodwill of the Moslems. But the journey was still sufficiently long and arduous to appeal to the common sense as well as to the religious feeling of medieval man. It was wise to remove a criminal for the space of a year or more from the scene of his crime. The discomforts and expense of his journey would be a punishment to him, while the achievement of his task and the emotional atmosphere of his goal would give him a feeling of spiritual cleansing and strength. He returned a better man.[1]

Casual references in the chroniclers tell us of frequent pilgrimages though the names of the actual pilgrims that we now possess are inevitably only those of the greater personages. From amongst the great lords and ladies of the West there came Hilda, Countess of Swabia, who died on her journey in 969, and Judith, Duchess of Bavaria, sister-in-law of the Emperor Otto I, whose tour took place in 970. The Counts of Ardèche, of Vienne, of Verdun, of Arcy, of Anhalt and of Gorizia, all were pilgrims. Leading ecclesiastics were even more assiduous. Saint Conrad, Bishop of Constance, made three separate journeys to Jerusalem, and Saint John, Bishop of Parma, no less than six. The Bishop of Olivola was there in 920. Pilgrim abbots included those of Saint-Cybar, of Flavigny, of Aurillac, of Saint-Aubin d'Angers and of Montier-en-Der. All these eminent travellers brought with them groups of humble men and women whose names were of no interest to the writers of the time.[2]

This activity was mainly the result of private enterprise. But a new force was appearing in European politics, which amongst its other work set about the organization of the pilgrim traffic. In 910 Count William I of Aquitaine founded the Abbey of Cluny. By the end of the century Cluny, ruled by a series of remarkable abbots, was the centre of a vast ecclesiastical nexus, well ordered, closely knit and intimately connected with the Papacy. The Cluniacs regarded themselves as the keepers of the conscience of western Christendom. Their doctrine approved of pilgrimage.

---

[1] See de Rozière, *Recueil général des Formules usitées dans l'Empire des Francs*, vol. II, pp. 939–41. A Frankish nobleman called Fromond, who with his brothers went to Palestine in order to expiate a crime in the mid-ninth century, is the first such penitent whose name is known. The *Peregrinatio Frotmundi* is given in the *Aa. Ss.* 24 October, Oct., vol. X, pp. 847 ff. See also van Cauwenbergh, *Les Pèlerinages expiatoires et judiciaires, passim,* and Villey, *La Croisade: Essai sur la Formation d'une Théorie juridique*, pp. 141 ff.

[2] See Bréhier, *L'Eglise et l'Orient au Moyen Age*, pp. 32–3, and Ebersolt, *Orient et Occident*, vol. I, pp. 72–3, who give references for these journeys.

They wished to give it practical assistance. By the beginning of the next century the pilgrimages to the great Spanish shrines were almost entirely under their control. At the same time they began to arrange and to popularize journeys to Jerusalem. It was owing to their persuasion that the Abbot of Stavelot set out for the Holy Land in 990 and the Count of Verdun in 997. Their influence is shown by the great increase in the eleventh century of pilgrims from France and Lorraine, from districts that were near to Cluny and her daughter houses. Though there were still many Germans amongst the pilgrims of the eleventh century, such as the Archbishops of Trier and Mainz and the Bishop of Bamberg, and many pilgrims from England, French and Lorraine pilgrims now by far outnumbered them. The two great dynasties of northern France, the Counts of Anjou and the Dukes of Normandy, were both, despite their mutual rivalry, the close friends of Cluny; and both patronized the eastern journey. The terrible Fulk Nerra of Anjou went to Jerusalem in 1002 and twice returned there later. Duke Richard III of Normandy sent alms there, and Duke Robert led a huge company there in 1035. All these pilgrimages were faithfully recorded by the Cluniac historian, the monk Glaber.[1]

The Normans followed their Dukes' example. They had a particular veneration for Saint Michael; and great numbers of them made the journey to Monte Gargano. From there the more enterprising would go on to Palestine. In the middle of the century they formed so large and so fervent a proportion of the Palestine pilgrims that the government at Constantinople, angry with the Normans for their raids on Byzantine Italy, began to show some ill will towards the pilgrim traffic.[2] Their cousins from Scandinavia

---

[1] Radulph Glaber in Bouquet, *R.H.F.* vol. x, pp. 20, 32, 52, 74, 106, 108. See Bréhier, *op. cit.* pp. 42–5; Ebersolt, *op. cit.* pp. 75–81.

[2] Bréhier, *op. cit.* p. 42, assumes that the 'schism' of Michael Cerularius created ill will between the Byzantines and the pilgrims. Riant, *Expéditions et Pèlerinages des Scandinaves*, p. 125, goes so far as to say that the Byzantine authorities deliberately closed the route to Palestine. This is apparently based on his interpretation of Lietbert of Cambrai's experience (see p. 49, and n. 1),

showed an almost equal enthusiasm. Scandinavians had long been used to visit Constantinople; and its wealth and wonders greatly impressed them. They talked in their northern homes of Micklegarth, as they called the great city; which they even at times identified with Asgard, the home of the gods. Already by 930 there were Norsemen in the Emperor's army. Early in the eleventh century there were so many of them that a special Norse regiment was formed, the famed Varangian Guard. The Varangians soon acquired the habit of spending a leave on a journey to Jerusalem. The first of whom we have a record was a certain Kolskeggr, who was in Palestine in 992. Harald Hardrada, most famous of the Varangians, was there in 1034. During the eleventh century there were many Norwegians, Icelanders and Danes who spent five or more years in the imperial service, then made the pilgrimage before they returned, rich with their savings, to their homes in the north. Stimulated by their tales their friends would come south merely to make the pilgrimage. The apostle to Iceland, Thorvald Kódransson Vidtförli, was in Jerusalem about the year 990. Several Norse pilgrims claimed to have seen there Olaf Tryggvason, first Christian king of Norway, after his mysterious disappearance in 1000. Olaf II intended to follow his example, but his voyage never took place except in legend. These Nordic princes were violent men, frequently guilty of murder and frequently in need of an act of penance. The half-Danish Swein Godwinsson set out with a body of Englishmen in 1051 to expiate a murder, but died of exposure in the Anatolian mountains next autumn. He had gone barefoot because of his sins. Lagman Gudrödsson, Norse king of Man, who had slain his brother, sought a similar pardon from God. Most Scandinavian pilgrims liked to make a round tour, coming by sea through the Straits of Gibraltar and returning overland through Russia.[1]

which is in fact explained by conditions in Syria at the time. But Pope Victor's letter (see p. 49, and n. 3) suggests that the imperial officials were not always cordial in their treatment of the pilgrims. Dislike of the Normans rather than any schism was the cause of the coldness.

[1] Riant, *op. cit.* pp. 97–129, gives a full account of the Norse pilgrims.

Tenth-century pilgrims from the West had been obliged to travel by sea across the Mediterranean to Constantinople or to Syria. But fares were high and berths not easy to obtain. In 975 the rulers of Hungary were converted to Christianity; and an overland route was opened, going down the Danube and across the Balkans to Constantinople. Till 1019, when Byzantium finally established control over the whole Balkan peninsula, this was a dangerous road; but thenceforward a pilgrim could travel with very little risk through Hungary to cross the Byzantine frontier at Belgrade and then proceed through Sofia and Adrianople to the capital. Alternatively, he could now go to Byzantine Italy and make the short sea-passage across from Bari to Dyrrhachium and then follow the old Roman Via Egnatia through Thessalonica to the Bosphorus. There were three good main roads that would take him across Asia Minor to Antioch. Thence he went down to the coast at Lattakieh and crossed into Fatimid territory near Tortosa. This was the only frontier that he had to pass since his arrival at Belgrade or at Termoli in Italy; and he could proceed without further hindrance to Jerusalem. Travel overland, though slow, was far cheaper and easier than travel by sea, and far better suited to large companies.

So long as the pilgrims were orderly they could count on hospitable treatment from the peasants of the Empire; and for the earlier part of their journey the Cluniacs were now building hostels along the route. There were several hospices in Italy, some restricted to the use of Norsemen. There was a great hospice at Melk in Austria.[1] At Constantinople the Hospice of Samson was reserved for the use of western pilgrims; and the Cluniacs kept up an establishment at Rodosto in the suburbs.[2] At Jerusalem itself pilgrims could stay at the Hospital of St John, founded by the merchants of Amalfi.[3] There was no objection to the great lords of the West bringing with them an armed escort, so long as it was

[1] Orderic Vitalis, *Historia Ecclesiastica* III, 4, vol. II, p. 64.
[2] See Riant, *op. cit.* p. 60.
[3] William of Tyre, XVIII, 4–5, I, pp. 822–6; Aimé, *Chronicon*, p. 320.

properly under control; and most pilgrims tried to join some such company. But it was not uncommon, nor particularly risky, for men to travel alone or in twos and threes. At times there might be difficulties. During Hakim's persecution it was uncomfortable to stay long in Palestine, though the flow of pilgrims was never wholly interrupted. In 1055 it was considered dangerous to cross the frontier into Moslem territory. Lietbert, Bishop of Cambrai, was not granted an exit-visa by the governor of Lattakieh and was forced to go to Cyprus.[1] In 1056 the Moslems, perhaps with the connivance of the Emperor, forbade westerners to enter the Holy Sepulchre and ejected some three hundred of them from Jerusalem.[2] Both Basil II and his niece the Empress Theodora caused offence by ordering their customs officers to levy a tax on pilgrims and their horses. Pope Victor II wrote to the Empress in December 1056, begging her to cancel the order; and his letter suggests that her officials were also to be found in Jerusalem itself.[3]

But such inconveniences were rare. Throughout the eleventh century till its last two decades, an unending stream of travellers poured eastward, sometimes travelling in parties numbering thousands, men and women of every age and every class, ready, in that leisurely age, to spend a year or more on the voyage. They would pause at Constantinople to admire the huge city, ten times greater than any city that they knew in the West, and to pay reverence to the relics that it housed. They could see there the Crown of Thorns, the Seamless Garment and all the major relics of the Passion. There was the cloth from Edessa on which Christ had imprinted His face, and Saint Luke's own portrait of the

[1] 'Vita Lietberti', in d'Achéry, *Spicilegium*, vol. IX, pp. 706–12. The great German pilgrimage of 1064–5, on which 7000 pilgrims travelled, found conditions south of the Byzantine frontier very uncomfortable. The account is given in *Annales Altahenses Majores*, p. 815. See Joranson, 'The Great German Pilgrimage of 1064–5'.

[2] 'Miracula Sancti Wolframni Senonensis', in *Acta Sanctorum Ordinis Sancti Benedicti*, saeculum III, pars I, pp. 381–2. Lietbert met travellers who had been turned out of Palestine ('Vita Lietberti', *loc. cit.*).

[3] Letter of Victor II, in *M.P.L.* vol. CXLIX, cols. 961–2, wrongly attributed to Victor III; Riant, *Inventaire critique des Lettres historiques des Croisades*, pp. 50–3.

Virgin; the hair of John the Baptist and the mantle of Elijah; the bodies of innumerable saints, prophets and martyrs; an endless store of the holiest things in Christendom.[1] Thence they went on to Palestine, to Nazareth and Mount Tabor, to the Jordan and to Bethlehem, and to all the shrines of Jerusalem. They gazed at them all and prayed at them all; then they made the long voyage homeward, returning edified and purified, to be greeted by their countrymen as the pilgrims of Christ who had made the most sacred of journeys.

But the success of the pilgrimage depended on two conditions: first, that life in Palestine should be orderly enough for the defenceless traveller to move and worship in safety; and secondly, that the way should be kept open and cheap. The former necessitated peace and good government in the Moslem world, the latter the prosperity and benevolence of Byzantium.

[1] Ebersolt, *Les Sanctuaires de Byzance*, pp. 105 ff.

CHAPTER IV

TOWARDS DISASTER

'In prosperity the destroyer shall come.'   JOB XV, 21

In the middle of the eleventh century the tranquillity of the east Mediterranean world seemed assured for many years to come. Its two great powers, Fatimid Egypt and Byzantium, were on good terms with each other. Neither was aggressive, and both wished to keep in check the Moslem states further to the east, where Turkish adventurers were stirring up trouble, without, however, seriously alarming the governments of Constantinople or Cairo. The Fatimids were friendly towards the Christians. Since Hakim's death there had been no persecution; and they were opening their ports to merchants from Byzantium and from Italy. Traders and pilgrims alike enjoyed their goodwill.

This goodwill was guaranteed by the power of Byzantium. Thanks to a series of great warrior Emperors the Empire now stretched from the Lebanon to the Danube and from Naples to the Caspian Sea. Despite occasional corruption and an occasional riot, it was better administered than any contemporary kingdom. Constantinople had never before been so wealthy. It was the unrivalled financial and commercial capital of the world. Traders from far and wide, from Italy and Germany, from Russia, from Egypt and the East, came crowding there to buy the luxuries produced by its factories and to exchange their own rougher wares. The bustling life of the vast city, far more extensive and populous than even Cairo or Baghdad, never failed to amaze the traveller with its crowded harbour, its full bazaars, its wide suburbs and its tremendous churches and palaces. The imperial court, dominated though it was at present by two wildly eccentric, elderly princesses, seemed to him the centre of the universe.

If art is the mirror of civilization, Byzantine civilization stood high. Its eleventh-century artists showed all the restraint and balance of their classical ancestors; but they added two qualities derived from Oriental tradition, the rich decorative formalism of the Iranians and the mystical intensity of the ancient East. The works of the age that survive, whether they be small ivories or great mosaic panels or provincial churches, such as those of Daphne or Holy Luke in Greece, all display the same triumphant synthesis of traditions merged into a perfect whole. The literature of the time, though more hampered by the overstrong memory of classical achievement, shows a variety all of excellent standard. We have the polished history of John Diaconus, the delicate lyrics of Christopher of Mitylene, the sweeping popular epic of Digenis Akritas, the rough, common-sense aphorisms of the soldier Cecaumenus and the witty, cynical court memoirs of Michael Psellus. The atmosphere almost has the complacency of the eighteenth century, but for an other-worldliness and a pessimism from which Byzantium never was freed.

The Greek has a subtle and difficult character, not to be recognized in the picture that popular students of the fifth century B.C. like to paint. The Byzantine complicated this character with the strains of eastern blood in him. The result was full of paradox. He was highly practical, with an aptitude for business and a taste for worldly honours; yet he was always ready to renounce the world for a life of monastic contemplation. He believed fervently in the divine mission of the Empire and the divine authority of the Emperor; yet he was an individualist, quick to rebel against a government that displeased him. He had a horror of heresy; yet his religion, most mystical of all the established forms of Christianity, allowed him, priest and layman alike, great philosophical latitude. He despised all his neighbours as barbarians; yet he easily adopted their habits and their ideas. Despite his sophistication and his pride his nerve was unsteady. Disaster had so often nearly overwhelmed

Byzantium that his confidence in things was sapped. In a sudden crisis he would panic and would indulge in savagery that in his calmer moments he disdained. The present might be peaceful and brilliant; but countless prophecies warned him that some day his city would perish, and he believed them to be true. Happiness and tranquillity could not be found in this dark transitory world, but only in the kingdom of Heaven.

His fears were justified. The foundations of Byzantine power were insufficiently sure. The great Empire had been organized for defence. The provinces were governed by military officials, themselves controlled by the civil administration at Constantinople. This system provided an efficient local militia that could defend its district in times of invasion and which could supplement the main imperial army on its great campaigns. But, with the danger of invasion over, it gave too much power to the provincial governor, especially if he were rich enough to ignore his paymaster at the capital. Moreover, prosperity was ruining the agrarian organization of Asia Minor. The backbone of Byzantium had been its communities of free peasants, holding their land directly from the State, often in return for military services. But, there as elsewhere in the Middle Ages, land was the only safe investment for wealth. Every rich man sought to acquire land. The Church persuaded its devotees to bequeath it land. Land was the usual reward given to successful generals or deserving ministers of state. So long as the Empire was winning back land from the enemy or repopulating areas emptied by raids and devastation, all seemed well; but its very success created a land-hunger. Magnates and monasteries could only increase their estates by buying out peasants that were in need of cash or by taking over whole villages, either as a gift from the state or by undertaking the responsibility for paying the taxes of the community. The wiser Emperors sought to prevent them, partly because the new landlord seldom resisted the temptation to turn his land into a sheep-ranch, and still more because the transference of peasant-soldiers' holdings gave to the landlord the power to raise a private army and weakened the army of the state. But their legislation failed. In the course of the tenth century there arose in Byzantium a hereditary land-owning aristocracy, rich and powerful enough to defy the central government. The Emperor Basil II, the greatest of the Macedonian dynasty, had with difficulty suppressed a revolt by members of this aristocracy early in his reign. He triumphed; and his prestige lasted on till his dynasty ended in 1056, at the death of his niece, Theodora. Had the Macedonian line produced male heirs, the hereditary principle might well have been established for the imperial throne, and Byzantium would have possessed a force capable of curbing the hereditary nobility. But, though loyalty to the dynasty enabled the Empress Zoe and her successive husbands to reign on in profligate insouciance for nearly thirty years and the aged Empress Theodora to rule alone, disruptive forces were growing all the while. When Theodora died, two parties in Byzantium faced each other in bitter opposition, the court clique which controlled the central administration and the noble families who controlled the army; while the Church, with a foot in both camps, attempted to hold the balance.[1]

Hardly had the septuagenarian Empress, trusting till the end in a prophecy that offered her a reign of many years, sunk into her final coma before the court had pushed on to the throne an elderly civil servant, Michael Stratioticus. The army refused to accept the new Emperor. It marched on Constantinople determined that its commander should succeed. Michael retired without a struggle; and the general, Isaac Comnenus, became Emperor. The military aristocracy had won the first round.

Isaac Comnenus, like many of his fellow-Byzantine noblemen, was an aristocrat of only the second generation. His father was a Thracian soldier, probably a Vlach, who had caught the fancy of

[1] For Byzantine civilization at this period see Iorga, *Histoire de la Vie Byzantine*, vol. II, pp. 230–49; Vasiliev, *Histoire de L'Empire Byzantin*, vol. I, pp. 476–92. For the agrarian problem in Byzantium, see Ostrogorsky, 'Agrarian Conditions in the Byzantine Empire', in *The Cambridge Economic History of Europe*, vol. I, pp. 204 ff. For the political history, see Bury, 'Roman Emperors from Basil II to Isaac Komnenos', in *Selected Essays*, pp. 126–214; Ostrogorsky, *Geschichte des byzantinischen Staates*, pp. 224–40.

Basil II and had been given by the Emperor lands in Paphlagonia, where he built a great castle known as *Castra Comnenôn,* and still to-day called Kastamuni. Isaac and his brother John inherited their father's lands and his military prowess, and both had married into the Byzantine aristocracy. Isaac's wife was a princess of the former royal house of Bulgaria, John's an heiress of the great family of the Dalasseni. But despite his wealth and his high command and the support of the army, Isaac found his government continually thwarted by the ill will of the civil service. After two years he gave up the struggle and retired to a monastery. He had no son; so he nominated as his successor Constantine Ducas. His sister-in-law, Anna Dalassena, never forgave him.

Constantine Ducas was head of probably the oldest and richest family of the Byzantine aristocracy; but he had made his career at court. Isaac hoped that he would therefore be acceptable to both parties. But he soon showed that his leanings were away from his caste. His treasury was empty; and the army was dangerously powerful. His solution was to reduce the armed forces. As a measure of internal policy this could be defended. But at no time in Byzantine history would it have been safe to weaken the Empire's defensive power; and at this moment such an action was fatal. Storm clouds were blowing up from the East; and in the West a storm had broken.[1]

For some decades past, the state of southern Italy had been turbulent and confused. The frontier of the Byzantine Empire officially ran from Terracina on the Tyrrhenian coast to Termoli on the Adriatic. But within that line only the provinces of Apulia and Calabria were under the direct rule of Byzantium. There the population was mainly Greek. On the west coast were the three merchant city-states of Gaeta, Naples and Amalfi. All three were nominally the vassals of the Emperor. The Amalfitans, who by now had a considerable trade with the Moslem East, found the Emperor's goodwill useful in their negotiations with the Fatimid

[1] Ostrogorsky, *op. cit.* pp. 238–42; Diehl and Marçais, *Le Monde Oriental de 395 à 1081,* pp. 523–31.

authorities; and they kept a permanent consul at Constantinople. The Neapolitans and the Gaetans, though equally ready to trade with the infidel, were less punctilious towards the Emperor. The interior of the country was held by the Lombard princes of Benevento and Salerno, acknowledging alternately the suzerainty of the eastern and the western emperor and equally disrespectful to both. Sicily was still held by the Moslems, despite many Byzantine attempts to reconquer the island; and raids along the Italian coasts from there and from Africa added to the chaos of the country.

Into these districts had come large numbers of Norman adventurers from northern France, pilgrims on their way to Jerusalem or to visit their favourite shrine of St Michael on Monte Gargano, many of them soldiers of fortune who stayed on to serve the Lombard princes. There was a land-hunger in Normandy, whose thickly populated estates offered no scope for ambitious and restless younger sons and landless knights. This impulse for expansion, which was soon to make them undertake the conquest of England, turned their eyes towards the East and all its riches; and they saw southern Italy as the key to a Mediterranean empire. Its confusion gave them their opportunity.

In 1040 six brothers, the sons of a petty Norman knight, Tancred de Hauteville, seized the town of Melfi in the Apulian hills and founded there a principality. The local Byzantine authorities did not take them seriously; but the western emperor, Henry III, eager to control a province for which the two empires had long contended, and the German Pope whom he had nominated, resentful that the Patriarch of Constantinople should rule over any Italian see, both gave the Normans their support. Within twelve years the sons of Tancred had established a mastery over the Lombard principalities. They had driven the Byzantines into the tip of Calabria and to the Apulian coast. They were threatening the cities of the west coast; and they were sending raids through Campania northward to the neighbourhood of Rome. The Byzantine government was alarmed. The governor of Apulia, Marianus Argyrus, was summoned home to report and sent out again with fuller powers to repair the situation. Militarily, Marianus achieved nothing. The Normans easily repulsed his small army. Diplomatically he was more successful; for the Pope, the Lorrainer Leo IX, was equally nervous. The Norman successes were greater than he or Henry III had envisaged. Henry was now occupied with a Hungarian campaign; but he sent help to the Pope. In the summer of 1053 Leo set out southward with an army of Germans and Italians, proclaiming that this was a holy war. A Byzantine contingent was to have joined him; but as he awaited it outside the little Apulian town of Civitate the Normans attacked him. His army was routed and he himself made prisoner. To obtain his release he disavowed his whole policy.

This was the last serious attempt to curb the sons of Tancred. Henry III died in 1056. His successor was the child Henry IV; and the regent, Agnes of Poitou, was too busy in Germany to concern herself with the south. The Papacy decided to be realist. In 1059, at the Council of Melfi, Pope Nicholas II recognized Robert Guiscard, 'Robert the Weasel', the eldest survivor of Tancred's sons, as 'Duke of Apulia and Calabria, by the grace of God and Saint Peter, and, by their help, of Sicily'. This recognition, considered by Rome but not by Robert to involve vassaldom to Saint Peter's heir, enabled the Normans easily to finish off their conquest. The maritime republics soon submitted to them; and by 1060 all that was left to the Byzantines in Italy was their capital, the coastal fortress of Bari. Meanwhile Robert's younger brother Roger began the slow but successful conquest of Sicily from the Arabs.[1]

So long as Bari held out, the Byzantines kept some check on further Norman expansion to the east. But the political troubles in Italy had inevitably led to religious troubles. The arrival of Latin conquerors in southern Italy brought up the question of the Greek Church in the province and the ancient dispute between

---

[1] The best accounts of the Norman infiltration into southern Italy and the conquest of the country are given in Chalandon, *Histoire de la Domination normande en Italie et en Sicile*, vol. I, chs. II–VII, and Gay, *L'Italie Méridionale et l'Empire Byzantin*, bk. V, chs. II–V.

Constantinople and Rome over its ecclesiastical allegiance. Reforms at Rome had resulted in the Papacy's determination to allow no compromise over any of its claims; while the Patriarchal see of Constantinople was now occupied by one of the most aggressive and ambitious of Greek Church statesmen, Michael Cerularius. The unhappy story of the visit of Pope Leo IX's legates to Constantinople in 1054 should be told in connection with the whole sequence of the relations between the eastern and western Churches. It ended in scenes of mutual excommunication, in spite of the Emperor's attempt to secure a compromise; and it made impossible any sincere co-operation between Rome and Constantinople as far as the immediate needs of Italy were concerned. But it did not cause the final schism which later historians have attributed to it. Political relations between the imperial courts were strained but unbroken. Cerularius soon lost his influence. Snubbed by the Empress Theodora, whom he had tried to exclude from her heritage, and deposed by the Emperor Isaac, he died an impotent exile. But in the end he triumphed. To subsequent generations of Byzantium he was seen as a champion of their independence; and, even at a moment when the Emperor and the Pope wrote to each other with renewed cordiality, the Empress Eudocia Macrembolitissa, his niece and the consort of Constantine Ducas, secured his canonization.[1]

To judge from the contemporary historians of Byzantium the quarrel was barely noticed by the rulers of the Empire. Trouble in the West was overshadowed in their eyes by the problems arising in the East.

The decline of the Abbasid Caliphate had not proved entirely beneficial to Byzantium. The growing impoverishment of Iraq began to alter the trade routes of the world. The far eastern merchant no longer brought his goods to the markets of Baghdad, from which much was carried on into the Empire, to be transhipped from the ports of Asia Minor or from Constantinople itself to the West. He preferred now to go by the Red Sea route to Egypt; and

[1] See below, pp. 96–8.

from Egypt his goods were taken to Europe by Italian merchant ships. Byzantium no longer lay across the route. Moreover, lawlessness in the outlying provinces of the Abbasid empire caused the closing down of the old caravan route from China that ran through Turkestan and northern Persia to Armenia and the sea at Trebizond. The alternative route, going to the north of the Caspian, was never secure for long. For the whole Mediterranean world, politically as well as commercially, the Abbasid power had been a benefactor, in providing an outer defence against the barbarians of central Asia.

The defences now were down. Central Asia was able once again to burst out over the lands of ancient civilization. The Turks had long played an important role in history. The Turkish empire of the sixth century had during its short life been a civilizing and stabilizing force in Asia. Outlying Turkish peoples, such as the Judaistic Khazars of the Volga or the Nestorian Christian Ouigours, later established on the frontier of China, showed themselves adaptable and capable of cultural progress. But in Turkestan itself there had been no advance since the seventh century. A few cities had grown up along the caravan routes, but the population of Turcomans remained for the most part pastoral and semi-nomadic; and its growing numbers gave it a continual desire to migrate beyond its boundaries. In the tenth century Turkestan was ruled by the Persian dynasty of the Samanids, whose chief role in history was their conversion of the Turks of central Asia to Islam. Henceforward the eyes of the Turks were directed towards the lands of south-western Asia and the eastern Mediterranean.

The Samanids were displaced by the first great Moslem Turk, Mahmud the Ghaznavid, who during the first decades of the eleventh century built up a great empire stretching from Ispahan to Bokhara and Lahore. Meanwhile Turkish soldiers of fortune were penetrating the whole Moslem world, much as the Normans were penetrating Christian Europe. Turkish regiments were maintained by the Caliph at Baghdad and by many other Moslem rulers. Amongst the subjects of the Ghaznavids was a clan of

Ghuzz Turks from the Aral steppes, called from the name of a semi-mythical ancestor the Seldjuks. The Seldjuk princes formed a group of adventurers, jealous of each other but uniting to secure the advancement of the family, not unlike the sons of Tancred de Hauteville. But, luckier than the Normans whose compatriots were few, they could call upon the support of the vast, restless hordes of Turcomans. After Mahmud's death in 1030 they rose against the Ghaznavids and by 1040 had driven them to take refuge in their Indian domains. In 1050 Tughril Bey, the senior prince of the house, entered Ispahan and made it the capital of a state comprising Persia and Khorassan, while his brothers and cousins established themselves on his northern borders, forming a loose confederation that acknowledged his overlordship and freely raiding the countries around. In 1055, on the invitation of the Abbasid Caliph, who had been terrified by the intrigues of his Turkish minister Basasiri with the Fatimids, Tughril entered Baghdad as the champion of Sunni Islam, and was made king of the East and the West, with supreme temporal power over all the lands that owed spiritual allegiance to the Caliph.[1]

There had been Turkish raids into Armenia as far back as the reign of Basil II, while the Seldjuks were still under Ghaznavid rule; and it was to protect his empire against the Turks that Basil had inaugurated the policy of the piecemeal annexation of Armenia. After the Seldjuk conquest of Persia the raids became more frequent. Tughril Bey himself only once took part, in 1054, when he devastated the country round Lake Van but failed to take the fortress of Manzikert. The raiding armies were usually led by his cousins, Asan and Ibrahim Inal. In 1047 they had been defeated by the Byzantines before Erzerum, and during the next years they concentrated on attacking the Georgian allies of the Empire. In 1052 they ravaged Kars; in 1056 and 1057 they were again in Armenia.

[1] The best summary of early Turkish history is given in the article 'Turks' by Barthold in the *Encyclopaedia of Islam*. See also the article 'Seljuks' by Houtsma in the *Encyclopaedia Britannica*, 11th ed. For Mahmud the Ghaznavid see Barthold, *Turkestan down to the Mongol Invasion*, pp. 18 ff.

In 1057 Melitene was sacked. In 1059 Turkish troops advanced for the first time into the heart of imperial territory, to the town of Sebastea.[1]

Tughril Bey died in 1063. He himself had not taken much interest in his north-western frontier. But his nephew and successor, Alp Arslan, nervous of a possible alliance between the Byzantines and the Fatimids, sought to protect himself from the former by the conquest of Armenia before he pursued his main objective against the latter. Raids into the Empire were intensified. In 1064 the old Armenian capital of Ani was destroyed; and the prince of Kars, the last independent Armenian ruler, gladly handed over his lands to the Emperor in return for estates in the Taurus mountains. Large numbers of Armenians accompanied him to his new home. From 1065 onwards the great frontier-fortress of Edessa was yearly attacked; but the Turks were as yet inexpert in siege warfare. In 1066 they occupied the passes of the Amanus mountains, and next spring they sacked the Cappadocian metropolis, Caesarea. Next winter Byzantine armies were defeated at Melitene and at Sebastea. These victories gave the Turks full control of Armenia. During the following years they raided far into the Empire, to Neocaesarea and Amorium in 1068, to Iconium in 1069, and in 1070 to Chonae, close to the Aegean coast.[2]

The imperial government was forced to take action. Constantine X, whose policy of reducing the armed forces was largely responsible for the serious situation, had died in 1067, leaving a young son, Michael VII, under the regency of the Empress-mother, Eudocia. Next year Eudocia married the commander-in-chief, Romanus Diogenes, and raised him to the throne. Romanus was a distinguished soldier and a sincere patriot; but the task before him required a man of genius. He saw that the safety of the Empire demanded the reconquest of Armenia. But the Byzantine army

---

[1] Laurent, *Byzance et les Turcs Seldjoucides*, pp. 16–24; Cahen, 'La première Pénétration turque en Asie Mineure', pp. 5–21, in *Byzantion*, vol. XVIII. See also Mukrimin Halil, *Türkiye Tarihi*, vol. I, *Anadolun Fethi*, *passim*.

[2] Laurent, *op. cit.* pp. 4–6; Cahen, *op. cit.* pp. 21–30.

was no longer the magnificent force it had been fifty years before. The provincial troops were inadequate to protect their own districts against the raiders; they could spare no troops for the Emperor's campaign. The noble families, who could have raised men from their estates, were suspicious and held aloof. The cavalry regiments, sixty thousand strong, that had patrolled the Syrian frontier till the middle of the century, were now disbanded. The imperial guards, hand-picked and highly trained Anatolians, were far below their old strength. The bulk of the army consisted now of foreign mercenaries, the Norsemen of the Varangian Guard, Normans and Franks from western Europe, Slavs from the north, and Turks from the steppes of southern Russia, Petcheneg, Cuman and Ghuzz. Out of these elements Romanus collected a force of nearly a hundred thousand men, of which perhaps half were Byzantine-born, but only a very few of these were professional soldiers and none was well-equipped. Of the mercenaries, the largest contingent was that of the Cuman Turks, under the leadership of the Turkish-born Joseph Tarchaniotes. The *corps d'élite* was the Frankish and Norman heavy cavalry, under the Norman, Roussel of Bailleul. The former Frankish commanders of the corps, Hervé and Crispin, had each in turn been deposed for open treachery; but the men would only serve under a compatriot. The chief Byzantine commander under the Emperor was Andronicus Ducas, the late Emperor's nephew and, like all his family, a bitter enemy of Romanus, who did not dare to leave him behind at Constantinople. With this large but untrustworthy army Romanus set out in the spring of 1071 to reconquer Armenia. As he was leaving the capital the news came through from Italy that Bari, the last Byzantine possession in the peninsula, had fallen to the Normans.

The chroniclers tell in tragic detail of the Emperor's march eastward along the great Byzantine military road. His intention was to capture and garrison the Armenian fortresses before the Turkish army should come up from the south. Alp Arslan was in Syria, near Aleppo, when he heard of the Byzantine advance. He realized how vital was the challenge; and he hurried northward to meet the

Emperor. Romanus entered Armenia along the southern branch of the upper Euphrates. Near Manzikert he divided his forces. He himself went on to Manzikert itself, while he sent his Franks and Cumans to secure the fortress of Akhlat, on the shores of Lake Van. At Manzikert he received news that Alp Arslan was approaching; and he swung to the south-west to reunite the army before the Turks should be on him. But, forgetful of the first principle of Byzantine tactics, he neglected to send out scouts. On Friday, 19 August, as he lay in a valley on the Akhlat road, awaiting his mercenaries, Alp Arslan fell on him. His mercenaries never came to his rescue. The Cumans, remembering that they were Turks and in arrears with their pay, had gone over in a body on the previous night to join the enemy; and Roussel and his Franks decided to take no part in the battle. The issue of the battle was not long in doubt. Romanus himself fought bravely; but Andronicus Ducas, seeing that his cause was lost and guessing that the next act of the drama would be played at Constantinople, drew the reserve troops under his command away from the battlefield and marched them westward, leaving the Emperor to his fate. By evening the Byzantine army was destroyed and Romanus wounded and a prisoner.[1]

[1] The fullest and best-referenced account is that given by Cahen, 'La Campagne de Mantzikert d'après les Sources Mussulmanes', in *Byzantion*, vol. IX, pp. 613–42. See also Laurent, *op. cit.* p. 43 and n. 10. The strategy and tactics of the battle are well described in Oman, *History of the Art of War*, pp. 217–19. Delbrück, *Geschichte der Kriegskunst*, vol. III, p. 206, and Lot, *L'Art Militaire et les Armées du Moyen Age*, vol. I, pp. 71–2, mock at Oman for accepting the enormous figures given in the eastern chroniclers for the strength of Romanus IV's army—100,000 men upwards—but the army was without doubt exceptionally large; only, as Laurent, *op. cit.* pp. 45–59, has pointed out, owing to Constantine X's economies on the army, its equipment was inadequate and the proportion of trained soldiers very small.

CHAPTER V

CONFUSION IN THE EAST

'Yea, though they have hired among the nations, now will I gather them, and they shall sorrow a little for the burden of the king of princes.' HOSEA VIII, IO

The Battle of Manzikert was the most decisive disaster in Byzantine history. The Byzantines themselves had no illusions about it. Again and again their historians refer to that dreadful day. To the later Crusaders it seemed that the Byzantines had forfeited on the battlefield their title as the protectors of Christendom. Manzikert justified the intervention of the West.[1]

The Turks made little immediate use of their victory. Alp Arslan had achieved his object. His flank was now protected; and he had removed the danger of a Byzantine-Fatimid alliance. All that he demanded of the captive Emperor was the evacuation of Armenia and a heavy ransom for his person. He then marched off to campaign in Transoxiana, where he died in 1072. Nor did his son and successor, Malik Shah, whose empire was to stretch from the Mediterranean to the boundaries of China, himself ever march into Asia Minor. But his Turcoman subjects were on the move. He had no wish to settle them in the ancient lands of the Caliphate; but the central plains of Anatolia, emptied and turned into sheep-farms by the Byzantine magnates themselves, were perfectly suited to them. He gave to his cousin, Suleiman

[1] William of Tyre, I, 2, vol. I, p. 29, considered that the disaster justified the Crusading movement as Byzantium could no longer protect eastern Christendom. Delbrück, *loc. cit.*, considers that the importance of the battle has been exaggerated; but it is clear from the evidence that as a result of it the Empire was unable to put an effective army into the field for many years to come. See Laurent, *loc. cit.*

ibn Kutulmish, the task of conquering the country for the Turkish people.[1]

The conquest was made easy by the Byzantines themselves. The next twenty years of their history were spent in a tangle of rebellion and intrigue. When the news reached Constantinople of the disaster and the Emperor's captivity, his stepson, Michael Ducas, declared himself of age and took over the government. The arrival of his cousin Andronicus with the remnants of the army confirmed his position. Michael VII was an intelligent, cultured youth, who in kindlier times would have been a worthy ruler. But the problems that faced him required a far greater man. Romanus Diogenes returned from his captivity to find himself deposed. He attempted to fight for his position but was easily defeated and taken as a prisoner to Constantinople. There they put out his eyes so savagely that he died a few days later. Michael could not afford to let him live; but Romanus's powerful relatives and the friends that his gallantry had won him were shocked and angry at the brutality of his end. Their resentment was soon to find its expression in treachery.[2]

The Turkish invasions of Asia Minor began seriously in 1073. They were neither concerted nor uniform. Suleiman himself wished to establish an orderly sultanate that he could govern under the suzerainty of Malik Shah. But there were lesser Turkish princes, men like Danishmend, Chaka or Menguchek, whose aim was to capture some town or fortress from which they could rule as brigand chieftains over whatever population might be there. Behind them, giving the invasion its full force, were the Turcoman

[1] Article 'Suleiman ben Qutulmush' by Zettersteen in *Encyclopaedia of Islam*; Laurent, *op. cit.* pp. 9–11; Cahen, 'La première Pénétration turque', in *Byzantion*, vol. XVIII, pp. 31–2. See also Wittek, 'Deux Chapitres de l'Histoire des Turcs de Roum', in *Byzantion*, vol. XI, pp. 285–319. For the question of the Turcomans, see Ramsay, 'Intermixture of Races in Asia Minor', in *Proc. Brit. Acad.* vol. VII, pp. 23–30, and Yakubovsky, 'Seldjuk Invasion and the Turcomans in the Eleventh Century' (in Russian), in *Proc. Acad. Sci. U.S.S.R.* 1936.

[2] The chief original source for this tangled period in Byzantine history is Nicephorus Bryennius, who covers it in detail. Modern résumés in Diehl and Marçais, *op. cit.* pp. 554 ff. and Ostrogorsky, *op. cit.* pp. 243–7.

nomads, travelling lightly armed, with their horses, their tents and their families, making for the upland prairies. The Christians fled before them, abandoning their villages to be burnt and their flocks and herds to be rounded up by the invaders. The Turcomans avoided the cities, but their presence and the destruction that they caused interrupted communications throughout the country and forced provincial governors into isolation and enabled the Turkish chieftains to follow their own desires. They formed the element that would render impossible any Byzantine attempt at reconquest.[1]

The Emperor Michael had tried to oppose the Turkish advance. The prudent treachery of Roussel of Bailleul had enabled his Franco-Norman regiment to survive the disaster at Manzikert. Unreliable though Roussel had proved himself, Michael was obliged to make use of him. To him he attached a small native army, under the young Isaac Comnenus, nephew of the former Emperor. The choice of Isaac was wise. He and his brother Alexius, who accompanied him, belonged to the family that most bitterly hated the Ducas clan; but, despite their mother's urging, they remained loyal to Michael throughout his reign, and both proved their worth as generals. But Isaac's loyalty was cancelled out by the perfidy of Roussel. Before the Byzantine army had met the Turks, Roussel and his troops threw off their allegiance. Isaac, attacked both by Turks and Franks and hopelessly outnumbered, was taken prisoner by the Seldjuks.

Roussel now made his intentions clear. Fired by the example of his compatriots in southern Italy, he planned himself to found a Norman state in Anatolia. He had only three thousand men with him; but they were devoted to him and well equipped and trained. Man to man they could outfight any Byzantine or Turkish soldier. To the Emperor, Roussel now seemed a more dangerous enemy than the Turks. Scraping together what troops he could gather, he sent them out under his uncle, the Caesar John Ducas. Roussel met them near Amorium and easily routed them, capturing the Caesar. To clothe himself with a legal excuse he proclaimed his

[1] See p. 65 n. 1 (references).

unwilling captive Emperor, and marched on Constantinople. He reached the Asiatic shore of the Bosphorus without hindrance, burning the suburb of Chrysopolis (Scutari) and camping amid its ruins. In despair Michael turned to the only power that could help him. An embassy was sent to the Seldjuk Sultan, Suleiman. Suleiman, with the approval of his suzerain, Malik Shah, promised assistance in return for the cession of the east Anatolian provinces that he already occupied. Roussel turned back to meet him; but his troops were surrounded by the Turks on Mount Sophon in Cappadocia. He himself with a few men managed to escape and to set himself up in Amasea, further to the north-east. Michael then sent Alexius Comnenus to deal with him. Alexius managed to outbid him for the support of the principal Turkish chieftain in the neighbourhood and induced him to surrender. But so efficient and popular had his government been that the citizens of Amasea only gave up their attempts to rescue him on the news of his being blinded. In truth Alexius could not bring himself so to mutilate him; and such was his charm that even the Emperor was glad to hear that he had not suffered that indignity.[1]

Roussel disappears from history. But the episode left its mark on the Byzantines. It taught them that the Normans were not to be trusted, that their ambition was not bounded by the shores of southern Italy but they wished to found principalities in the East. It goes far to explain Byzantine policy twenty years later. In the meantime Normans were discouraged from entering the imperial service; and even their Scandinavian cousins were suspect. The Varangian Guard was henceforward recruited from a people that had suffered from the Normans, the Anglo-Saxons of Britain.[2]

Fear of the Normans and the constant need for foreign mercenaries prompted Michael to adopt a policy of appeasement towards

---

[1] Roussel's career is told by Bryennius, pp. 73–96, and Attaliates, pp. 183 ff. See Schlumberger, 'Deux Chefs normands', in *Revue Historique*, vol. XVI.

[2] For the English in the Varangian Guard, see Vasilievsky, *Works* (in Russian), vol. I, pp. 355–77; Vasiliev, 'Opening Stages of the Anglo-Saxon Immigration to Byzantium', in *Seminarium Kondakovianum*, vol. IX, pp. 39–70.

the West. The loss of southern Italy was irreparable; nor could he afford to continue the war there. The ambassador that he sent to make peace with the Normans, John Italus, an Italian-born philosopher, was considered by many Byzantines to have betrayed the interests of the Empire. But Michael was satisfied, and, knowing the desire of the upstart house of Hauteville to make grand marriage alliances, he suggested that Guiscard's daughter, Helen, be sent as a bride for his own infant son Constantine. At the same time he sought and obtained the cordial friendship of the great Pope Gregory VII. His policy preserved peace on his western frontier.[1]

But in Anatolia confusion grew worse. The imperial government lost control; and though a few loyal generals, such as Isaac Comnenus, now in command of Antioch, maintained the Emperor's authority, communications were interrupted and there was no concerted policy. At last, in 1078, Nicephorus Boteniates, governor of the great Anatolic Theme in west-central Asia Minor, partly from personal ambition and partly from genuine exasperation at the weakness of Michael's rule, rose up in revolt. But Nicephorus was a general without an army. To secure himself the force that he needed he enrolled large numbers of Turks under his standard and used them to garrison the towns that he took on his way to the capital: Cyzicus, Nicaea, Nicomedia, Chalcedon and Chrysopolis. For the first time, Turkish hordes found themselves inside the great cities of western Anatolia. They might be the mercenaries of the new Emperor; but he would not find it easy to dislodge them. Michael made no resistance. When Nicephorus entered the capital he retired into a monastery. There he found his true vocation. Luckier than most fallen emperors, within a few years he had risen, entirely on his merits, to an archiepiscopal throne. His deserted wife, the Caucasian Maria of Alania, the loveliest princess of her day, wisely offered her hand to the usurper.

Nicephorus found a rebel's life easier than a ruler's. Other generals followed his example. In the west of the Balkans Nicephorus Bryennius, the governor of Dyrrhachium, declared

[1] Chalandon, *op. cit.* vol. I, pp. 264–5; Gay, *Les Papes du XIe Siècle*, pp. 311–12.

himself Emperor and attracted the soldiers of the European provinces to his standard. Alexius Comnenus was sent against him with a small force of untrained Greek soldiers and a few Franks; who, as usual, deserted. It was only through the timely arrival of some Turkish mercenaries that he was able to defeat Bryennius. No sooner was this campaign ended than Alexius had to go to Thessaly to crush another usurper, Basilacius. Meanwhile, the Turkish garrison of Nicaea rose in revolt. Pope Gregory, on the news of the fall of his ally Michael, had excommunicated the new Emperor; and Robert Guiscard, encouraged by the Papacy and himself furious at the rupture of his daughter's engagement, planned to cross the Adriatic. In May he landed in full force at Avlona and marched on Dyrrhachium. Early that same spring the leading general in Asia, Nicephorus Melissenus, revolted and made an alliance with the Turkish Sultan Suleiman; thanks to which Suleiman was enabled to march unchallenged into Bithynia, where the Turkish garrisons left by Boteniates welcomed him. When Melissenus failed to capture Constantinople Suleiman refused to hand back the cities that he occupied. Instead, he established himself in Nicaea; and Nicaea, one of the most venerated cities of Christendom, situated within a hundred miles of Constantinople itself, became the capital of the Turkish sultanate.

In Constantinople the Emperor Nicephorus threw away his only chance of survival by quarrelling with the family of the Comneni. Isaac and Alexius had served him loyally and had hoped to keep his goodwill by a close friendship with the Empress, whose cousin Isaac had married and whose lover Alexius was thought to be. But she could not control the court intrigues that turned Nicephorus against them. For their own safety the brothers were forced into rebellion; and Alexius, recognized by his family as the abler of the two, proclaimed himself Emperor. Nicephorus fell as easily as the Emperor that he had dislodged. On the advice of the Patriarch he retired, weary and humiliated, to end his days as a monk.[1]

[1] The best summary of the reign of Boteniates is given in Chalandon, *Essai sur le Règne d'Alexis Comnène*, pp. 35-50.

Alexius Comnenus was to reign for thirty-seven years and was to prove the greatest statesman of his time. But in the year 1081 it seemed certain that neither he nor his Empire could survive. He was a young man, probably not yet thirty years of age, but he had had many years' experience as a general, usually as a general with inadequate forces, whose success depended on his wits and his diplomacy. His presence was impressive; he was not tall, but well-built, with a dignified air. His manner was gracious and easy, and his self-control was remarkable; but he combined a genuine kindliness with a cynical readiness to use trickery and terror if the interests of his country required. He had few assets beyond his personal qualities and the affection of his troops. His family, with its connections branching through the Byzantine aristocracy, had undoubtedly helped him into power; and he had strengthened his position by marrying a lady of the Ducas house. But the intrigues and jealousies of his relatives, especially the hatred that his domineering mother bore for his wife and all her clan, only added to his problems. The court was filled with members of former imperial families or the families of would-be usurpers, whom Alexius sought to bind to him by marriage alliances. There was the Empress Maria, desperately jealous of the new Empress, Irene; and Maria's son, Constantine Ducas, whom he made his junior colleague and soon betrothed to his eldest child, Anna; there were the sons of Romanus Diogenes, one of whom he married to his sister Theodora; there was the son of Nicephorus Bryennius, who actually married Anna Comnena after the early death of Constantine Ducas; there was Nicephorus Melissenus, already married to his sister Eudocia, who yielded his claims to the Empire to his brother-in-law in return for the title of Caesar. Over all of them Alexius had to keep a watchful eye, calming their quarrels and forestalling their treachery. An elaborate system of titles was created to satisfy their pretensions. The nobility and the higher civil service were equally unreliable. Alexius continually discovered conspiracies against his government and was in constant danger of assassination. Both from policy and from temperament he was gentle in his punishments; and this clemency and the calm long-sightedness of all his actions are the more remarkable in view of the personal insecurity in which his whole life was spent.[1]

The state of the Empire in 1081 was such that only a man of great courage or of great stupidity would have undertaken its government. There was no money in the treasury. Recent Emperors had been spendthrift; the loss of Anatolia and rebellions in Europe had sadly diminished the revenue; the old system of tax-collection had broken down. Alexius was no financier; his methods would have left a modern economist aghast. Yet somehow, by taxing his subjects to their utmost limits, by exacting forced loans and confiscating property from the magnates and the Church, by punishing with fines rather than imprisonment, by selling privileges and by developing the palace industries, he managed to pay for a large administrative organization and to rebuild the army and the navy, and at the same time to maintain a sumptuous court and to make lavish gifts to loyal subjects and visiting envoys and princes. For he realized that in the East prestige depends entirely on splendour and magnificence. Niggardliness is the one unforgiven sin. But Alexius was guilty of two great errors. In return for immediate aid he gave commercial advantages to foreign merchants, to the detriment of his own subjects; and at one crucial moment he debased the imperial coinage, the coinage that for seven centuries had provided the only stable currency in a chaotic world.

In foreign affairs the situation was even more desperate—if 'foreign' was still an applicable epithet; for on all sides enemies had penetrated far into the Empire. In Europe the Emperor maintained a precarious hold over the Balkan peninsula; but the Slavs of Serbia and Dalmatia had risen in revolt. The Turkish tribe of Petchenegs, roaming beyond the Danube, continually crossed the river to raid. And in the West Robert Guiscard and the Normans

---

[1] Anna Comnena describes her father's personal appearance in flattering terms in the *Alexiad*, III, ii, 5, vol. I, pp. 106–7. His character is summarized in Chalandon, *op. cit.* pp. 51–2. The anonymous *Synopsis Chronicon*, which is not always well disposed towards him, calls him 'μεγαλόβουλος καὶ μεγαλουργός', 'great in will and in action' (p. 185).

had captured Avlona and were besieging Dyrrhachium. In Asia little was left to Byzantium except the Black Sea coasts, a few isolated cities on the south coast and the great fortified metropolis of Antioch; but communications with these further cities were uncertain and rare. Several cities in the interior were still in Christian hands; but their rulers were entirely cut off from the central government. The bulk of the country was in the hands of the Seldjuk Sultan Suleiman, who ruled from Nicaea domains stretching from the Bosphorus to the Syrian frontier; but his state had no organized administration and no fixed frontiers. Other cities were in the power of pettier Turkish princes, some of them acknowledging the suzerainty of Suleiman, but most of them admitting no master but Malik Shah. Of these the most important were the house of Danishmend, now in possession of Caesarea, Sebastea and Amasea; Menguchek, the lord of Erzindjan and Colonea; and, most dangerous of all, the adventurer Chaka who had captured Smyrna and the Aegean littoral. The Turkish chieftains had established some sort of order round their main cities; but the countryside was still overrun by nomad Turcoman hordes, while bodies of Greek and Armenian refugees added to the confusion. Large numbers of Christians adopted Islam and were gradually merged into the Turkish race. A few Greek communities lingered on in mountain districts; and the Christian Turks, settled some centuries before round Caesarea in Cappadocia, retained their identity and their religion right down to modern times. But the majority of the Greek population made its way as best it could to the shores of the Black Sea and the Aegean.[1]

[1] For the Petchenegs, see Vasilievsky, *Works* (in Russian), vol. I, pp. 38 ff. For Suleiman, see *art. cit.* in the *Encyclopaedia of Islam*, and the article 'Izniq' *ibid.* by Honigmann. For the Danishmends, see article 'Danişmend' by Mukrimin Halil in the Turkish *Islam Ansiklopedisi*, and Cahen, 'La première Pénétration turque', *op. cit.* pp. 46–7, 58–60. For Menguchek see the article 'Menguchek' by Houtsma in the *Encyclopaedia of Islam*. For Chaka, who is only known to us from Anna Comnena, *Alexiad*, VII, viii, 1–8, vol. II, pp. 110–16; for his early career see the article 'Izmir' by Mordtmann in the *Encyclopaedia of Islam*. For the indigenous population, see Bogiatzides, Ἱστορικαὶ Μελέται, vol. I, pt. I, *passim*, and Köprülü, *Les Origines de l'Empire Ottoman*, pp. 48 ff.

The migration of the Armenians was more deliberate and orderly. The various Armenian princes dispossessed by the Byzantines had been given estates in Cappadocia, especially in the south, towards the Taurus mountains. Many of their retainers had accompanied them; and when the Seldjuk invasions began in earnest a continual stream of Armenians left their homes to join these new colonies, till almost half of the population of Armenia was on the move south-westward. The Turkish penetration of Cappadocia drove them further into the Taurus mountains and the Anti-Taurus; and they spread out into the valley of the middle Euphrates, to which the Turks had not yet come. The districts that they had abandoned were soon filled not by Turks but by Moslem Kurds from the hills of Assyria and north-west Iran. The last Armenian prince of the old Bagratid dynasty, a dynasty that proudly claimed descent from David and Bathsheba, was killed by Byzantine orders in 1079, after his own peculiarly atrocious murder of the Archbishop of Caesarea; whereupon one of his relatives, by name Roupen, rebelled from the Empire and set himself up in the hills of north-west Cilicia. About the same time another Armenian chieftain, Oshin, son of Hethoum, founded a similar lordship a little further to the west. Both the Roupenian and the Hethoumian dynasties had parts to play in later history; but at the time Roupen and Oshin were outshone by the Armenian Vahram, whom the Greeks called Philaretus.

Philaretus had been in Byzantine service and had been appointed by Romanus Diogenes to the governorship of Germanicia (Marash). When Romanus fell he refused to recognize Michael Ducas and declared himself independent. During the chaos of Michael's reign he conquered the chief cities of Cilicia, Tarsus, Mamistra and Anazarbus. In 1077 one of his lieutenants, after a siege of six months, took Edessa from the Byzantines. In 1078 the citizens of Antioch, whose governor, the successor to Isaac Comnenus, had just been assassinated, begged Philaretus to take over the city to save it from the Turks. His dominion now stretched from Tarsus to the lands beyond the Euphrates; and both Roupen and Oshin became his vassals. But he felt insecure. Unlike most of his contemporaries he was Orthodox, and he did not wish to separate himself entirely from the Empire. On Michael's abdication he announced his allegiance to Nicephorus Boteniates, who left him as governor of the lands that he had conquered. He apparently recognized Alexius also; but he took the additional precaution of paying some sort of homage to the Arab lords of Aleppo.[1]

Alexius on his accession was obliged to decide against which of his enemies it was necessary first to campaign. Calculating that the Turks could only be driven back by a long sustained effort for which he was not yet ready and that in the meantime they were likely to quarrel amongst themselves, he considered it more urgent to defeat the Norman attack. It took longer than he had thought. In the summer of 1081 Robert Guiscard, accompanied by his Amazon wife, Sigelgaita of Salerno, and by his eldest son, Bohemond, laid siege to Dyrrhachium. In October Alexius, with an army whose chief regiment was the Anglo-Saxon Varangian Guard, went to relieve the fortress. But there, as at Hastings, fifteen years before, the Anglo-Saxons were no match for the Normans. Alexius was decisively beaten. Dyrrhachium held out over the winter but fell in February 1082, enabling Robert in the spring to march along the great main road, the Via Egnatia, towards Constantinople. Italian affairs soon obliged him to return home; but he left his army under Bohemond to secure Macedonia and Greece. Bohemond twice defeated Alexius, who was obliged to borrow men from the Turks and ships from the Venetians. While the latter interrupted Norman communications, the former enabled the Emperor to deliver Thessaly. Bohemond retired to Italy in 1083 but returned with his father next year, destroying the Venetian fleet off Corfu. The war only ended when Robert died in Cephalonia in 1085, and his sons quarrelled over his inheritance.[2]

---

[1] Laurent, *op. cit.* pp. 81 ff.; *idem*, 'Des Grecs aux Croisés', pp. 368–403; Grousset, *Histoire des Croisades*, pp. xl–xliv. Philaretus's career is known to us chiefly from the hostile account given by Matthew of Edessa (II, cvi ff. pp. 173 ff.), who hated him as an Orthodox Christian.

[2] For the Norman war, see Chalandon, *op. cit.* pp. 58–94.

The authority of the Emperor was at last established over the European provinces; but during those four years the eastern provinces were lost. Philaretus fatally involved himself in Turkish intrigues. Early in 1085 Antioch was betrayed by his son to the Sultan Suleiman, together with his Cilician cities. Edessa fell in 1087 to a Turkish chieftain, Buzan, but was recaptured later in 1094 by an Armenian, Thoros, who had been a vassal of Malik Shah and was at first kept in order by a Turkish garrison in the citadel. Melitene meanwhile was occupied by another Armenian, his father-in-law, Gabriel, who, like Thoros, belonged to the Orthodox rite. Quarrels between the Orthodox and the Jacobite and Armenian Churches increased the disorder throughout northern Syria. To the latter the decline of Byzantine power was a matter for rejoicing. They preferred the rule of the Turk.[1]

In southern Syria Seldjuk domination was now complete. Ever since Tughril Bey had entered Baghdad in 1055 the Syrian possession of the Fatimites had been threatened; and growing alarm and suspense there had resulted in disorder and petty rebellions. When in 1056 the Byzantine frontier officials at Lattakieh had refused to allow the pilgrim Bishop of Cambrai to proceed southward, their motive was not, as the westerners suspected, just to be unpleasant to a Latin (though there was probably a ban on Norman pilgrims); they were informed that Syria was unsafe for Christian travellers. The experience of the German bishops who eight years later insisted on crossing the frontier against local advice shows that the Byzantine officials were justified.[2]

In 1071, the year of Manzikert and the fall of Bari, a Turkish adventurer, Atsiz ibn Abaq, nominally vassal to Alp Arslan, captured Jerusalem without a struggle and soon occupied all Palestine down to the frontier fortress of Ascalon. In 1075 he took possession of Damascus and the Damascene. In 1076 the

---

[1] Laurent, 'Des Grecs aux Croisés', pp. 403–10 (references); also article 'Malatya' by Honigmann in the *Encyclopaedia of Islam*.
[2] See above, p. 49 nn. 1 and 2.

Fatimids recovered Jerusalem, from which Atsiz drove them again after a siege of several months and a massacre of the Moslem inhabitants. Only the Christians, safe within their walled quarter, were spared. Despite this, the Fatimids were soon able to attack Atsiz at Damascus; and he was obliged to call in the help of the Seldjuk prince, Tutush, the brother of Malik Shah, who was trying, with his brother's approval, to build himself a sultanate in Syria. In 1079 Tutush had Atsiz murdered and became sole ruler of a state stretching from Aleppo, which remained still under its Arab dynasty, to the borders of Egypt. Tutush, and his lieutenant Ortoq, governor of Jerusalem, seem to have provided an orderly government. There was no special animosity shown against the Christians, though the Orthodox Patriarch of Jerusalem seems to have spent much of his time in Constantinople, where his colleague from Antioch now took up residence.[1]

In 1085 the Emperor Alexius, freed from the Norman danger, turned his attention to the Turkish problem. Hitherto it had only been by unceasing intrigues, setting one Turkish prince against another, that he had been able to keep any check on them. Now, combining his diplomacy with a show of arms, he secured a treaty that restored to the Empire Nicomedia and the Anatolian shores of the Marmora. Next year his patience was rewarded still further. Suleiman ibn-Kutulmish, having taken Antioch, marched on Aleppo, whose Arab ruler called on Tutush to rescue him. In

---

[1] See articles 'Tutush' by Houtsma and 'Ortoqids' by Honigmann in the *Encyclopaedia of Islam*. The Coptic *History of the Patriarchs of Alexandria* compares Turkish rule very favourably to the Frankish rule that followed in Palestine (pp. 181, 207). The famous arrow that Ortoq fired at the roof of the Holy Sepulchre was not intended as an insult but as a sign of suzerainty. See Cahen, 'La Tughra Seldjucide', in *Journal Asiatique*, vol. CXXXIV, pp. 167–73. The Patriarch Euthymius of Jerusalem was in Constantinople at the end of 1082, when he went to Thessalonica on an embassy to Bohemond, and his successor, Symeon, was at the Council there in 1086 which condemned Leo of Chalcedon. (See Dölger, *Regesten*, no. 1087, vol. II, p. 30 and Montfaucon, *Bibliotheca Coisliniana*, pp. 102 ff. for the Church Council at Constantinople that year.) But he was back in Jerusalem in 1089. The Patriarch of Antioch was present at this Council. See below, p. 103 n. 1.

a battle fought outside the city, Tutush was victorious and Suleiman was slain.

The death of Suleiman brought chaos to the Turks in Anatolia; and Alexius was in his element, plotting with one chieftain against another, playing on their mutual jealousies, offering each in turn bribes and hints of a marriage alliance. Nicaea was held for six years by the Turkish rebel, Abu'l Kasim; but in 1092 Malik Shah was able to replace him by the son of Suleiman, Kilij Arslan I. Meanwhile Alexius had been able to consolidate his position. It was not easy. The only territory that he could recover was the town of Cyzicus; and he could not prevent the Danishmends from extending their dominion westward and taking his own family home, Kastamuni, in Paphlagonia. Palace conspiracies hampered him; and in 1087 he had to meet a serious invasion from over the Danube, led by the Petchenegs with Hungarian help. It was not till 1091 that his diplomacy, aided by one tremendous victory, permanently freed him from the threat of barbarian inroads from the north.

More alarming still was Chaka, the Turkish Emir of Smyrna. Chaka, more ambitious than most of his compatriots, aimed at succeeding to the Empire. He employed Greeks rather than Turks, for he realized the need for sea-power; but at the same time he attempted to organize the Turkish princes into an alliance and married his daughter to the young Kilij Arslan. Between 1080 and 1090 he made himself master of the Aegean coast and the islands of Lesbos, Chios, Samos and Rhodes. Alexius, one of whose first cares had been to recreate the Byzantine fleet, managed at last to defeat him on the sea at the entrance to the Marmora; but the menace remained till in 1092 Chaka was murdered by his son-in-law, Kilij Arslan, at a banquet at Nicaea. The murder was the result of the Emperor's advice to the Sultan, who feared to see another Turk grow greater than himself.[1]

[1] Chaka's death is described in Anna Comnena, IX, iii, 3, vol. II, pp. 165–6, but a new Chaka appears in her history (IX, v, 3, vol. III, pp. 24–5). He was probably the son of the first Chaka and known as Ibn Chaka, which Anna

With Suleiman and Chaka dead, Alexius could contemplate a more aggressive policy. He himself was now secure in Constantinople; and the European provinces were quiet. His fleet was efficient; his treasury was temporarily full. But his army was very small. He had few native troops on which to draw, with Anatolia lost to him. His need was for trained foreign mercenaries.

Certainly, by about the year 1095, it seemed that the Seldjuk power was at last declining. Malik Shah, who had kept some control over the whole Turkish empire, died in 1092; and his death was followed by civil war between his young sons. For the next ten years, till they could agree to a division of their inheritance, the main attention of the Turks was given to this struggle. Meanwhile Arab and Kurdish chieftains arose in Iraq. In Syria, where Tutush died in 1095, his sons, Ridwan of Aleppo and Duqaq of Damascus, proved themselves incapable of keeping order. Jerusalem passed to the sons of Ortoq. Their government was ineffectual and oppressive. The Orthodox Patriarch Symeon and his higher clergy retired to Cyprus. At Tripoli a Shiite clan, the Banū 'Ammār, set up a principality. The Fatimids began to reconquer southern Palestine. In the north a Turkish general, Kerbogha, Atabeg of Mosul under the Abbasid Caliph, gradually encroached upon Ridwan's territory of Aleppo. To the travellers of the time it seemed that every city had a different master.[1]

It is remarkable that there were still travellers, not only Moslems but also Christian pilgrims from the West. The pilgrim traffic had never entirely ceased, but the journey was now very difficult. In Jerusalem, till Ortoq's death, the life of the Christians seems to have been very little affected; and Palestine, except when Turks and Egyptians were actually engaged in fighting there, was usually

simplifies as Chaka. Similarly the Sultan Kilij Arslan is called Suleiman by western authors who were used to hearing him called Ibn Suleiman. Chaka's war with Alexius is described in Chalandon, *op. cit.* pp. 126 ff.

[1] See the article 'Sukman ibn Ortok' by Zettersteen in the *Encyclopaedia of Islam*. William of Tyre, I, 8, vol. I, pp. 25–6, describes the impression of the pilgrims of the time. Symeon of Jerusalem had retired to Cyprus well before the commencement of the Crusade, but the actual date is unknown.

quiet. But Anatolia could now be traversed only if the voyager took an armed escort; and even so the way was full of danger, and wars or hostile authorities often held him up. Syria was little better. Everywhere there were brigands on the roads; and at each small town the local lord tried to levy a tax on passers-by. The pilgrims that succeeded in overcoming all the difficulties returned to the West weary and impoverished, with a dreadful tale to tell.

BOOK II

THE PREACHING OF
THE CRUSADE

CHAPTER I

HOLY PEACE AND HOLY WAR

'We looked for peace, but no good came.'   JEREMIAH VIII, 15

The Christian citizen has a fundamental problem to face: is he entitled to fight for his country? His religion is a religion of peace; and war means slaughter and destruction. The earlier Christian Fathers had no doubts. To them a war was wholesale murder. But after the triumph of the Cross, after the Empire had become Christendom, ought not its citizens to be ready to take up arms for its welfare?

The eastern Church thought not. Its great canonist, Saint Basil, while he realized that the soldier must obey orders, yet maintained that anyone guilty of killing in war should refrain for three years from taking communion as a sign of repentance.[1] This counsel was too strict. The Byzantine soldier was not in fact treated as a murderer. But his profession brought him no glamour. Death in battle was not considered glorious, nor was death in battle against the infidel considered martyrdom; the martyr died armed only with his faith. To fight against the infidel was deplorable though it might at times be unavoidable; to fight against fellow-Christians was doubly bad. Indeed, Byzantine history was remarkably free of wars of aggression. Justinian's campaigns had been undertaken to liberate Romans from heretic barbarian governors Basil II's against the Bulgars to recover imperial provinces and to remove a danger that menaced Constantinople. Peaceful methods were always preferable, even if they involved tortuous diplomacy or the payment of money. To western historians, accustomed to admire martial valour, the actions of many Byzantine statesmen

[1] Saint Basil, letter no. 188, in *M.P.G.* vol. XXXII, col. 681.

appear cowardly or sly; but the motive was usually a genuine desire to avoid bloodshed. The princess Anna Comnena, one of the most typical of Byzantines, makes it clear in her history that, deep as was her interest in military questions and much as she appreciated her father's successes in battle, she considered war a shameful thing, a last resort when all else had failed, indeed in itself a confession of failure.[1]

The western point of view was less enlightened. Saint Augustine himself had admitted that wars might be waged by the command of God;[2] and the military society that had emerged in the West out of the barbarian invasions inevitably sought to justify its habitual pastime. The code of chivalry that was developing, supported by popular epics, gave prestige to the military hero; and the pacifist acquired a disrepute from which he has never recovered. Against this sentiment the Church could do little. It sought, rather, to direct bellicose energy into paths that would lead to its own advantage. The holy war, that is to say, war in the interests of the Church, became permissible, even desirable. Pope Leo IV, in the mid-ninth century, declared that anyone dying in battle for the defence of the Church would receive a heavenly reward.[3] Pope John VIII, a few years later, ranked the victims of a holy war as martyrs; if they died armed in battle their sins would be remitted. But the soldier should be pure at heart.[4] Nicholas I laid down that men under the sentence of the Church for their sins should not bear arms, except to fight against the infidel.[5]

But, though the highest ecclesiastical authorities thus did not condemn fighting, there were thinkers in the West whom it shocked. The German Bruno of Querfurt, martyred by the

---

[1] For Anna Comnena's attitude, see Buckler, *Anna Comnena*, pp. 97–9.

[2] Saint Augustine, *De Civitate Dei*, in *M.P.L.* vol. XLI, col. 35.

[3] Mansi, *Concilia*, vol. XIV, p. 888.

[4] John VIII, letters, in *M.P.L.* vol. CXXVI, cols. 696, 717, 816; Mansi, *Concilia*, vol. XVII, p. 104.

[5] Letter of Nicholas I in *Monumenta Germaniae Historica, Epistolae*, vol. VI, p. 658. This letter was incorporated in the canonical collections of Burchard and Gratian.

heathen Prussians in 1009, had been outraged by the wars waged by the emperors of his time against fellow-Christians, Otto II against the French king, and Henry II against the Poles.[1] A movement for peace had already been inaugurated in France. The Council of Charroux, in 989, where the bishops of Aquitaine met to protect the immunity of the clergy, suggested that the Church should guarantee that the poor might live in peace.[2] At the Council of Le Puy next year the suggestion was repeated more firmly. Guy of Anjou, Bishop of Le Puy, declared that without peace no one would behold the Lord, and therefore urged all men to become the sons of peace.[3] A few years later, William the Great, Duke of Guienne, carried the idea further. At the Council of Poitiers, which he summoned in 1000, it was laid down that disputes should no longer be decided by arms but by recourse to justice, and that all who refused to conform to this rule should be excommunicated. The Duke and his nobility solemnly subscribed to it; and Robert the Pious, king of France, followed suit with a similar rule for his dominions.[4] The Church was still mainly concerned with the movement in order to preserve its own property from the ravages and exactions of war; and a series of councils were held to this end. At Verdun-sur-le-Doubs, in 1016, a formula was evolved with which the nobility swore neither to impress clerics nor peasants into their forces, nor to raid their crops, nor confiscate their beasts. The oath was taken freely throughout France, while the assembled priests and congregation shouted: 'Peace, peace, peace.'[5]

This success incited some enthusiastic bishops to go further. In

[1] See Erdmann, *Die Entstehung des Kreuzzugsgedankens*, p. 97 n. 35, giving references to the relevant texts.

[2] Mansi, *Concilia*, vol. XIX, pp. 89–90.

[3] *Cartulaire de Saint-Chaffre*, p. 152.

[4] Mansi, *Concilia*, vol. XIX, pp. 267–8; Fulbert of Chartres, letter in Bouquet, *Historiens de la France*, vol. X, p. 463.

[5] Hefele-Leclercq, *Histoire des Conciles*, vol. IV, pt. 2, p. 1409; Radulph Glaber, in Bouquet, *R.H.F.* vol. X, pp. 27–8. See Pfister, *Etudes sur le Règne de Robert le Pieux*, p. lx; Huberti, *Studien zur Rechtsgeschichte der Gottesfrieden und Landfrieden*, p. 165.

1038 Aymon, Archbishop of Bourges, ordered every Christian of more than fifteen years of age to declare himself an enemy of all that broke the peace and ready if need be to take up arms against them. Leagues of Peace were organized and were at first effective; but the second half of the Archbishop's command proved more attractive than the first. Castles belonging to recalcitrant nobles were destroyed by troops of armed peasants led by the clergy; and this improvised militia soon became so irresponsible and so destructive that the authorities were obliged to suppress it. After a great League of Peace had burnt down the village of Bénécy, Count Odo of Déols routed it on the banks of the Cher. We are told that no fewer than seven hundred clerics perished in the battle.[1]

Meanwhile a more practical attempt to limit warfare was being made. In 1027 Oliba, Bishop of Vich, held a synod at Toulouges in Roussillon, which prohibited all warfare during the hours of the Sabbath.[2] This idea of a truce to cover holy days was enlarged when, under the influence of the great abbot of Cluny, Odilo, the bishops of Provence, claiming to speak in the name of the whole Church of Gaul, sent a letter in 1041 to the Church of Italy, demanding that the Truce of God should be extended to include Good Friday, Holy Saturday and Ascension Day.[3] The Church of Aquitaine had already followed the Provençal lead. But the duchy of Burgundy went further, reserving for the Truce the whole week between Wednesday evening and Monday morning, and adding the period from Advent to the first Sunday after Epiphany, and Lent and Holy Week to the octave of Easter.[4] In 1042 William the Conqueror, legislating for Normandy, included as well the period from the Rogation days to the octave of Pentecost.[5] In 1050 a council at Toulouges recommended the further inclusion

---

[1] *Miracles de Saint-Benoît*, ed. by de Certain, p. 192.
[2] Mansi, *Concilia*, vol. XIX, pp. 483–8.   [3] *Ibid.* pp. 593–6.
[4] *M.G.H., Constitutiones et Acta Publica Imperatorum et Regum*, vol. I, p. 599. See Huberti, *op. cit.* pp. 296, 303.
[5] Mansi, *Concilia*, vol. XIX, pp. 597–600.

of the three feast-days of the Virgin and the major saints' days.[1]
By the middle of the century the idea of the Truce of God seemed
thus to be well established; and the great Council of Narbonne,
held in 1054, sought to co-ordinate it with the idea of the Peace of
God, protecting the goods of the Church and of the poor from the
effects of war. Both were to be obeyed under the penalty of excommunication; and it was further laid down that no Christian
should slay another Christian, 'for he that slays a Christian sheds
the blood of Christ'.[2]

Movements for peace are seldom as impressive in fact as in
theory; and those of the eleventh century were no exception to
the rule. The princes that had most strongly advocated the Truce
of God did not abide by its provisions. It was on a Saturday that
William the Conqueror fought his fellow-Christian Harold at
Hastings; and Anna Comnena was to note with horror that while
her Church tried honestly to avoid warfare on holy days the
western knights attacked Constantinople in Holy Week; while
their armies were full of armed and fighting priests.[3] Nor, as the
Popes themselves knew from experience, was Church property
ever immune from attacks by the laity. The bellicosity of the
West and its taste for military glory could not be so easily quenched.
It was wiser to revert to the older policy and to make use of this
energy by diverting it into warfare against the heathen.

To the countries of the West the Moslem menace was far more
frightening than it had been to Byzantines till the Turkish invasions;
and the Turks alarmed the Byzantines as barbarians rather than as
infidels. Since the Arab failure before Constantinople early in the
eighth century, war on the eastern frontier of Christendom had
been endemic but never serious enough to threaten the integrity
of the Empire; and it never for long interrupted commercial and
intellectual exchanges. The Arab, almost as much as the Byzantine,
was an heir of Graeco-Roman civilization. His way of life was not

[1] *Ibid.* p. 1042.   [2] *Ibid.* pp. 827–32.
[3] Anna Comnena, *Alexiad*, x, viii, 8, vol. II, pp. 218–19; x, ix, 5–6, vol. II,
p. 222.

very different. A Byzantine felt far more at home at Cairo or Baghdad than he would feel at Paris or Goslar, or even at Rome. Except in rare times of crisis and reprisals the authorities in the Empire and the Caliphate agreed not to force conversions on either side and to allow the free worship of the other religion. Boastful Caliphs might speak slightingly of the Christian Emperors and might at times exact tribute from them; but, as the late tenth century had shown, the Byzantine was a formidable and well-organized foe.

The western Christian could not share the Byzantine's tolerance and sense of security. He was proud to be a Christian, and, as he thought, the heir of Rome; yet he was uneasily aware that in most respects Moslem civilization was higher than his own. Moslem power dominated the western Mediterranean from Catalonia to Tunis. Moslem pirates preyed upon his shipping. Rome had been sacked by the Moslems. They had built robber castles in Italy and in Provence. From their strongholds in Spain it seemed that they might again emerge to cross the frontiers and pour over the Pyrenees into France. Western Christendom had no organization that could have met such an attack. Individual heroes, from the days of Charles Martel onwards, had defeated Saracen raids; and the Carolingian empire for a time provided the necessary bulwark. In 915 Pope John X had co-operated with the court of Constantinople in forming a league of Christian princes to drive the Moslems from their castle on the Garigliano.[1] In 941 the Byzantines joined Hugh of Provence in an attack on their castle at Fréjus. This was unsuccessful, owing to Hugh's last-minute tergiversation; but in 972 a league of Provençal and Italian princes completed the work.[2] But such leagues were local, sporadic and ephemeral. There was need of greater co-ordination and a more concentrated effort. And

---

[1] Liudprand, *Antapodosis*, pp. 61–2; Leo of Ostia, pp. 50 ff. See Gay, *L'Italie Méridionale et l'Empire Byzantin*, p. 161, who establishes the date 915; Runciman, *The Emperor Romanus Lecapenus*, pp. 184–5.

[2] Liudprand, *op. cit.* pp. 135, 139; Poupardin, *Le Royaume de Bourgogne*, pp. 94 ff.

nowhere was the need better realized than in Rome, ever mindful of the sack of St Peter's church in 846.

In the tenth century the Moslems of Spain represented a very real threat to Christendom. The ground previously gained by the Christians was lost. In the middle of the century the great Caliph, Abd ar-Rahman III, was unquestioned master of the peninsula. His death in 961 brought some relief, as his successor, Hakam II, was pacific and was troubled by wars with the Fatimids and with the Idrisids of Morocco. But after Hakam's death in 976 the scene was dominated by a warlike vizier, Mahomet ibn Abi Amir, surnamed al-Mansur, the Victorious, and known to the Spaniards as Almanzor. The leading Christian power in Spain was the kingdom of Leon. It bore the brunt of Almanzor's attacks. In 981 he took Zamora, in the south of the kingdom. In 996 he sacked Leon itself and next year burnt the city of St James at Compostella, which ranked third as a place of pilgrimage after Jerusalem and Rome. He was careful, however, to respect the shrine itself. Already in 986 he had captured Barcelona. It seemed that he would soon be crossing the Pyrenees, when in 1002 he died.[1] After his death the Moslem power began to decline. Pirates from Africa were able to sack Antibes in 1003, Pisa in 1005 and again in 1016, and Narbonne in 1020. But organized Moslem aggression had ended for the moment. It was time for a counter-attack.[2]

The counter-attack was planned by Sancho III, called the Great, king of Navarre. In 1014 he attempted to organize a league of Christian princes to fight the infidel. His colleagues in Leon and Castile were willing to help; and he found an eager ally in Sancho-William, Duke of Gascony. But King Robert of France gave no answer to his appeal. Nothing concrete was achieved; but meanwhile Sancho had secured the interest of a far more valuable ally. The tremendous organization of Cluny, under two great abbots whose rule extended for 115 years, Odilo, who succeeded in 994

---

[1] For Almanzor see Dozy, *Histoire des Musulmanes en Espagne*, rev. ed., vol. II, pp. 235 ff.
[2] Ballesteros, *Historia de España*, vol. II, pp. 389 ff.

and died in 1048, and Hugh, who followed him and lived till 1109, began to pay special attention to Spanish affairs. Cluny was always concerned with the welfare of pilgrims and was glad to have some say in managing the pilgrim route to Compostella, and to help in the whole safeguarding of Spanish Christendom. It was probably Cluniac influence that brought Roger of Tosni from Normandy, though his own Norman adventurousness may have helped, to the aid of the Countess Erselinde of Barcelona in 1018, when the Moslems threatened her. Under Sancho and his successors the Cluniac hold on the Spanish Church was strengthened, carrying it into the fore of the reform movement. The Papacy could not therefore fail to view with especial approval any attempt to enlarge the boundaries of Christendom in Spain. Cluniac and Papal blessing accompanied Sancho-William of Gascony when he joined with Sancho of Navarre in an attack on the Emir of Saragossa and encouraged Raymond-Berengar I of Barcelona as he pushed the Moslems southward.[1]

War against the infidel in Spain thus acquired the status of a holy war; and soon the Popes themselves took a hand in its direction. In 1063 the king of Aragon, Ramiro I, at the outset of a great offensive against the Moslems, was murdered by a Moslem at Grados. His death stirred the imagination of Europe. Pope Alexander II at once promised an indulgence for all who fought for the Cross in Spain and set about collecting an army to carry on Ramiro's work. A Norman soldier in his service, William of Montreuil, recruited troops in northern Italy. In northern France Count Ebles of Roucy, brother of the Aragonese queen Felicia, gathered an army; and the largest contingent was brought by Guy-

---

[1] Boissonnade, *Du nouveau sur la Chanson de Roland*, pp. 6–22. Both Boissonnade and Hatem (*Les Poèmes Epiques des Croisades*, pp. 43–63) are considered by Fliche, in *L'Europe Occidentale de 888 à 1125*, pp. 551–3, to have exaggerated the role of Cluny in organizing holy wars in Spain. Halphen, in a series of lectures at the Ecole des Hautes Etudes at Paris, which has not yet been published, has fully discussed the question and considers that Cluny's role was important but that it did not actually organize military expeditions. See also Rousset, *Les Origines et les Caractères de la première Croisade*, pp. 31–5.

Geoffrey, Count of Aquitaine, who was given command of the expedition. Very little was achieved. The town of Barbastro was captured with a large booty, but was soon lost again.[1] But henceforward French knights streamed over the Pyrenees to carry on the work. In 1073 a new expedition was organized by Ebles of Roucy. Pope Gregory VII invited the princes of Christendom to join in it, and, while reminding the world that the Spanish kingdom belonged to the see of St Peter, declared that Christian knights might enjoy the lands that they conquered from the infidel.[2] In 1078 Hugh I, Duke of Burgundy, led an army to aid his brother-in-law, Alfonso VI of Castile.[3] In 1080 Gregory VII gave his personal encouragement to an expedition led by Guy-Geoffrey. During the next years all went well. The Castilians captured Toledo itself in 1085.[4] There followed a Moslem revival, led by the fanatical Almoravids; and from 1087 onward Christian knights were urgently summoned to Spain to oppose them. Pope Urban II gave his anxious support and even told intending pilgrims to Palestine that they could spend their money more usefully on the reconstruction of Spanish towns rescued from Moslem ravages.[5] Till the end of the century Spanish campaigns continued to attract adventurous Christian knights from the north, till the capture of Huesca in 1096 and Barbastro in 1101 brought this series of campaigns to an end.

By the close of the eleventh century the idea of the holy war had thus been carried into practice. Christian knights and soldiers were encouraged by the authorities of the Church to leave their petty quarrels and to journey to the frontiers of Christendom to fight against the infidel. To reward them for their service they might take possession of the lands that they reconquered, and they received spiritual benefits. What exactly these benefits were is

---

[1] Boissonnade, *op. cit.* pp. 22–8; Fliche, *op. cit.* pp. 551-2.
[2] Gregory VII, *Registrum*, I, 7, pp. 11–12. See also Villey, *La Croisade: Essai sur la Formation d'une Théorie juridique*, p. 71.
[3] Boissonnade, *op. cit.* pp. 29–31.   [4] *Ibid.* pp. 31-2.
[5] Riant, *Inventaire critique*, pp. 68–9.

uncertain. Alexander II seems to have offered an indulgence to the campaigners of 1064;[1] but Gregory VII only gave absolution to all who died in battle for the Cross.[2] He had given similar absolution to the soldiers of Rudolf of Swabia fighting against the excommunicated Henry IV of Germany.[3] The Papacy was taking over the direction of the holy wars. It often launched them and often named the commander. The land that was conquered had to be held under ultimate Papal suzerainty.

Though the great princes were apt to remain aloof, western knights responded readily to the appeal of the holy war. Their motives were in part genuinely religious. They were ashamed to continue fighting amongst themselves; they wanted to fight for the Cross. But there was also a land-hunger to incite them, especially in northern France, where the practice of primogeniture was being established. As a lord grew unwilling to divide his property and its offices, now beginning to be concentrated round a stone-built castle, his younger sons had to seek their fortunes elsewhere. There was a general restlessness and taste for adventure in the knightly class in France, most marked among the Normans, who were only a few generations removed from nomadic freebooters. The opportunity for combining Christian duty with the acquisition of land in a southern climate was very attractive. The Church had reason to be pleased with the progress of the movement. Could it not be applied also to the eastern frontier of Christendom?

[1] Jaffé-Wattenbach, *Regesta*, no. 4530, vol. 1, p. 573.
[2] Gregory VII, *loc. cit.*
[3] *Ibid.* vii, 14 b, pp. 480 ff.

CHAPTER II

THE ROCK OF SAINT PETER

'By me kings reign, and princes decree justice.'　　PROVERBS VIII, 15

As the tide of Islam receded in Spain the Pope had little difficulty in establishing his authority over the Church of the reconquered lands. The Donation of Constantine, widely if incorrectly accepted as genuine by western Christendom, gave him temporal suzerainty over many countries, to which the addition of the Iberian peninsula passed unnoticed. Nor was there any ecclesiastical power in Spain that could challenge him. But eastern Christendom was differently organized. The Patriarchates of Alexandria and Antioch, the latter founded by Saint Peter and the former by Saint Mark, were as old as the see of Rome. The Patriarchate of Jerusalem, the Church of Saint James, though younger possessed the prestige that was due to the world's most sacred city. And the Patriarchate of Constantinople was the most formidable rival of all. Despite its alleged foundation by Saint Andrew, it could not claim the same authority of age. But Constantinople was New Rome. It had superseded the older capital. It was the seat of the unbroken line of Christian Emperors. It was by far the greatest city in Christendom. Its Patriarch might reasonably call himself Oecumenical, the chief ecclesiastical magistrate of the civilized world. The religious opposition in Byzantium might at times seek to use the authority of Old Rome as a counter against the increasing domination of the Emperor; but no one in the East seriously thought that the bishop of the shrunken western city, so often in the power of its turbulent petty nobles or of barbarous potentates from the north, should hold any jurisdiction over the eastern churches, with their long-established and enduring traditions. Yet Rome could still command a special respect. Though her claim to supremacy was ignored, she was almost universally allowed a primacy amongst the great sees of Christendom, even by the Oecumenical Patriarch. Nor was anyone ready to challenge the belief that Christendom was and should be one.

After the Arab conquest, the Patriarchates of the south-east had lost much of their power; and Constantinople emerged as the champion of the eastern churches. There had been many controversies and quarrels between Rome and Constantinople on ecclesiastical affairs, though none of them had been so serious and prolonged as later polemists came to believe.[1] The unity of Christendom was still generally accepted. But in the eleventh century the organization of the Roman Church was overhauled. The reforms had been largely suggested by monastic influences from Cluny and from Lorraine and had been at first carried out by the lay authorities that had at the time dominated Rome. The emperor Henry III had been particularly active, and had given them such momentum that after his death the Church was able to continue and develop them independently of and eventually in opposition to the lay government; and out of the movement there emerged theories that insisted on the universal spiritual dominance of Rome and its ultimate superiority over secular princes. These in their turn provoked new controversies with the East.

The fundamental issue lay in the reaffirmation of the Roman claim to supremacy. But disputes began over details of doctrine and of usage. In its desire to establish its authority, the Papacy sought to make the usages of the Church uniform. Not only did it, for political as well as for spiritual reasons, desire to abolish the marriage of the secular clergy, but it attempted to standardize the liturgy and ritual. Such reforms were possible in the West; but the usages of the eastern churches were different. There were Greek churches in the Roman sphere just as there were Latin churches in

[1] The best general account of the relations between Rome and Constantinople is to be found in Every, *The Byzantine Patriarchate, passim.*

the sphere of Constantinople; and in southern Italy the frontier between the two spheres had long been under discussion. At the same time German influence at Rome had led to the insertion there of the word *filioque* in the Creed in connection with the Procession of the Holy Ghost. The reforming Popes were less willing to compromise or to remain tactfully silent on such matters than their predecessors had been. Clashes were inevitable.

Pope Sergius IV, in his systatic letter, the declaration of faith sent by a Pope or Patriarch to his colleagues on his accession, included the word *filioque*. The Patriarch Sergius II of Constantinople thereupon refused to commemorate his name in the diptychs of the Patriarchal churches at Constantinople. To the Byzantines this indicated that the Pope personally was considered unorthodox on a point of doctrine; it did not impugn the orthodoxy of the whole western Church. But to the Pope, and to the western churches, accustomed to regard him as the source of orthodox doctrine, the insult seemed more general and far-reaching. The Patriarch came to realize that there was bargaining power in an offer to restore the name.[1]

In 1024 a suggestion reached Pope John XIX from Constantinople that points at issue between the Churches might be solved by the acceptance of a formula ingeniously worded to grant Rome titular supremacy and to leave Constantinople with full practical independence. It declared that 'with the consent of the Roman pontiff the Church of Constantinople be accounted universal in her sphere as that of Rome was in the universe'. John himself was ready to agree; but the Cluniac abbot of St Benignus at Dijon wrote hastily and sternly to remind him that the power to bind and loose in Heaven and on earth belonged to the office of Saint Peter and his successors alone, and urged him to show more vigour in his government of the universal Church. Byzantium

---

[1] For this incident, see Michel, *Humbert und Kerularios*, vol. I, pp. 20-40. There is evidence that the *filioque* was introduced into the Creed at Rome at the time of the coronation of Henry II there in 1014. Berno, *Libellus de Officio Missae*, in *M.P.L.* vol. CXLII, cols. 1061-2.

was to learn that the reformed Papacy would tolerate no such compromise.[1]

In the middle of the century the Norman invasions of southern Italy made desirable a political alliance between the Pope and the eastern Emperor. But by now the reformed Papacy was committed to a policy of standardization and wished to abolish usages current in Greek churches in southern Italy and copied by many Italian churches as far north as Milan. In 1043 a proud, ambitious man, Michael Cerularius, had become Patriarch of Constantinople and was equally eager to standardize usages within his sphere. His original motive was to absorb more easily the churches of the newly occupied Armenian provinces, where divergent customs, such as the use of unleavened bread, were practised. But his policy affected also the Latin churches in Byzantine Italy and those that existed in Constantinople itself for the benefit of merchants, pilgrims and soldiers of the Varangian Guard. When these latter churches refused to conform, they were closed by order of the Patriarch, whose court began to issue tracts denouncing the usages of the Latins.

Cerularius was not, it seems, interested in the theological issue. He was ready to restore the Pope's name to the diptychs in return for reciprocal treatment at Rome. The dispute was over usages; and it therefore raised the problem of the ecclesiastical frontier in Italy, a problem made more acute by the invasion of the Normans, themselves members of the Latin Church. Negotiations were undertaken by the governor of Byzantine Italy, the Lombard Argyrus, a Byzantine subject who followed the Latin rite. The Emperor trusted him, but Cerularius inevitably was suspicious; and circumstances played into his hand. In 1053, before legates had been appointed to go from Rome to Constantinople, Pope Leo IX was captured by Normans. When his legates, led by the Cardinal Humbert of Silva Candida, arrived in Constantinople in

[1] Radulph Glaber, in Bouquet, *R.H.F.* vol. x, pp. 44–5. No Greek source mentions these negotiations, but there is no reason for doubting their occurrence.

January 1054, they were honourably received by the Emperor; but Cerularius questioned whether they had in fact been appointed by the Pope and whether the Pope in his captivity could implement any promises that they made. In April, before the discussions had gone far, Leo suddenly died; and the legates lost whatever official backing they might have possessed. It was a year before the next Pope was elected; and no one knew what his policy might be. Cerularius refused to continue the negotiations. In spite of the Emperor's desire for an accord, feelings ran high; till at last the legates departed in fury, leaving on the altar of St Sophia a bull excommunicating the Patriarch and his advisers but expressly admitting the orthodoxy of the Byzantine Church. In answer the Patriarch held a synod condemning the bull as the work of three irresponsible persons, and deploring the addition of *filioque* to the Creed and the persecution of married clergy, but making no mention of the Roman Church as a whole nor of the other usages in dispute. There was, in fact, no change at all in the situation, except that bitterness had been aroused.

The churches of Alexandria and Jerusalem had taken no part in the episode. The Patriarch of Antioch, Peter III, definitely thought that Cerularius had been unnecessarily difficult. His Church had continued to commemorate the Pope's name in its diptychs; and he saw no reason why that practice should cease. He may have feared that Cerularius, whose ambitions he suspected, had designs against the independence of his see. He probably sympathized with the Emperor's policy. Moreover, he could not support the standardization of ritual and usage; for his diocese contained churches where a Syrian liturgy was in use, and many of them lay beyond the political frontiers of the Empire. He could not have enforced uniformity there, even had he desired it. He kept himself outside of the quarrel.[1]

---

[1] For the so-called 'schism' of Cerularius, see Michel, *op. cit. passim*, especially vol. I, pp. 43–65; Jugie, *Le Schisme Byzantin*, especially pp. 187 ff.; Leib, *Rome, Kiev et Byzance*, pp. 27 ff.; Every, *op. cit.* pp. 153–72. Jugie, *op. cit.* p. 188, deduces that the Patriarch was willing to restore the Pope's name to the

During the next decade relations slightly improved. Michael Cerularius was deposed in 1059. Soon after his disappearance the Latin churches in Constantinople were reopened. In southern Italy the growing success of the Normans, since 1059 the faithful allies of the Papacy, made it impracticable for Byzantium to press its ecclesiastical claims there. In 1061 Roger the Norman embarked on the conquest of Sicily from the Arabs, a holy war encouraged by the Pope. There too Byzantium had to face the loss of the control of the Christian congregations. By 1073 the Emperor Michael VII decided that a cordial understanding with Rome must be achieved. After the Norman conquest of Bari in 1071 he feared further aggression, which papal influence might prevent. The Turcoman irruption into Asia Minor had begun. Michael was in desperate need of soldiers; and recruitment in the West would be eased if the Papacy were cordial. In 1073 the Cardinal Hildebrand, already famed for his vigour and integrity, was elected Pope under the name of Gregory VII. Gregory was convinced of the supremacy of his see and therefore omitted to send a systatic letter to any of the Patriarchs of the East. But Michael thought it prudent to make a friendly gesture. He sent the new Pope a letter of congratulations, hinting at his wish for a closer connection. Pleased, Gregory sent Dominicus, Patriarch of Grado, as legate to Constantinople to report on conditions there.[1]

Informed by Dominicus, Gregory convinced himself that Michael was sincere. He also learnt of the situation in Asia Minor. This bore seriously on the pilgrim traffic. Palestine itself was not yet closed to pilgrims; but the journey thither across Anatolia

diptychs from Leo IX's letter to Cerularius in *M.P.L.* vol. cxliii, cols. 773–4, and Cerularius's letter to Peter of Antioch in *M.P.G.* vol. cxx, col. 784. Peter of Antioch's motive must remain conjectural; but his attitude is clear from his correspondence with Cerularius. See their letters in *M.P.G.* vol. cxx, cols. 756–820.

[1] See Gregory VII's letters in his *Registra*, I, 46, 49, II, 37, vol. I, pp. 70, 75, 173. The visit of Dominicus to Constantinople is reported *ibid.* I, 18, pp. 31–2. It is probable that Gregory failed to send a systatic letter to the eastern Patriarchs on his accession. See Dvornik, *The Photian Schism*, pp. 327–8.

would soon be impossible if the Turcoman invasions were not checked. In a stroke of imaginative statesmanship Gregory planned a new policy. The holy war, which was being so successfully waged in Spain, should be extended into Asia. His friends in Byzantium were in need of military aid. He would send them an army of Christian knights, under the orders of the Church. And on this occasion, because there were ecclesiastical problems to solve, the Pope would lead them in person. His troops would drive the infidel out of Asia Minor; and he would then hold a council at Constantinople where the Christians of the East would resolve their quarrels in grateful humility and acknowledge the supremacy of Rome.[1]

Whether the Emperor Michael knew of the Pope's intention and whether he would have welcomed it we cannot tell. For Gregory was never able to carry his scheme into effect. The unyielding integrity of his policy led him further and further into trouble in the West. His eastern ambitions had to be abandoned. But he never forgot them nor lost his interest there.

In 1078 Michael VII was deposed. On hearing the news Gregory had at once excommunicated the usurper, Nicephorus Boteniates. A short time afterwards an adventurer appeared in Italy declaring that he was the fallen Emperor. The Normans for a while affected to believe in him; and Gregory lent him his support. When Nicephorus in his turn was replaced in April 1081 by Alexius Comnenus, the excommunication was extended to the new Emperor. In June Alexius wrote to the Pope seeking to recover his goodwill and to secure his help in restraining the aggression of Robert Guiscard; but there was no response. The Emperor found a more promising ally in Henry IV of Germany. In the meantime he closed the Latin churches in Constantinople. It seemed clear to the Byzantines that the Pope was in league with the treacherous and godless Normans. They told each other fantastic stories of his pride and lack of charity; and when he died, caught in the net of

---

[1] Jaffé, *Monumenta Gregoriana*, I, 46, 49, II, 3, 137, *Bibliotheca Rerum Germanicarum*, vol. II, pp. 64-5, 69-70, 111-12, 150-1.

disasters woven by his policy, they welcomed the news as a judgement from on high.[1]

In 1085, the year of Gregory's death, relations between eastern and western Christendom had never before been so cold. The eastern Emperor had been excommunicated by the Pope, who was openly encouraging unscrupulous adventurers to attack their fellow-Christians; while the Pope's chief enemy, the king of Germany, was openly receiving subsidies from the Byzantines. Bitterness and resentment were growing on either side. But there was as yet no actual schism. Statesmanship might still preserve the unity of Christendom. In the Emperor Alexius the East possessed a statesman of sufficient elasticity and wisdom. A statesman of similar calibre was now to arise in the West.

Odo de Lagery was born of a noble family in Châtillon-sur-Marne in about the year 1042. For his education he was sent to the cathedral school at Reims, where his headmaster was Saint Bruno, later the founder of the Carthusian Order. He stayed on at Reims, to become canon, then archdeacon of the cathedral; but it did not satisfy him. Suddenly he decided to retire to the community at Cluny. In 1070 he was professed by the abbot Hugh, who recognized his ability. After acting for a while as prior he was transferred to Rome. He soon made his mark there; and in 1078 Gregory VII appointed him Cardinal-Bishop of Ostia. From 1082 to 1085 he was legate in France and in Germany and came back to remain with Gregory during the last unhappy years of his pontificate. On Gregory's death in exile, with the anti-Pope Guibert reigning in Rome, the loyal cardinals elected in his stead the weak unwilling abbot of Monte Cassino, who took the name of Victor III. The Cardinal of Ostia disapproved of the election and showed his disapproval. But Victor bore him no malice, and on his death-bed, in September 1087, recommended him to the cardinals as his

---

[1] Anna Comnena, *Alexiad*, III, x, 1–8, vol. I, pp. 132–6; Malaterra, *Historia Sicula*, in *M.P.L.* vol. CXLIX, col. 1192. Anna Comnena, *op. cit.* I, xiii, 1–10, vol. I, pp. 47–51, gives a hostile and libellous account of Gregory's quarrel with Henry IV.

successor. Gregory VII also was known to have wished for his succession; but it was not till March 1088 that a conclave could meet at Terracina, to elect him as Urban II.[1]

Urban was well fitted for his task. He was an impressive man, tall, with a handsome, bearded face, courteously mannered and persuasive in his speech. If he lacked the fire and singleness of purpose of Gregory VII, he excelled him in breadth of vision and in the handling of men. Nor was he as proud nor as obstinate as Gregory; but he was not weak. He had suffered imprisonment in Germany at the hands of Henry IV for his loyalty to the Pope and to his beliefs. He could be stern and relentless, but he preferred to be gentle; he preferred to avoid controversy that might arouse bitterness and strife.

He came into a difficult heritage. He could live safely only in Norman territory; and the Normans were selfish, unreliable allies. Rome was held by the anti-Pope Guibert. Urban might penetrate to the suburbs, but he could not go further without bloodshed; and that he refused to provoke. Further north Matilda of Tuscany staunchly supported him throughout her vast domains; and in 1089 she strengthened her position by a cynical marriage with a German prince, Welf of Bavaria, a boy of less than half her age. But in 1091 her troops were routed by Henry of Germany at the battle of Trisontai. Henry was at the height of his power. Crowned emperor by the anti-Pope in 1084, he was now master of Germany and triumphant in northern Italy. A Pope as insecurely placed as Urban could not hope to command obedience further afield.

But Urban worked on steadily and tactfully, till in 1093 all was changed. By the use of money rather than of arms, he was enabled to spend Christmas that year in Rome and next spring took up his residence in the Lateran. The emperor Henry was weakened by the revolt of his own son, Conrad, whose dissatisfaction Urban had quietly encouraged. In France, his native country, he succeeded, by his powers of organization, in bringing the whole ecclesiastical

[1] For Urban's early career, see Leib, *op. cit.* pp. 1-4, and Gay, *Les Papes du XIe siècle*, pp. 356-8.

structure under his control. In Spain his influence was supreme; and gradually the more distant countries of the West came to recognize his spiritual authority. He omitted to press the claims for political suzerainty made by Gregory VII. With the lay princes everywhere, except with his outspoken enemies, he showed forbearance stretched to its utmost limits. By 1095 he was spiritual master of western Christendom.[1]

Meanwhile he had turned his attention to eastern Christendom. On Robert Guiscard's death his brother, Roger of Sicily, had emerged as the chief power amongst the Normans; and Roger had no wish further to offend Byzantium. With his goodwill, Urban opened negotiations with the Byzantine court. At the Council of Melfi, in September 1089, in the presence of ambassadors from the Emperor, he lifted the ban of excommunication against Alexius. Alexius responded to this gesture by holding that same month a synod at Constantinople; where it was found that the Pope's name had been omitted from the diptychs 'not by any canonical decision but, as it were, from carelessness', and it was proposed that it should be restored on the receipt of a systatic letter from the Pope. There was no real cause, the synod considered, for any dispute between the Churches, and it recommended that the Patriarchs of Alexandria and Jerusalem should be consulted. The Patriarch of Antioch was present in person. The Patriarch Nicholas III of Constantinople wrote to Urban to inform him of these decisions and to ask him to send his systatic letter within eighteen months. He assured him that the Latin churches in Constantinople were free to follow their own usages. No mention was made of any theological issue. This was not to the liking of the Emperor's ambassadors in Italy, Basil, Metropolitan of Trani, and Romanus, Archbishop of Rossano, Greek clerics who were alarmed by papal encroachments into their territory and who had been shocked when the Pope claimed, with some historical justification, that his diocese ought really to include Thessalonica. They would have preferred Alexius to support the anti-Pope. But Alexius had

[1] Gay, *op. cit.* pp. 358–63.

decided which was the better man and was realist enough to accept the loss of Byzantine Italy; while Guibert soon offended his Greek friends by holding a council at Rome which condemned clerical marriage.[1]

Urban did not in fact ever send a systatic letter, probably because he was unwilling to raise questions of theology; nor was his name ever inserted into the Constantinople diptychs. But good relations were restored. An embassy from Alexius visited Urban in 1090, bearing a message of cordial friendship. The official Byzantine point of view was shown in a treatise written by Theophylact, Archbishop of Bulgaria. He begged his readers not to exaggerate the importance of uniformity in usage. He regretted the addition of the word *filioque* to the Creed, but explained that the poverty of the Latin language in theological terms was apt to cause misunderstanding. He did not take seriously the papal claim of authority over the eastern churches.[2] Indeed, there was no reason at all why a schism should ever develop. Other eastern theologians continued to discuss differences in usage; but their polemics were mild in tone. Among these writers was the Patriarch of Jerusalem, Symeon II, who condemned the Latin use of unleavened bread in the Communion, but in terms that were in no way acrimonious.[3]

Early in 1095 Pope Urban II moved northward from Rome and summoned representatives of all the western Church to meet him at the first great council of his pontificate, to be held in March at

---

[1] The report of the synod is given, with relevant letters, in Holtzmann, 'Unionsverhandlungen zwischen Kaiser Alexios I und Papst Urban II im Jahre 1089', in *Byzantinische Zeitschrift*, vol. xxviii, pp. 60–7. The wording of the findings of the synod quoted above must mean that the Patriarch Sergius II had acted in 1009 without referring the matter to a synod or consulting his fellow-Patriarchs. For Guibert's council, see Jaffé-Loewenfeld, *Regesta*, vol. i, p. 652.

[2] For the report of Alexius's embassy to Urban, see Holtzmann, *op. cit.* pp. 64–7. Theophylact's treatise is published in *M.P.G.* vol. cxxvi, cols. 222–50.

[3] Symeon's treatise is published by Leib, *Deux Inédits Byzantins sur les Azymites*, pp. 85–107. Leib doubted Symeon's authorship, as the treatise seems to answer one written by Bruno of Segni in about 1108. But Michel, *Amalfi und Jerusalem im griechischen Kirchenstreit*, has shown that the treatise is in answer to one by a certain Laycus, which Bruno plagiarized.

Piacenza. There the assembled clergy passed decrees against simony and clerical marriages and against schism within the Church. The adultery of King Philip of France was discussed; but it was decided to take no action till Urban himself could visit France. Messengers came from the emperor Henry's son, Conrad, to arrange for his meeting with the Pope at Cremona. Henry's empress, Praxedis of Russia, of the Scandinavian house that ruled at Kiev, arrived in person to tell of the indignities that she suffered at the hands of her husband. The Council acted as the supreme court of western Christendom, with the Pope as presiding judge.

Amongst the visitors attending the Council were envoys from the Emperor Alexius. His wars against the Turks were faring well. Seldjuk power was in an obvious decline. A few well-timed campaigns might break it for ever. But his Empire was still short of soldiers. The old Anatolian recruiting grounds were disorganized and many of them lost. He was largely dependent on foreign mercenaries, on regiments composed of Petchenegs and other tribes from the steppes, which he used mainly as frontier guards and military police, on the Varangian Guard, still mainly filled by Anglo-Saxon exiles from Norman England, and on companies of adventurers from the West who took temporary service in his army. Most eminent of these had been Count Robert I of Flanders, who had fought for him in the year 1090. But, even with the native troops that he still could raise, his needs were unsatisfied. He had the long Danube frontier to guard against attacks from the northern barbarians. On the north-west the Serbs were restive; and his Bulgarian subjects were seldom quiescent for long. There was always the danger of Norman aggression from Italy. In Asia Minor the defence of the ill-defined frontier and its outposts and the general maintenance of order and communications used up his remaining resources. If he were to take the offensive he must have more recruits. His policy towards the Papacy would bear fruit if he could use papal influence to find him these recruits. Urban was sympathetic. It was part of the papal programme to persuade the quarrelsome knights of the West to use their arms in a distant and a holier cause. The Byzantine ambassadors were invited to address the assembly.

Their speeches have not survived. But it seems that, in order to convince their audience that it was meritorious to serve under the Emperor, they laid special emphasis on the hardships that the Christians of the East must endure till the infidel was driven back. If recruitment was to be encouraged by the Church, the inducement of good pay was insufficient. The appeal to Christian duty made a stronger argument. It was not the moment for an exact appraisal of Byzantine achievements and intentions. But let the bishops return to their homes believing that the safety of Christendom still was threatened, and they would be eager to send members of their flocks eastward to fight in the Christian army.

The bishops were impressed, and likewise the Pope. As he journeyed to Cremona to receive the homage of young Conrad, and on over the Alpine passes to France, he began to turn over in his mind a vaster and more glorious scheme, envisaging a holy war.[1]

---

[1] Bernold of Constance, ad ann. 1095, p. 161; Hefele-Leclercq, *Histoire des Conciles*, vol. v, pt. I, pp. 394–5. See also Munro in *American Historical Review*, vol. xxvII, pp. 731–3.

CHAPTER III

THE SUMMONING

'Hearken unto me, ye stouthearted, that are far from righteousness.'   ISAIAH XLVI, 12

Pope Urban arrived in France in the late summer of 1095. On 5 August he was at Valence and on 11 August he reached Le Puy. From there he sent letters to the bishops of France and the neighbouring lands, requesting them to meet him at Clermont in November. Meanwhile he turned south, to spend September in Provence, at Avignon and Saint-Gilles. Early in October he was at Lyons and thence moved on into Burgundy. At Cluny, on 25 October, he consecrated the high altar of the great basilica that Abbot Hugh had begun to build. From Cluny he went to Souvigny, near Moulins, to pay his respects at the tomb of the holiest of Cluniac abbots, Saint Maiolus. There the Bishop of Clermont joined him, to escort him to his episcopal city, in readiness for the Council.[1]

As he travelled Urban busied himself with the affairs of the Church in France, organizing and correcting, giving praise and blame where they were due. But his journeyings enabled him also to pursue his further scheme. We do not know whether, while he was in the south, he met in person Raymond of Saint-Gilles, Count of Toulouse and Marquis of Provence, already celebrated for his leadership of the holy wars in Spain. But he was in touch with him and must have heard of his experiences. At Cluny he could talk with men that were concerned with the pilgrim traffic, both to Compostella and to Jerusalem. They could tell him of the

---

[1] For Urban's movements, see Gay, *op. cit.* pp. 369–72; Chalandon, *Histoire de la première Croisade*, pp. 19–22.

overwhelming difficulties that pilgrims to Palestine had now to endure with the disintegration of Turkish authority there. He learnt that not only were the roads across Asia Minor blocked, but the Holy Land itself was virtually closed to pilgrims.

The Council of Clermont sat from 18 November to 28 November 1095. Some three hundred clerics were present and their work covered a wide range. In general, decrees against lay investiture, simony and clerical marriage were repeated and the Truce of God was advocated. In particular, King Philip was excommunicated for adultery and the Bishop of Cambrai for simony, and the primacy of the see of Lyons over those of Sens and Reims was established.[1] But the Pope wished to use the occasion for a more momentous purpose. It was announced that on Tuesday, 27 November, he would hold a public session, to make a great announcement. The crowds, clerical and lay, that assembled were too huge to be contained within the cathedral, where hitherto the Council had met. The Papal throne was set up on a platform in an open field outside the eastern gate of the city; and there, when the multitudes were gathered, Urban rose to his feet to address them.

Four contemporary chroniclers have reported the Pope's words for us. One of them, Robert the Monk, claims to have been present at the meeting. Baudri of Dol and Fulcher of Chartres write as though they had been present. The fourth, Guibert of Nogent, probably obtained his version at second hand. But none of them professes to give an accurate verbal account; and each wrote his chronicle a few years later and coloured his account in the light of subsequent events. We can only know approximately what Urban in fact said. It seems that he began his speech by telling his hearers of the necessity for aiding their brethren in the East. Eastern Christendom had appealed for help; for the Turks were advancing into the heart of Christian lands, maltreating the inhabitants and desecrating their shrines. But it was not only of Romania (which is Byzantium) that he spoke. He stressed the

[1] Hefele-Leclercq, *op. cit.* vol. v, pt. 1, pp. 399–403; Mansi, *Concilia*, vol. xx, pp. 695–6, 815 ff.

special holiness of Jerusalem and described the sufferings of the pilgrims that journeyed there. Having painted the sombre picture, he made his great appeal. Let western Christendom march to the rescue of the East. Rich and poor alike should go. They should leave off slaying each other and fight instead a righteous war, doing the work of God; and God would lead them. For those that died in battle there would be absolution and the remission of sins. Life was miserable and evil here, with men wearing themselves out to the ruin of their bodies and their souls. Here they were poor and unhappy; there they would be joyful and prosperous and true friends of God. There must be no delay. Let them be ready to set out when the summer had come, with God to be their guide.[1]

Urban spoke with fervour and with all the art of a great orator. The response was immediate and tremendous. Cries of 'Deus le volt!'—'God wills it!'—interrupted the speech. Scarcely had the Pope ended his words before the Bishop of Le Puy rose from his seat and, kneeling before the throne, begged permission to join in the holy expedition. Hundreds crowded up to follow his example. Then the Cardinal Gregory fell on his knees and loudly repeated the *Confiteor*; and all the vast audience echoed it after him. When the prayer was over Urban rose once more and pronounced the absolution and bade his hearers go home.[2]

The enthusiasm was greater than Urban had expected. His plans for its direction were not yet fully made. No great lay lord had

[1] Urban's speech is given in five of the chroniclers, Fulcher of Chartres, I, iii, pp. 130–8; Robert the Monk, I, i–ii, pp. 727–9; Baudri, *Historia Jezoso-limitana* I, iv, pp. 12–15; Guibert of Nogent, II, iv, pp. 137–40; and William of Malmesbury, *Gesta Regum*, vol. II, pp. 393–8. William wrote some thirty years afterwards; but the other four wrote as though they were present. Baudri, indeed, claims definitely to have been there. But both Baudri and Guibert admit that their versions of his words may not be exactly correct. All the versions vary considerably. Munro, 'The Speech of Pope Urban II at Clermont', in the *American Historical Review*, vol. XI, pp. 231 ff. analyses the differences between the versions and hopes to find the actual text by collecting the points on which they agree. But it is clear that each author wrote the speech that he thought that the Pope ought to have made and added his own favourite rhetorical tricks.

[2] Robert the Monk, I, ii–iii, pp. 15–16; Baudri, I, v, p. 15.

been present at Clermont. The recruits were all humbler men. It would be necessary to secure more solid secular support. In the meantime Urban reassembled his bishops for further consultation. The Council had probably already at his request passed a general decree giving remission from temporal penalties for the sins of all that took part with pious intentions in the holy war. It was now added that the worldly belongings of the participants should be placed under the protection of the Church during their absence at the war. The local bishop should be responsible for their safe-keeping and should return them intact when the warrior came home. Each member of the expedition was to wear the sign of the Cross, as a symbol of his dedication; a cross of red material should be sewn on to the shoulder of his surcoat. Anyone that took the Cross should vow to go to Jerusalem. If he turned back too soon or failed to set out, he would suffer excommunication. Clerics and monks were not to take the Cross without the permission of their bishop or abbot. The elderly and infirm must be discouraged from attempting the expedition; and no one at all should go without consulting his spiritual adviser. It was not to be a war of mere conquest. In all towns conquered from the infidel the churches of the East were to have all their rights and possessions restored to them. Everyone should be ready to leave his home by the Feast of the Assumption (15 August) next year, when the harvests should have been gathered; and the armies should assemble at Constantinople.[1]

Next, a leader must be appointed. Urban wished to make it clear that the expedition was under the control of the Church. Its head must be an ecclesiastic, his legate. With the unanimous consent of the Council he nominated the Bishop of Le Puy.

Adhemar de Monteil, Bishop of Le Puy, belonged to the family

[1] The canons of the Council of Clermont are given by Lambert of Arras in Mansi, *Concilia*, vol. xx, pp. 815-20. Only the 33rd and last directly concerns the Crusade; and, though Gratian attributes it to the Council, it is not found in the canons of the Council of Rouen, which reproduces those of Clermont. See Hefele-Leclercq, *op. cit.* vol. v, p. 339. Chalandon, *op. cit.* pp. 44-6, analyses the Pope's arrangements from the various somewhat confused sources.

of the Counts of Valentinois. He was a middle-aged man, who had already made the pilgrimage to Jerusalem nine years before. He had earned his leadership by coming forward as the first to answer Urban's appeal; but as he had already entertained Urban at Le Puy in August and must have talked to him there of eastern affairs, it is possible that his stirring gesture was not entirely spontaneous. It was a wise appointment. Subsequent experience proved him to be a fine preacher and a tactful diplomat, broad-minded, calm and kindly, a man whom all would respect but who sought to persuade rather than to command. His influence was unfailingly used to curb passions and to spread goodwill, but it was not always firm enough to control the magnates that were nominally to be under his orders.[1]

The first of the magnates to ask to join the expedition was Count Raymond of Toulouse. On 1 December, while Urban was still at Clermont, messengers arrived there to say that the Count and many of his nobility were eager to take the Cross. Raymond, who was at Toulouse, could not have heard reports of the great speech at Clermont. He must have had forewarning. As the first to be told of the project and the first to take the vow, he considered that he should be given the secular leadership over the other great lords. He wished to be Moses to Adhemar's Aaron. Urban would not admit this pretension; but Raymond never entirely abandoned it. In the meantime he planned to co-operate loyally with Adhemar.[2]

Urban left Clermont on 2 December. After visiting various Cluniac houses he spent Christmas at Limoges, where he preached the Crusade in the cathedral, then passed northward through Poitiers to the valley of the Loire. In March he was at Tours, where he held a council; and one Sunday he summoned a congregation to meet him in a meadow by the banks of the river. Standing on an improvised platform he preached a long and solemn sermon, exhorting his hearers to repent and to go on the Crusade.

[1] Robert the Monk, I, iv, p. 731; Guibert, II, v, p. 140. For Adhemar's past history, see the texts collected in Chevalier, *Cartulaire de Saint-Chaffre*, pp. 13–14, 139, 161–3.   [2] Baudri, I, v, p. 16.

From Tours he turned southward again through Aquitaine, past
Saintes and Bordeaux to Toulouse. Toulouse was his headquarters
in May and June; and he had many opportunities for discussing
the Crusade with his host, Count Raymond. Late in June he
moved on to Provence. Raymond accompanied him to Nîmes.

In August the Pope recrossed the Alps into Lombardy. His
journey had been no holiday. All the time he was interviewing
churchmen and writing letters, seeking to complete his reorganiza-
tion of the Church in France and, above all, continuing his plans
for the Crusade. Synodal letters embodying the decisions taken
at Clermont were sent round to the bishops of the West. In some
cases provincial councils were held to receive them and to consider
local action. It is probable that the chief lay powers were also
officially informed of the Pope's desires.[1] From Limoges at the end
of 1095 Urban wrote to all the faithful in Flanders referring them
to the acts of the Council at Clermont and asking for their support.[2]
He had every reason to be satisfied with the response that came
from Flanders and the neighbouring lands. In July 1096, while he
was at Nîmes, he received a message from King Philip announcing
his absolute submission on the matter of his adultery and probably
telling at the same time of the adhesion of his brother, Hugh of
Vermandois, to the Crusade.[3] During the same month Raymond
of Toulouse gave proof of his intentions by handing over many of
his possessions to the monastery of Saint-Gilles.[4] It was perhaps on
Raymond's advice that Urban decided that the help of a maritime
power would be necessary in order to maintain the expedition's

[1] Orderic Vitalis, *Historia Ecclesiastica*, IX, 3, vol. III, p. 470; Riant, *Inventaire*, p. 109. Riant, *op. cit.* p. 113, quotes a sixteenth-century text, based apparently on some lost document, which tells of the Pope informing lay lords
of his wishes. His movements are given in detail by Crozet, 'Le Voyage
d'Urbain II', in *Revue Historique*, vol. CLXXIX, pp. 271–310.

[2] The letter is given in Hagenmeyer, *Die Kreuzzugsbriefe*, pp. 136–7. In it
Urban gives the date of 15 August for the departure of the Crusade.

[3] Jaffé-Loewenfeld, *Regesta*, vol. I, p. 688. Philip's promises of repentance
were not kept.

[4] Document given in d'Achéry, *Spicilegium*, 2nd ed. vol. I, p. 630, and Mansi,
Concilia, vol. XX, p. 938.

supplies. Two legates set out with letters to the republic of Genoa to ask for its co-operation. The republic agreed to provide twelve galleys and a transport, but cautiously delayed their dispatch till it could tell whether the Crusade was a serious movement. It was only in July 1097 that this fleet set sail from Genoa. Meanwhile many Genoese took the Cross.[1]

By the time that Urban was back in Italy he was assured of the success of his scheme. His summons was eagerly obeyed. From as far afield as Scotland, Denmark and Spain, men hastened to make their vows. Some raised money for the journey by pawning their possessions and their lands. Others, expecting never to return, gave everything over to the Church. A sufficient number of great nobles had adhered to the Crusade to give it a formidable military backing. Beside Raymond of Toulouse and Hugh of Vermandois, Robert II of Flanders, Robert, Duke of Normandy, and the latter's brother-in-law Stephen, Count of Blois, were making preparations to set out. More remarkable was the adherence of men devoted to the emperor Henry IV. Chief amongst these was Godfrey of Bouillon, Duke of Lower Lorraine, who took the Cross with his brothers, Eustace, Count of Boulogne, and Baldwin. Grouped round these leaders were many of the lesser nobility and a few eminent ecclesiastics, such as the Bishop of Bayeux.[2]

In Italy Urban found similar enthusiasm. In September 1096 he wrote to the city of Bologna to thank its citizens for their zeal and to caution them not to leave for the East without their priests' permission. Nor should newly married husbands leave without their wives' consent. Meanwhile news of the project had reached southern Italy and was warmly welcomed by many of the Normans there, who were always ready to start on a new adventure. The princes at first held back, but Guiscard's son Bohemond, now prince of Taranto but thwarted in his ambitions in Italy by his brother Roger Borsa and his uncle Roger of Sicily, soon realized the possibilities that the Crusade would open out for him. Together

---

[1] Caffaro, *De Liberatione*, pp. 49–50.
[2] For fuller lists of the Crusaders, see below, Book III, ch. L.

with many of his family and his friends, he took the Cross. Their participation brought to the movement many of the most experienced and enterprising soldiers in Europe. When Urban returned to Rome in time for Christmas 1096, he could feel assured that the Crusade was truly launched.[1]

He had in fact launched a movement greater than he knew. It might have been better if fewer great lords had answered his appeal. For, though with all of them except Bohemond genuine religious fervour was the strongest motive, soon their terrestrial schemes and rivalries would create troubles far beyond the papal legate's control. Still more uncontrollable was the response shown by humbler folk throughout France and Flanders and the Rhineland.

The Pope had asked his bishops to preach the Crusade; but far more effective preaching was done by poorer men, by evangelicals such as Robert of Arbrissel, founder of the Order of Fontevrault, and still more by an itinerant monk called Peter. Peter was an oldish man, born somewhere near Amiens. He had probably tried to make the pilgrimage to Jerusalem a few years previously, but had been maltreated by the Turks and forced to turn back. His contemporaries knew him as Little Peter—*chtou* or *kiokio* in the Picard dialect—but later the hermit's cape that he habitually wore brought him the surname of 'the Hermit', by which he is better known to history. He was a man of short stature, swarthy and with a long, lean face, horribly like the donkey that he always rode and which was revered almost as much as himself. He went barefoot; and his clothes were filthy. He ate neither bread nor meat, but fish, and he drank wine. Despite his lowly appearance he had the power to move men. There was an air of strange authority about him. 'Whatever he said or did', Guibert of Nogent, who knew him personally, tells us, ' it seemed like something half-divine.'[2]

---

[1] Urban II, *Letter to the Bolognese*, in Hagenmeyer, *op. cit.* pp. 137–8. For the Normans, see above, pp. 56–8.

[2] Guibert, I, vii, p. 142. The fullest discussion of Peter's origin and early career is given in Hagenmeyer, *Le Vrai et le Faux sur Pierre l'Hermite*, trans. by Furcy Raynaud, pp. 17–63. Guibert describes him in II, viii, p. 142; Orderic Vitalis, IX, 4, vol. III, p. 477, gives the number of 15,000 for his followers.

Peter probably had not assisted at the Council of Clermont; but before the year 1095 was out he was already preaching the Crusade. He began his tour in Berry, then moved during February and March through Orléannais and Champagne into Lorraine, and thence past the cities of the Meuse and Aachen to Cologne, where he spent Easter. He gathered disciples whom he sent to the districts that he could not himself visit. Among them were the Frenchmen Walter Sans-Avoir, Rainald of Breis, Geoffrey Burel and Walter of Breteuil, and the Germans Orel and Gottschalk. Wherever he or his lieutenants went, men and women left their homes to follow him. By the time that he reached Cologne his train was estimated at about 15,000 persons; and many more joined him in Germany.[1]

The extraordinary success of his preaching was due to many causes. Life for a peasant in north-western Europe was grim and insecure. Much land had gone out of cultivation during the barbarian invasions and the raids of the Norsemen. Dykes had been broken, and the sea and rivers had encroached on to the fields. The lords often opposed the clearing of the forests in which they hunted for their game. A village unprotected by a lord's castle was liable to be robbed or burnt by outlaws or by soldiers fighting petty civil wars. The Church sought to protect the poor peasants and to establish *bourgs* in empty lands; but its help was fitful and often unavailing. Greater lords might encourage the growth of towns, but lesser barons opposed it. The organization of the demesne was breaking down, but no orderly system was taking its place. Though actual serfdom had vanished, men were tied to the land by obligations that they could not easily escape. Meanwhile the population was increasing, and holdings in a village could not be subdivided beyond a certain limit. 'In this land', said Urban at Clermont, according to Robert the Monk, 'you can scarcely feed the inhabitants. That is why you use up its goods and excite endless wars amongst yourselves.' Recent years had been especially difficult. Floods and pestilence in 1094 had been followed by drought and a famine in 1095. It was a moment when emigration seemed very

[1] Hagenmeyer, *op. cit.* pp. 127–51; Chalandon, *op. cit.* pp. 57–9.

attractive. Already in April 1095 a shower of meteorites had presaged a great movement of peoples.[1]

Apocalyptic teaching added to the economic inducement. It was an age of visions; and Peter was thought to be a visionary. Medieval man was convinced that the Second Coming was at hand. He must repent while yet there was time and must go out to do good. The Church taught that sin could be expiated by pilgrimage and prophecies declared that the Holy Land must be recovered for the faith before Christ could come again. Further, to ignorant minds the distinction between Jerusalem and the New Jerusalem was not very clearly defined. Many of Peter's hearers believed that he was promising to lead them out of their present miseries to the land flowing with milk and honey of which the scriptures spoke. The journey would be hard; there were the legions of Antichrist to be overcome. But the goal was Jerusalem the golden.[2]

What Pope Urban thought of Peter and the success of his preaching no one now knows. His letter to the Bolognese suggests that he was a little nervous of uncontrolled enthusiasm; but he did not, or could not, prevent it from spreading in Italy. Throughout the summer of 1096 a casual but constant stream of pilgrims without leaders or any form of organization began to flow to the East. No doubt he hoped that they and Peter's followers would safely reach Constantinople and there would await the coming of his legate and the military chieftains, who would incorporate them into the orderly ranks of the great Christian army.

Urban's insistence that the expedition should assemble at Constantinople shows how confident he was that the Emperor Alexius would welcome it. Byzantium had asked for soldiers from the

---

[1] Ekkehard, *Chronicon*, ad ann. 1094, p. 207; Sigebert of Gembloux, *Chronicon*, ad ann. 1095, p. 367; Robert the Monk, I, i, p. 728. The shower of meteorites, interpreted by Bishop Gislebert of Lisieux to foretell a mass-movement towards the holy places, is reported by Orderic Vitalis, IX, 4, vol. III, pp. 461–2.

[2] The apocalyptic evangelism of Robert of Arbrissel (whose life, by Baudri, is given in the *Aa. Ss.* 23 February, vol. III) is typical of the spirit of the time. Robert also preached the Crusade, at Urban's request (*ibid.* p. 695).

West; and here they were answering the summons, not as a few individual mercenaries but in whole powerful armies. His confidence was ingenuous. No government is unwilling to make allies. But when these allies send large armies, over which it has no control, to invade its territory, expecting to be fed and housed and provided with every amenity, then it questions whether the alliance is worth while. When news of the Crusading movement reached Constantinople it aroused feelings of disquiet and alarm.

In 1096 the Byzantine Empire had been enjoying for some months a rare interval of repose. The Emperor had recently defeated a Cuman invasion of the Balkans so decisively that none of the barbarian tribes of the steppes was likely now to attempt to cross the frontier. In Asia Minor, thanks to civil wars encouraged by Byzantine diplomacy, the Seldjuk empire was beginning to disintegrate. Alexius hoped soon to take the offensive against it, but he wished to choose his own time. He still needed a breathing-space in which he could repair his strained resources. The problem of man-power worried him. He wished for mercenaries from the West; and no doubt he hoped that his ambassadors in Italy were successful in their recruitment. Now he was informed that instead of the individual knights or small companies that he expected to join his forces, whole Frankish armies were on the move. He was not pleased, as he knew from experience that the Franks were an unstable race, greedy for money and unscrupulous in keeping agreements. They were formidable in attack; but under the circumstances that was a doubtful advantage. It was with some apprehension that the imperial court learnt, in the words of the princess Anna Comnena, that 'all the West and all the barbarian tribes from beyond the Adriatic as far as the Pillars of Hercules were moving in a body through Europe towards Asia, bringing whole families with them'. Not only the Emperor but his subjects were uneasy. As a monitory portent great hordes of locusts swept over the Empire, leaving the corn untouched but devouring the vines. Inspired, perhaps, by a hint from the authorities who were anxious not to spread despondency, popular soothsayers interpreted this to mean that the Franks would do no harm to good Christians, whose symbol was the corn, the source of the bread of life, but would destroy the Saracens, a people whose sensuality might well be symbolized by the vine. The Princess Anna was a little sceptical of the interpretation; but the likeness of the Franks to locusts was certainly apparent.[1]

The Emperor Alexius set about calmly making his preparations. The Frankish armies would have to be fed as they travelled through the Empire; and precautions must be taken to keep them from ravaging the countryside and robbing the inhabitants. Stores of provisions were accumulated in each main centre through which they would pass, and a police force was detailed to meet each detachment when it arrived within the Empire and to accompany it to Constantinople. There were two great roads across the Balkan peninsula, the north road that crossed the frontier at Belgrade and struck south-east through Nish, Sofia, Philippopolis and Adrianople, and the Via Egnatia, from Dyrrhachium through Ochrida and Edessa (Vodena) to Thessalonica and on through Mosynopolis and Selymbria to the capital. Since the great German pilgrimage of 1064 the former road had seldom been used by travellers from the West. The total number of pilgrims had declined and those that had attempted the journey had preferred the alternative route. Moreover, Alexius received his information about the Crusade from Italy. He therefore anticipated that the Frankish armies would cross the Adriatic and make use of the Via Egnatia. Supplies were sent to Dyrrhachium and the intervening cities; and the governor of Dyrrhachium, the Emperor's nephew John Comnenus, was instructed to give the Frankish leaders a cordial welcome, but to see that they and their armies were all the time supervised by the military police. High-ranking envoys from Constantinople would be sent to greet each leader in turn. Meanwhile the admiral Nicholas Mavrocatacalon took a flotilla to Adriatic waters to

---

[1] Anna Comnena, *Alexiad*, x, v, 4–7, vol. II, pp. 206–8. Anna credits Peter with having organized the Crusade, probably because her first contact with the Crusaders was with Peter's rabble, who themselves gave him the credit.

watch the coasts and give warning of the approach of the Frankish transports.

The Emperor himself remained at Constantinople, awaiting further news. Knowing that the Pope had fixed 15 August as the date of departure for the expedition he did not hurry over his preparations, when suddenly, at the end of May 1096, a messenger came posting from the north to say that the first Frankish army had come down through Hungary and had entered the Empire at Belgrade.

BOOK III

THE JOURNEY TO THE WARS

CHAPTER I

THE PEOPLE'S EXPEDITION

'The Lord was not able to bring them into the land which he promised them.'   DEUTERONOMY IX, 28

Peter the Hermit arrived with his followers at Cologne on Holy Saturday, 12 April 1096.[1] There he began to realize the difficulties that beset the leader of a popular expedition. The vast motley collection of enthusiasts that he had gathered together consisted of men from many districts and of many types. Some brought their women with them, some even their children. Most of them were peasants, but there were townsfolk among them, there were junior members of knightly families, there were former brigands and criminals. Their only link was the fervour of their faith. All of them had given up everything to follow Peter; and they were eager to continue on their way. It was, moreover, essential to keep them on the move if they were to be fed; for few districts in medieval Europe had a sufficient surplus of foodstuffs to supply for long the needs of so large a company. But Cologne was set in a rich countryside with good river communications. Peter wished to take advantage of the facilities that it provided to pause a while

[1] The only detailed original account of Peter the Hermit's and Walter Sans-Avoir's journeys is that given by Albert of Aix. His veracity (see below, Appendix I, p. 331) has been severely questioned; but it seems quite clear that he derived his information from an eyewitness who had probably taken notes. Some of his numbers are unconvincing; and Peter's behaviour at times does not show consistency; but the author probably wished to make him appear always in a good light, regardless of consistency. The *Chronicle of Zimmern* provides some additional information, but seems to muddle the Crusades of 1096 and 1101. There is a short notice in the *Chronicle of Bari*, p. 147. The whole story has been studied in detail by Hagenmeyer, *op. cit.* pp. 151–241. In the main I accept his findings.

and preach to the Germans. He was probably anxious to attract some of the local nobility to his Crusade. In France and Flanders the knights preferred to join the company of some great lord. But no great German lord was going to the holy war. His preaching was successful. Among the many Germans that answered his call were several of the lesser nobility, led by Count Hugh of Tübingen, Count Henry of Schwarzenberg, Walter of Teck and the three sons of the Count of Zimmern.[1]

But the Frenchmen were impatient. Walter Sans-Avoir decided that he would not wait at Cologne. With a few thousand compatriots he left the city as soon as the Easter Feast was over, probably on Easter Tuesday, and set out on the road to Hungary. Marching up the Rhine and the Neckar and down the Danube, he reached the Hungarian frontier on 8 May. There he sent to King Coloman to ask for permission to cross the kingdom and for help in obtaining provisions for his men. Coloman proved friendly. The army passed through Hungary without an untoward incident. About the end of the month it reached Semlin on the further frontier, and crossed the Rive Save into Byzantine territory at Belgrade.

The military commander at Belgrade was taken by surprise. He had received no instructions how to deal with such an invasion. He sent post-haste to Nish, where the governor of the Bulgarian province resided, to inform him of Walter's arrival. The governor, a conscientious but undistinguished official called Nicetas, was equally uninstructed. In his turn he dispatched a messenger to take the news as quickly as possible to Constantinople. Meanwhile Walter at Belgrade demanded food for his followers. The harvests were not yet gathered, and the garrison had none to spare; so Walter and his troops began to pillage the countryside. His temper was inflamed owing to an unfortunate occurrence at Semlin, where

---

[1] See Hagenmeyer, *op. cit.* pp. 158–60 and 165–6, especially p. 160 n. 2, and p. 166 n. 1, for the German lords who joined Peter. Ekkehard, *Hierosolymita*, pp. 18–19, reports that the Crusade was not officially preached in Germany owing to the schism.

sixteen of his men, who had not crossed the river with their companions, tried to rob a bazaar. The Hungarians captured them and stripped them of their arms and their clothing, which were hung on the walls of Semlin as a warning, and sent them on naked across to Belgrade. When the pillaging round Belgrade began the commander resorted to arms. In the fighting several of Walter's men were killed and others were burnt alive in a church.

Walter was eventually able to march on to Nish, where Nicetas received him kindly and provided food, keeping him there till he received an answer from Constantinople. The Emperor, who had believed that the Crusade would not leave the West before the Feast of the Assumption, was forced to speed up his arrangements. Nicetas was requested to send Walter on under escort. Accompanied by this escort Walter and his army continued their journey in peace. Early in July they reached Philippopolis, where Walter's uncle, Walter of Poissy, died; and by the middle of the month they were in Constantinople.[1]

From Walter Nicetas must have learnt that Peter was not far behind, with a far larger company. He therefore moved up to Belgrade to meet him and made contact with the Hungarian governor of Semlin.

Peter left Cologne on about 20 April. The Germans at first had mocked at his preaching; but by now many thousands had joined him, till his followers probably numbered close on 20,000 men and women. Other Germans, fired by his enthusiasm, planned to follow later, under Gottschalk and Count Emich of Leisingen. From Cologne Peter took the usual road up the Rhine and the Neckar to the Danube. When they reached the Danube, some of his company decided to travel by boat down the river; but Peter and his main body marched by the road running south of Lake Ferto and entered Hungary at Oedenburg. Peter himself rode on his donkey, and the German knights on horseback, while lumbering wagons carried such stores as he possessed and the chest of money

[1] Walter's journey is given in Albert of Aix, I, 6, pp. 274–6, and, more briefly, in Orderic Vitalis, IX, 4, vol. III, pp. 478–9.

that he had collected for the journey. But the vast majority travelled on foot. Where the roads were good they managed to cover twenty-five miles a day.

King Coloman received Peter's emissaries with the same bene-volence that he had shown to Walter, warning them only that any attempt to pillage would be punished. The army moved peaceably through Hungary during late May and early June. At some point, probably near Karlovci, it was rejoined by the detachments that had travelled by boat. On 20 June it reached Semlin.[1]

There its troubles began. What actually happened is obscure. It seems that the governor, who was a Ghuzz Turk in origin, was alarmed by the size of the army. Together with his colleague across the frontier he attempted to tighten up police regulations. Peter's army was suspicious. It heard rumours of the sufferings of Walter's men; it feared that the two governors were plotting against it; and it was shocked by the sight of the arms of Walter's sixteen miscreants still hanging on the city walls. But all might have been well had not a dispute arisen over the sale of a pair of shoes. This led to a riot, which turned into a pitched battle. Probably against Peter's wishes, his men, led by Geoffrey Burel, attacked the town and succeeded in storming the citadel. Four thousand Hungarians were killed and a large store of provisions captured. Then, terrified of the vengeance of the Hungarian king, they made all haste to cross the river Save.

They took all the wood that they could collect from the houses, with which to build themselves rafts. Nicetas, watching anxiously from Belgrade, tried to control the crossing of the river, and to oblige them to use one ford only. His troops were mainly com-posed of Petcheneg mercenaries, men that could be trusted to obey his orders blindly. They were sent in barges to prevent any crossing except at the proper place. He himself, recognizing that he had

[1] Albert of Aix, I, 7, p. 276. Malavilla is certainly to be identified with Semlin (Hagenmeyer, *op. cit.* p. 169 n. 1); Guibert, II, viii, pp. 142–3, says that Peter had trouble when crossing through Hungary, but seems to confuse him with Emich.

insufficient troops for dealing with such a horde, retired back to Nish, where the military headquarters of the province were placed. On his departure the inhabitants of Belgrade deserted the town and took to the mountains.[1]

On 26 June Peter's army forced its way across the Save. When the Petchenegs tried to restrict them to one passage, they were attacked. Several of the boats were sunk and the soldiers aboard captured and put to death. The army entered Belgrade and set fire to it, after a wholesale pillage. Then it marched on for seven days through the forests and arrived at Nish on 3 July. Peter sent at once to Nicetas to ask for supplies of food.[2]

Nicetas had informed Constantinople of Peter's approach, and was awaiting the officials and military escort that were coming to convoy the westerners on to the capital. He had a large garrison at Nish; and he had strengthened it by recruiting locally additional Petcheneg and Hungarian mercenaries.[3] But he probably could

[1] Albert of Aix, I, 7, 8, pp. 276–8. Albert here makes Peter, who elsewhere appears as a pacific character, thirst for revenge, probably because his informant thought such ferocity to be to Peter's credit. The recurrent number 7, in connection with the Petcheneg frontier guards, is equally not to be taken literally. Albert confuses the rivers Morava and Save.

[2] Albert of Aix, I, 9, p. 278. I follow Hagenmeyer's dating (*Chronologie*, pp. 30–1).

[3] The escort sent from Constantinople to meet Peter joined him at Sofia on 9 or 10 July, having travelled well over 400 miles. Even though it was probably a cavalry escort, and therefore travelled fast, it must have left the capital before any messenger, sent from Nish after Peter's arrival there on 3 July, could have reached the imperial court. According to Jireček, *Die Heerstrasse von Belgrad nach Constantinopel*, p. 9, the Tartars who carried the Austrian imperial mail in the early nineteenth century took five days over the journey, travelling at full gallop and using relays. (The distance is rather more than 650 miles.) The Byzantine roads were rather better than the Ottoman, but the relays were probably not so well organized. A special messenger may have taken five or six days to reach Constantinople from Nish at this time. Nicetas must therefore have sent to inform the capital of Peter's coming before he actually crossed the frontier. Nicetas, whom the western sources call Nichita, is also known to us from one seal, recorded in Schlumberger, *Sigillographie de l'Empire Byzantin*, p. 239. He must not be confused with Leo Nicerites, Duke of Paristrium, with whom Chalandon, *Essai sur le Règne d'Alexis Comnène*, p. 167 n. 4, wrongly identifies him.

not spare any men to act as Peter's escort until the troops from Constantinople should meet him. On the other hand it was impracticable and dangerous to allow so vast a company to linger long at Nish. Peter was requested therefore to provide hostages while food was collected for his men and then to move on as soon as possible. All went well at first. Geoffrey Burel and Walter of Breteuil were handed over as hostages. The local inhabitants not only allowed the Crusaders to acquire the supplies that they needed, but many of them gave alms to the poorer pilgrims. Some even asked to join the pilgrimage.

Next morning the Crusaders started out along the road to Sofia. As they were leaving the town some Germans who had quarrelled with a townsman on the previous night wantonly set fire to a group of mills by the river. Hearing of this, Nicetas sent troops to attack the rearguard and to take some prisoners whom he could hold as hostages. Peter was riding his donkey about a mile ahead and knew nothing of all this till a man called Lambert ran up from the rear to tell him. He hurried back to interview Nicetas and to arrange for the ransom of the captives. But while they were conferring, rumours of fighting and of treachery spread round the army. A company of hotheads thereupon turned and assailed the fortifications of the town. The garrison drove them off and counterattacked; then while Peter, who had gone to restrain his men, tried to re-establish contact with Nicetas, another group insisted upon renewing the attack. Nicetas therefore let all his forces loose on the Crusaders, who were completely routed and scattered. Many of them were slain; many were captured, men, women and children, and spent the rest of their days in captivity in the neighbourhood. Amongst other things Peter lost his money-chest. Peter himself, with Rainald of Breis and Walter of Breteuil and about five hundred men, fled up a mountain-side, believing that they alone survived. But next morning seven thousand others caught them up; and they continued on the road. At the deserted town of Bela Palanka they paused to gather the local harvest, as they had no food left. There many more stragglers joined them.

When they continued on their march they found that a quarter of their company had been lost.[1]

They reached Sofia on 12 July. There they met the envoys and the escort, sent from Constantinople with orders to keep them fully supplied and to see that they never delayed anywhere for more than three days. Thenceforward their journey passed smoothly. The local population was friendly. At Philippopolis the Greeks were so deeply moved by the stories of their suffering that they freely gave them money, horses and mules. Two days outside Adrianople more envoys greeted Peter with a gracious message from the Emperor. It was decided that the expedition should be forgiven for its crimes, as it had been already sufficiently punished. Peter wept with joy at the favour shown him by so great a potentate.[2]

The Emperor's kindly interest did not cease when the Crusaders arrived at Constantinople on 1 August. He was curious to see its leader; and Peter was summoned to an audience at the court, where he was given money and good advice. To Alexius's experienced eye the expedition was not impressive. He feared that if it crossed into Asia it would soon be destroyed by the Turks. But its indiscipline obliged him to move it as soon as possible from the neighbourhood of Constantinople. The westerners committed endless thefts. They broke into the palaces and villas in the suburbs; they even stole the lead from the roofs of churches. Though their entry into Constantinople itself was strictly controlled, only small parties of sightseers being admitted through the gates, it was impossible to police the whole neighbourhood.

Walter Sans-Avoir and his men were already at Constantinople, and various bands of Italian pilgrims arrived there about the same time. They joined up with Peter's expedition; and on 6 August the whole of his forces were conveyed across the Bosphorus. From

[1] Albert of Aix, I, 9–12, pp. 278–82. He says that 30,000 were left out of an army of 40,000.
[2] *Ibid.* I, 13–15, pp. 282–3; Anna Comnena, *Alexiad*, x, v–vi, vol. II, p. 210.

the Asiatic shore they marched in an unruly manner, pillaging houses and churches, along the coast of the Sea of Marmora to Nicomedia, which lay deserted since its sack by the Turks fifteen years before. There a quarrel broke out between the Germans and the Italians on the one side and the French on the other. The former broke away from Peter's command and elected as their leader an Italian lord called Rainald. At Nicomedia the two parts of the army turned westward along the south coast of the Gulf of Nicomedia to a fortified camp called Cibotos by the Greeks and Civetot by the Crusaders, which Alexius had prepared for the use of his own English mercenaries in the neighbourhood of Helenopolis. It was a convenient camping-ground, as the district was fertile and further supplies could easily be brought by sea from Constantinople.[1]

Alexius had urged Peter to await the coming of the main Crusading armies before attempting any attack on the infidel; and Peter was impressed by his advice. But Peter's authority was waning. Both the Germans and Italians, under Rainald, and his own Frenchmen, over whom Geoffrey Burel seems to have held the chief influence, instead of quietly recuperating their strength, vied with each other in raiding the countryside. First they pillaged the immediate neighbourhood; then they cautiously advanced into territory held by the Turks, making forays and robbing the villagers, who were all Christian Greeks. In the middle of September several thousand of the Frenchmen ventured as far as the gates of Nicaea, the capital of the Seldjuk Sultan, Kilij Arslan ibn-Suleiman. They sacked the villages in the suburbs, rounding up the flocks and herds that they found and torturing and massacring the Christian inhabitants with horrifying savagery. It was said that they roasted babies on spits. A Turkish detachment

---

[1] Albert of Aix, I, 15, pp. 283-4; *Gesta Francorum*, I, 2, p. 6, where the rowdy behaviour of the army is mentioned; Anna Comnena, *loc. cit.* Orderic Vitalis, IX, 5, vol. III, pp. 490-1, tells us that Alexius had prepared Civetot for his English troops, See Vasilievsky, *Works* (in Russian), vol. I, pp. 363-4. For dating, see Hagenmeyer, *Chronologie*, p. 32.

sent out from the city was driven off after a fierce combat. They then returned to Civetot, where they sold their booty

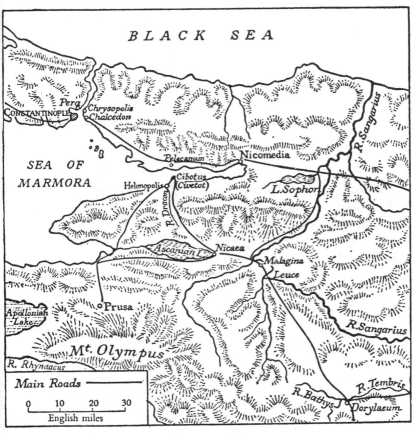

Environs of Constantinople and Nicaea at the time of
the First Crusade

to their comrades and to the Greek sailors who were about the camp.

This profitable French raid roused the jealousy of the Germans. Towards the end of September Rainald set out with a German expedition of some six thousand men, including priests and even bishops. They marched beyond Nicaea, pillaging as they went, but, kinder than the Frenchmen, sparing the Christians, till they came to a castle called Xerigordon. This they managed to capture; and, finding it well stocked with provisions of every sort, they planned to make it a centre from which they could raid the countryside. On hearing of the Crusaders' exploit, the Sultan sent a high military commander with a large force to recapture the castle. Xerigordon was set on a hill, and its water supply came from a well just outside the walls and a spring in the valley below. The Turkish army, arriving before the castle on St Michael's Day, 29 September, defeated an ambush laid by Rainald and, taking possession of the spring and the well, kept the Germans closely invested within the castle. Soon the besieged grew desperate from thirst. They tried to suck moisture from the earth; they cut the veins of their horses and donkeys to drink their blood; they even drank each other's urine. Their priests tried vainly to comfort and encourage them. After eight days of agony Rainald decided to surrender. He opened the gates to the enemy on receiving a promise that his life would be spared if he renounced Christianity. Everyone that remained true to the faith was slaughtered. Rainald and those that apostasized with him were sent into captivity, to Antioch and to Aleppo and far into Khorassan.

News of the capture of Xerigordon by the Germans had reached the camp at Civetot early in October. It was followed by a rumour, spread by two Turkish spies, that they had taken Nicaea itself and were dividing up the booty for their benefit. As the Turks expected, this caused tumultuous excitement in the camp. The soldiers clamoured to be allowed to hasten to Nicaea, along roads that the Sultan had carefully ambushed. Their leaders had difficulty in restraining them, till suddenly the truth was discovered about the fate of Rainald's expedition. The excitement was changed to panic; and the chiefs of the army met to discuss what next to do. Peter had gone to Constantinople. His authority over the army had vanished. He hoped to revive it by obtaining some important material aid from the Emperor. There was a movement in the army to go out to avenge Xerigordon. But Walter Sans-Avoir persuaded his colleagues to await Peter's return, which was due in eight days' time. Peter, however, did not return; and meanwhile it was reported that the Turks were approaching in force towards Civetot. The army council met again. The more responsible leaders, Walter Sans-Avoir, Rainald of Breis, Walter of Breteuil and Fulk of Orleans, and the Germans, Hugh of Tübingen and Walter of Teck, still urged that nothing should be done till Peter arrived. But Geoffrey Burel, with the public opinion of the army behind him, insisted that it would be cowardly and foolish not to advance against the enemy. He had his way. On 21 October, at dawn, the whole army of the Crusaders, numbering over 20,000 men, marched out from Civetot, leaving behind them only old men, women and children and the sick.

Barely three miles from the camp, where the road to Nicaea entered a narrow wooded valley, by a village called Dracon, the Turks were lying in ambush. The Crusaders marched noisily and carelessly, the knights on horseback at their head. Suddenly a hail of arrows from the woods killed or maimed the horses; and as they plunged in confusion, unseating their riders, the Turks attacked. The cavalry, pursued by the Turks, was flung back on to the infantry. Many of the knights fought bravely, but they could not stop the panic that seized the army. In a few minutes the whole host was fleeing in utter disorder to Civetot. There in the camp the daily round was just beginning. Some of the older folk were still asleep in their beds. Here and there a priest was celebrating early mass. Into its midst there burst a horde of terrified fugitives with the enemy on their heels. There was no real resistance. Soldiers, women and priests were massacred before they had time to move. Some fled into the forests around, others into the sea, but few of them escaped for long. Others defended themselves for a while by lighting bonfires which the wind blew into the Turks' faces. Only young boys and girls whose appearance pleased the Turks were spared, together with a few captives made after the first heat of the fighting was over. These were taken away into slavery. Some three thousand, luckier than the rest, managed to reach an old castle that stood by the sea. It had long been out of use, and its doors and windows were dismantled. But the refugees, with the energy of despair, improvised fortifications from the wood that lay about and reinforced them with bones, and were able to beat off the attacks of the enemy.

The castle held out; but elsewhere on the field by midday all was over. Corpses covered the ground from the pass of Dracon to the sea. Amongst the dead were Walter Sans-Avoir, Rainald of Breis, Fulk of Orleans, Hugh of Tübingen, Walter of Teck, Conrad and Albert of Zimmern and many other of the German knights. The only leaders to survive were Geoffrey Burel, whose impetuousness had caused the disaster, Walter of Breteuil and William of Poissy, Henry of Schwarzenberg, Frederick of Zimmern and Rudolf of Brandis, almost all of whom were badly wounded.

When dusk fell a Greek who was with the army succeeded in finding a boat and set sail for Constantinople, to tell Peter and the Emperor of the battle. Of Peter's feelings we have no record; but Alexius at once ordered some men-of-war, with strong forces aboard, to sail for Civetot. On the arrival of the Byzantine battle-squadron the Turks raised the siege of the castle and retired inland. The survivors were taken off to the ships and returned to Constantinople. There they were given quarters in the suburbs; but their arms were removed from them.[1]

---

[1] Albert of Aix, I, 16–22, pp. 284–9, and *Gesta Francorum*, I, 2, pp. 6–12, both give full accounts of the raids and final disaster of Peter's army. The author of the *Gesta*, who must have derived his version from a survivor whom he met at Constantinople, says throughout that Alexius was hostile to Peter and delighted by the massacre of his men, though he again admits that they behaved badly and burnt churches. Albert's version shows gratitude to the Emperor for his generosity, his good advice and his prompt rescue of the survivors. Anna Comnena, x, vi, 1–6, gives a shorter account in which she complains of the behaviour of the Franks and says that Peter, whom she wrongly supposes to

The Failure of the People's Crusade

The People's Crusade was over. It had cost many thousands of lives; it had tried the patience of the Emperor and his subjects; and it had taught that faith alone, without wisdom and discipline, would not open the road to Jerusalem.

have been with the army, blamed the disaster on the ungodly behaviour of those of its members who would not obey him. The *Chronicle of Zimmern* gives a list of the Germans killed at Civetot (p. 29).

CHAPTER II

THE GERMAN CRUSADE

*'Ah Lord God! wilt thou destroy all the residue
of Israel?'*　　　　　　　　EZEKIEL IX, 8

Peter the Hermit's departure for the East had not ended Crusading
enthusiasm in Germany. He had left behind him his disciple
Gottschalk to collect a further army; and many other preachers
and leaders prepared to follow his example. But, though the
Germans responded in thousands to the appeal, they were less
eager than the French had been to hurry to the Holy Land. There
was work to be done first nearer home.

Jewish colonies had been established for centuries past along the
trade routes of western Europe. Their inhabitants were Sephardic
Jews, whose ancestors had spread out from the Mediterranean
basin throughout the Dark Ages. They kept up connections with
their co-religionists in Byzantium and in Arab lands, and were
thus enabled to play a large part in international trade, more
especially the trade between Moslem and Christian countries. The
prohibition of usury in western Christian countries and its strict
control in Byzantium left them an open field for the establishment
of money-lending houses throughout Christendom. Their technical
skill and long traditions made them pre-eminent also in the practice
of medicine. Except long ago in Visigothic Spain they had never
undergone serious persecution in the West. They had no civic
rights; but both lay and ecclesiastical authorities were pleased to
give special protection to such useful members of the community.
The kings of France and Germany had always befriended them;
and they were shown particular favour by the archbishops of the
great cities of the Rhineland. But the peasants and poorer townsmen, increasingly in need of money as a cash economy replaced

the older economy of services, fell more and more into their debt and in consequence felt more and more resentment against them; while the Jews, lacking legal security, charged high rates of interest and extracted exorbitant profits wherever the benevolence of the local ruler supported them.

Their unpopularity grew throughout the eleventh century, as more classes of the community began to borrow money from them; and the beginnings of the Crusading movement added to it. It was expensive for a knight to equip himself for a Crusade; if he had no land and no possessions to pledge, he must borrow money from the Jews. But was it right that in order to go and fight for Christendom he must fall into the clutches of members of the race that crucified Christ? The poorer Crusader was often already in debt to the Jews. Was it right that he should be hampered in his Christian duty by obligations to one of the impious race? The evangelical preaching of the Crusade laid stress on Jerusalem, the scene of the Crucifixion. It inevitably drew attention to the people at whose hands Christ had suffered. The Moslems were the present enemy; they were persecuting Christ's followers. But the Jews were surely worse; they had persecuted Christ Himself.[1]

Already in the Spanish wars there had been some inclination on the part of Christian armies to maltreat the Jews. At the time of the expedition to Barbastro Pope Alexander II wrote to the bishops in Spain to remind them that there was all the difference in the world between the Moslems and the Jews. The former were irreconcilable enemies to the Christians, but the latter were ready to work for them. But in Spain the Jews had enjoyed such favour from the hands of the Moslems that the Christian conquerors could not bring themselves to trust them.[2]

In December 1095 the Jewish communities of northern France wrote to their co-religionists in Germany to warn them that the

---

[1] For the position of the Jews at this period see Graetz, *Geschichte der Juden*, vol. VI, pp. 89 ff.

[2] Letter in *M.P.L.* vol. CLXVI, col. 1387.

Crusading movement was likely to cause trouble to their race.[1] There were reports of a massacre of the Jews at Rouen. It is unlikely that such a massacre in fact occurred; but the Jews were sufficiently alarmed for Peter the Hermit to bring off a successful stroke of business. Hinting, no doubt, that otherwise he might find it difficult to restrain his followers, he obtained from the French Jews letters of introduction to the Jewish communities throughout Europe, calling upon them to welcome him and to supply him and his army with all the provisions that he might require.[2]

About the same time Godfrey of Bouillon, Duke of Lower Lorraine, began his preparations to start out on the Crusade. A rumour ran round the province that he had vowed before he left to avenge the death of Christ with the blood of the Jews. In terror the Jews of the Rhineland induced Kalonymos, chief Rabbi of Mainz, to write to Godfrey's overlord, the emperor Henry IV, who had always shown himself a friend to their race, to urge him so forbid the persecution. At the same time, to be on the safe side, the Jewish communities of Mainz and Cologne each offered the Duke the sum of five hundred pieces of silver. Henry wrote to his chief vassals, lay and ecclesiastic, to bid them guarantee the safety of all the Jews on their lands. Godfrey, having already succeeded in his blackmail, answered that nothing was further from his thoughts than persecution, and gladly gave the requested guarantee.[3]

If the Jews hoped to escape so cheaply from the threat of Christian fervour, they were soon to be disillusioned. At the end of April 1096, a certain Volkmar, of whose origins we know nothing, set out from the Rhineland with over ten thousand men to join Peter in the East. He took the road to Hungary that ran

[1] Hagenmeyer, *Chronologie*, p. 11; Anonymous of Mainz-Darmstadt, in Neubauer and Stern, *Quellen zur Geschichte der Juden*, vol. II, p. 169.
[2] Salomon bar Simeon, *Relation*, in Neubauer and Stern, *op. cit.* pp. 25, 131. The *Notitiae Duae Lemovicenses de Praedicatione Crucis in Aquitania*, p. 351, alludes in vague terms to massacres in several French cities.
[3] Salomon bar Simeon, p. 87; Ekkehard, *Chronicon*, ad ann. 1098, p. 208.

through Bohemia.[1] A few days later Peter's old disciple Gotts-chalk, with a slightly larger company, left along the main road that Peter had taken, up the Rhine and through Bavaria.[2] Mean-while a third army had been collected by a petty lord of the Rhineland, Count Emich of Leisingen, who had already acquired a certain reputation for lawlessness and brigandage. Emich now claimed to have a cross miraculously branded on his flesh. At the same time, as a soldier of known experience, he attracted to his banner a greater and more formidable variety of recruits than the preachers Volkmar and Gottschalk could command. A multitude of simple enthusiastic pilgrims joined him, some of them following a goose that had been inspired by God. But his army included members of the French and German nobility, such as the lords of Zweibrücken, Salm and Viernenberger, Hartmann of Dillingen, Drogo of Nesle, Clarambald of Vendeuil, Thomas of La Fère and William, Viscount of Melun, surnamed the Carpenter because of his huge physical strength.[3]

It was perhaps the example of Peter and of Duke Godfrey that suggested to Emich how easily religious fervour could be used to the personal profit of himself and his associates. Ignoring the special orders of the emperor Henry, he persuaded his followers to begin their Crusade on 3 May with an attack on the Jewish community at Spier, close to his home. It was not a very impressive attack. The Bishop of Spier, whose sympathies were won by a handsome present, placed the Jews under his protection. Only twelve were taken by the Crusaders and slain after their refusal to embrace Christianity; and one Jewess committed suicide to preserve her virtue. The bishop saved the rest and even managed to capture several of the murderers, whose hands were cut off in punishment.[4]

[1] Ekkehard, *Hierosolymita*, p. 20; Cosmas of Prague, *Chronicon*, III, 4, p. 103.
[2] Albert of Aix, I, 23, pp. 289–90; Ekkehard, *op. cit.* p. 20.
[3] Albert of Aix, I, 27, 28, pp. 292–4, 30, p. 295, 31, p. 299; Ekkehard, *op. cit.* pp. 20–1.
[4] Salomon bar Simeon, Eliezer bar Nathan and Anonymous of Mainz-Darmstadt, in Neubauer and Stern, *op. cit.* vol. II, pp. 84, 154–6, 171; Bernold, *Chronicon*, p. 465.

Small as was the massacre at Spier, it whetted the appetite. On 18 May Emich and his troops arrived at Worms. Soon afterwards a rumour went round that the Jews had taken a Christian and drowned him and used the water in which they had kept his corpse to poison the city wells. The Jews were not popular at Worms nor in the countryside around; and the rumour brought townsfolk and peasants to join with Emich's men in attacks on the Jewish quarter. Every Jew that was captured was put to death. As at Spier the bishop intervened and opened his palace to Jewish refugees. But Emich and the angry crowds with him forced the gates and broke into the sanctuary. There, despite the bishop's protests, they slaughtered all his guests, to the number of about five hundred.[1]

The massacre at Worms took place on 20 May. On 25 May Emich arrived before the great city of Mainz. He found the gates closed against him by order of Archbishop Rothard. But the news of his coming provoked anti-Jewish riots within the city, in the course of which a Christian was killed. So on 26 May friends within the city opened the gates to him. The Jews, who had assembled at the synagogue, sent gifts of two hundred marks of silver to the archbishop and to the chief lay lord of the city, asking to be taken into their respective palaces. At the same time a Jewish emissary went to Emich and for seven gold pounds bought from him a promise that he would spare the community. The money was wasted. Next day he attacked the archbishop's palace. Rothard, alarmed by the temper of the assailants, hastened to flee with all his staff. On his departure Emich's men broke into the building. The Jews attempted to resist but were soon overcome and slain. Their lay protector, whose name has not survived, may have been more courageous. But Emich succeeded in setting fire to his palace and forced its inmates to evacuate it. Several Jews saved their lives by abjuring their faith. The remainder were killed. The massacre lasted for two more days, while refugees were rounded up. Some of the apostates repented of their weakness and committed suicide.

[1] Salomon bar Simeon, p. 84; Eliezer bar Nathan, pp. 155–6; Anonymous of Mainz-Darmstadt, p. 172.

One, before slaying himself and his family, burnt down the synagogue to keep it from further desecration. The chief Rabbi, Kalonymos, with about fifty companions, had escaped from the city to Rüdesheim and begged asylum from the archbishop who was staying at his country villa there. To the archbishop, seeing the terror of his visitors, it seemed a propitious moment to attempt their conversion. This was more than Kalonymos could bear. He snatched up a knife and flung himself on his host. He was beaten off; but the outrage cost him and his comrades their lives. In the course of the massacre at Mainz about a thousand Jews had perished.[1]

Emich next proceeded towards Cologne. There had already been anti-Jewish riots there in April; and now the Jews, panic-stricken by the news from Mainz, scattered themselves among the neighbouring villages and the houses of their Christian acquaintances, who kept them hidden over Whit-Sunday, 1 June, and the following day, while Emich was in the neighbourhood. The synagogue was burnt and a Jew and a Jewess who refused to apostasize were slain; but the archbishop's influence was able to prevent further excesses.[2]

At Cologne Emich decided that his work in the Rhineland was completed. Early in June he set out with the bulk of his forces up the Main towards Hungary. But a large party of his followers thought that the Moselle valley also should be purged of Jews. They broke off from his army at Mainz and on 1 June they arrived at Trier. Most of the Jewish community there was safely given refuge by the archbishop in his palace; but as the Crusaders approached some Jews in panic began to fight among themselves, while others threw themselves into the Moselle and were drowned. Their persecutors then moved on to Metz, where twenty-two Jews perished. About the middle of June they returned to Cologne, hoping to rejoin Emich; but, finding him gone, they proceeded down the

---

[1] Salomon bar Simeon, pp. 87–91; Eliezer bar Nathan, pp. 157–8; Anonymous of Mainz-Darmstadt, pp. 178–80; Albert of Aix, I, 27, pp. 292–3, places the Mainz massacre after that at Cologne.

[2] Salomon bar Simeon, pp. 116–17; *Martyrology of Nuremburg*, p. 109; Albert of Aix, I, 26, p. 292.

Rhine, spending from 24 to 27 June in massacring the Jews at Neuss, Wevelinghofen, Eller and Xanten. Then they dispersed, some returning home, others probably merging with the army of Godfrey of Bouillon.[1]

News of Emich's exploits reached the parties that had already left Germany for the East. Volkmar and his followers arrived at Prague at the end of May. On 30 June they began to massacre the Jews in the city. The lay authorities were unable to curb them; and the vehement protests of Bishop Cosmas were unheeded. From Prague Volkmar marched on into Hungary. At Nitra, the first large town across the frontier, he probably attempted to take similar action. But the Hungarians would not permit such behaviour. Finding the Crusaders incorrigibly unruly they attacked and scattered them. Many were slain and others captured. What happened to the survivors and to Volkmar himself is unknown.[2]

Gottschalk and his men, who had taken the road through Bavaria, had paused at Ratisbon to massacre the Jews there. A few days later they entered Hungary at Wiesselburg (Moson). King Coloman issued orders that they should be given facilities for revictualling so long as they behaved themselves. But from the outset they began to pillage the countryside, stealing wine and corn and sheep and oxen. The Hungarian peasants resisted these exactions. There was fighting; several deaths occurred and a young Hungarian boy was impaled by the Crusaders. Coloman brought up troops to control them and surrounded them at the village of Stuhlweissenburg, a little further to the east. The Crusaders were obliged to surrender all their arms and all the goods that they had stolen. But trouble continued. Possibly they made some attempt to resist; possibly Coloman had heard by now of the events at Nitra and would not trust them even disarmed. As they lay at its mercy, the Hungarian army fell on them. Gottschalk was the first to flee but was soon taken. All his men perished in the massacre.[3]

[1] Salomon bar Simeon, pp. 117–37; Eliezer bar Nathan, pp. 160–3.
[2] Cosmas of Prague, *loc. cit.*
[3] Ekkehard, *op. cit.* pp. 20–1; Albert of Aix, I, 23–4, pp. 289–91.

Some few weeks later Emich's army approached the Hungarian frontier. It was larger and more formidable than Gottschalk's; and King Coloman, after his recent experiences, was seriously alarmed. When Emich sent to ask for permission to pass through his kingdom, Coloman refused the request and sent troops to defend the bridge that led across a branch of the Danube to Wiesselburg. But Emich was not to be deflected. For six weeks his men fought the Hungarians in a series of petty skirmishes in front of the bridge, while they set about building an alternative bridge for themselves. In the meantime they pillaged the country on their side of the river. At last the Crusaders were able to force their way across the bridge that they had built and laid siege to the fortress of Wiesselburg itself. Their army was well equipped and possessed siege-engines of such power that the fall of the town seemed imminent. But, probably on the rumour that the king was coming up in full strength, a sudden panic flung the Crusaders into disorder. The garrison thereupon made a sortie and fell on the Crusaders' camp. Emich was unable to rally his men. After a short battle they were utterly routed. Most of them fell on the field; but Emich himself and a few knights were able to escape owing to the speed of their horses. Emich and his German companions eventually retired to their homes. The French knights, Clarambald of Vendeuil, Thomas of La Fère and William the Carpenter, joined other expeditions bound for Palestine.[1]

The collapse of Emich's Crusade, following so soon after the collapse of Volkmar's and Gottschalk's Crusades, deeply impressed western Christendom. To most good Christians it appeared as a punishment meted out from on high to the murderers of the Jews. Others, who had thought the whole Crusading movement to be foolish and wrong, saw in these disasters God's open disavowal of it all. Nothing had yet occurred to justify the cry that echoed at Clermont, 'Deus le volt'.[2]

[1] Ekkehard, *op. cit. loc. cit.*; Albert of Aix, I, 28–9, pp. 293–5.
[2] Albert of Aix, I, 29, p. 259. Ekkehard, *Hierosolymita*, p. 21, says that many people thought the idea of the Crusade vain and frivolous.

CHAPTER III

THE PRINCES AND THE EMPEROR

'Will he make many supplications unto thee? will he speak soft words unto thee? Will he make a covenant with thee?' JOB XLI, 3, 4

The western princes that had taken the Cross were less impatient than Peter and his friends. They were ready to abide by the Pope's time-table. Their troops had to be gathered and equipped. Money had to be raised for the purpose. They must arrange for the government of their lands during an absence that might last for years. None of them was prepared to start out before the end of August.

The first to leave his home was Hugh, Count of Vermandois, known as Le Maisné, the younger, a surname translated most inappropriately by the Latin chroniclers even in his own time as Magnus. He was the younger son of King Henry I of France and of a princess of Scandinavian origin, Anne of Kiev; a man of some forty years of age, of greater rank than wealth, who had acquired his small county by marriage with its heiress, and had never played a prominent part in French politics. He was proud of his lineage but ineffectual in action. We cannot tell what were his motives in joining the Crusade. No doubt he inherited the restlessness of his Scandinavian ancestors. Perhaps he felt that in the East he could acquire the power and riches that befitted his high birth. Probably his brother, King Philip, encouraged his decision in order to ingratiate his family with the Papacy. Leaving his lands in the care of his countess, he set out in late August for Italy, with a small army composed of his vassals and some knights from his brother's domains. Before his departure he sent a special messenger ahead of him to Constantinople, requesting the Emperor to arrange for his reception with the honours due to a prince of royal blood. As

The Balkan Peninsula at the time of the First Crusade

BLACK SEA

CONSTANTINOPLE

Selymbria

Rodosto

Mesembria

Roussa

ADRIANOPLE

PARISTRIUM

R. Danube

Philippopolis

Comatine

Balkan Mountains

Rhodope Mountains

Sofia

Bela Palanka

Nish

R. Morava

Serbian Forest

Belgrade

R. Danube

R. Sava

R. Drina

BULGARIA

R. Struma

R. Vardar

Serres

THESSALONICA

Vodena

Monastir

Ochrida

Black Drin R.

Scodra

R. Devol

R. Viusa

Castoria

Mt. Olympus

Larissa

THESSALY

EUBOEA

C. Palli

Dyrrhachium

Avlona

Otranto

Chimarra

CORFU

Brindisi

Bari

Taranto

Melfi

Mt. Gargano

ADRIATIC SEA

0 20 40 60 80 100
English miles

Via Egnatia
(followed by Raymond, Robert of Flanders,
Robert of Normandy and Stephen of Blois
from Dyrrhachium to Constantinople, and
by Bohemond from Vodena)

· · · · · · · · ·   Route followed by Peter the Hermit and by
Godfrey

— — — —   Route followed by Raymond to Dyrrhachium

— · — · —   Route followed by Bohemond to Vodena

· — · · — · ·   Boundary of Byzantine Empire in 1096–7

he journeyed southward he was joined by Drogo of Nesle and Clarambald of Vendeuil and William the Carpenter and other French knights returning from Emich's disastrous expedition.[1]

Hugh and his company passed by Rome and arrived at Bari early in October. In southern Italy they found the Norman princes themselves preparing for the Crusade; and Bohemond's nephew William decided not to wait for his relatives but to cross the sea with Hugh. From Bari Hugh sent an embassy of twenty-four knights, led by William the Carpenter, across to Dyrrhachium to inform the governor that he was about to arrive and to repeat his demand for a suitable reception. The governor, John Comnenus, was thus able to warn the Emperor of his approach and himself prepared to welcome him. But Hugh's actual arrival was not as dignified as he had hoped. A storm wrecked the small flotilla that he had hired for the crossing. Some of his ships foundered with all their passengers. Hugh himself was cast ashore on Cape Palli, a few miles to the north of Dyrrhachium. John's envoys found him there bewildered and bedraggled, and escorted him to their master; who at once re-equipped him and feasted him and showed him every attention, but kept him under strict surveillance. Hugh was pleased with the flattering regard shown to him; but to some of his followers it seemed that he was being kept a prisoner. He remained at Dyrrhachium till a high official, the admiral Manuel Butumites, arrived from the Emperor to escort him to Constantinople. His journey thither was achieved in comfort, though he was obliged to take a roundabout route through Philippopolis, as the Emperor did not wish to let him make contact with the Italian pilgrims that were crowding along the Via Egnatia. At Constantinople Alexius greeted him warmly and showered presents on him but continued to restrict his liberty.[2]

---

[1] Anna Comnena, *Alexiad*, x, vii, 1, vol. II, p. 213; *Gesta Francorum*, p. 14; Fulcher of Chartres, pp. 144–5. Anna tells us (x, vii, 3, p. 213) that the Count 'Τзερπεντήριος' accompanied his expedition, and Albert of Aix (II, 7, p. 304) that Drogo and Clarambald were with him. Anna calls Hugh 'Uvos'.

[2] Anna Comnena, x, vii, 2–5, vol. II, pp. 213–15. She admits that John Comnenus did not leave Hugh in complete liberty; but her story is full and

Hugh's arrival forced Alexius to declare his policy towards the western princes. The information that he had acquired and his memory of the career of Roussel of Bailleul convinced him that, whatever might be the official reasons for the Crusade, the real object of the Franks was to secure for themselves principalities in the East. He did not object to this. So long as the Empire recovered all the lands that it had held before the Turkish invasions, there was much to be said in favour of the creation of Christian buffer-states on its perimeter. That small states could be independent was unthought-of at the time. But Alexius wished to be sure that he would be clearly regarded as overlord of any that might be erected. Knowing that in the West allegiance was established by a solemn oath, he decided to demand such an oath from all the western leaders to cover their future conquests. To win their compliance he was ready to pour gifts and subsidies on them, while he would emphasize his own wealth and glory, that they might not feel their dignity lowered in becoming his men. Hugh, dazzled by the magnificence and the generosity of the Emperor, fell in willingly with his plans. But the next to arrive from the West was not so easily persuaded.

Godfrey of Bouillon, Duke of Lower Lorraine, appears in later legend as the perfect Christian knight, the peerless hero of the whole Crusading epic. A scrupulous study of history must modify the verdict. He was born about the year 1060, the second son of Count Eustace II of Boulogne and of Ida, daughter of Godfrey II, Duke of Lower Lorraine, who was descended in the female line from Charlemagne. He had been designated as the heir to the possessions of his mother's family; but on her father's death the emperor Henry IV confiscated the duchy, leaving Godfrey only the county of Antwerp and the lordship of Bouillon in the Ardennes. Godfrey, however, served Henry so loyally in his German and Italian campaigns that in 1082 he was invested with

convincing. The western sources, *Gesta Francorum*, Fulcher and Albert (*loc. cit.*) declare that he was kept a complete and unwilling prisoner. His subsequent behaviour does not bear this out.

the duchy, but as an office, not as a hereditary fief. Lorraine was impregnated with Cluniac influences; and, though Godfrey remained loyal to the emperor, it is possible that Cluniac teaching, with its strong papal sympathies, began to trouble his conscience. His administration of Lorraine was not very efficient. There seems to have been some doubt whether Henry would continue to employ him. It was therefore partly from despondency about his future in Lorraine, partly from uneasiness over his religious loyalties, and partly from genuine enthusiasm that he answered the call to the Crusade. He made his preparations very thoroughly. After raising money by blackmailing the Jews, he sold his estates of Rosay and Stenay on the Meuse, and pledged his castle of Bouillon to the Bishop of Liège, and was thus able to equip an army of considerable size. The number of his troops and his former high office gave Godfrey a prestige that was enhanced by his pleasant manners and his handsome appearance. For he was tall, well-built and fair, with a yellow beard and hair, the ideal picture of a northern knight. But he was indifferent as a soldier, and as a personality he was overshadowed by his younger brother, Baldwin.

Godfrey's two brothers had also taken the Cross. The elder, Eustace III, Count of Boulogne, was an unenthusiastic Crusader, always eager to return to his rich lands that lay on both sides of the English Channel. His contribution of soldiers was far smaller than Godfrey's, whom he was therefore content to regard as leader. He probably travelled out separately, going through Italy. The younger brother, Baldwin, who accompanied Godfrey, was of a different type. He had been destined for the Church and so had not been allotted any of the family estates. But, though his training at the great school at Reims left him with a lasting taste for culture, his temperament was not that of a churchman. He returned to lay life and apparently took service under his brother Godfrey in Lorraine. The brothers formed a striking contrast. Baldwin was even taller than Godfrey. His hair was as dark as the other's was fair; but his skin was very white. While Godfrey was gracious in manner,

Baldwin was haughty and cold. Godfrey's tastes were simple, but Baldwin, though he could endure great hardships, loved pomp and luxury. Godfrey's private life was chaste, Baldwin's given over to venery. Baldwin welcomed the Crusade with delight. His home-land offered him no future; but in the East he might find himself a kingdom. When he set out he took with him his Norman wife, Godvere of Tosni, and their little children. He did not intend to return.

Godfrey and his brothers were joined by many leading knights from Walloon and Lotharingian territory; their cousin, Baldwin of Rethel, lord of Le Bourg, Baldwin II, Count of Hainault, Rainald, Count of Toul, Warner of Gray, Dudo of Konz-Saarburg, Baldwin of Stavelot, Peter of Stenay and the brothers Henry and Geoffrey of Esch.[1]

Perhaps because he felt some embarrassment as an imperialist in his relations with the Papacy, Godfrey decided not to travel through Italy by the route that the other crusading leaders were planning to take. Instead, he would go through Hungary, following not only the popular Crusades but also, according to the legend that was now spreading through the West, his ancestor Charlemagne himself on his pilgrimage to Jerusalem. He left Lorraine at the end of August, and after a few weeks' marching up the Rhine and down the Danube he arrived at the beginning of October at the Hungarian frontier on the river Leitha. From there he sent an embassy, headed by Geoffrey of Esch, who had previous experience of the Hungarian court, to King Coloman to ask for permission to cross his territory. Coloman had recently suffered too severely at the hands of

[1] For Godfrey of Lorraine's early career, see Breysig, 'Gottfried von Bouillon vor dem Kreuzzuge', in *Westdeutsche Zeitschrift für Geschichte*, vol. XVII, pp. 169 ff. Albert of Aix, II, I, p. 229, gives a list of his companions. His appearance is described by William of Tyre (IX, 5, p. 371) and Baldwin's *ibid.* (X, 2, pp. 401–2). According to Albert (II, 21, p. 314), Eustace of Boulogne travelled out with the northern French army; but Fulcher, who travelled with that army and is full of information about it, does not mention his presence. Probably he was one of the knights that arrived at Constantinople soon after Godfrey, having travelled by sea.

Crusaders to welcome a new invasion. He kept the embassy for eight days, then announced that he would meet Godfrey at Oedenburg for an interview. Godfrey came with a few of his knights and was invited to spend some days at the Hungarian court. The impression that Coloman received from this visit decided him to allow the passage of Godfrey's army through Hungary, provided that Baldwin, whom he guessed to be its most dangerous member, was left with him as a hostage, together with his wife and children. When Godfrey returned to his army, Baldwin at first refused to give himself up; but he later consented; and Godfrey and his troops entered the kingdom at Oedenburg. Coloman promised to provide them with provisions at reasonable prices; while Godfrey sent heralds round his army to announce that any act of violence would be punished by death. After these precautions had been taken the Crusaders marched peaceably through Hungary, the king and his army keeping close watch on them all the way. After spending three days revictualling at Mangjeloz, close to the Byzantine frontier, Godfrey reached Semlin towards the end of November and took his troops in an orderly manner across the Save to Belgrade. As soon as they were all across, the hostages were returned to him.

The imperial authorities, probably forewarned by the Hungarians, were ready to welcome him. Belgrade itself had lain deserted since its pillage by Peter, five months before. But a frontier guard hurried to Nish, where the governor Nicetas was residing and where an escort for Godfrey was waiting. The escort set out at once and met him in the Serbian forest, half-way between Nish and Belgrade. Arrangements for provisioning the army had already been made; and it moved on without trouble through the Balkan peninsula. At Philippopolis news reached it of the arrival of Hugh of Vermandois at Constantinople and of the wonderful gifts that he and his comrades had received. Baldwin of Hainault and Henry of Esch were so deeply impressed that they decided to hasten on ahead of the army to the capital in order to secure their share in the gifts before the others came. But rumour also reported, not entirely without foundation, that Hugh was being kept a prisoner, Godfrey was somewhat disquieted.[1]

On about 12 December Godfrey's army halted at Selymbria, on the Sea of Marmora. There its discipline, which had hitherto been excellent, suddenly broke down; and for eight days it ravaged the countryside. The reason for this disorder is unknown; but Godfrey sought to excuse it as reprisals for Hugh's imprisonment. The Emperor Alexius promptly sent two Frenchmen in his service, Radulph Peeldelau and Roger, son of Dagobert, to remonstrate with Godfrey and to persuade him to continue his march in peace. They succeeded; and on 23 December Godfrey's army arrived at Constantinople and encamped, at the request of the Emperor, outside the city along the upper waters of the Golden Horn.

Godfrey's arrival with a large and well-equipped army presented a difficult problem to the imperial government. In pursuit of his policy, Alexius wished to make sure of Godfrey's allegiance and then to send him on as soon as possible out of the dangerous neighbourhood of the capital. It is doubtful whether he really suspected, as his daughter Anna suggests, that Godfrey had designs on Constantinople. But the suburbs of the city had already suffered severely from the ravages of Peter the Hermit's followers. It was dangerous to expose them to the attentions of an army that had proved itself equally lawless and was far better armed. But he had first to secure Godfrey's oath of homage. Accordingly, as soon as Godfrey was settled in his camp, Hugh of Vermandois was sent to visit him, to persuade him to come to see the Emperor. Hugh, so far from resenting his treatment at the Emperor's hands, willingly undertook the mission.

Godfrey refused the Emperor's invitation. He felt out of his depth. Hugh's attitude puzzled him. His troops had already made contact with the remnants of Peter's forces, most of whom justified their recent disaster by attributing it to imperial treachery; and he

---

[1] Godfrey's journey is described fully by Albert of Aix, II, 1-9, pp. 299-305. The *Chronicle of Zimmern*, pp. 21-2, gives a short account. No Greek source mentions the actual journey.

was affected by their propaganda. As Duke of Lower Lorraine he had taken a personal oath of allegiance to the emperor Henry IV, and may have thought that this precluded an oath to the rival eastern Emperor. Moreover, he did not wish to take any important step till he could consult the other Crusading leaders whom he knew to be soon arriving. Hugh returned to the palace without an answer for Alexius.

Alexius was angry, and unwisely thought to bring Godfrey to reason by shutting off the supplies that he had promised to provide for his troops. While Godfrey hesitated, Baldwin at once began to raid the suburbs, till Alexius promised to lift the blockade. At the same time Godfrey agreed to move his camp down the Golden Horn to Pera, where it would be better sheltered from the winter winds, and where the imperial police could watch it more closely. For some time neither side took further action. The Emperor supplied the western troops with sufficient provisions; and Godfrey for his part saw that discipline was maintained. At the end of January Alexius again invited Godfrey to visit him; but Godfrey was still unwilling to commit himself till other Crusading leaders should join him. He sent his cousin, Baldwin of Le Bourg, Conon of Montaigu and Geoffrey of Esch to the palace to hear the Emperor's proposals, but on their return gave no answer. Alexius was unwilling to provoke Godfrey lest he should again ravage the suburbs. After ensuring that the Lorrainers had no communication with the outside world, he waited till Godfrey should grow impatient and come to terms.

At the end of March Alexius learnt that other Crusading armies would soon arrive at Constantinople. He felt obliged to bring matters to a head, and began to reduce the supplies sent to the Crusaders' camp. First he withheld fodder for their horses, then, as Holy Week approached, their fish and finally bread. The Crusaders responded by making daily raids on the neighbouring villages and eventually came into conflict with the Petcheneg troops that acted as police in the district. In revenge Baldwin set an ambush for the police. Sixty were captured and many of them were put to death. Encouraged by the small success and feeling that he was now committed to fight, Godfrey decided to move his camp and to attack the city itself. After carefully plundering and burning the houses in Pera in which his men had been lodged, he led them across a bridge over the head waters of the Golden Horn, drew them up outside the city walls and began to attack the gate that led to the palace quarter of Blachernae. It is doubtful whether he meant to do more than put pressure on the Emperor; but the Greeks suspected that he aimed at seizing the Empire.

It was the Thursday in Holy Week, 2 April; and Constantinople was quite unprepared for such an onslaught. There were signs of a panic in the city, which was only stilled by the presence and the cool behaviour of the Emperor. He was genuinely shocked by the necessity for fighting on so holy a day. He ordered his troops to make a demonstration outside the gates without coming to blows with the enemy, while his archers on the walls were told to fire over their heads. The Crusaders did not press their attack and soon retired, having slain only seven of the Byzantines. Next day Hugh of Vermandois again went out to remonstrate with Godfrey, who retorted by taunting him with slavishness for having so readily accepted vassaldom. When envoys were sent by Alexius to the camp later in the day to suggest that Godfrey's troops should cross over to Asia even before Godfrey took the oath, the Crusaders advanced to attack them without waiting to hear what they might say. Thereupon Alexius decided to finish the affair, and flung in more of his men to meet the attack. The Crusaders were no match for the seasoned imperial soldiers. After a brief contest they turned and fled. His defeat brought Godfrey at last to recognize his weakness. He consented both to take the oath of allegiance and to have his army transported across the Bosphorus.

The ceremony of the oath-taking was held probably two days later, on Easter Sunday. Godfrey, Baldwin and their leading lords swore to acknowledge the Emperor as overlord of any conquests that they might make and to hand over to the Emperor's officials any reconquered land that had previously belonged to the Emperor. They then received huge gifts of money and were entertained by the Emperor at a banquet. As soon as the ceremonies were over, Godfrey and his troops were shipped across to Chalcedon and marched on to an encampment at Pelecanum, on the road to Nicomedia.[1]

Alexius had very little time to spare. Already a miscellaneous army, probably composed of various vassals of Godfrey who had preferred to travel through Italy and were probably led by the Count of Toul, had arrived at the outer suburbs of the city and were waiting on the shores of the Marmora, near Sosthenium. They showed the same truculence as Godfrey, and were anxious to wait for Bohemond and the Normans, whom they knew to be close behind; while the Emperor was determined to prevent their

[1] The two fullest accounts of Godfrey's behaviour at Constantinople are those given in Anna Comnena, *Alexiad*, x, ix, 1-11, vol. II, pp. 220-6 and Albert of Aix, II, 9-16, pp. 305-11. As Chalandon, *Histoire de la première Croisade*, pp. 119-29, has pointed out, Anna's account is far more convincing than Albert's, and may be accepted as true, apart from her exaggeration of the strength of Godfrey's army. There is a shorter and highly prejudiced account in the *Gesta Francorum*, I, 3, pp. 14-18. The exact site of Pelecanum is uncertain. Leib, in his edition of Anna Comnena (vol. II, p. 226 n. 2) identifies it with Hereke, some sixteen miles west of Nicomedia. Ramsay, *Historical Geography of Asia Minor*, p. 185, implies that it was nearer to Chalcedon. It is clear from Anna (see below, p. 175) that it was close to the ferry to Civetot and conveniently placed for keeping in touch with Constantinople. John Cantacuzenus, the only other Byzantine writer to mention it, places it east of Dacibyza, the modern Gebze (vol. I, pp. 342 ff.). The ferry to Civetot left from Aegiali, midway between Gebze and Hereke, about six miles from each. According to Anna (XI, iii, 1, vol. III, p. 16) it was at Pelecanum that Alexius received the Crusaders after the fall of Nicaea; but Stephen of Blois (Hagenmeyer, *Die Kreuzzugsbriefe*, p. 140) says that Alexius was on an island when he saw him on that occasion. It is clear that Pelecanum, wherever it was, was not an island; nor can it have been the peninsula of Aegiali, to which Anna gives its correct name. Stephen's evidence on such a point is reliable. It is probable, therefore, that Pelecanum itself was close to Aegiali, but that Alexius had moved back to one of the islands off the coast, either the island opposite to Tuzla (twelve miles west of Aegiali), where there are still considerable ruins dating from Byzantine times, or the island of Sts Peter and Paul, opposite to Pendik, which was a known Byzantine resort.

junction with Godfrey. It was only after some fighting that he could keep control over their movements; and as soon as Godfrey was safely across the Bosphorus he conveyed them by sea to the capital, where they joined other small groups of Crusaders that had straggled across the Balkans. All the Emperor's tact and many gifts were needed to persuade their leaders to take the oath of allegiance. When at last they consented, Alexius enhanced the solemnity of the occasion by bringing over Godfrey and Baldwin to witness the ceremony. The western lords were grudging and unruly. One of them sat himself down on the Emperor's throne; whereupon Baldwin sharply reproved him, reminding him that he had just become the Emperor's vassal and telling him to observe the customs of the country. The westerner angrily muttered that it was boorish of the Emperor to sit when so many valiant captains were standing. Alexius, who overheard the remark and had it translated for him, asked to speak with the knight; and when the latter began to boast of his unbeaten prowess in single combat, Alexius gently advised him to try other tactics when fighting the Turks.[1]

The incident typified the relations between the Emperor and the Franks. The crude knights from the West were inevitably impressed by the splendour of the palace and by its smooth, careful ceremonial and the quiet, polished manners of the courtiers. But they resented it all. Their wounded pride made them obstreperous and rude, like naughty children.

[1] Anna Comnena, x, x, 1–7, vol. II, pp. 226–30. She calls the leader of this group 'Count Raoul'—'ὁ 'Ραοὺλ καλούμενος Κόμης'; his identity is unknown as he is nowhere else mentioned. From the fact that the Emperor thought it worth while to have Godfrey assist at the ceremony of oath-taking by this company, I believe that they consisted of men from parts of Lorraine and not from France, to impress whom Hugh's presence would have been more suitable. We know that Rainald of Toul came to the Crusade under Godfrey's auspices. Albert of Aix mentions him as one of Godfrey's party from the start; but it is not necessary to take his evidence too literally. Anna was not good at learning Frankish names, and, as in the case of Raymond, whom she calls 'Isangeles', sometimes calls the Counts by their titles. But 'Raoul' was a name of which she had previous experience from Guiscard's ambassador Raoul. She may therefore have telescoped 'Rainald de Toul' into a form that was familiar to her.

When their oaths were taken the knights and their men were transported across the straits to join Godfrey's army on the coast of Asia. The Emperor had acted just in time. On 9 April Bohemond of Taranto arrived at Constantinople.

The Normans of southern Italy had not at first taken much notice of Urban's preaching of the Crusade. Intermittent civil war had dragged on there ever since Robert Guiscard's death. Robert had divorced his first wife, Bohemond's mother, and left his duchy of Apulia to his son by Sigelgaita, Roger Borsa. Bohemond revolted against his brother and managed to secure Taranto and the Terra d'Otranto in the heel of the peninsula before their uncle, Roger of Sicily, could patch up an uneasy truce between them. Bohemond never accepted the truce as final and continued surreptitiously to embarrass Roger Borsa. But in the summer of 1096 the whole family had come together to punish the rebel city of Amalfi. The papal decrees about the Crusade had already been published; and small bands of southern Italians had already crossed the sea for the East. But it was only the arrival in Italy of enthusiastic armies of Crusaders from France that made Bohemond realize the importance of the movement. He saw then that it could be used for his advantage. His uncle, Roger of Sicily, would never allow him to annex the whole Apulian duchy. He would do better to find a kingdom in the Levant. The zeal of the French Crusaders affected the Norman troops before Amalfi; and Bohemond encouraged them. He announced that he too would take the Cross and he summoned all good Christians to join him. In front of his assembled army he took off his rich scarlet cloak and tore it into pieces to make crosses for his captains. His vassals hastened to follow his lead, and with them many of his brother's vassals and of the vassals of his uncle of Sicily; who was left complaining that the movement had robbed him of his army.[1]

Bohemond's nephew William started off at once with the French Crusaders; but Bohemond himself needed a little time to

[1] *Gesta Francorum*, I, 4, pp. 18–20. See Chalandon, *Histoire de la Domination normande en Italie*, vol. II, p. 302.

prepare his forces. He left his lands under safeguards in his brother's care, and raised sufficient money to pay for the expenses of all that came with him. The expedition sailed from Bari in October. With Bohemond were his nephew Tancred, William's elder brother, son of his sister Emma and the Marquis Odo; his cousins Richard[1] and Rainulf of Salerno and Rainulf's son Richard; Geoffrey, Count of Rossignuolo, and his brothers; Robert of Ansa, Herman of Cannae, Humphrey of Monte Scabioso, Albered of Cagnano and Bishop Girard of Ariano, among the Normans from Sicily; while Normans from France that joined Bohemond included Robert of Sourdeval and Boel of Chartres. His army was smaller than Godfrey's, but it was well equipped and well trained.[2]

The expedition landed in Epirus at various points along the coast between Dyrrhachium and Avlona, and reassembled at a village called Dropoli, up the valley of the river Viusa. The arrangements for landing had doubtless been made after consultation with the Byzantine authorities at Dyrrhachium, who may have wished not to strain any further the resources of the towns along the Via Egnatia; but the choice of the route that his army was to follow was probably Bohemond's. His campaigns fifteen years before had given him some knowledge of the country to the south of the main road; and he may have hoped by taking a less usual route to avoid the supervision of the Byzantines. John Comnenus had no troops to spare; and Bohemond was able to start on his journey without an imperial police escort. But there seems to have been no ill feeling; for ample supplies were provided for the Normans, while Bohemond impressed upon all his men that they were to pass through a Christian land and must refrain from pillage and disorder.

Travelling right over the passes of the Pindus, the army reached Castoria, in western Macedonia, shortly before Christmas. It is impossible to trace his route; but it cannot have been easy and must have led him over land more than four thousand feet above sea-level. At Castoria he endeavoured to secure provisions; but the inhabitants were unwilling to spare anything from their small

---

[1] Known as Richard of the Principate.   [2] *Gesta Francorum*, I, 4, p. 20.

stores for those unexpected visitors whom they remembered as ruthless enemies a few years ago. The army therefore took the cattle that it required, together with horses and donkeys, since many of the pack-animals must have perished on the passes of the Pindus. Christmas was spent at Castoria; then Bohemond led his men eastward towards the river Vardar. They paused to attack a village of Paulician heretics close to their road, burning the houses and their inmates, and eventually reached the river in the middle of February, having taken some seven weeks to cover a distance of little more than a hundred miles.[1]

Bohemond's route probably brought him through Edessa (Vodena) where he joined the Via Egnatia. Thenceforward he was accompanied by an escort of Petcheneg soldiers, with the usual orders from the Emperor to prevent raiding and straggling and to see that the Crusaders never remained more than three days at any one place. The Vardar was crossed without delay by the main portion of the army; but the Count of Rossignuolo and his brothers delayed with a small party on the western bank. The Petchenegs therefore attacked them to urge them on. On hearing of the battle Tancred at once recrossed the river to rescue them. He drove off the Petchenegs and made some captives, whom he brought before Bohemond. Bohemond questioned them; and when he heard that they were carrying out imperial orders he promptly let them go. His policy was to behave perfectly correctly towards the Emperor.[2]

In his desire to be correct he had already, probably when he first landed in Epirus, sent ambassadors ahead to the Emperor. When his army had passed by the walls of Thessalonica and was on the road to Serres, these ambassadors met him on their return from Constantinople, bringing with them a high imperial official, whose

---

[1] *Gesta Francorum*, I, 4, pp. 20–2. Bohemond probably took the road that runs inside the present Albanian frontier, through Premeti and Koritsa, and follows a northward curve before crossing the frontier and falling south-eastward to Castoria.

[2] *Ibid.* pp. 22–4.

relations with Bohemond soon became cordial. Food was provided in plenty for the army; and in return Bohemond not only promised not to try to enter any of the towns on his route but also agreed to restore all the beasts that his men had taken on their journey. His followers would have liked more than once to raid the country-side; but Bohemond sternly forbade them.

The army reached Roussa (the modern Keshan) in Thrace on 1 April. Bohemond now decided to hurry on to Constantinople, to find out what was being negotiated there between the Emperor and the western leaders that had already arrived. He left his men under the command of Tancred; who took them to a rich valley off the main road, where they spent the Easter week-end. Bohemond came to Constantinople on 9 April. He was lodged outside the walls, at the monastery of St Cosmas and St Damian, and next day was admitted to the presence of the Emperor.[1]

To Alexius Bohemond seemed by far the most dangerous of the Crusaders. Past experience had taught the Byzantines that the Normans were formidable enemies, ambitious, wily and un-scrupulous; and Bohemond had shown himself in previous cam-paigns to be a worthy leader for them. His troops were well organized, well equipped and well disciplined; he had their complete confidence. As a strategist he was perhaps over-sure of himself and not always wise; but as a diplomat he was subtle and persuasive, and far-sighted as a politician. His person was very impressive. Anna Comnena, who knew him and hated him passionately, could not but admit his charm and wrote enthusi-astically of his good looks. He was immensely tall; and though he was already over forty years of age, he had the figure and complexion of a young man, broad-shouldered and narrow-waisted, with a clear skin and ruddy cheeks. He wore his yellow hair shorter than was the fashion with western knights and was clean-shaven. He had stooped slightly from his childhood, but

[1] *Gesta Francorum*, II, 5, pp. 24–8. The date of Bohemond's arrival at Con-stantinople is established by Hagenmeyer, *Chronologie de la Première Croisade*, p. 64.

without impairing his air of health and strength. There was, says Anna, something hard in his expression and sinister in his smile; but being, like all Greeks down the ages, susceptible to human beauty, she could not withhold her admiration.[1]

Alexius arranged first to see Bohemond alone, while he discovered what was his attitude; but, finding him perfectly friendly and helpful, he admitted Godfrey and Baldwin, who were still staying in the palace, to take part in the discussions. Bohemond's correctness of behaviour was deliberate. He knew, far better than the other Crusaders, that Byzantium was still very powerful and that without its help nothing could be achieved. To quarrel with it would only lead to disaster; but a wise use of its alliance could be turned to his advantage. He wished to lead the campaign, but he had no authority from the Pope to do so and he would have to contend with the rivalry of the other Crusading chieftains. If he could obtain an official charge from the Emperor he would be in a position from which he could direct operations. He would be in control of the Crusaders' dealings with the Emperor; he would be the functionary to whom the Crusaders would have to hand over the lands reconquered for the Empire. He would be the pivot on which the whole Christian alliance would turn. Without hesitation he took the oath of allegiance to the Emperor and then suggested that he might be appointed to the post of Grand Domestic of the East, that is, commander-in-chief of all the imperial forces in Asia.

The request embarrassed Alexius. He feared and distrusted Bohemond, but was anxious to retain his goodwill. He had already shown him particular generosity and honours, and he continued to pour money on him. But he prevaricated over the request. It was not yet the moment, he said, to make such an appointment, but Bohemond would doubtless earn it by his energy and his loyalty. Bohemond had to be satisfied with this vague promise, which encouraged him to maintain his policy of co-operation. Meanwhile Alexius promised to send troops to

[1] See Anna Comnena, *Alexiad*, XIII, x, 4–5, vol. III, pp. 122–4, for a portrait of Bohemond.

accompany the Crusading armies, to repay them for their expenses and to ensure their revictualling and their communications.[1]

Bohemond's army was then summoned to Constantinople and on 26 April it was conveyed across the Bosphorus to join Godfrey's at Pelecanum. Tancred, who disliked and did not understand his uncle's policy, passed through the city by night with his cousin, Richard of Salerno, in order to avoid having to take the oath.[2] That same day Count Raymond of Toulouse arrived at Constantinople and was received by the Emperor.

Raymond IV, Count of Toulouse, usually known from his favourite property as the Count of Saint-Gilles, was already a man of mature age, probably approaching his sixtieth year. His ancestral county was one of the richest in France, and he had recently inherited the equally rich marquisate of Provence. By his marriage with the princess Elvira of Aragon he was connected with the royal houses of Spain; and he had taken part in several holy wars against the Spanish Moslems. He was the only great noble with whom Pope Urban had personally discussed his project of the Crusade, and he was the first to announce his adherence. He therefore considered himself with some justification to be entitled to its lay command. But the Pope, anxious to keep the movement under spiritual control, had never admitted this claim. Raymond probably hoped that the need for a lay leader would become apparent. In the meantime he planned to set out for the East in the company of its spiritual chief, the Bishop of Le Puy.

Raymond had taken the Cross at the time of Clermont, in November 1095; but it was not till next October that he was ready to leave his lands. He vowed to spend the rest of his days in the

---

[1] *Ibid.* x, xi, 1–7, vol. II, pp. 230–4. *Gesta Francorum*, II, 6, pp. 28–32, gives, as usual, an account very hostile to the Emperor. The passage in which it tells of a secret treaty between the Emperor and Bohemond over Antioch (p. 30, ll. 14–20, 'Fortissimo autem...preteriret') is a later interpolation into the text, made on Bohemond's orders. See Krey, 'A Neglected Passage in the *Gesta*', pp. 57–78. Albert of Aix, II, 18, p. 312, says that Bohemond took the oath unwillingly. This seems to be incorrect.

[2] *Gesta Francorum*, II, 7, pp. 32–4; Albert of Aix, II, 19, p. 313.

Holy Land; but it is possible that the vow was made with reservations; for, while he left his lands in France to be administered by his natural son, Bertrand, he carefully did not abdicate his rights. His wife and his legitimate heir, Alfonso, were to accompany him. He sold or pledged some of his lands in order to raise money for his expedition; but he seems to have shown a certain economy in its equipment. His personality is difficult to assess. His actions show him as being vain, obstinate and somewhat rapacious. But his courteous manners impressed the Byzantines, who found him rather more civilized than his colleagues. He also struck them as being more reliable and honest. Anna Comnena, whom later events prejudiced in his favour, commended the superiority of his nature and the purity of his life. Adhemar of Le Puy, who was certainly a man of high standards, clearly regarded him as a worthy friend.

Several noblemen from southern France joined Raymond's Crusade. Amongst these were Rambald, Count of Orange, Gaston of Béarn, Gerard of Roussillon, William of Montpelier, Raymond of Le Forez and Isoard of Gap. Adhemar of Le Puy brought with him his brothers, Francis-Lambert of Monteil, lord of Peyrins, and William-Hugh of Monteil, and all his men. After Adhemar the chief ecclesiastic to come was William, Bishop of Orange.[1]

The expedition crossed the Alps by the Col de Genèvre and travelled through northern Italy to the head of the Adriatic. Perhaps from motives of economy Raymond had decided not to go by sea across the Adriatic but to follow its eastern shore through Istria and Dalmatia. It was an unwise decision; for the Dalmatian roads were very bad and the population rough and unfriendly. Istria was crossed without incident; then for forty winter days the army struggled along the rocky Dalmatian tracks, continually harassed by wild Slav tribes that hung on its rear. Raymond him-

[1] For Raymond's early career, see Vaissète, *Histoire de Languedoc*, vol. III, pp. 466–77, and Manteyer, *La Provence du Ier au XIIe Siècle*, pp. 303 ff. The names of the chief southern French lords that came on the Crusade are given in the rather muddled list in Albert of Aix, II, 22–3, pp. 315–16. For Adhemar and his family see references above, pp. 109–10.

self remained with the rearguard to protect it, and on one occasion only saved his men by erecting across the road a barrier made of Slav prisoners that he had captured and cruelly mutilated. He had started out well supplied with foodstuffs; and none of his men perished on the journey from hunger nor in the fighting. When at last they reached Skodra, supplies were running low. Raymond obtained an interview with the local Serbian prince, Bodin, who in return for costly presents agreed to allow the Crusaders to buy freely in the markets of the town. But no food was available. The army had to continue on its way in growing hunger and misery till it reached the imperial frontier north of Dyrrhachium early in February. Raymond and Adhemar now hoped that their troubles were at an end.

John Comnenus welcomed the Crusaders at Dyrrhachium, where imperial envoys and a Petcheneg escort were waiting to convey them along the Via Egnatia. Raymond sent an embassy ahead to Constantinople to announce his arrival; and after a few days' rest at Dyrrhachium the army set out again. Adhemar's brother, the Lord of Peyrins, was left behind to recover from an illness caused by the hardships of the journey. Raymond's men were unruly and ill-disciplined. They resented the presence of Petcheneg police watching them on every side; and their incorrigible taste for marauding brought them into frequent conflict with their escort. Before many days had passed two Provençal barons were killed in one of these skirmishes. Soon afterwards the Bishop of Le Puy himself strayed from the road and was wounded and captured by the Petchenegs before they realized who he was. He was promptly returned to the army, and seems to have borne no resentment for the incident; but the troops were deeply shocked. Their ill temper increased when Raymond himself was attacked in similar circumstances near Edessa.

At Thessalonica the Bishop of Le Puy left the army in order to receive proper treatment for his wounds. He remained there till his brother was able to join him from Dyrrhachium. Without his restraining influence the discipline of the army worsened; but there was no serious mishap till it reached Roussa in Thrace. Bohemond's men had been delighted with their reception at this town a fortnight earlier; but, perhaps because the townsfolk had no provisions left for sale, Raymond's men took offence at something. Crying 'Toulouse, Toulouse' they attacked the walls and forced an entrance and pillaged all the houses. At Rodosto a few days later they were met by Raymond's ambassadors returning from Constantinople with an envoy from the Emperor and cordial messages urging Raymond to hasten to the capital and adding that Bohemond and Godfrey were eager for his presence. It was probably the latter part of the message and the fear of being absent while important decisions were made that induced Raymond to accept the invitation. He left his army and hurried ahead to Constantinople where he arrived on 21 April.

With his departure there was no one to keep the army in order. It began at once to raid the countryside. But now there was more than a small Petcheneg escort to oppose it. Regiments of the Byzantine army, stationed nearby, moved up to attack the raiders. In the battle that followed Raymond's men were thoroughly defeated and fled, leaving their arms and their baggage in the hands of the Byzantines. The news of the disaster reached Raymond just as he was setting out to interview the Emperor.[1]

Raymond had been well received at Constantinople. He was housed in a palace just outside the walls but was begged to come as soon as possible to the palace, where it was suggested that he should take the oath of allegiance. But the experiences of his journey and the news that he had just received had put him in an ill temper; and he was puzzled and displeased by the situation that he found in the palace. His everlasting aim was to be recognized as military leader of the whole Crusading expedition. But his authority, such as it was, came from the Pope and from his connection with the papal representative, the Bishop of Le Puy. The bishop was absent. Raymond lacked both the support and the

---

[1] Raymond's journey to Constantinople is described at length by Raymond of Aguilers, I–II, pp. 235–8, in a tone of great bitterness against the Byzantines.

advice that his presence would have given. Without him he was
unwilling to commit himself; the more so, as to take the oath
of allegiance as the other Crusaders had done would mean the
abandonment of his special relation towards the Papacy. He
would reduce himself to the same level as the others. There was
a further danger. He was intelligent enough to see at once that
Bohemond was his most dangerous rival. Bohemond seemed to
be enjoying the particular favours of the Emperor; and it was
rumoured that he was to be appointed to a high imperial command.
To take the oath might mean that not only would Raymond lose
his priority but he might well find himself under the jurisdiction
of Bohemond as the Emperor's representative. He declared that
he had come to the East to do God's work and that God was now
his only suzerain, implying thereby that he was the lay delegate of
the Pope. But he added that if the Emperor were himself to lead
the united Christian forces, he would serve under him. The concession shows that it was not the Emperor but Bohemond that he
resented. The Emperor could only reply that unfortunately the
state of the Empire would not permit him to leave it. In vain the
other western leaders, fearing that the success of the whole campaign was in jeopardy, begged Raymond to change his mind.
Bohemond, hoping still for the imperial command and eager to
please the Emperor, went so far as to say that he would support
the Emperor should Raymond openly quarrel with him; while
even Godfrey pointed out the harm that his attitude was doing to
the Christian cause. Alexius himself kept apart from the discussions,
though he withheld from Raymond such gifts as he had given to
the other princes. At last, on 26 April, Raymond agreed to swear
a modified oath, promising to respect the life and honour of the
Emperor and to see that nothing was done, by himself or by his
men, that would be to his hurt. This type of oath was not unusual
for vassals to take in southern France; and with it Alexius was
satisfied.

It was when these negotiations were over that Bohemond and
his army crossed into Asia. Meanwhile, Raymond's army had

reassembled, rather crestfallen, at Rodosto, where it awaited the arrival of the Bishop of Le Puy who was to lead it on to Constantinople. Of Adhemar's activities in the capital we know nothing. Presumably he saw the chief Greek ecclesiastics; and he certainly had an audience with the Emperor. These interviews were very friendly. He may have helped to reconcile Raymond with Alexius; for their relations quickly improved. But it is probable that Bohemond's departure was of greater assistance. The Emperor was able to see Raymond in private and to explain to him that he too had no love for the Normans and that Bohemond would in fact never receive an imperial command. Raymond took his army across the Bosphorus two days after taking his oath, but returned to spend a fortnight at the court. When he left he was on cordial terms with Alexius, in whom he knew now that he had a powerful ally against Bohemond. His attitude towards the Empire was altered.[1]

The fourth great western army to go on the Crusade set out from northern France in October 1096, shortly after Raymond had left his home. It was under the joint leadership of Robert, Duke of Normandy, his brother-in-law Stephen, Count of Blois,

---

[1] Raymond's negotiations with the Emperor are given in Raymond of Aguilers, II, p. 238, and *Gesta Francorum*, II, 6, p. 52. The accounts agree that Raymond was anxious to avenge himself for the defeat of his army at Rodosto, and that it was with difficulty that the other princes persuaded him to take some sort of oath. Both also agree on the terms of the oath that he took. Raymond of Aguilers alone provides the significant information that the Count was prepared to serve under Alexius in person. I believe that his motives are easily explained by his jealousy of Bohemond. Anna Comnena, whom later events prejudiced in Raymond's favour, says nothing at all about these negotiations but merely says that her father liked and respected 'Isangeles'—i.e. the Count of Saint-Gilles—for his courtesy and his honesty. She adds that Alexius had long conversations with the Count, and quotes a speech of the latter warning the Emperor against Bohemond and promising to work with the Byzantines (*Alexiad*, X, xi, 9, vol. II, pp. 234–5). I see no reason to assume that she was confusing this visit with the visit that Raymond paid to Alexius in 1100; Albert of Aix, whose information came from one of Godfrey's soldiers, agrees that Raymond left Constantinople on the best terms with Alexius after remaining behind there for a fortnight (II, 20, p. 314). Instances of the use of the oath of non-prejudice in Languedoc are given in Vaissète, *Histoire de Languedoc*, vols. V, pp. 372, 381, and VII, pp. 134 ff.

and his cousin Robert II, Count of Flanders. Robert of Normandy was the eldest son of William the Conqueror. He was a man of forty, mild-mannered and somewhat ineffectual, but not without personal courage and charm. Ever since his father's death he had been carrying on a desultory war with his brother, William Rufus of England, who had several times invaded his duchy. Urban's preaching of the Crusade had deeply moved him; and he soon declared his adhesion. In return the Pope, while he was still in northern France, arranged a reconciliation between him and his brother. But Robert took several months to plan his Crusade and was eventually only able to raise the money that he required by pledging his duchy to William for ten thousand silver marks. The act confirming the pledge was signed in September 1096. A few days later Robert set out with his army for Pontarlier, where he was joined by Stephen of Blois and Robert of Flanders. With him were Odo, Bishop of Bayeux, Walter, Count of Saint-Valéry, the heirs of the Counts of Montgomery and Mortagne, Girard of Gournay, Hugh of Saint-Pol and the sons of Hugh of Grant-Mesnil, and a number of knights and infantrymen not only from Normandy but also from England, Scotland and Brittany; though the only English nobleman to accompany the Crusade, Ralph Guader, Earl of Norfolk, was at the time an exile, living on his mother's estates in Brittany.[1]

Stephen of Blois had no desire to join the Crusade. But he had married Adela, daughter of William the Conqueror; and in their household it was she who made the decisions. She wished him to go; and he went. With him were his chief vassals, Everard of Le Puits, Guerin Gueronat, Caro Asini, Geoffrey Guerin, and his chaplain Alexander. Amongst the party was the cleric Fulcher of Chartres, the future historian. Stephen, who was one of the wealthiest men in France, raised the money for his journey without great difficulty. He left his lands in the competent management of his wife.[2]

---

[1] For Robert of Normandy, see David, *Robert Curthose, passim.* In Appendix D, pp. 221–9, he gives a full list of Robert's companions.
[2] For Stephen of Blois, see Hagenmeyer, *Die Kreuzzugsbriefe,* pp. 48–56.

The Count of Flanders was a slightly younger man but possessed a more formidable personality. His father, Robert I, had made the pilgrimage to Jerusalem in 1086, and on his way back had taken service for a while under the Emperor Alexius, with whom he remained in touch until his death in 1093. It was therefore natural that Robert II should wish to carry on his work against the infidel. His army was a little smaller than Raymond's or Godfrey's but was of high quality. He was accompanied by troops from Brabant, under Baldwin of Alost, Count of Ghent. His lands were to be administered in his absence by his countess, Clementia of Burgundy.[1]

From Pontarlier the united army moved southward across the Alps into Italy. Passing through Lucca in November it met Pope Urban, who was staying there a few days on his way from Cremona to Rome. Urban received the leaders in audience and gave them his special blessing. The army went on to Rome, to visit the tomb of Saint Peter, but refused to interfere in the struggle between Urban's followers and the followers of the anti-Pope Guibert which was troubling the city. From Rome it passed, by way of Monte Cassino, into the Norman duchy in the south. There it was well received by the Duke of Apulia, Roger Borsa, whose wife, Adela, the widowed queen of Denmark, was the Count of Flanders' sister, and who acknowledged the Duke of Normandy as the head of his race. Roger offered his brother-in-law many costly gifts; but the latter would only accept a present of holy relics, the hair of the Virgin and the bones of Saint Matthew and Saint Nicholas, which he sent to his wife to place in the abbey of Watten.[2]

Robert of Normandy and Stephen of Blois decided to spend the winter comfortably in Calabria. But Robert of Flanders moved

---

[1] For Robert and Clementia of Flanders, see *ibid.* pp. 247–9. The names of northern French knights in the Crusading army are given in Albert of Aix's list (II, 22–3, pp. 315–16).

[2] Fulcher of Chartres, I, vii, pp. 163–8; charter of Clementia, Countess of Flanders, in Hagenmeyer, *op. cit.* pp. 142–3.

on almost at once to Bari with his men and crossed over into Epirus, early in December. He reached Constantinople without any untoward incident about the same time as Bohemond. But the Count of Alost, who had attempted to land near Chimarra, further south than the accepted ports of disembarkation, found his way blocked by a Byzantine squadron. There was a slight sea-battle, recounted at length in Anna Comnena's history, as its hero, Marianus Mavrocatacalon, the son of the admiral, was a friend of hers. In spite of the prowess of a Latin priest, whose warlike disregard of his cloth shocked the Byzantines, the Brabançon ship was boarded and captured; and the Count and his men were landed at Dyrrhachium.[1] The Flemish party apparently made no difficulty about the oath of allegiance to Alexius. Count Robert was among the princes that urged Raymond to comply.[2]

Robert of Normandy and Stephen of Blois lingered on in southern Italy till the spring. Their lack of enthusiasm affected their followers, many of whom began to wander back towards their homes. At last, in March, the army moved to Brindisi, and on 5 April it prepared to embark. Unfortunately, the first ship to set sail capsized and foundered, losing some four hundred passengers, with their horses and mules and many chests of money. The tactful discovery that the corpses washed up on the shore were miraculously marked with crosses on their shoulder-blades, while it edified the faithful, did not discourage many more timorous folk

---

[1] Fulcher of Chartres, *loc. cit.* p. 168; Anna Comnena, *Alexiad*, X, viii, 2–10, vol. II, pp. 215–20. Maricq, 'Un "Comte de Brabant" et des "Brabançons" dans deux textes byzantins', in the *Bulletin de la Classe des Lettres* of the Royal Academy of Belgium, vol. XXXIV, pp. 463 ff., has satisfactorily identified Anna's 'ὁ Κόμης Πρεβέντζας' with Baldwin II, Count of Alost, thus superseding Grégoire's earlier suggestion that he was Richard of the Principate ('Notes sur Anne Comnène', in *Byzantion*, vol. III, pp. 312–13, which also contains an interesting discussion on the word τζάγγρα mentioned here by Anna). Ducange's theory that the 'Κόμης Πρεβέντζας' is Raymond of Toulouse, who was also Marquis of Provence, which is followed by Mrs Buckler, *Anna Comnena*, p. 465, is impossible, as Anna always calls Raymond 'Isangeles', and his movements are well known to us.

[2] Raymond of Aguilers, II, p. 238.

from abandoning the expedition. But the bulk of the army safely embarked and after a rough voyage of four days landed at Dyrrhachium. The Byzantine authorities received them well and provided them with an escort to take them along the Via Egnatia to Constantinople. Apart from an accident while the army was crossing a stream in the Pindus, when a sudden flood swept away several pilgrims, the journey passed pleasantly. After a delay of four days before the walls of Thessalonica, Constantinople was reached early in May. A camp was provided for the army just outside the walls; and parties of five or six at a time were admitted daily into the city to see its sights and worship at its shrines. The earlier Crusading armies had all by now been transferred across the Bosphorus; and these latecomers found no malcontents to spoil their relations with the Byzantines. They were struck with admiration at the beauty and splendour of the city; they enjoyed the rest and comfort that it provided. They were grateful for the Emperor's distribution of coins and of silk garments and for the food and the horses that he provided. Their leaders at once took the oath of allegiance to the Emperor and were rewarded with magnificent presents. Stephen of Blois, writing next month to his wife, to whom he was a dutiful correspondent, was in ecstasies over his reception by the Emperor. He stayed for ten days at the palace, where the Emperor treated him like a son, giving him much good advice and many superb gifts and offering to educate his youngest son. Stephen was particularly impressed by the Emperor's generosity to all ranks in the Crusading army and by his lavish and efficient organization of supplies for the troops already in the field. 'Your father, my love', he wrote, alluding to William the Conqueror, 'made many great gifts, but he was almost nothing compared to this man.'

The army spent a fortnight at Constantinople before it was transported to Asia. Even the crossing of the Bosphorus pleased Stephen, who had heard that the channel was dangerous but found it no more so than the Marne or the Seine. They marched along the Gulf of Nicomedia, past Nicomedia itself, to join the main

Crusading armies, who were already beginning the siege of Nicaea.[1]

Alexius could breathe again. He had wished for mercenaries from the West. Instead, he had been sent large armies, each with its own leaders. No government really cares to find numbers of independent allied forces invading its territory, particularly when they are on a lower level of civilization. Food had to be provided; marauding had to be prevented. The actual size of the Crusading armies can only be conjectured. Medieval estimates are always exaggerated; but Peter the Hermit's rabble, including its many non-combatants, probably approached twenty thousand. The chief Crusading armies, Raymond's, Godfrey's and the northern French, each numbered well over ten thousand, including non-combatants. Bohemond's was a little smaller; and there were other lesser groups. But in all from sixty to a hundred thousand persons must have entered the Empire from the West between the summer of 1096 and the spring of 1097.[2] On the whole the Emperor's arrangements for dealing with them had succeeded. None of the Crusaders had suffered from lack of food when crossing the Balkans. The only raids made to secure food were those of Walter Sans-Avoir at Belgrade and Peter at Bela Palanka, both under exceptional circumstances, and of Bohemond at Castoria, when he was travelling in midwinter along an unsuitable road. Petty marauding and one or two wanton attacks on towns had been impossible to prevent, as Alexius had insufficient troops for the purpose. But his Petcheneg squadrons, by their blind uncompromising obedience to orders, irritating though it must have been to the Crusaders, proved an efficient police force; while his special envoys usually handled the western princes with tact. The growing success of the Emperor's methods is shown by the smooth passage of the last of the

---

[1] Fulcher of Chartres, ii, viii, pp. 168–76; letter of Stephen of Blois to his wife, in Hagenmeyer, *op. cit.* pp. 138–40. This letter was written from Nicaea. An earlier letter, written from Constantinople and describing the journey there, to which Stephen here refers, is unfortunately lost.

[2] See Appendix II, pp. 336–41.

armies, composed of northern Frenchmen, who were not a well-disciplined people and were led by weak and incompetent leaders.

At Constantinople Alexius had obtained an oath of allegiance from all the princes except Raymond, with whom he had achieved a private understanding. He had no illusions about the practical value of the oath nor about the reliability of the men that had sworn it. But at least it gave him a juridical advantage that might well prove important. The result had not been easy to achieve; for though the wiser leaders, such as Bohemond, and intelligent observers, such as Fulcher of Chartres, saw the necessity for co-operation with Byzantium, to the lesser knights and the rank and file the oath seemed to be an humiliation and even a betrayal of trust.[1] They had been prejudiced against the Byzantines by the chilly welcome that they had received from the countryfolk, whom they thought that they were coming to save. Constantinople, that vast, splendid city, with all its wealth, its busy population of merchants and manufacturers, its courtly nobles in their civilian robes and the richly dressed, painted great ladies with their trains of eunuchs and slaves, roused in them contempt mixed with an uncomfortable sense of inferiority. They could not understand the language nor the customs of the country. Even the church services were alien to them.

The Byzantines returned their dislike. To the citizens of the capital these rough, unruly brigands, encamped for so long in their suburbs, were an unmitigated nuisance; while the attitude of the countryfolk is shown in a letter written by Theophylact, Archbishop of Bulgaria, from his see of Ochrida, on the Via Egnatia. Theophylact, who was notoriously broad-minded towards the West, speaks of the trouble caused by the passage of the Crusaders through his diocese, but adds that now he and his folk were learning to bear the burden with patience.[2] The opening of the Crusade did not augur well for the good relations between East and West.

[1] Fulcher of Chartres, I, viii, 9, pp. 175–6, I, ix, 3, p. 179.
[2] Letter of Theophylact of Bulgaria, in *M.P.G.* vol. cxxvi, cols. 324–5.

Nevertheless, Alexius was probably not ill satisfied. The danger to Constantinople was over; and the great Crusading army had set out to fight against the Turks. He intended genuinely to co-operate with the Crusade, but with one qualification. He would not sacrifice the interests of the Empire to the interests of the western knights. His duty was first to his own people. Moreover, like all Byzantines, he believed that the welfare of Christendom depended on the welfare of the historic Christian Empire. His belief was correct.

BOOK IV

THE WAR AGAINST THE TURKS

CHAPTER I

THE CAMPAIGN IN ASIA MINOR

*'And thou shalt come from thy place out of the north parts, thou, and many
people with thee, all of them riding upon horses, a great company, and a
mighty army.'*   EZEKIEL XXXVIII, 15

However much the Emperor and the Crusader princes might
quarrel over their ultimate rights and the distribution of conquests
to come, there could be no dissension about the opening stages of
the campaign against the infidel. If the Crusade was to reach
Jerusalem, the roads across Asia Minor must be cleared; and to
drive the Turk out of Asia Minor was the chief aim of Byzantine
policy. There was complete agreement on strategy; and as yet,
with a Byzantine army by their side, the Crusaders were willing
to defer to its experienced generals on matters of tactics.

The first objective was the Seldjuk capital, Nicaea. Nicaea lay
on the shores of the Ascanian lake, not far from the Sea of Marmora.
The old Byzantine military road ran through it, though there was
an alternative route passing a little further to the east. To leave this
great fortress in enemy hands would endanger all communications
across the country. Alexius was eager to move the Crusaders on as
soon as possible, as summer was advancing; and the Crusaders themselves were impatient. In the last days of April, before the northern
French army had arrived at Constantinople, orders were given to
prepare to strike the camp at Pelecanum and to advance on Nicaea.[1]

[1] The movements of the princes are complicated to trace. Godfrey's army
had been at Pelecanum since early in April, and had been joined there by
Bohemond's. These two armies probably moved on, Godfrey's three days
before Bohemond's, before Raymond's army arrived there, on 29 or 30 April,
so as not to overcrowd the camp. Raymond's army waited for him at Pelecanum, while he returned to visit the Emperor.

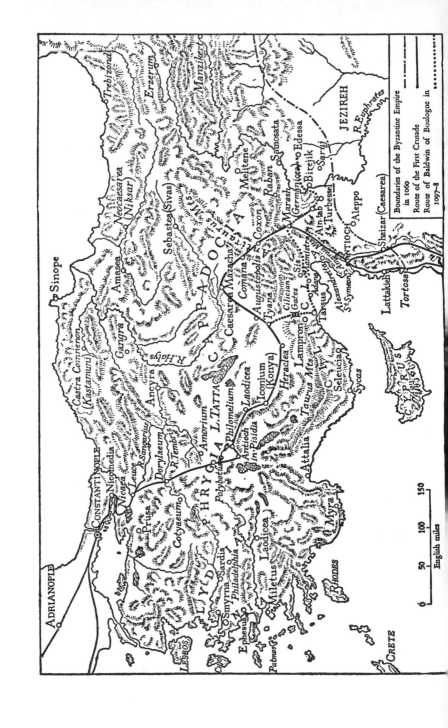

ADRIANOPLE

CONSTANTINOPLE

Sinope

Trebizond

Erzerum

Manzikert

JEZIREH

R. Euphrates

Aleppo

ANTIOCH

Lattakieh

Tortosa

Shaizar (Caesarea)

CYPRUS

CRETE

RHODES

LESBOS

Samos

Cos

Patmos

Myra

Attalia

Seleucia

Sycas

Miletus

Ephesus

Smyrna

Sardis

Philadelphia

Laodicea

L Y D I A

Cotyaeum

Prusa

Nicomedia

Nicaea

Leuce

R. Sangarius

R. Tembris

Dorylaeum

Amorium

P H R Y G I A

L. TATTA

Polybotus

Philomelium

Laodicea

Antioch in. Pisidia

Iconium (Konya)

Heraclea

Lampron

Cilician Gates

Tarsus

Adana

Mamistra

Alexandretta

St Symeon

Castra Comnenon (Kastamuni)

Gangra

Ancyra

R. Halys

Augustopolis

Tyana

Coxon

Comana

Caesarea Mazacha

Amasea

Neocaesarea (Niksar)

Sebastea (Sivas)

C A P P A D O C I A

Melitene

Marash

Germanicea

Raban

Samosata

Edessa

Sarūj

Turbessel

Birejik

Coele

Sis

Tarsus

T a u r u s M t s.

Taurus Mts.

Anti-Taurus

Boundaries of the Byzantine Empire in 1060

Route of the First Crusade

Route of Baldwin of Boulogne in 1097–8

0   50   100   150

English miles

The moment was well chosen; for the Seldjuk Sultan, Kilij Arslan I, was away on his eastern frontier, contesting with the Danishmend princes for the suzerainty of Melitene, whose Armenian ruler, Gabriel, was busily embroiling the neighbouring potentates with each other. Kilij Arslan did not take seriously this new menace from the West. His easy defeat of Peter the Hermit's rabble taught him to despise the Crusaders; and perhaps his spies in Constantinople, wishing to please their master, gave him exaggerated accounts of the quarrels between the Emperor and the western princes. Believing that the Crusade would never penetrate to Nicaea, he left his wife and children and all his treasure inside its walls. It was only when he received news of the enemy concentration at Pelecanum that he sent part of his army hurrying back westward, following himself as soon as he could arrange his affairs in the east. His troops arrived too late to interfere with the Crusaders' march on Nicaea.[1]

Godfrey of Lorraine's army left Pelecanum on about 26 April, and marched to Nicomedia, where it waited for three days and was joined by Bohemond's army, under the command of Tancred, and by Peter the Hermit and the remains of his rabble. Bohemond himself stayed on for a few days at Constantinople, to arrange with the Emperor for the provision of supplies to the army. A small Byzantine detachment of engineers with siege engines accompanied the troops, under the leadership of Manuel Butumites. From Nicomedia Godfrey led the army to Civetot, then turned south through the defile where Peter's men had perished. Their bones still covered the entrance to the pass; and, warned by their fate and by the advice of the Emperor, Godfrey moved cautiously, sending scouts and engineers in front, to clear and widen the track; which was then marked by a series of wooden crosses, to serve as a guide for future pilgrims. On 6 May he arrived before Nicaea. The city had been strongly fortified since the fourth century; and its walls,

[1] Matthew of Edessa, II, cxlix–cl, pp. 211–12, 215, describes Kilij Arslan's attack on Melitene, and says that he was engaged there when the Franks attacked Nicaea.

some four miles in length, with their two hundred and forty towers, had been kept in constant repair by the Byzantines. It lay on the eastern end of the Ascanian Lake, its west walls rising straight out of the shallow water, and it formed an uneven pentagon. Godfrey encamped outside the northern wall and Tancred outside the eastern wall. The southern wall was left for Raymond's army.

The Turkish garrison was large but needed reinforcements. Messengers, one of whom was intercepted by the Crusaders, were sent to the Sultan to urge him to rush troops into the city through the south gates, before its investment was complete. But the Turkish army was still too far away. Before its vanguard could approach, Raymond arrived, on 16 May, and spread his army before the southern wall. Bohemond had joined his army two or three days sooner. Till he came, insufficient provisions had weakened the Crusaders; but, thanks to his arrangements with Alexius, henceforward supplies flowed freely to the besiegers, coming both by land and by sea. When Robert of Normandy and Stephen of Blois arrived with their forces on 3 June, the whole Crusading army was assembled. It worked together as a single unit, though there was no one supreme commander. Decisions were taken by the princes acting in council. As yet there was no serious discord between them. Meanwhile the Emperor moved out to Pelecanum, where he could keep in touch both with his capital and with Nicaea.[1]

The first Turkish relieving force reached Nicaea immediately after Raymond, to find the city entirely blockaded by land. After

---

[1] *Gesta Francorum*, II, 7, p. 34, describes Godfrey's march to Nicaea. Anna Comnena, XI, i, 1, vol. III, p. 7, says that some of the army went by sea direct from Pelecanum to Civetot. Albert of Aix says that Godfrey reached 'Rufinel' the night that he left the camp (at Pelecanum) and stopped there to receive a message from Raymond at Constantinople and to be joined by Peter the Hermit (Albert, II, 20, pp. 313–14). By 'Rufinel' he must mean Nicomedia, which is a day's journey from Pelecanum. Raymond's arrival on 16 May is reported by *Gesta Francorum*, II, 8, p. 36, and that of the northern French, *ibid.* p. 38, and by Fulcher of Chartres, I, x, 3, p. 182, who gives the date.

PLATE I

A PILGRIM OF THE LATE ELEVENTH CENTURY

PLATE II

THE EMPEROR ALEXIUS I BEFORE CHRIST

PLATE III

ANTIOCH FROM ACROSS THE RIVER ORONTES

The fortified bridge is in the foreground. The section of the wall where the Crusaders entered the city
is on the right, on the slope behind the city buildings.

PLATE IV

RAMLEII

PLATE V

THE PORT OF JAFFA

PLATE VI

JERUSALEM FROM THE SOUTH

PLATE VII

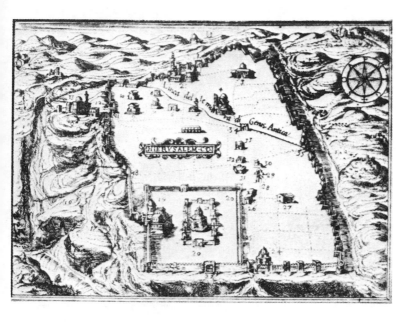

1	Porta di Giaffa.	13	Il S Cenacolo. (cor. della V.M	25	Probatica Piscina.
2	Castello de Pisani.	14	Doue i Giu. volsero pigliare il	26	Casa di Pilato.
3	Monast rio de'Catolici.	15	Doue S Piet o pianse.	27	Casa del Re Herode.
4	Chiesa del S. Sepolcro.	16	Fonte di Siloe.	28	L'arco di Pilato.
5	Casa di Zebedeo.	17	Fonte di Maria Verg.	29	Chiesa del Spasmo.
6	Porta Ferrea.	18	Porta Sterquilina.	30	Simon Cireneo.
7	Casa di S Marco.	19	Chiesa della Prese. della V.M.	31	Casa dell'Epulone.
8	Casa di S Thomaso.	20	Piazza del Tempio.	32	Casa del Fariseo.
9	Chiesa di S Iacomo.	21	Tempio di Salomone.	33	Casa di Veronica.
10	Casa d'Anna Pontef.	22	Porta Aurea.	34	Porta Iudicialis.
11	Porta Dauid.	23	Porta di S Stephano.	35	Porta Efraim.
12	Casa di Caipha Pontef.	24	Chiesa di S. Anna.	36	Basarre.

PLAN OF JERUSALEM

PLATE VIII

a brief, unsuccessful skirmish with Raymond's troops it withdrew, to await the main Turkish army which was approaching under the leadership of the Sultan. Alexius had instructed Butumites to establish contact with the besieged garrison. When it saw its relief retreating, its leaders invited Butumites under a safe-conduct into the town, to discuss terms of surrender. He accepted; but almost at once news came that the Sultan was not far away; and negotiations were broken off.

It was on about 21 May that the Sultan and his army came up from the south and at once attacked the Crusaders in an attempt to force an entrance into the city. Raymond, with the Bishop of Le Puy in command of his right flank, bore the brunt of the attack; for neither Godfrey nor Bohemond could venture to leave his section of the walls unguarded. But Robert of Flanders and his troops came to Raymond's aid. The battle raged fiercely all day; but the Turks could make no headway. When night fell the Sultan decided to retreat. The Crusader army was stronger than he had thought; and, man for man, his Turks were no match for the well-armed westerners in the open ground in front of the city. It was better strategy to retreat into the mountains and to leave the city to its fate.[1]

The Crusaders' losses had been heavy. Many had been killed, including Baldwin, Count of Ghent; and almost all the surviving participants in the battle had been wounded. But the victory filled them with elation. To their delight they found among the Turkish dead the ropes brought to bind the prisoners that the Sultan had hoped to take. To weaken the morale of the besieged garrison they cut off the heads of many of the enemy corpses and threw them over the walls or fixed them on pikes to parade them before the gates.[2]

[1] Anna Comnena, XI, i, 3-4, vol. III, pp. 8-9, makes it clear that the Turks sent two separate forces to relieve Nicaea. Albert of Aix, II, 25-6, pp. 318-19, tells of the capture of Turkish spies just before the main Turkish attack. The battle is described in *Gesta Francorum*, II, 8, pp. 36-8, and by Raymond of Aguilers, III, p. 239, and Albert of Aix, II, 27, pp. 319-20.
[2] *Gesta Francorum*, *loc. cit.*; Albert of Aix, II, 28, pp. 320-1. Baldwin of Ghent's death is reported by Stephen of Blois, Hagenmeyer, *op. cit.* p. 139.

Then, with no more danger to fear from outside, they concentrated on the siege. But the fortifications were formidable. In vain Raymond and Adhemar attempted to mine one of the southern towers by sending sappers to dig beneath it and there to light a huge fire. The little damage that was done was repaired during the night by the garrison. Moreover it was found that the blockade was incomplete; for supplies still reached the city from across the lake.[1] The Crusaders were obliged to ask the Emperor to come to their help and to provide boats to intercept this water route. Alexius was probably well aware of the position but wished the western princes to discover how necessary his co-operation was to them. At their request he provided a small flotilla for the lake, under the command of Butumites.[2]

The Sultan, when he retired, had told the garrison to do as it thought best, as he could give no more aid. When it saw the Byzantine ships on the lake and understood that the Emperor was fully assisting the Crusaders it decided upon surrender. This was what Alexius had hoped. He had no wish to add a half-destroyed city to his dominions nor that his future subjects should undergo the horrors of a sack, especially as the majority of the citizens were Christians; for the Turks comprised only the soldiers and a small court nobility. Contact was re-established with Butumites, and the terms of surrender were discussed. But the Turks still hesitated, hoping, perhaps, that the Sultan would return. It was only on the news that the Crusaders were planning a general assault that at last they gave in.

The assault was ordered for 19 June. But when morning broke the Crusaders saw the Emperor's standard waving over the city towers. The Turks had surrendered during the night; and imperial troops, mainly Petcheneg, had entered the city through the gates

[1] *Gesta Francorum, loc. cit.*; Albert of Aix, II, 31, pp. 322–3; Anna Comnena, XI, i, 6–7, vol. III, pp. 9–10.
[2] *Gesta Francorum, ibid.* p. 40; Albert of Aix, II, 32, pp. 323–4. Anna Comnena, XI, ii, 3–4, vol. III, pp. 11–12, hints at her father's motives in at last sending ships on to the lake, and says that at the same time he despatched troops under Taticius and Tzitas to help the Crusaders on land.

on the lakeside. It is unlikely that the Crusading leaders had not been informed of the negotiations; nor did they disapprove, for they saw that it was pointless to waste time and men on storming a town that would not be theirs to hold. But they were deliberately kept in ignorance of the final stages; while the rank and file considered themselves cheated of their prey. They had hoped to pillage the riches of Nicaea. Instead, they were only allowed in small groups into the city, closely surveyed by the Emperor's police. They had hoped to hold the Turkish nobles up to ransom. Instead, they saw them conveyed under escort, with their movable possessions, to Constantinople or to the Emperor at Pelecanum. Their resentment against the Emperor grew more bitter.[1]

To some extent it was mitigated by the Emperor's generosity. For Alexius promptly ordered that a gift of food should be made to every Crusading soldier, while the leaders were summoned to Pelecanum, to be presented with gold and with jewels from the Sultan's treasury. Stephen of Blois, who travelled there with Raymond of Toulouse, was awe-stricken by the mountain of gold that was his portion. He did not share the view, held by some of his comrades, that the Emperor should have come in person to Nicaea, for he understood that the demonstration that the liberated city would make to receive its sovereign might prove embarrassing to him. In return for his presents Alexius required the knights who had not yet taken the oath of allegiance to him to do so now. Many lesser lords, about whom he had not troubled when they passed through Constantinople, complied. Raymond was not, it seems, asked to do more than he had already done; but Tancred's case was taken more seriously. Tancred at first was truculent. He declared that unless the Emperor's great tent was given to him filled to the brim with gold, as well as an amount equal to all the gold given to the other princes, he would swear nothing. When

---

[1] Anna Comnena, XI, ii, 4–6, vol. III, pp. 12–13, gives a full account of the surrender of the town, frankly admitting that the Byzantines deceived the Crusaders. The western sources merely say that Nicaea surrendered to the Emperor.

the Emperor's brother-in-law, George Palaeologus, protested at his rudeness, he turned roughly on him and began to manhandle him. The Emperor rose to intervene, and Bohemond sharply reproved his nephew. In the end Tancred grudgingly paid homage.[1]

The Crusaders were shocked by the Emperor's treatment of his Turkish captives. The court officials and the commanders were allowed to buy their freedom; while the Sultana, the daughter of the Emir Chaka, was received with royal honours at Constantinople, where she was to remain till a message should come from her husband stating where he wished her to join him. She and her children were then to be dispatched to him without ransom. Alexius was a kindly man, and he well knew the value of courtesy to a defeated enemy; but to the western princes his attitude seemed double-faced and disloyal.[2]

Nevertheless, in spite of some disappointment that they had not themselves captured the city nor helped themselves to its riches,

---

[1] Raymond of Aguilers, III, pp. 239–40, says that the Emperor had promised the princes all the booty taken in Nicaea and had undertaken to found a Latin monastery and hostel there; and his failure to do so caused great bitterness. But Fulcher of Chartres, I, x, 10, pp. 188–9, Anselm of Ribemont, Hagenmeyer, *op. cit.* p. 145, and Stephen of Blois, Hagenmeyer, *op. cit.* p. 140, speak of his great generosity, the latter saying that in fact he distributed the best of the booty to the princes, and food to the poorer soldiers; and even the *Gesta Francorum* says (III, 9, p. 42) that he gave abundant alms to the poor Franks. Anna Comnena, XI, iii, 1–2, vol. III, pp. 16–17, tells of the second oath-taking. Grousset, *Histoire des Croisades*, vol. I, p. 31, for no apparent reason assumes that Tancred still refused to take the oath, and even Chalandon, *Essai sur le Règne d'Alexis Comnène*, p. 123 n. 4, believes that he cannot have done so, because Alexius never actually accused him later of having broken an oath. But Anna's story is clear and convincing. On the other hand, Radulph of Caen's version of the episode (XVIII–XIX, pp. 619–20) is clearly fanciful, representing the story that Tancred liked to imagine was true. See Nicholson, *Tancred*, p. 32 n. 5. Anselm, *loc. cit.*, admits that some of the princes were displeased with the Emperor. Albert of Aix, II, 28, p. 321, reports a distribution of gifts by Alexius to the princes during the siege. See above, p. 152 n. 1, for the site of the ceremony.

[2] The author of the *Gesta Francorum* (II, 8, pp. 40–2) declares that the Emperor treated the captives generously simply in order that they might vex the Crusaders later. For the Sultana's subsequent movements, see p. 194.

the liberation of Nicaea filled the Crusaders with joy and with hope for the future. Letters went westward to announce that this venerable place was Christian once more; and the news was received with enthusiasm. The Crusade was proved to be a success. More recruits came forward; and the Italian cities, hitherto rather cautious and dilatory with their promised aid, began to take the movement more seriously. In the Crusader camp the knights were eager to continue their journey. Stephen of Blois was full of optimism. 'In five weeks' time', he wrote to his wife, 'we shall be at Jerusalem; unless', he added, more prophetically than he knew, 'we are held up at Antioch.'[1]

From Nicaea the Crusaders set out along the old Byzantine main road across Asia Minor. The road from Chalcedon and Nicomedia joined the road from Helenopolis and Nicaea on the banks of the river Sangarius. It soon left the river to climb up a tributary valley to the south, past the modern Biledjik, then wound over a pass to Dorylaeum, near the modern Eskishehir. There it split into three. The great military road of the Byzantines ran due east, probably by-passing Ancyra to the south, and dividing again, after it crossed the Halys, one branch continuing straight past Sebastea (Sivas) into Armenia, the other turning towards Caesarea Mazacha. From there several roads led across the passes of the Anti-Taurus range into the Euphrates valley, while another road doubled back to the south-west, through Tyana to the Cilician Gates. The second road from Dorylaeum led directly across the great salt desert in the centre of Asia Minor, just south of Lake Tatta, from Amorium to the Cilician Gates. It was a road that could only be used by swiftly moving companies; for it passed through a desolate country entirely lacking in water. The third road skirted the southern edge of the salt desert, running from Philomelium, the modern Akshehir, to Iconium and Heraclea and the Cilician Gates. One branch road led from near Philomelium to the Mediterranean at Attalia,

---

[1] Stephen of Blois, *loc. cit.* The Crusaders were allowed to visit Nicaea in groups of ten persons (Anna Comnena, XI, ii, 10, vol. III, p. 16).

another from just beyond Iconium to the Mediterranean at Seleucia.[1]

Whichever road the Crusading forces should decide to take, they must first reach Dorylaeum. On 26 June, a week after the fall of Nicaea, the vanguard began to move, followed during the next two days by the various divisions of the army, to reassemble at the bridge across the Blue River, where the road leaves the Sangarius valley to climb up into the plateau. A small Byzantine detachment under the experienced general Taticius accompanied the Crusaders. A certain number of the Crusaders, probably for the most part those that had been wounded at Nicaea, stayed behind and took service with the Emperor. They were put under Butumites and employed to repair and to garrison Nicaea.[2]

By the bridge, at a village called Leuce, the princes took counsel. It was decided to divide the army into two sections, in order to ease the problem of supplies, one section to precede the other at about a day's interval. The first army consisted of the Normans of southern Italy and of northern France, with the troops of the Counts of Flanders and of Blois and the Byzantines, who were providing the guides. The second army included the southern French and the Lorrainers, with the troops of the Count of Vermandois. Bohemond was regarded as leader of the first group and Raymond of Toulouse of the second. As soon as the division was made, Bohemond's army set out along the road to Dorylaeum.[3]

After his failure to relieve Nicaea the Sultan Kilij Arslan had withdrawn eastward, to gather his own forces and to conclude peace and an alliance with the Danishmend Emir against this new

---

[1] For the roads across Asia Minor, see Ramsay, *Historical Geography of Asia Minor*, pp. 74–82.

[2] Bohemond's army set out on 26 June (*Gesta Francorum*, III, 9, p. 44), Raymond's on 28 June (Raymond of Aguilers, III, p. 240; Anselm of Ribemont, *loc. cit.*), and the northern French on 29 June (Fulcher of Chartres, I, xi, 1; p. 190). Anna Comnena, XI, iii, 3, vol. III, pp. 16–17, mentions that some of the Franks remained with Butumites.

[3] Anna Comnena, XI, iii, 4, vol. III, p. 18; *Gesta Francorum*, III, 9, p. 44; Albert of Aix, II, 38, pp. 328–9.

menace. The loss of Nicaea had alarmed him; and the loss of his treasury there had been serious. But the Turks were still nomadic by instinct. The Sultan's real capital was his tent. In the last days of June he returned towards the west, with all his own troops, with his vassal Hasan, Emir of the Cappadocian Turks, and with the Danishmend army, under its Emir. On 30 June he was waiting in a valley by Dorylaeum, ready to attack the Crusaders as they came down over the pass.

That evening the first Crusading army encamped in the plain not far from Dorylaeum. At sunrise the Turks swooped down over the hill-side, shouting their battle-cry. Bohemond was not unprepared. The non-combatant pilgrims were quickly assembled in the centre of the camp, where there were springs of water; and the women were given the task of carrying water up to the front line. Tents were quickly dressed, and the knights were told to dismount from their horses. Meanwhile a messenger was sent galloping down to the second army, urging it to make haste, while Bohemond addressed his captains, telling them to prepare for a difficult fight and to remain at first on the defensive. Only one of them disobeyed his orders, the same knight that had boldly seated himself on the Emperor's throne at Constantinople. With forty of his men he charged the enemy, to be driven back in ignominy covered with wounds. The camp was soon surrounded by the Turks, whose numbers seemed to the Christians to be infinite, and who followed their favourite tactics of running archers to the front line to discharge their arrows and then at once to make room for others.

As the hot July morning advanced the Crusaders began to doubt whether they could hold out against the ceaseless rain of missiles. But, surrounded as they were, flight was impossible and surrender would mean captivity and slavery. They all determined if need be to suffer martyrdom together. At last, about midday, they saw their comrades of the second army arrive, Godfrey and Hugh and their men in front and Raymond and his men close behind. The Turks had not realized that they had not entrapped the whole Crusading force. At the sight of the newcomers they faltered and could not prevent the two armies from making a juncture. The Crusaders were heartened. Forming a long front with Bohemond, Robert of Normandy and Stephen of Blois on the left, with Raymond and Robert of Flanders in the centre, and with Godfrey and Hugh on their right, they began to take the offensive, reminding each other of the riches that they would acquire if they were victorious. The Turks were unprepared to meet an attack and were probably running short of ammunition. Their hesitation was turned to panic by the sudden appearance of the Bishop of Le Puy and a contingent of the southern French on the hills behind them. Adhemar had himself planned this diversion and found guides to take him over the mountain paths. His intervention ensured the Crusaders' triumph. The Turks broke their lines and soon were in full flight to the east. In their haste they abandoned their encampment intact; and the tents of the Sultan and the Emirs fell, with all their treasure, into the hands of the Christians.[1]

[1] Anna Comnena, *loc. cit.* telling of the French knight; *Gesta Francorum*, III, 9, pp. 44–8; Raymond of Aguilers, IV, pp. 240–1, describing Adhemar's role; Fulcher of Chartres, I, xi, 3–10, pp. 189–97; Albert of Aix, II, 39–42, pp. 329–32; letter of the princes to Urban II in Hagenmeyer, *Die Kreuzzugsbriefe*, p. 161. Dorylaeum, from which the battle is usually named, lay about two miles northwest of the modern Eskishehir. The exact site of the battle is disputed. Anna calls it the 'plain of Dorylaeum'; the princes in their letter to Urban the 'valley of Dorotilla', by which Dorylaeum must be meant; Raymond of Aguilers the 'Campus Floridus', and Albert of Aix the 'valley of Degorganhi which is now called Ozellis'. Hagenmeyer, *Chronologie de la Première Croisade*, pp. 86–7, considers that the Crusaders could not reach Dorylaeum itself by the night of 30 June, as it is 22 hours' marching distance from Leuce. He places the battle near the modern 'Bosuzuk' (he means Bosoyuk) or Inönü. But the direct Byzantine road by-passed both these places, running through Söğüt, and entered the plain about eight miles north-west of Dorylaeum. The Turks made a surprise attack. They must therefore have been hidden by hills; while Adhemar also used some hills to take the Turks in the rear. Before the road enters the plain the mountains are too abrupt to allow of such manoeuvres. But the plain of the Sari-su, the Greek Bathys, into which the road comes, is divided from that of the Porsuk, the Greek Tembris, by a low range of hills, easy to cross, running to the junction of the streams, just above Dorylaeum. If the Crusaders camped in the Sari-su valley, the Turks could make a surprise attack from the Porsuk valley, while an observation-post on the heights of Karadjashehir, just south of the Porsuk, would enable them to watch the Crusaders' movements. Adhemar

It was a great victory. Many Christian lives had been lost, including those of Tancred's brother William, of Humphrey of Monte Scabioso and of Robert of Paris; and the Franks had been taught to pay a proper respect to the Turks as soldiers. Perhaps to enhance their achievement, they willingly gave to the Turks an admiration which they withheld from the Byzantines, whose more scientific methods of warfare they regarded as decadent. Nor did they acknowledge the share taken by the Byzantines in the battle. The anonymous Norman author of the *Gesta* considered that the Turks would be the finest of races if only they were Christians; and he recalled the legend that made the Franks and Turks akin, being both the descendants of the Trojans—a legend based rather on a common rivalry against the Greeks than on any ethnological foundation.[1] But, admirable though the Turkish soldiery might be, their defeat ensured the safe passage of the Crusaders across Asia Minor. The Sultan, robbed first of his capital city and now of his royal tent and the greater part of his treasure, decided that it was useless to attempt to hold them up. Meeting in his flight a company of Syrian Turks who had come up too late for the battle, he explained that the numbers and strength of the Franks were greater than he had expected and that he could not oppose them. He and his people took to the hills after pillaging and deserting the cities that they had occupied and ravaging the countryside, that the Crusaders might find it impossible to feed themselves as they advanced.[2]

The Crusading army rested for two days at Dorylaeum, to recover from the battle and to plan the next stages of the march.

also probably crossed into the Porsuk valley to take the Turks in the rear. As the result of a personal inspection of the countryside I place the battle in the plain of the Sari-su, where the direct road from Leuce entered it. To reach this point the vanguard would have had to cover some 85 miles in four days, as it left Nicaea on the morning of 26 June, but paused perhaps for a whole day at Leuce. The rearguard left Nicaea two days later but apparently did not pause at Leuce. After a forced march it was able to catch up with the vanguard on the afternoon of the battle. The leaders of the rearguard, being on horseback, probably reached Leuce for discussions with their colleagues before their infantry arrived.

[1] *Gesta Francorum*, III, 9, pp. 50–2.   [2] *Ibid*. IV, 10, pp. 52–4.

The choice of the road to be taken was not difficult. The military road to the east ran too far into country controlled by the Danishmends and by Emirs whose power had not been broken. The army was too large and too slow-moving to cut straight across the salt desert. It had to follow the slower road along the edge of the mountains to the south of the desert. This was no doubt the advice given by Taticius and the guides that he provided. But, even so, the road was uncertain. With the Turcoman invasions and twenty years of warfare, villages had been destroyed and fields gone out of cultivation; wells had become impure or been allowed to dry; bridges had fallen or been destroyed. Information could not always be extracted from the sparse and terrified population. Yet if anything went wrong the Franks at once suspected the Greek guides of treachery, while the Greeks were embittered by Frankish indiscipline and ingratitude. Taticius found his role increasingly unpleasant and difficult.[1]

Starting out on 3 July in one continuous body, to avoid a recurrence of the risk run at Dorylaeum, the army toiled south-eastward across the Anatolian plateau. It could not keep to the old main road. After passing through Polybotus it turned off to Pisidian Antioch, which had probably escaped devastation by the Turks, and where supplies could therefore be obtained. Thence the Crusaders crossed over the bare passes of the Sultan Dagh to rejoin the main road at Philomelium. From Philomelium their way ran through desolate country between the mountains and the desert. In the relentless heat of high summer the heavily armed knights and their horses and the foot-soldiers all suffered terribly. There was no water to be seen except the salt marshes of the desert and no vegetation except thorn-bushes, whose branches they chewed in a vain attempt to find moisture. They could see the old

---

[1] There are no complaints against Taticius and the Byzantines till the army reaches Antioch; but by that time he has become 'inimicus' (*Gesta Francorum*, VI, 16, p. 78). See below, p. 224 and n. 1. Resentment must have been growing against him to make Bohemond's propaganda so immediately successful.

Byzantine cisterns by the roadside; but they had all been ruined by the Turks. The horses were the first to perish. Many knights were forced to go on foot; others could be seen riding on oxen; while sheep and goats and dogs were collected to pull the baggage trains. But the morale of the army remained high. To Fulcher of Chartres the comradeship of the soldiers, coming from so many different lands and speaking so many different languages, seemed something inspired by God.[1]

In the middle of August the Crusaders reached Iconium. Iconium, the Konya of to-day, had been in Turkish hands for thirteen years; and Kilij Arslan was soon to choose it as his new capital. But at the moment it was deserted. The Turks had fled into the mountains with all their movable possessions. But they could not destroy the streams and orchards in the delicious valley of Meram, behind the city. Its fertility enchanted the weary Christians. They rested there for several days to recover their strength. All of them were in need of rest. Even their leaders were worn out. Godfrey had been wounded a few days earlier by a bear that he was hunting. Raymond of Toulouse was gravely ill, and was thought to be dying. The Bishop of Orange gave him extreme unction; but the sojourn at Iconium restored him, and he was able to march with the army when it moved on. Taking the advice of the small population of Armenians living near Iconium, the soldiers took with them sufficient water to last them till they reached the fertile valley of Heraclea.[2]

At Heraclea they found a Turkish army, under the Emir Hasan and the Danishmend Emir. The two Emirs, anxious for their possessions in Cappadocia, probably hoped by their presence to force the Crusaders to attempt to cross the Taurus mountains to the coast. But at the sight of the Turks the Crusaders at once attacked, led by

---

[1] *Gesta Francorum*, IV, 10, p. 55; Fulcher of Chartres, I, xiii, 1–5, pp. 199–203; Albert of Aix, III, 1–3, pp. 339–41.

[2] *Gesta Francorum*, *ibid.* p. 56; Fulcher of Chartres, *ibid.* p. 200. Raymond of Aguilers, IV, p. 241, reports Raymond's illness, which must be dated here, and Albert of Aix, III, 4, pp. 341–2, Godfrey's accident.

Bohemond, who sought out the Danishmend Emir himself. The Turks had no desire for a pitched battle and swiftly retired to the north, abandoning the towns to the Christians. A comet flaring through the sky illuminated the victory.[1]

It was now necessary to discuss again the route to be followed. A little to the east of Heraclea the main road led across the Taurus mountains, through the tremendous pass of the Cilician Gates, into Cilicia. This was the direct route to Antioch; but it offered disadvantages. The Cilician Gates are not easy to cross. At times the road is so steep and so narrow that a small hostile party in command of the heights can quickly cause havoc to a slow-moving army. Cilicia was in Turkish hands; and the climate there in September, as the Byzantine guides could report, is at its deadliest. Moreover, an army going from Cilicia to Antioch must cross over the Amanus range, by the difficult pass known as the Syrian Gates. On the other hand, the recent defeat of the Turks opened the road to Caesarea Mazacha. From there a continuation of the great Byzantine military road led across Anti-Taurus to Marash (Germanicea) and down over the low broad pass of the Amanus Gates into the plain of Antioch. This was the road that traffic from Antioch to Constantinople had mainly taken in the years before the Turkish invasions; and at the moment it had the advantage of passing through country held by Christians, Armenian princelings, for the most part nominal vassals of the Emperor and likely to be well disposed. It is probable that this latter route was recommended by Taticius and the Byzantines, but their suggestion was opposed by those of the princes that were hostile to the Emperor, led by Tancred. The majority decided to take the road through Caesarea. But Tancred, with a body of the Normans of southern Italy, and Godfrey's brother Baldwin, with some of the Flemish and of the Lorrainers, determined to split from the main army and to cross into Cilicia.

[1] *Gesta Francorum, loc. cit.*; Anna Comnena, XI, iii, 5, vol. III, pp. 18–19. She mentions Bohemond's prowess at this battle. Her informant must have been Taticius. Fulcher of Chartres, I, xiv, pp. 203–5, mentions the comet.

About 10 September Tancred and Baldwin set off by two separate routes for the Taurus passes,[1] and the main army moved north-eastward towards Caesarea. At the village of Augustopolis it caught up with Hasan's troops and inflicted another defeat on them; but, wishing to avoid delay, it did not attempt to capture a castle of the Emir's that stood not far from the road; though several small villages were occupied and were given to a local Armenian lord, by name Symeon, at his own request, to hold under the Emperor. At the end of the month the Crusaders reached Caesarea, which had been deserted by the Turks. They did not stop there but moved on to Comana (Placentia), a pros-perous town inhabited by Armenians, which the Danishmend Turks were engaged in besieging. At their approach, the Turks vanished; and though Bohemond set out to pursue them he could not establish contact. The citizens gladly welcomed their rescuers; who invited Taticius to nominate a governor to rule the city in the Emperor's name. Taticius gave the post to Peter of Aulps, a Provençal knight who had first come to the east with Guiscard and then had entered the service of the Emperor. It was a tactful choice; and the episode showed that the Franks and Byzantines were still able to co-operate and to carry out together the treaty made between the princes and the Emperor.[2]

From Comana the army advanced south-east to Coxon, the modern Güksün, a prosperous town full of Armenians, set in a fertile valley below the Anti-Taurus range. There it remained for three days. The inhabitants were very friendly; and the Crusaders were able to secure plentiful provisions for the next stage of their march, across the mountains. A rumour now reached the army that the Turks had abandoned Antioch. Bohemond was still absent, pursuing the Danishmends; so Raymond of Toulouse at once, without consulting more than his own staff, sent five hundred knights under Peter of Castillon to hurry ahead and occupy the

---

[1] See below, pp. 197–8.
[2] *Gesta Francorum*, IV, 11, pp. 60–2; Stephen of Blois, in Hagenmeyer, *op. cit.* p. 150; Baudri, VII, pp. 38–9; Anna Comnena, XI, iii, 6, vol. III, p. 19.

city. The knights travelled at full speed; but as they reached a castle held by Paulician heretics not far from the Orontes, they learnt that it was a false rumour and that on the contrary the Turks were pouring in reinforcements. Peter of Castillon apparently rode back to rejoin the army; but one of his knights, Peter of Roaix, slipped away with a few comrades, and, after a skirmish with the Turks of the locality, took over some forts and villages in the valley of Rusia, towards Aleppo, with the glad help of the local Armenians. Raymond's manoeuvre may not have been intended to secure the lordship of Antioch for himself but only the glory and the loot that would accrue to the first-comer. But Bohemond, when he returned to the army, learnt of it with suspicion; and it showed the growing breach between the princes.[1]

The journey on from Coxon was the most difficult that the Crusaders had to face. It was now early October, and the autumn rains had begun. The road over the Anti-Taurus was in appalling disrepair; and for miles there was only a muddy path leading up steep inclines and skirting precipices. Horse after horse slipped and fell over the edge; whole lines of baggage animals, roped together, dragged each other down into the abyss. No one dared to ride. The knights, struggling on foot under their heavy accoutrement, eagerly tried to sell their arms to more lightly equipped men, or threw them away in despair. The mountains seemed accursed. They took more lives than ever the Turks had done. It was with joy that the army emerged at last into the valley that surrounded Marash.

At Marash, where again they found a friendly Armenian population, the Crusaders waited for a few days. An Armenian prince called Thatoul, who had been formerly a Byzantine official, was ruler of the town and was confirmed in his authority. Bohemond rejoined them there, after his fruitless pursuit of the Turks; and Baldwin came hurrying up from Cilicia, to see his wife Godvere, who was dying. After her death he departed again, making now

[1] *Gesta Francorum*, IV, II, p. 62.

for the east.[1] Leaving Marash about 15 October, the main army marched, strengthened and refreshed, down into the plain of Antioch. On the 20th it arrived at the Iron Bridge, at three hours' distance from the city.[2]

Four months had passed since the Crusade had set out for Nicaea. For a large army, with a numerous following of non-combatants, travelling in the heat of summer over country that was mainly barren, always liable to be attacked by a formidable and swiftly moving enemy, the achievement was remarkable. The Crusaders were helped by their faith and by their burning desire to reach the Holy Land. The hope of finding plunder and perhaps a lordship was an added spur. But some credit too must be given to the Byzantines that accompanied the expedition, whose experience in fighting the Turks enabled them to give good advice, and without whose guidance the route across Asia Minor could never have been traced. The guides may have made some errors, as in the choice of their road from Coxon to Marash; but, after twenty years of neglect and occasional deliberate destruction, it was impossible to tell in what state any road might be. Taticius had a difficult part to play; but, till the army reached Antioch, his relations with the western princes remained friendly. The humbler Crusading soldiery might be distrustful of the Greeks; but, in so far as the direction of the movement was concerned, everything still ran smoothly.

Meanwhile the Emperor Alexius, who was to be responsible for the maintenance of communications across Asia Minor, was consolidating the Christian position in the rear of the Crusade. The success of the Franks had reconciled the Seldjuks with the Danishmends, thus creating, as soon as the shock of the first defeat was over, a strong potential Turkish force in the centre and east of the peninsula. The Emperor's policy was, therefore, to recover the

---

[1] See below, pp. 200–1. The death of Baldwin's wife, Godvere (or Godhild) of Tosni, is recorded by Albert of Aix, III, 27, p. 358.

[2] The journey from Coxon to Antioch is described in the *Gesta Francorum*, IV, 11, p. 64, which emphasizes the horror of the mountain road, and by Albert of Aix, III, 27–9, pp. 358–9. Thatoul's installation as ruler of Marash is mentioned by Matthew of Edessa, II, clxvi, pp. 229–30.

west of the peninsula, where, with the aid of his growing maritime power, he could open up a road to the south coast which it would be possible to keep under his permanent control. After refortifying Nicaea and securing the fortresses commanding the road to Dorylaeum, he sent his brother-in-law, the Caesar John Ducas, supported by a squadron under the admiral Caspax, to reconquer Ionia and Phrygia. The main objective was Smyrna, where Chaka's son still ruled over an emirate that included most of the Ionian coastline and the islands of Lesbos, Chios and Samos, while vassal Emirs held Ephesus and other towns near the coast. Phrygia was under Seldjuk chieftains, now cut off from contact with the Sultan. To impress the Turks, John took with him the Sultana, Chaka's daughter, for whom arrangements had not yet been made to join her husband. The combined land and sea attack was too much for the Emir of Smyrna, who promptly surrendered his states in return for permission to retire free to the east. He seems to have escorted his sister to the Sultan's court, where he disappears from history. Ephesus fell next, with hardly a struggle; and while Caspax and his fleet reoccupied the coast and the islands, John Ducas marched inland, capturing one by one the chief Lydian cities, Sardis, Philadelphia and Laodicea. The province was in his hands by the end of the autumn of 1097; and he was ready, as soon as the winter should be over, to advance into Phrygia, as far as the main road down which the Crusaders had travelled. His aim was probably to re-establish Byzantine control of the road that led from Polybotus and Philomelium due south to Attalia, and thence along the coast eastward, where sea-power would give protection and junction could be made with the Armenian princes that were now settled in the Taurus mountains. A route would thus be ensured by which supplies could reach the Christians battling in Syria, and the united effort of Christendom could continue.[1]

---

[1] Anna Comnena, XI, v, 1–6, vol. III, pp. 23–7.

CHAPTER II

ARMENIAN INTERLUDE

'Trust ye not in a friend.'   MICAH VII, 5

The Armenian migration to the south-west, begun when the Seldjuk invasions made life in the Araxes valley and by Lake Van no longer secure, continued throughout the last years of the eleventh century. When the Crusaders arrived in eastern Asia Minor there was a series of small Armenian principalities stretching from beyond the middle Euphrates to the heart of the Taurus mountains. The ephemeral state that the Armenian Philaretus had founded had crumbled even before his death in 1090. But Thoros still held Edessa, where he had recently managed to eject the Turkish garrison from the citadel; and his father-in-law, Gabriel, still held Melitene.[1] At Marash the leading Christian citizen, Thatoul, was recognized as governor by the Byzantine authorities to whom the Crusaders restored the town.[2] At Raban and Kaisun, between Marash and the Euphrates, an Armenian called Kogh Vasil, Vasil the Robber, had set up a small principality.[3] Thoros and Gabriel, and probably Thatoul also, had been lieutenants of Philaretus and like him had started their public careers in the Byzantine administrative service. Not only did they belong to the Orthodox Church, and not to the separated Armenian Church, but they

[1] For Thoros, see Laurent, 'Des Grecs aux Croises', pp. 405–10; for Gabriel, see *ibid.* p. 410, and article 'Malatya' by Honigmann in the *Encyclopaedia of Islam*. See above, pp. 75, 177.

[2] See above, pp. 192–3.

[3] For Kogh Vasil, see Chalandon, *Les Comnènes*, pp. 99 ff. As the leading Armenian prince belonging to the Armenian Church he offered refuge to the Armenian Catholicus, Gregory Vahram (Matthew of Edessa, II, clxxxviii, p. 258). There was a rival Catholicus, Basil, now at Ani (*ibid.* II, cxxxiv, pp. 201–2).

continued to use the titles that they had received long ago from the Emperor; and, whenever possible, they re-established relations with the court at Constantinople, reaffirming their allegiance. Thoros had, indeed, received from Alexius the high title of curopalates. This imperial connection gave to their government a certain legitimacy; but a more solid base was provided by their readiness to accept the suzerainty of neighbouring Turkish chieftains. Thoros played off these potential suzerains one against the other with surprising agility; while Gabriel had sent his wife on a mission to Baghdad to obtain recognition from the highest Moslem authorities. But all these princes were in a precarious position. With the exception of Kogh Vasil, they were separated by their religion from most of their compatriots and hated by the Syrian Christians who still were plentiful in their territories; and all were distrusted by the Turks, whose disunion alone enabled them to survive.

The Armenians in the Taurus were less exposed to danger; for the territory in which they were settled was hard of access and easy to defend. Oshin, son of Hethoum, now controlled the mountains to the west of the Cilician Gates, with his headquarters at the impregnable castle of Lampron on a high spur overlooking Tarsus and the Cilician plain. He kept up a fitful connection with Constantinople and had been given by the Emperor the title of stratopedarch of Cilicia. Though not, it seems, a member of the Orthodox Church, he had served under Alexius in the past; and it was probably with the Emperor's approval that he had taken over Lampron from its unconquered Byzantine garrison. He made frequent excursions into the Cilician plain; and in 1097 he took advantage of the Turkish preoccupation with the advance of the Crusaders to capture part of the town of Adana.[1] East of the Cilician Gates the mountains were in the possession of Constantine, son of Roupen, with his headquarters at the castle of Partzerpert,

---

[1] Oshin's career is mentioned in Matthew of Edessa, II, cli, p. 216. See Laurent, 'Les Arméniens de Cilicie', in *Mélanges Schlumberger*, vol. I, pp. 159–68. According to Matthew, Oshin's brother Pazouni was still living. In Radulph of Caen, XI, pp. 634–5, Oshin is called Ursinus.

to the north-west of Sis. He had, since his father's death, extended his power eastward towards the Anti-Taurus and had captured the great castle of Vahka, on the Göksü river, from its isolated Byzantine garrison. He was a passionate adherent of the separated Armenian Church and, like his father, as heir of the Bagratid dynasty kept up a family feud against Byzantium. He, too, hoped to use the embarrassment of the Turks to establish himself in the rich Cilician plain, where already the population was largely Armenian.[1]

Baldwin of Boulogne had for some time past interested himself in the Armenian question. At Nicaea he had struck up a close friendship with an Armenian, formerly in the Emperor's service, Bagrat, the brother of Kogh Vasil; and Bagrat had joined his staff. It is probable that Bagrat was anxious to secure Baldwin's help for the Armenian principalities near the Euphrates where his family connections lay.[2] But when at Heraclea Tancred announced his intention of leaving the main army to try his fortune in Cilicia, Baldwin decided that it would be unwise to allow any other western prince to be the first to embark on an Armenian venture, if he was to reap the advantage of being the chief friend of that race. It is unlikely that he and Tancred had come to any understanding together. Both were junior members of a princely family, without any future at home; and both frankly wished to found lordships in the East. But while Baldwin had already decided upon an Armenian state, Tancred was ready to set himself up wherever it seemed most convenient. He opposed the detour to Caesarea because it was a Byzantine suggestion from which the Byzantines were to benefit; and the presence of a friendly Christian population close at hand offered him an opportunity.

About 15 September Tancred, with a small group of a hundred knights and two hundred infantrymen, left the Crusader camp at Heraclea and made straight for the Cilician Gates. Immediately

---

[1] For Constantine, see Matthew of Edessa, *loc. cit.*; Sembat, *Chronicle*, p. 610.
[2] Bagrat's early career and connection with Baldwin are mentioned by Albert of Aix, III, 17, pp. 350–1. William of Tyre, VII, 5, vol. I, pp. 383–4, mentions his relationship to Kogh Vasil.

afterwards Baldwin set out, with his cousin Baldwin of Le Bourg, Rainald of Toul and Peter of Stenay and five hundred knights and two thousand infantrymen. Neither expedition burdened itself with non-combatants; and Baldwin's wife, Godvere, and her children remained with the main army. Tancred seems to have taken the direct road for the pass, travelling as the railway does to-day past Ulukishla; but Baldwin, with his heavier army, preferred the old main road which came down to Podandus, at the head of the pass, from Tyana, further to the east. He was therefore three days behind Tancred in going through the defile.

On descending into the plain, Tancred marched on Tarsus, which was still the chief city of Cilicia. Meanwhile he sent back to the main army to ask for reinforcements. Tarsus was held by a Turkish garrison, which at once made a sortie to drive off the invaders but was severely repulsed. The Christian inhabitants of the city, Armenians and Greeks, then made contact with Tancred and begged him to take possession of it. But the Turks held out till, three days later, Baldwin and his army came into sight. Then, finding themselves outnumbered, they waited till nightfall and fled under cover of the darkness. Next morning the Christians opened the gates to Tancred; and Baldwin arrived to see Tancred's banner waving from the towers. Tancred was unaccompanied by any Byzantine official and certainly had no intention of handing over any conquest that he might make to the Emperor. But in Baldwin he discovered a more dangerous competitor who was equally careless of the treaty made at Constantinople. Baldwin demanded that Tarsus should be transferred to his authority; and Tancred, furious but powerless in face of his rival's greater strength, was forced to agree. He withdrew his troops and marched eastward towards Adana.

Baldwin had hardly taken possession of Tarsus when three hundred Normans arrived before the city, having come from the main army to reinforce Tancred. Despite their supplication, he refused to allow them to enter inside the walls; and while they were encamped outside they were attacked at night by the former

Turkish garrison, which was now roaming the countryside, and were massacred to a man. The episode shocked the Crusaders. Baldwin was blamed for their fate even by his own army; and his position might have been badly damaged had not news come of the unexpected appearance of a Christian fleet in the bay of Mersin, at the mouth of the river Cydnus, just below the city, under the command of Guynemer of Boulogne.

Guynemer was a professional pirate who had been astute enough to see that the Crusade would need naval help. Collecting a group of fellow-pirates, Danes, Frisians and Flemings, he had sailed from the Netherlands in the late spring and, having reached Levantine waters, was seeking to make contact with the Crusaders. He retained a sentiment of loyalty for his home town. He was therefore delighted to find close at hand an army whose general was the brother of his Count. He sailed up the river to Tarsus and paid homage to Baldwin. In return Baldwin borrowed three hundred of his men to serve as a garrison of the town and probably nominated Guynemer to act as his lieutenant there while he himself prepared to march on to the east.

Meanwhile Tancred had found Adana in a state of confusion. Oshin of Lampron had recently raided the town and left a force there that was disputing it with the Turks; while a Burgundian knight called Welf, who had probably started out with Baldwin's army but had broken off to see what he could gain, had also forced his way in and now held the citadel. On Tancred's arrival the Turks withdrew; and Welf, who welcomed his troops into the citadel, was confirmed in his possession of the town. Oshin was probably only concerned in extracting his own men from a risky adventure. He was grateful for Tancred's intervention; but he urged him to go on to Mamistra, the ancient Mopsuesta, where a wholly Armenian population was longing for deliverance from the Turks. He was eager to see the Franks pass on into the sphere of influence coveted by his rival, Constantine the Roupenian.

Tancred reached Mamistra early in October. As at Adana, the Turks fled on his appearance; and the Christians gladly let him into the town. While he was there, Baldwin and his army came up. Baldwin seems to have decided already that his future principality would not be in Cilicia. Possibly the climate, steamy and malarial in September, had deterred him. Possibly he felt it to be too close to the Emperor's growing power. His adviser Bagrat was urging him eastward, where the Armenians were appealing for his help. He had at any rate damaged Tancred's chances of founding a strong Cilician state. Now he was on his way back to the main army, to consult with his brother and his friends before embarking on a fresh campaign. But Tancred was reasonably suspicious. He would not permit Baldwin to enter into Mamistra but obliged him to camp on the far side of the river Jihan. He was ready, however, to allow victuals to be sent off to the camp from the town. But many of the Normans, led by Tancred's brother-in-law, Richard of the Principate, could not endure that Baldwin should go unpunished for his crime at Tarsus. They persuaded Tancred to join them in a surprise attack on his camp. It was an unwise move. Baldwin's troops were too numerous and too strong for them and soon drove them back in disorder across the river. The unedifying conflict provoked a reaction; and Baldwin and Tancred allowed themselves to be reconciled. But the harm was done. It had become painfully clear that the Crusading princes were not prepared to co-operate for the good of Christendom when a chance arose for acquiring personal possessions; and the native Christians were quick to realize that their Frankish rescuers were only superficially moved by altruistic sentiment and to learn that their best advantage lay in the easy game of playing off one Frank against another.[1]

After the reconciliation at Mamistra, Baldwin moved quickly on to rejoin the main army at Marash. News had reached him that Godvere was dying; and their children too, it seemed, were sick

[1] The story of the Cilician campaign is given in detail by Albert of Aix, III, 5–17, pp. 342–50, and by Radulph of Caen, XXXIII–XLVII, pp. 629–41. A shorter account, sympathetic to Tancred, is given in *Gesta Francorum*, IV, 10, pp. 55–60. Radulph (p. 634) says that Ursinus (Oshin) then held Adana, but Albert (p. 346) says that it was in the possession of Welf. Albert (pp. 348–9) tells of Guynemer's arrival.

and did not long survive. Baldwin only remained a few days with his brothers and the other chiefs of the army. Then, when the main force set out southward to Antioch, he went off to the east, to try his fortune in the valley of the Euphrates and the lands beyond. A far smaller company travelled with him than had gone on the Cilician expedition. Maybe his popularity as a leader had not recovered from the events at Tarsus; maybe his brothers, anxious for the capture of Antioch, could not now spare troops for him. He had only a hundred horsemen; but his Armenian adviser, Bagrat, still was with him; and he added a new chaplain to his staff, the historian Fulcher of Chartres.[1]

Tancred did not remain long at Mamistra after Baldwin's departure. Leaving a small garrison there, he turned southward round the head of the Gulf of Issus to Alexandretta. As he journeyed he sent envoys to Guynemer, whose headquarters were probably still at Tarsus, asking for his co-operation. Guynemer responded gladly and came with his fleet to join Tancred before Alexandretta. A combined assault gave them the town, which Tancred garrisoned. He then marched over the Amanus range through the Syrian Gates to unite with the Christian army before Antioch.[2]

The Cilician adventure had done little good either to Baldwin or to Tancred. Neither had found it worth while to found a state there. The small Frankish garrisons left in the three Cilician towns, Guynemer's at Tarsus, Welf's at Adana and Tancred's at Mamistra, would not be able to withstand any serious attack. The dispersal of the Turkish garrisons had, however, been of some value to the Crusade as a whole in preventing the use of Cilicia as a base from which the Turks could launch a flank attack on the Franks during

[1] According to Matthew of Edessa, II, cliv, p. 219, Baldwin had 100 horsemen with him when he took Turbessel and sixty when he went on to Edessa. Fulcher of Chartres, who accompanied him (I, xiv, 2, p. 206, 15, p. 215) says that he had 'milites paucos' when he set out (I, xiv, 4, p. 208) and eighty when he crossed the Euphrates (I, xiv, 7, p. 210).

[2] William of Tyre, III, 25, I, p. 149, mentions that the sailors stayed on with Tancred.

their operations at Antioch; while the capture of Alexandretta provided the Franks with a useful port through which supplies could pass. But the chief beneficiaries of the whole affair were the Armenian princes of the hills. The collapse of Turkish power in the plain enabled them slowly to penetrate its villages and towns and to lay the foundations of the Cilician kingdom of Little Armenia.

When Baldwin left the main army at Marash, it was about to start upon its southward march to Antioch; and at first Baldwin took a parallel road a few miles to the east, so as to protect its left flank. It was perhaps by promising to undertake this task that he had obtained permission again to separate from the army; and, indeed, he could justify his whole expedition for the protection that it would give to the Crusade; for the easiest road by which reinforcements from Khorassan could reach the Turks at Antioch lay through the territory that he intended to invade. Moreover, its rich lands might provide the Crusade with the supplies of food that it required.

At Ain-tab Baldwin turned sharply to the east. It is doubtful if he had any planned course of action beyond a general determination to found a principality upon the Euphrates, which might be of profit to himself and to the whole Crusading movement. The circumstances were favourable. He would not have to conquer the country from the infidel; for it was already in friendly Armenian hands. He was in touch with its Armenian princes. Through Bagrat he must have entered into relations with Bagrat's brother, Kogh Vasil, whose lordship lay due east from Marash. Gabriel of Melitene, in permanent danger from the Danishmend Turks, was probably appealing for Frankish aid; while Thoros of Edessa was certainly in communication with the Crusaders. Indeed, Baldwin's decision to leave Cilicia was said to have been due to a message that he or Bagrat received there from Thoros, inviting him urgently to Edessa. The Armenians had long hoped to obtain succour from the West. Twenty years before, when Pope Gregory VII was known to be contemplating an expedition to rescue eastern Christendom, an Armenian bishop had travelled to Rome to secure his interest.[1] Western allies had always seemed more attractive to them, even to the princes that bore Byzantine titles, than anything that might increase their dependence upon the hated Empire. The presence of a Frankish army fighting victoriously for Christendom on their very borders offered them the opportunity, for which they had prayed, to establish their independence once and for all from both Turkish and Byzantine domination. They eagerly welcomed Baldwin and his men as liberators.

We know nowadays to distrust the hopeful word 'liberation'. The Armenians learnt the lesson before us. As Baldwin moved towards the river Euphrates, the Armenian population rose up to greet him. The Turkish garrisons that remained in the district either fled or were massacred by the Christians. The only Turkish lord of any importance in the neighbourhood, the Emir Balduk of Samosata, who controlled the road from Edessa to Melitene, attempted to organize resistance but could not take any offensive measures. Two local Armenian nobles, called by the Latins Fer and Nicusus, joined Baldwin with their small levies. During the early winter of 1097 Baldwin completed his conquest of the land up to the Euphrates, capturing the two chief fortresses, Ravendel and Turbessel, as the Latins adapted the Arabic names Ruwandan and Tel-Basheir. Ravendel, which commanded his communications with Antioch, he put under the governorship of his Armenian adviser, Bagrat; while the command of Turbessel, important for its proximity to the historic ford across the Euphrates at Carchemish, was given to the Armenian, Fer.[2]

While Baldwin was still at Turbessel, probably about the new year, an embassy reached him from Edessa. Thoros was impatient for the arrival of the Franks, whom he now saw delaying on the west bank of the Euphrates. His position was always precarious; and he was alarmed by the news that Kerbogha, the terrible Turkish

[1] Letter of Gregory in Jaffé, *Monumenta Gregoriana*, VIII, i, *Bibliotheca Rerum Germanicarum*, vol. II, pp. 423–4.
[2] Albert of Aix, III, 17–18, pp. 350–1.

Emir of Mosul, was collecting a huge army which was destined for the relief of Antioch, but which could easily mop up Edessa and the Armenian states on its way. But Baldwin was not going on to Edessa except on terms that suited him. Thoros had expected to use him as a mercenary, paying him with money and rich gifts; but it was clear now that Baldwin wanted more than that. The Edessene embassy at Turbessel was now empowered to offer more; Thoros would adopt Baldwin as his son and heir and would at once co-opt him as partner in the government of his lands. To Thoros, who was childless and ageing, it seemed the only solution. It was not what he would have chosen but, unpopular at home and threatened by his neighbours, he could not afford to choose.[1] But the less short-sighted amongst the Armenians were disquieted. It was not for this that Bagrat had schooled Baldwin in Armenian affairs. Bagrat himself was the first to show his discontent. While the Franks were still at Turbessel, Fer, who doubtless wished to succeed Bagrat in Baldwin's confidence, reported that he was intriguing with the Turks. It is probable that his intrigues were only with his brother, Kogh Vasil, with whom he was consulting about the new menace to Armenian freedom. Perhaps he hoped, too, to make himself prince of Ravendel. But Baldwin was taking no risks. Troops were rushed to Ravendel to arrest Bagrat, who was brought before Baldwin and tortured to confess what he had done. He had little to confess and soon escaped, to take refuge in the mountains, protected by his brother, Kogh Vasil, till he too was driven to join him in the wilderness.[2]

At the beginning of February 1098, Baldwin left Turbessel for Edessa. Only eighty knights were with him. The Turks of Samosata laid an ambush for him where he was expected to cross the Euphrates, probably at Birejik, but he eluded them, slipping over a ford further to the north. He arrived at Edessa on 6 February, and was received with the greatest enthusiasm both by Thoros and

---

[1] Albert of Aix, III, 19, p. 352; Fulcher of Chartres, I, xiv, 5–6, pp. 209–10; Matthew of Edessa, II, cliv, pp. 218–21; Laurent, *op. cit.* pp. 418–23.
[2] Albert of Aix, III, 18, p. 351.

by the whole Christian population. Almost immediately Thoros formally adopted him as his son. The ceremony, following the usual ritual of the Armenians of the time, was better suited to the adoption of a child than of a grown man; for Baldwin was stripped to the waist, while Thoros put on a doubly wide shirt, which he passed over Baldwin's head; and the new father and son rubbed their bare breasts against each other. Baldwin then repeated the ceremony with the princess, Thoros's wife.[1]

Once established as heir and co-regent of Edessa, Baldwin saw that his first task must be to destroy the Turkish emirate of Samosata, which could too easily interrupt his communications with the west. The Edessenes gladly supported his scheme for an expedition, as the Emir Balduk was the closest and most persistent of their enemies, continually raiding their flocks and fields and occasionally extracting tribute from the city itself. The Edessene militia accompanied Baldwin and his knights against Samosata, together with an Armenian princeling, Constantine of Gargar, who was vassal to Thoros. The expedition, which took place between 14 and 20 February, was not a success. The Edessenes were poor soldiers. They were surprised by the Turks and a thousand of them were slain; whereupon the army withdrew. But Baldwin captured and fortified a village called St John, close to the Emir's capital, and installed the greater number of his knights there, to control the movements of the Turks. As a result there was a decline in the number of Turkish raids; for which the Armenians rightly gave Baldwin the credit.[2]

Soon after Baldwin's return to Edessa a conspiracy against Thoros began to be hatched in the city, with the support of Constantine of Gargar. To what extent Baldwin was involved can never be known. His friends denied it; but according to the testimony of the Armenian writer Matthew he was informed by the conspirators

---

[1] Albert of Aix, III, 19–21, pp. 352–4; Fulcher of Chartres, I, xiv, 7–12, pp. 210–13. Guibert, XIV, p. 165, also describes the adoption ceremony.
[2] Albert of Aix, III, 21, pp. 353–4. Matthew of Edessa, II, cliv, pp. 218–21, merely says that the expedition was a disaster.

of their intention to dethrone Thoros in his favour. The people of Edessa had no love for Thoros nor any gratitude for the agility with which he had preserved the independence of their city. They disliked him for being a member of the Orthodox Church and a titular official of the Empire. He had not been able to protect their harvests nor their merchandise from raiders; and he had extorted high taxation from them. But, till Baldwin appeared, they could not afford to dispense with him. Now they had a more efficient protector. It needed therefore no prompting from the Franks to provoke a conspiracy; but it is hard to believe that the conspirators would have ventured to go far without securing the approval of the Franks. On Sunday, 7 March, the conspirators struck. They whipped up the populace to attack the houses in which Thoros's officials lived, then marched on the prince's palace in the citadel. Thoros was deserted by his troops; and his adopted son did not come to his rescue but merely advised him to surrender. Thoros agreed and asked only that he and his wife might be free to retire to her father at Melitene. Though Baldwin apparently guaranteed his life, Thoros was not allowed to go. Finding himself imprisoned in his palace, he attempted on the Tuesday to escape from a window but was captured and torn to pieces by the crowd. The fate of the princess, Baldwin's adoptive mother, is unknown. On Wednesday, 10 March, Baldwin was invited by the people of Edessa to assume the government.

Baldwin had achieved his ambition of obtaining a principality. Edessa was not, indeed, in the Holy Land; but a Frankish state on the middle Euphrates could be a valuable element of defence for any state that might be set up in Palestine. Baldwin could justify himself on the lines of broad Crusading policy. But he could not legally justify himself before all Christendom. Edessa, as a city that had belonged to the Emperor before the Turkish invasions, was covered by the oath that he had sworn at Constantinople. He had moreover acquired it by displacing and conniving at the murder of a governor who was, officially at least, a recognized servant of the Empire. But Baldwin had shown already in Cilicia that his oath meant nothing to him; while at Edessa Thoros himself was ready to barter away his rights without reference to his distant suzerain. But the episode was not unnoticed by Alexius, who reserved his rights till he should be in a position to enforce them.

Later Armenian historians, writing when it was clear that the Frankish domination had brought about the utter ruin of the Armenians of the Euphrates, were severe in their condemnation of Baldwin. But they were unjust. There is no moral excuse for Baldwin's treatment of Thoros, as the embarrassed attitude of the Latin chroniclers well shows. Thoros had behaved in a similar manner to the Turk Alphilag, whom he had invited to save him from the Danishmends three or four years before and had caused to be murdered; but he acted then to save his city and his people from infidel tyranny; nor had Alphilag adopted him as his son. It is true that adoption was a less serious thing in Armenian custom than in western law; but that cannot lessen Baldwin's moral guilt. But the Armenians should not blame him; for it was by Armenians that Thoros was actually murdered; and Baldwin was invited to take his place with the almost unanimous approval of their race. The Armenian princes whom the Crusaders were to eject and who alone distrusted the value of their aid were men who had served the Empire in olden days. They were disliked by their compatriots for their allegiance to the Emperor, and, still more, for having become members of the Orthodox Church. These former Byzantine officials such as Thoros and Gabriel alone had had sufficient experience in government to preserve the existence of Armenian independence on the Euphrates. But their ungrateful subjects, with their loathing of Byzantium, with their readiness to forgive in a Latin the heretical errors that damned a Greek eternally in their eyes, had only themselves to blame if their Frankish friends were to lure them to disaster.[1]

[1] Matthew of Edessa, *loc. cit.* emphasizing Baldwin's treachery; Fulcher of Chartres, I, xiv, 13–14, pp. 213–15, whose account is short and rather embarrassed; Albert of Aix, III, 22–3, pp. 354–5. See Laurent, *op. cit.* pp. 428–38, who maintains convincingly that Matthew was present at Edessa at the time.

For the moment all was rosy. Baldwin took the title of Count of Edessa and made it clear that he intended to rule alone. But his Frankish troops were few in number; he was forced to rely upon Armenians to work for him. He found several that he could trust; and his task was made easier by the discovery in the citadel of a vast store of treasure, much of which dated from the days of the Byzantines and to which Thoros by his exactions had greatly added. The new-gotten wealth enabled him not only to buy support but to carry off a master-stroke of diplomacy. The Emir Balduk of Samosata had been frightened by the news of Baldwin's accession. When he saw preparations being made for a fresh attack on his capital he hastily sent to Edessa offering to sell his emirate for the sum of ten thousand bezants. Baldwin accepted, and entered Samosata in triumph. In the citadel there he found many hostages that Balduk had taken from Edessa. He promptly restored them to their families. This action, together with his elimination of the Turkish menace from Samosata, enormously increased his popularity. Balduk was invited to take up residence at Edessa with his bodyguard, as mercenaries of the Count.[1]

As Baldwin's successes became generally known, several western knights, on their way to reinforce the Crusading army at Antioch, turned aside to share in his fortune, while others left the dreary siege of Antioch to join him. Amongst these were Drogo of Nesle and Rainald of Toul and Raymond's vassal, Gaston of Béarn. Baldwin rewarded them with handsome gifts from his treasury and, to settle them, encouraged them to marry Armenian heiresses. He himself, a widower and childless now, set the example. His new countess was the daughter of a chieftain known to the Latin chroniclers as Taphnuz or Tafroc. He was a wealthy prince owning territory nearby and apparently was related to Constantine of Gargar; and he had connections with Constantinople, whither he ultimately retired. It is possible that he was the same as Thatoul, the ruler of Marash, whose alliance would certainly be of value to Baldwin. He gave his daughter a dowry of sixty thousand bezants

[1] Albert of Aix, III, 24, pp. 355–6.

and a vague promise that she should inherit his lands. But the marriage brought her no happiness; and no children were born of it.[1]

Baldwin thus laid down the principles of the policy that he was later to establish for the kingdom of Jerusalem. The control of the government was to be kept by the Frankish prince and his Frankish vassals; but orientals, both Christian and Moslems, were invited to play their part in the state, which a general fusion of races would in the end blend into a corporate whole. It was the policy of a clear-sighted statesman; but to knights newly come from the West, pledged to dedicate themselves to the Cross and to extirpate the infidel, it seemed almost a betrayal of the vows of a Crusader. It was not to set up Baldwin and his like in semi-oriental monarchies that Urban had appealed to the faithful at Clermont.

Nor was it at first an easy policy to follow. The Moslems regarded Baldwin as a transitory adventurer of whom use might be made. Between Edessa and the Euphrates, to the south-west of the city, lay the Moslem town of Saruj. It was tributary to an Ortoqid prince, Balak ibn Bahram, but had recently revolted. Balak now wrote to Baldwin asking to hire his services for its reduction; and Baldwin, delighted by the opportunity thus opened to him, agreed to perform the task. The citizens of Saruj thereupon sent secretly

---

[1] The identity of Baldwin's father-in-law cannot be absolutely established. Albert of Aix, III, 31, p. 361, calls him Taphnuz and says that he was the brother of Constantine. William of Tyre, X, i, 1, p. 402, calls him Tafroc. Dulaurier, p. 431 n. 2, in his edition of Matthew of Edessa, assumes that he must be a brother of Constantine the Roupenian, called Thoros; but he admits that Constantine had no known brother of that name. Hagenmeyer, p. 421 n. 7, in his edition of Fulcher of Chartres, accepts the identification. But it is clear that the Constantine of whom Albert was thinking was Constantine of Gargar. Honigmann, article 'Marash' in the *Encyclopaedia of Islam*, suggests that Taphnuz is really Thatoul. In support of this, we know that Thatoul retired to Constantinople in 1104 (Matthew of Edessa, III, clxxxvi, p. 257), and that Baldwin's wife asked permission to join her parents in Constantinople soon after she had been repudiated by him in 1104 (William of Tyre, XI, i, 1, pp. 451–2). There is no reason for supposing her to have had the name of Arda, which she is sometimes given. See Hagenmeyer's edition of Fulcher, *loc. cit.* Albert of Aix, v, 15, pp. 441–2, names the knights that joined Baldwin.

to Balduk to come and save them. Balduk and his troops slipped
out of Edessa and were admitted to Saruj. But Baldwin followed
on his heels, bringing with him a number of siege engines. Balduk
and the men of Saruj lost heart. The latter at once offered to give
up their town to him and to pay him tribute, while the former
came out to meet him, declaring that he had hurried ahead merely
to take over the town for him. Baldwin was undeceived. He
accepted Balduk's apology and apparently restored him to favour;
but a few days later he demanded that the Emir's wife and children
should be handed to him as hostages. When Balduk demurred, he
arrested him and cut off his head. Meanwhile a Frankish garrison
was placed in Saruj, under Fulk of Chartres; who is not to be confused with the historian Fulcher. The episode taught Baldwin that
the Moslems could not be trusted. Henceforward he saw to it that
any of them dwelling in his territory should be leaderless; but he
allowed them freedom of worship. If he was to hold a town like
Saruj, where the population was almost entirely Arab and Moslem,
he could not do otherwise. But his tolerance shocked western
opinion.[1]

The capture of Saruj, which was followed a few months later
by that of Birejik, with its ford over the Euphrates, by clearing the
roads between Edessa and his fortresses of Turbessel and Ravendel,
consolidated Baldwin's county and ensured his communications
with the main Crusade. At the same time it taught the Moslems
that the Count of Edessa was a power to be taken seriously; and
they concentrated on his destruction. Their determination and the
value of a Frankish Edessa to the Crusades were illustrated in May,
when Kerbogha, on his way to relieve Antioch, paused to eliminate
Baldwin. For three weeks he battled vainly against the walls of
Edessa before he abandoned the attack. His failure raised Baldwin's
prestige; and the time that he had lost saved the Crusade.[2]

The Armenians also had not taken Baldwin seriously enough.

[1] Albert of Aix, III, 25, pp. 356-7.
[2] *Idem*, IV, 10-12, pp. 396-7; Fulcher of Chartres, I, xix, pp. 242-3; Matthew
of Edessa, II, clv, p. 221.

They resented the flow of Frankish knights into their territory, and the favours that Baldwin bestowed on them. Nor did the Frankish knights placate the Armenians, whom they treated with disdain and often with violence. The notables of Edessa found themselves excluded from the Count's council where only Franks were represented; but the taxes that they paid were no lower than in Thoros's day. Moreover Armenian estates in the countryside were being granted to the new-comers; and the farmers were bound to them by the tighter feudal custom of the west. Late in 1098 an Armenian revealed to Baldwin a plot against his life. Twelve of the chief citizens of the town were said to have been in touch with the Turkish Emirs of the Diarbekir district. Baldwin's father-in-law, Taphnuz, was at Edessa at the time; his daughter's wedding had taken place only a short time before. It was said that the conspirators wished to put him in Baldwin's place or at least to oblige Baldwin to share the government with him. On hearing the report Baldwin struck at once. The two leading plotters were arrested and blinded; their chief associates had their noses or their feet cut off. A large number of Armenians suspected of complicity were flung into gaol and their fortunes were confiscated. But, after the manner of wise orientals, they had hidden their money well enough for it to elude Baldwin's inspectors; so Baldwin graciously allowed them to buy their freedom at prices ranging from twenty to sixty thousand bezants a head. Taphnuz, whose association with the plot could not be proved, nevertheless thought it wise to hasten back to his mountains away from his terrible son-in-law. He took with him most of the countess's dowry, of which he had only handed over seven hundred bezants.[1]

Baldwin's fierce crushing of the conspiracy ended the risk of trouble from his Armenian subjects. He continued to employ a few of them in high posts, such as Abu'l Gharib, whom he made governor of Birejik. But as more Franks joined him, attracted by his renown, he could afford to ignore the orientals. His renown was now, less than a year after his coming to Edessa, already

[1] Albert of Aix, v, 16–18, pp. 442–3.

tremendous. While the main Crusading army was still toiling on the way to Jerusalem, he had founded a rich and powerful state deep in Asia and was feared and respected throughout the eastern world. He had started out on the Crusade a youngest son, penniless and dependent on the charity of his brothers. He had been utterly overshadowed by great nobles such as Raymond of Toulouse or Hugh of Vermandois or by experienced adventurers such as Bohemond. Already he was a greater potentate than any of them. In him the Crusade could recognize the ablest and most astute of its statesmen.

CHAPTER III

BEFORE THE WALLS OF ANTIOCH

'Only the trees which thou knowest that they be not trees for meat, thou shalt destroy and cut them down; and thou shalt build bulwarks against the city that maketh war with thee, until it be subdued.' DEUTERONOMY XX, 20

The city of Antioch lies on the river Orontes, some twelve miles from the sea. It was founded in the year 300 B.C. by Seleucus I of Syria and called after his father. It soon rose to be the chief city in Asia; and under the Roman Empire it was the third city in the world. To the Christians it was especially holy; for there they had first been given the name of Christian; and there Saint Peter had founded his first bishopric. In the sixth century A.D. earthquakes and a sack by the Persians had diminished its splendour; and after the Arab conquest it had declined, to the profit of its inland rival Aleppo. Its recovery by Byzantium in the tenth century restored some of its greatness. It became the chief meeting place of Greek and Moslem commerce and the most formidable fortress on the Syrian frontier. Suleiman ibn Kutulmish captured it in 1085. On his death it passed to the Sultan Malik Shah, who installed as governor the Turcoman Yaghi-Siyan. Yaghi-Siyan had now ruled the city for ten years. Since Malik Shah's death his nominal suzerain had been the Emir Ridwan of Aleppo; but he was an un-dutiful vassal and preserved practical independence by playing off against Ridwan his rivals Duqaq of Damascus and Kerbogha of Mosul. In 1096 Yaghi-Siyan had even betrayed Ridwan during a war against Duqaq whom he now called his overlord; but his aid had not enabled Duqaq to take Aleppo, whose Emir never forgave him.

The news of the Christian advance alarmed Yaghi-Siyan. Antioch was the acknowledged objective of the Crusaders; and, indeed, they could not hope to be able to march southward towards Palestine unless the great fortress was in their hands. Yaghi-Siyan's subjects were most of them Christians, Greeks, Armenians and Syrians. The Syrian Christians, hating Greeks and Armenians alike,

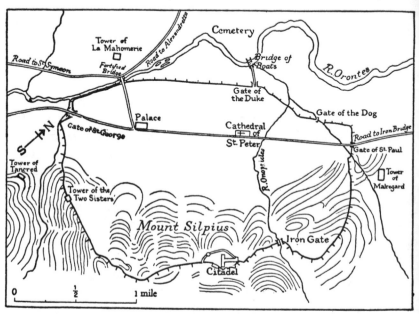

Plan of Antioch in 1098

might remain loyal; but he could not trust the others. Hitherto it seems that he was tolerant towards the Christians. The Orthodox Patriarch, John the Oxite, was permitted to reside in the city, whose great churches had not been turned into mosques. But with the approach of the Crusade he began restrictive measures. The Patriarch, the head of the most important community in Antioch, was thrown into prison. Many leading Christians were ejected from the city; others fled. The Cathedral of St Peter was desecrated and became a stable for the Emir's horses. Some persecution was carried on in the villages outside the city; which had for a result the prompt massacre of the Turkish garrisons by the villagers as soon as the Crusaders were at hand.[1]

Next Yaghi-Siyan searched for allies. Ridwan of Aleppo would do nothing to help him, in short-sighted revenge for his treachery the previous year. But Duqaq of Damascus, to whom Yaghi-Siyan's son, Shams ad-Daula, had gone personally to appeal, prepared an expedition for his rescue; and his *atabeg*, the Turcoman Toghtekin, and the Emir Janah ad-Daula of Homs, offered their support. Another envoy went to the court of Kerbogha, *atabeg* of Mosul. Kerbogha was now the leading prince in upper Mesopotamia and the Jezireh. He was wise enough to see the threat of the Crusade to the whole Moslem world; and he had long had his eye on Aleppo. If he could acquire Antioch, Ridwan would be encircled and in his power. He, too, prepared an army to rescue the city; and, behind him, the Sultans of Baghdad and Persia promised support. Meanwhile Yaghi-Siyan collected his own considerable forces within the fortress and began to supply it with provisions against a long blockade.[2]

The Crusaders entered Yaghi-Siyan's territory at the small town of Marata, the Turkish garrison fleeing at their approach. From Marata a detachment under Robert of Flanders went off to the south-west to liberate the town of Artah, whose Christian population had massacred the garrison. Meanwhile, on 20 October, the main army reached the Orontes at the Iron Bridge, where the roads from Marash and Aleppo united to cross the river. The bridge was heavily fortified, with two towers flanking its entrance. But the Crusaders attacked it at once, the Bishop of Le Puy directing the operations, and after a sharp struggle forced their way across. The victory enabled them to capture a huge convoy of cattle, sheep and corn on its way to provision Yaghi-Siyan's army. The road

---

[1] Abu'l Feda, *Annales*, p. 3; Ibn al-Athir, *Kamil at-Tawarikh*, p. 192; Kemal ad-Din, *Chronicle of Aleppo*, pp. 578-9.
[2] Kemal ad-Din, *loc. cit.*

now lay open to Antioch, whose citadel they could see in the distance. Next day Bohemond at the head of the vanguard arrived before the city walls; and the whole army followed close behind.[1]

The Crusaders were filled with awe at the sight of the great city. The houses and bazaars of Antioch covered a plain nearly three miles long and a mile deep between the Orontes and Mount Silpius; and the villas and palaces of the wealthy dotted the hillside. Round it all rose the huge fortifications constructed by Justinian and repaired only a century ago by the Byzantines with the latest devices of their technical skill. To the north the walls rose out of the low marshy ground along the river, but to the east and west they climbed steeply up the slopes of the mountain, and to the south they ran along the summit of the ridge, carried audaciously across the chasm through which the torrent called Onopnicles broke its way into the plain, and over a narrow postern called the Iron Gate, and culminated in the superb citadel a thousand feet above the town. Four hundred towers rose from them, spaced so as to bring every yard of them within bowshot. At the north-east corner the Gate of St Paul admitted the road from the Iron Bridge and Aleppo. At the north-west corner the Gate of St George admitted the road from Lattakieh and the Lebanese coast. The roads to Alexandretta and the port of St Symeon, the modern Suadiye, left the city through a great gate on the river-bank and across a fortified bridge. Smaller gates, the Gate of the Duke and the Gate of the Dog, led to the river further to the east. Inside the enceinte water was abundant; there were market-gardens and rough pasture ground for flocks. A whole army could be housed there and provisioned against a long siege. Nor was it possible entirely to surround the city; for no troops could be stationed on the wild precipitous terrain to the south.[2]

[1] Albert of Aix, III, 28-35, pp. 358-64; *Gesta Francorum*, V, 12, pp. 66-7.
[2] Fulcher (I, xv, 2-4, pp. 217-18) and Raymond of Aguilers (V, pp. 241-2) give a short description of Antioch. William of Tyre (IV, 9-10, I, pp. 165-9) describes it more fully. The western chroniclers call the river Orontes the

It was only through treachery that the Turks had taken Antioch in 1085; and treachery was the only danger that Yaghi-Siyan had to face. But he was nervous. If the Crusaders were not able to encircle the city, he on his side had not enough soldiers to man all its walls. Till reinforcements came up he could not risk losing any of his men. He made no attempt to attack the Crusaders as they moved up into position, and for a fortnight he left them unmolested.

On their arrival the Crusaders installed themselves outside the north-east corner of the walls. Bohemond occupied the sector opposite the Gate of St Paul, Raymond that opposite the Gate of the Dog, with Godfrey on his right, opposite the Gate of the Duke. The remaining armies waited behind Bohemond, ready to move up where they might be required. The Bridge Gate and the Gate of St George were for the moment left uncovered. But work was at once started on a bridge of boats to cross the river from Godfrey's camp to the village of Talenki, where the Moslem cemetery lay. This bridge enabled the army to reach the roads to Alexandretta and St Symeon; and a camp was soon established on the north of the river.[1]

Yaghi-Siyan had expected an immediate assault on the city. But, amongst the Crusading leaders, only Raymond advised that they should try to storm the walls. God, he said, who had protected them so far, would surely give them the victory.[2] His faith was not shared by the others. The fortifications daunted them; their troops were tired; they could not afford heavy losses now. Moreover, if they delayed, reinforcements would join them. Tancred was due to arrive from Alexandretta. Perhaps the Emperor would soon come with his admirable siege engines. Guynemer's fleet

Ferrins (Fulcher of Chartres, I, xv, I, p. 216—'Orontes or Ferrins'), the Far (William of Tyre, IV, 8, I, p. 164, who calls it a vulgar mistake) or the Farfar (*Gesta Francorum*, x, 34, p. 180) or Pharpar (Albert of Aix, *loc. cit.*).

[1] Albert of Aix, III, 38–9, pp. 365–6, gives the disposition of the troops. *Gesta Francorum*, v, 12, pp. 66–8, describes the inaction of the garrison and Raymond of Aguilers (v, pp. 242–3) the building of the bridge and the establishment of Raymond's camp.

[2] Raymond of Aguilers, IV, p. 241.

might spare them men; and there were rumours of a Genoese fleet in the offing. Bohemond, whose counsel carried most weight among them, had his private reasons for opposing Raymond's suggestion. His ambitions were now centred on the possession of Antioch for himself. Not only would he prefer not to see it looted by the rapacity of an army eager for the pleasure of looting a rich city; but, more seriously, he feared that were it captured by the united effort of the Crusade he could never establish an exclusive claim to it. He had learnt the lesson taught by Alexius at Nicaea. If he could arrange for its surrender to himself, his title would be far harder to dispute. In a little time he should be able to make such an arrangement; for he had some knowledge of Oriental methods of treachery. Under his influence Raymond's advice was ignored; Raymond's hatred of him grew greater; and the one chance of quickly capturing Antioch was lost. For, had the first attack met with any success, Yaghi-Siyan, whose nerve was shaking, would have put up a poor resistance. The delay restored his confidence.

Bohemond and his friends had no difficulty in finding intermediaries through whom they could make connections with the enemy. The Christian refugees and exiles from the city kept close touch with their relatives within the walls, owing to the gaps in both blockade and the defence. The Crusaders were well informed of all that passed inside Antioch. But the system worked both ways; for many of the local Christians, in particular the Syrians, doubted whether Byzantine or Frankish rule was preferable to Turkish. They were prepared to ingratiate themselves with Yaghi-Siyan by keeping him equally well informed of all that went on in the Crusaders' camp. From them he learnt of the Crusaders' reluctance to attack. He began to organize sorties. His men would creep out from the western gate and cut off any small band of foraging Franks that they could find separated from the army. He communicated with his garrison out at Harenc, across the Iron Bridge on the road to Aleppo, and encouraged it to harass the Franks in the rear. Meanwhile he heard that his son's mission to Damascus had succeeded and that an army was coming to relieve him.[1]

As autumn turned to winter, the Crusaders, who had been unduly cheered by Yaghi-Siyan's preliminary inaction, began to lose heart, despite some minor successes. In the middle of November an expedition led by Bohemond managed to lure the garrison of Harenc from their fortress and to exterminate it completely.[2] Almost the same day a Genoese squadron of thirteen vessels appeared at the port of St Symeon, which the Crusaders were thereupon able to occupy. It brought reinforcements in men and armaments, in belated response to Pope Urban's appeal to the city of Genoa, made nearly two years before. Its arrival gave the Crusaders the comfortable knowledge that they now could communicate by sea with their homes. But these successes were overshadowed by the problem of feeding the army. When the Crusaders had first entered the plain of Antioch, they had found it full of provisions. Sheep and cattle were plentiful, and the village granaries still contained most of the year's harvest. They had fed well and neglected to lay in supplies for the winter months. Troops were now obliged to go foraging over an ever larger radius, and were all the more liable to be cut off by Turks coming down from the mountains. It was soon discovered that the raiders from Antioch would creep through the gorge of the Onopnicles and wait on the hill above Bohemond's camp to attack stragglers returning late to their quarters. To counter this, the leaders decided to build a fortified tower on the hill, which each of them guaranteed to garrison in turn. The tower was soon constructed and named Malregard.[3]

About Christmas time 1097, the army's stocks of food were almost exhausted; and there was nothing more to be obtained in the neighbouring countryside. The princes held a council at which it was decided that a portion of the army should be sent under

---

[1] *Gesta Francorum*, v, 12, p. 68; Kemal ad-Din, *op. cit.* p. 577.
[2] *Gesta Francorum, ibid.* pp. 68–70.
[3] *Ibid.* v, 13, p. 70; Raymond of Aguilers, v, p. 242; Caffaro, *De Liberatione*, p. 50.

Bohemond and Robert of Flanders up the Orontes valley towards Hama, to raid the villages there and carry off all the provisions on which they could lay hands. The conduct of the siege should be meantime left in the hands of Raymond and the Bishop of Le Puy. Godfrey at the time was seriously ill. Bohemond and Robert set out on 28 December, taking with them some twenty thousand men. Their departure was at once known to Yaghi-Siyan. He waited till they were well away, then, on the night of the 29th, made a sortie in strength across the bridge and fell on the Crusaders encamped north of the river. These were probably Raymond's troops, who had moved from their first station when the winter rains made the low ground between the river and the walls no longer habitable. The attack was unexpected; but Raymond's alertness saved the situation. He hastily collected a group of knights and charged out of the darkness on the Turks; who turned and fled back across the bridge. So hotly did Raymond pursue them that for a moment his men obtained a foothold across the bridge before the gates could be swung shut. It seemed that Raymond was about to justify his belief that the city could be stormed, when a horse that had thrown its rider suddenly bolted back, pushing the knights crowded on the bridge into confusion. It was too dark to see what was happening; and a panic arose among the Crusaders. In their turn they fled, pursued by the Turks, till they rallied at their camp by the bridge of boats; and the Turks returned to the city. Many lives were lost on both sides, but especially among the Frankish knights, whom the Crusade ill could spare. Among them was Adhemar's own standard-bearer.[1]

Meantime Bohemond was riding with Robert of Flanders southward, totally ignorant of how nearly Antioch had fallen to his rival, Raymond, and ignorant, too, that a great Moslem relief force was moving up towards him. Duqaq of Damascus had left his capital, with his *atabeg* Toghtekin and with Yaghi-Siyan's son Shams and a considerable army, about the middle of the month. At Hama the Emir joined them with his forces. On 30 December they were

[1] Raymond of Aguilers, v, pp. 243–4; *Gesta Francorum*, VI, 14, pp. 74–6.

at Shaizar, where they learnt that a Crusading army was close by. They marched on at once and next morning came upon the enemy at the village of Albara. The Crusaders were taken by surprise; and Robert, whose army was a little ahead of Bohemond's, was all but surrounded. But Bohemond, seeing what was happening, kept the bulk of his troops in reserve, to charge upon the Moslems at the moment when they thought that the battle was won. His intervention saved Robert and inflicted such heavy losses on the Damascene army that it fell back on Hama. But the Crusaders, though they claimed the victory and had indeed prevented the relief of Antioch, were themselves too seriously weakened to continue their foraging. After sacking one or two villages and burning a mosque, they returned, almost empty-handed, to the camp before Antioch.[1]

They found their comrades deep in gloom. The disastrous battle on the night of the 29th had been followed next day by a severe earth-tremor, which was felt even at Edessa; and that evening the aurora borealis illuminated the sky. During the next weeks torrential rain poured down incessantly, and it grew steadily colder. Stephen of Blois could not understand why anyone complained of excessive sunshine in Syria. It was clear that God was displeased with His warriors, for their pride, their luxuriousness and their brigandage. Adhemar of Le Puy ordered a solemn fast for three days; but with famine already approaching the fast made little difference; and now the failure of the foraging expedition would mean starvation for many. Soon one man in every seven was dying of hunger. Envoys in search of food were sent as far as the Taurus mountains, where the Roupenian princes consented to provide what they could. Some supplies came from the Armenian monks settled out on the Amanus mountains; while local Christians, Armenian and Syrian, collected everything edible that they could find and brought it to the camp. But their motive was not philanthropy but gain. For one donkey-load

[1] *Gesta Francorum*, v, 13, pp. 70–2; Albert of Aix, III, 50–1, pp. 373–4; Kemal ad-Din, *op. cit.* p. 580.

of provisions eight bezants were charged; and these were prices that only the wealthiest soldiers could afford. The horses suffered even worse than the men, till only some seven hundred were left with the army.[1]

A more generous helper was found in the island of Cyprus. The Bishop of Le Puy, acting no doubt on Pope Urban's instructions, had been assiduous in establishing good relations with the Orthodox Church dignitaries of the East; whom he treated with a respect that belies the theory that the Pope envisaged the Crusade as a means for bringing them under his control. For the Patriarch of Antioch, imprisoned within the city, this friendship was as yet of little value; for the Turks would from time to time put him in a cage and hang him over the walls. But the Patriarch Symeon of Jerusalem, who had retired from his see when Ortoq's death made life there too insecure, was now in Cyprus. As soon as communications were opened, Adhemar made contact with him. Symeon was no friend of Latin usages, against which he had published a firm but moderate treatise; but he was glad to co-operate with the western Church for the good of Christendom. Already in October he had joined with Adhemar in sending a report on the Crusade to the Christians of the West. Now, hearing of the plight of the army, he regularly dispatched across to it all the food and wine that the island could spare.[2]

---

[1] Anselm of Ribemont, letter in Hagenmeyer, *Die Kreuzzugsbriefe*, p. 157 (especially mentioning the horses); Stephen of Blois, *ibid.* p. 150 (mentioning the appalling weather); Fulcher of Chartres, I, xv, 2–xvi, 6, pp. 221–8 (a rhetorical account blaming the Crusaders for their sins); Raymond of Aguilers, VI, p. 245 (mentioning the aurora and the fast); *Gesta Francorum*, VI, 14, p. 76 (giving the prices charged by the native speculators); Matthew of Edessa, II, cli, p. 217 (telling of the generosity of the Armenian princes and monks).

[2] Albert of Aix, VI, 39, p. 489. Symeon sent the Crusaders gifts of pomegranates, 'apples of the cedars of Lebanon', bacon and wine. The letter dated October, sent from Antioch to report to the western Church on the progress of the Crusade, runs in the name of Symeon and of Adhemar, 'and principally the latter, who was given charge of the Christian army by Pope Urban', Hagenmeyer, *op. cit.* pp. 141–2. For Symeon see above, pp. 78, 103.

The Patriarch's food parcels, plentiful though they were, could do little to alleviate the general misery. Pressed by hunger, men began to desert from the camp to seek refuge in richer districts or to attempt the long road home. At first the deserters were obscure private soldiers; but one January morning it was found that Peter the Hermit himself had fled, accompanied by William the Carpenter. William was an adventurer with no desire to waste his time on a hopeless Crusade; he had already deserted an expedition in Spain; but why Peter should have lost his nerve is hard to understand. The refugees were pursued by Tancred and brought back in ignominy. Peter, whose reputation it was advisable to preserve, was pardoned in silence; but William was kept standing all night in Bohemond's tent and in the morning received from him a harsh and menacing lecture. He swore that he would never leave the army again till it reached Jerusalem; but he later broke his oath. Peter's prestige inevitably suffered; but he was soon to be given a chance to redeem it.[1]

With the army daily diminishing from famine and from flight, Adhemar considered that a strong appeal for reinforcements must be made to the West. To give it the utmost authority, he drafted it in the name of the Patriarch of Jerusalem, whose permission he had presumably secured. The language of the appeal is significant for the light that it throws on Adhemar's ecclesiastical policy. The Patriarch addresses all the faithful of the West as leader of the bishops now in the East, both Greek and Latin. He entitles himself 'Apostolic'; he takes it upon himself to excommunicate any Christian who fails in his Crusading vows. It is the language of an independent pontiff. Adhemar could never have put it into the mouth of one who was intended to be made subject to the Bishop of Rome. Whatever Urban's ultimate plans might be for the government of the eastern Churches, his legate was not preaching papal supremacy. We do not know what response the Patriarch's letter evoked in the West.[2]

[1] *Gesta Francorum*, VI, 15, pp. 76–8.
[2] Letter in Hagenmeyer, *op. cit.* pp. 146–9.

While the Crusaders showed a proper respect for the hierarchs of eastern Orthodoxy, their relations with its lay overlord deteriorated. Early in February the Emperor's representative Taticius suddenly left the army. He had accompanied the Crusade from Nicaea with a small staff and a company mainly of guides and engineers, and had apparently been on good terms with its leaders. At Comana and at Coxon they had correctly handed over their conquests to him; and he in his reports paid generous tribute to their fighting qualities. Several explanations were given at the time for his departure; but there is no need to reject the story that he told on his return to Constantinople. According to him, Bohemond sent for him one day, when it was already known that the Turks were about to make another effort to relieve Antioch, and told him in strict confidence that the other leaders believed the Emperor to be responsible for encouraging the Turks and were plotting to revenge themselves by taking his life. Taticius allowed himself to be convinced. Indeed, the temper of the army at this moment was such that a scapegoat might well be desired. Besides, he believed that the Crusaders, weakened and demoralized by hunger, could not now hope to take the great fortress. His advice that it should be starved into surrender by the occupation of the castles that commanded its more distant approaches had been ignored. He therefore announced that he must return to imperial territory to arrange for a more satisfactory system of revictualment and took a ship at the port of St Symeon for Cyprus. To show that he intended to return, he left most of his staff behind with the army. But as soon as he was gone Bohemond's propagandists suggested that he had fled from cowardice in face of the coming Turkish attack, if not from actual treachery. When the Emperor's representative acted so dishonourably, surely the Crusade was freed from any obligation towards the Empire. That is to say, Antioch need not be restored to it.[1]

---

[1] Raymond of Aguilers, v, pp. 254–6, says that Taticius suggested a closer blockade. His idea was not taken up; and soon after he treacherously fled, having allotted the towns of Mamistra, Tarsus and Adana to Bohemond. This

Next, Bohemond put it about that he was himself contemplating his departure from the army. He could not much longer ignore his obligations at home. Hitherto he had played a leading part in all the military operations of the Crusade; and, as he calculated, the prospect of losing his aid at this critical juncture terrified the army. He therefore allowed it to be understood that if he were given the lordship of Antioch it would compensate him for any losses that he might suffer owing to his absence from Italy. His fellow-princes were not taken in by these manoeuvres; but among the rank and file he won much sympathy.[1]

Meanwhile the Turks were massing again for the relief of Antioch. When Duqaq failed to bring the aid that he had promised, Yaghi-Siyan turned again to his former suzerain, Ridwan of Aleppo. Ridwan by now regretted his own inaction that had permitted the Franks to penetrate to Antioch. When Yaghi-Siyan readmitted his suzerainty, he prepared to come to his rescue, assisted by his cousin, Soqman the Ortoqid, from Diarbekir, and by his father-in-law, the Emir of Hama. Early in February the allies reoccupied Harenc, where they assembled for their attack on the Crusaders' camp. On hearing the news, the Crusading princes held a council in Adhemar's tent, where Bohemond proposed that while the infantry should remain in the camp to contain any sortie from the city, the knights, of whom there were only seven hundred now fit for service, should make a surprise onslaught on the invading army. His advice was taken. On 8 February, at nightfall, the Frankish cavalry slipped out across the bridge of boats and took up its position between the river and the Lake of Antioch, from

highly improbable gift must have been invented by Bohemond and put about the army. *Gesta Francorum*, VI, 16, pp. 78–80, says that he fled from sheer cowardice, on the excuse of trying to arrange for a better provisioning of the army. Albert of Aix says that he had kept his tent on the edge of the camp, as he always intended to flee. When he fled he falsely promised to return (III, 38, p. 366, IV, 38, p. 416). Anna Comnena's story, which must be based on Taticius's own reports, is the most convincing version (XI, iv, 3, vol. II, p. 20).

[1] Raymond of Aguilers, *loc. cit.*

which it could fall on the Turks as they advanced to cross the Iron Bridge. At daybreak the Turkish army came in sight; and at once the first line of the Crusaders charged, before the Turkish archers could be formed into line. The charge could not break the mass of the Turks; and the knights withdrew, luring the enemy to their chosen battleground, where the lake on the left and the river on the right prevented the great numbers of the Turks from outflanking them. On this narrow terrain the knights charged again, this time in full force. Before their weight, the more lightly armed Turks broke and fled, spreading confusion in the packed lines behind them. Soon the whole of Ridwan's army was in full disorderly retreat back to Aleppo. As they passed through Harenc, its garrison joined the fugitives, leaving the town for the native Christians to hand back to the Crusaders.

While the cavalry were winning this spectacular victory, the infantry were fighting a harder battle. Yaghi-Siyan made a sortie in full strength against the camp; whose defenders were beginning to lose ground, when, in the afternoon, the triumphant knights were seen approaching. As they drew near Yaghi-Siyan understood that the army of relief was beaten. He called his men back within the walls.[1]

The defeat of the second relieving army, though it raised the morale of the Crusaders, did nothing to improve their immediate situation. Food was still very short, though supplies were beginning to arrive at the port of St Symeon, coming largely from Cyprus, where the Patriarch Symeon, and probably also the unappreciated Taticius, collected all that was available. But the road down to the sea was perpetually raided by parties slipping out of the city, who ambushed the smaller convoys; while the city itself received provisions through the still unguarded Gate of St George and across the fortified bridge. To control the bridge and so to make the passage to St Symeon safe, Raymond proposed to build a tower on the north bank close by. But the project was held back

[1] *Gesta Francorum*, VI, 17, pp. 80–6; Raymond of Aguilers, VII, pp. 246–8.

owing to the lack of materials and of masons. On 4 March a fleet manned by Englishmen and commanded by the exiled claimant to the throne, Edgar Atheling, sailed into St Symeon. It brought pilgrims from Italy, but had called on its way at Constantinople, where Edgar had joined it, placing himself under the orders of the Emperor. There it had been loaded with siege materials and mechanics, whose arrival was very timely. The fact that they were provided by the Emperor was carefully disregarded by the Crusaders.

Hearing that the fleet had put in, Raymond and Bohemond set out together, neither trusting the other alone, to recruit as many fighting-men as possible from its passengers and to escort the mechanics and material up to the camp. On 6 March, as they were returning laden along the road from St Symeon, they were ambushed by a detachment from the garrison of the city. Their troops were taken by surprise and fled in panic, leaving their loads in the hands of the enemy. A few stragglers rushed into the camp and spread the rumour that both Raymond and Bohemond were killed. At the news Godfrey prepared to go out to rescue the defeated army, when the Turks made a sudden sortie from the city against the camp, to provide cover under which the ambushers, now heavy with booty, could reach the gates. Godfrey's men, already armed to set out along the road to the sea, were able to hold the attack till Raymond and Bohemond appeared unexpectedly with the remnant of their forces. Their arrival, weakened though they were, enabled Godfrey to drive the Turks back into the city. The princes then united to intercept the raiders as they returned. Their tactics were entirely successful. The raiders, handicapped by their loads, were outmanoeuvred and massacred as they struggled to reach the bridge; and the precious building materials were recovered. It was said that fifteen hundred Turks were slain, many of them drowned while trying to cross the river. Among the dead were nine Emirs. That evening members of the garrison crept out to bury the dead in the Moslem cemetery on the north bank of the river. The Crusaders saw them and left them in peace, but next morning they dug up the corpses for the sake of the gold and silver ornaments that they wore.[1]

The result of the Crusaders' victory was to complete the blockade of Antioch. With the workmen and materials now provided the planned fortress was built to command the approach to the fortified bridge. It was built close to a mosque by the Moslem cemetery and was officially called the castle of La Mahomerie, from the old French word for 'mosque'. But when the leaders debated in whose charge the castle should be placed, Raymond, whose idea it was to erect it, claimed its control for himself; and it was usually known as the castle of Raymond. The building was finished by 19 March. It soon proved its value in preventing any access to the bridge-gate. But the Gate of St George was still open. To bring it too under control it was next resolved to build a castle on the site of an old convent on the hill that faced it. The construction was completed in April and the castle entrusted to Tancred, who was allowed the sum of three hundred marks for his expenses. Henceforward no convoys of food were able to reach the city, nor could its inhabitants send, as had been their custom hitherto, their flocks to pasture outside the walls. Individual raiders could still climb over the walls on Mount Silpius or through the narrow Iron

---

[1] *Gesta Francorum*, VII, 18, pp. 88–96; Raymond of Aguilers, VII–VIII, pp. 248–9; Albert of Aix, III, 53–5, pp. 383–6; letter of Stephen of Blois in Hagenmeyer, *op. cit.* pp. 151–2; letter of Anselm of Ribemont in Hagenmeyer, *op. cit.* pp. 158–9; letter of the clergy of Lucca in Hagenmeyer, *op. cit.* pp. 165–7, where it is stated that a Lucchese citizen called Bruno arrived at St Symeon at this moment, travelling with an English fleet. David, *Robert Curthose*, pp. 236–7, doubts whether Edgar Atheling can have been with this fleet, as he was still in Scotland in the autumn of 1097, and it must have left England before that date. But the fleet was almost certainly composed of English 'Varangians', who had left England long ago and were cruising in the Mediterranean under the orders of the Emperor, for whom we find them acting later. (See below, p. 255.) Edgar could quite well have travelled quickly out to Constantinople, to hire his services temporarily to the Emperor, and joined the fleet there. Orderic Vitalis (X, 11, vol. IV, pp. 70–2) is positive that he was with the fleet and captured Lattakieh during the time of the siege, though William of Malmesbury (II, p. 310) places his capture of Lattakieh at a slightly later date. See below, *loc. cit.*

Gate, but could no longer attempt an organized sortie. While the garrison began to suffer from hunger, the Crusaders' problem of commissariat was eased. The better weather as spring came on, the possibility of foraging without the risk of sudden Turkish attacks and the readiness of merchants that had hitherto sold their goods at high prices to the garrison to do business now with the camp made more provisions available and raised the morale of the Franks. Soon after his castle had been built Tancred had captured a huge consignment of food destined for Yaghi-Siyan and conveyed by Christian merchants, Syrian and Armenian. Such successes led the Crusaders to hope that Antioch might now be starved into surrender. But it must be done quickly, for the terrible Kerbogha of Mosul was gathering his forces.[1]

While they were still at Constantinople the Emperor Alexius had advised the Crusaders to arrive at some sort of understanding with the Fatimids of Egypt. The Fatimids were uncompromising enemies to the Turks; they were tolerant towards their Christian subjects and had always been ready to treat with the Christian powers. The Crusaders probably had not followed this advice; but in the early spring an Egyptian embassy arrived at the camp before Antioch, sent by al-Afdal, the all-powerful vizier of the boy Caliph, al-Mustali. His proposal seems to have been that a division should be made of the Seldjuk empire; the Franks should take northern Syria and Egypt should take Palestine. Al-Afdal no doubt regarded the Crusaders merely as the mercenaries of the Emperor and assumed therefore that such a division, based on the state of affairs before the Turkish invasions, would be perfectly acceptable. The western princes received the ambassadors with cordiality, though they did not commit themselves to any specific arrangement. The Egyptians stayed for some weeks at the camp and returned home accompanied by a small Frankish embassy and laden with gifts, chiefly derived from the booty captured in the

[1] *Gesta Francorum*, VII, 18, VIII, 19, pp. 88, 96–8; Raymond of Aguilers, VIII, pp. 249–50; letter of Anselm of Ribemont in Hagenmeyer, *op. cit.* pp. 158–9; letter of the clergy of Lucca, *ibid.* p. 166.

battle on 6 March. The negotiations taught the Crusaders the advantages that might emerge from intrigues with the Moslem powers. Laying aside their religious prejudices they next, on the news of Kerbogha's preparations, sent to Duqaq of Damascus, asking for his neutrality and declaring that they had no designs on his territory. Duqaq, who regarded his brother Ridwan of Aleppo as his chief enemy and saw that Ridwan had reverted to his former neutrality, did not acquiesce with their wishes.[1]

Early in May it was known that Kerbogha was on the march. Besides his own troops, men had been provided by the Sultans of Baghdad and of Persia and from the Ortoqid princes of northern Mesopotamia; Duqaq was waiting to join him; and at Antioch Yaghi-Siyan, though hard pressed, was still holding out. Amongst the Crusaders tension grew. They knew that unless they captured the city first they would be crushed between the garrison and the huge relieving army. The Emperor Alexius was now campaigning in Asia Minor. A desperate appeal was sent to him to hurry to their rescue. Bohemond, determined to win Antioch for himself, had special cause for worry. If the Emperor arrived before Antioch fell or if Kerbogha were defeated only with the Emperor's help, then it would be impossible not to restore Antioch to the Empire. Most of the princes were prepared to give Bohemond the city; but Raymond of Toulouse, probably supported by the Bishop of Le Puy, would not agree. Raymond's motives have often been discussed. He, alone of the princes, was not bound by an explicit oath to the Emperor; but he had left Constantinople on good terms with the Emperor; he hated and suspected Bohemond as his

---

[1] According to the *Historia Belli Sacri* (*Tudebodus Imitatus*), p. 181, the Crusaders had already sent an embassy to Egypt from Nicaea, on the advice of Alexius. The list of ambassadors is suspect; possibly they formed the embassy sent from Antioch. But it is probable that the Emperor's advice was remembered. The Egyptian embassy to Antioch is mentioned by Raymond of Aguilers, VII, p. 247, by Stephen of Blois, in Hagenmeyer, *op. cit.* p. 151, by Anselm of Ribemont, in Hagenmeyer, *op. cit.* p. 160, and by the *Gesta Francorum*, VI, 17, p. 86, VII, 19, p. 96. Ibn al-Athir mentions the negotiations of the Crusaders with Duqaq (*op. cit.* p. 193).

chief rival for the military leadership of the Crusade; and both he and the legate may have considered that if the oath was invalid, the Church, of which Adhemar was the representative, should alone be able to allot territory. After some discussion and intrigue a compromise was reached. If Bohemond were the prince whose troops first entered the city, and if the Emperor never came, he should receive it for himself. Even so, Raymond demurred, but Bohemond already had reason to be satisfied.[1]

Kerbogha's own miscalculation gave the Crusade a breathing-space. He did not like to advance on Antioch leaving a Frankish army in Edessa in a position to threaten his right flank. He did not realize that Baldwin was too weak for offensive action but was too strong in his great fortress to be easily displaced. For the last three weeks of May he paused in front of Edessa, vainly attacking its walls, before he decided that the effort and the time lost were not worth while.[2]

During these three precious weeks Bohemond was hard at work. At some time he had established a connection with a captain inside the city of Antioch, whose name was Firouz. Firouz was apparently an Armenian converted to Islam, who had risen to a high position in Yaghi-Siyan's government. Though outwardly loyal he was jealous of his master, who had recently fined him for hoarding grain; and he kept in touch with his former co-religionists. Through them he reached an understanding with Bohemond and agreed to sell the city. The secret of the transaction was well kept. Bohemond took no one into his confidence. Instead, he publicly emphasized the dangers ahead in order to increase the value of his coming triumph.[3]

---

[1] *Gesta Francorum*, VIII, 19, pp. 100–2, corroborated by Anna Comnena, XI, iv, 4, vol. III, p. 21. William of Tyre's account (V, 17, 1, pp. 220–1) records Raymond's disagreement.

[2] See above, p. 210, and references given *ibid.* n. 2.

[3] *Gesta Francorum*, VIII, 20, p. 100. The author calls him 'Pirrus' and says that he was a Turk. Anna Comnena, XI, iv, 2, vol. II, p. 19, calls him 'a certain Armenian'. Radulph of Caen, LXII, pp. 651–2, calls him 'a rich Armenian'; Matthew of Edessa, 'one of the chief men of the city', giving no race (II, civ,

His propaganda was only too successful. At the end of May Kerbogha abandoned the profitless siege of Edessa and continued his advance. As he approached, panic began to spread in the Crusaders' camp. Deserters began to slip away in such numbers that it was useless to try to stop them. At last, on 2 June, a large body of the northern French took the road to Alexandretta, led by Stephen of Blois. Only two months before Stephen had written cheerfully to his wife from the camp, to tell her of the difficulties of the siege but also to describe the triumphant battle of 6 March and to emphasize his own importance in the army. But now, with the city still untaken and Kerbogha's host at hand, it seemed to him mere folly to await for certain massacre. He had never been a great fighting man, but at least he would live to fight another day. Of all the princes Stephen had been most enthusiastic in his admiration for the Emperor. Bohemond must have smiled to see him go; but he could not foretell how useful this flight would be to his cause.[1]

p. 222); Raymond of Aguilers, VIII, p. 251, calls him 'quidam de Turcatis', probably meaning by this phrase a renegade Christian. The Arabic sources, Kemal ad-Din (*op. cit.* pp. 581–2) and Ibn al-Athir (*op. cit.* p. 192), give him no special race; the latter calls him Firouz. The former says that he was an armourer, known as 'Zarrad', the maker of cuirasses, whom Yaghi-Siyan had punished for hoarding. William of Tyre, V, 11, I, pp. 212–13, relying apparently on Arabic sources, says that he belonged to the corporation of the 'Beni Zarra; *quod in lingua latina interpretatur filii loricatoris'.* He belonged to a good family. The Old French translation of William adds that he was 'Hermin'—an Armenian.

[1] Fulcher of Chartres, I, xvi, 7, p. 228, says that Stephen's departure took place the day before the fall of Antioch, i.e. 2 June. He states it with regret but does not attribute it to cowardice. *Gesta Francorum*, IX, 27, p. 140, says that he fled on the plea of illness. Raymond of Aguilers, XI, p. 258, attributes the flight to cowardice, which seems to have been the general impression. Guibert of Nogent, XXV, pp. 199–200, feels it necessary to make excuses for him. Stephen had been elected 'ductor' of the army (*Gesta Francorum, loc. cit.*) or 'dictator' (Raymond of Aguilers, *loc. cit.*) or 'dominus atque omnium actuum provisor atque gubernator' (Stephen of Blois, letter in Hagenmeyer, *op. cit.* p. 149). This certainly cannot mean that he was appointed commander-in-chief or political leader of the Crusade, as he never took the lead in military operations, while Adhemar was the only person to be recognized as having any political authority over the princes. It is probable that Stephen was put in charge of the administrative side of the army and was responsible for the organization of supplies.

Had Stephen delayed his departure for only a few hours he would have changed his mind. On that very day Firouz sent his son to Bohemond to say that he was ready for the act of treachery. It was later rumoured that he had been hesitating right up till the evening before, when he discovered that his wife was compromised with one of his Turkish colleagues. He was now in command or the Tower of the Two Sisters and the adjoining section of the wall of the city on the outside, facing the castle of Tancred. He therefore urged Bohemond to assemble the Crusading army that afternoon and lead it out eastward, as though he were going to intercept Kerbogha; then, after dark, the troops should creep back to the western wall, bringing their ladders to scale the tower where he would be watching for them. If Bohemond agreed to this, he would send back his son as a hostage that evening as a sign that he was prepared.

Bohemond took his advice. As the day drew on he sent one of his infantrymen, whose name was Male Couronne, round the camp as a herald to bid the army be ready to set out at sunset for a raid in enemy territory. Then he invited the chief princes to see him, Adhemar, Raymond, Godfrey and Robert of Flanders, and, for the first time, told them of his plot. 'Tonight', he said, 'if God favours us, Antioch will be given into our hands.' Whatever jealousy Raymond may have felt was left unspoken. He and his colleagues gave their loyal support to the scheme.

As the sun set the Crusading army set out eastward, the cavalry riding up the valley in front of the city and the infantry toiling over the hill-paths behind it. The Turks within the city saw them go and relaxed, in expectation of a quiet night. But in the middle of the night orders were given throughout the army to turn back to the west and north-west walls. Just before dawn Bohemond's troops arrived before the Tower of the Two Sisters. A ladder was placed against the tower; and, one after the other, sixty knights climbed up, led by Fulk of Chartres, and entered through a window high on the wall into a room where Firouz was nervously waiting. As they first entered he thought their numbers insufficient. 'We

have so few Franks', he cried out in Greek, 'where is Bohemond?'
He need not have worried. From the Two Sisters the knights took
over the other two towers under his control, enabling their friends
to set ladders against the intervening stretches of the wall, while
an Italian infantryman went to tell Bohemond that it was time for
him to climb into the city. The ladder broke behind him; but while
some of the soldiers ran along the wall, surprising the garrisons in
their towers, others descended into the city and roused the Christian
inhabitants and with their help flung open the Gate of St George
and the great Gate of the Bridge, across which the bulk of the army
was waiting. The Crusaders now poured in through the gates,
meeting with little opposition. Greeks and Armenians joined them
in massacring all the Turks that they saw, women as well as men,
including Firouz's own brother. Many Christians perished in the
confusion. Yaghi-Siyan himself, awakening to the clamour, at once
concluded that all was lost. With his bodyguard he fled on horseback up the gorge that led to the Iron Gate and out on to the hill-
side. But his son Shams ad-Daula kept his head. Gathering what
men he could find he made his way up to the citadel before the
Franks could overtake him. Bohemond followed but failed to force
an entrance; so he planted his purple banner on the highest point
that he could reach. The sight of it, waving in the light of the rising
sun, cheered the Crusaders far below as they entered into the city.

When he had gathered enough men Bohemond attempted a
serious assault on the citadel. But he was driven back and was
himself wounded. His men preferred to return to the more
agreeable task of sacking and looting the city streets; while he was
soon consoled by receiving from an Armenian peasant the head of
Yaghi-Siyan. Yaghi-Siyan had been thrown from his horse on
a mountain path as he fled. His escort had deserted him; and as
he lay there exhausted and half-stunned some Armenians had
found him and recognized him. They killed him at once; and
while one earned a handsome reward by bringing Bohemond his
head the others sold his belt and his scimitar-sheath for sixty
bezants apiece.

The Capture of the City

By nightfall on 3 June there was no Turk left alive in Antioch; and even from neighbouring villages to which the Franks had never penetrated the Turkish population had fled, to seek refuge with Kerbogha. The houses of the citizens of Antioch, of Christians as well as of Moslems, were pillaged. The treasures and the arms found there were scattered or wantonly destroyed. You could not walk on the streets without treading on corpses, all of them rotting rapidly in the summer heat. But Antioch was Christian once more.[1]

---

[1] The most vivid account of the capture of Antioch is given in the *Gesta Francorum*, VIII, 20, pp. 100–10, though it omits Bohemond's failure to capture the citadel. Raymond of Aguilers in his account supplies this information, and says that the first Crusader to enter the city was Fulk of Chartres (IX, pp. 251–3). Radulph of Caen calls him Gouel of Chartres (LXVI, p. 654). Fulcher of Chartres (I, xviii, pp. 230–3), gives a briefer account. William of Tyre's account (v, 18–23, vol. I, pt. I, pp. 222–3) is long but full of unreliable details. He supplies the story of the incident of Firouz's wife. Ibn al-Athir tells of Yaghi-Siyan's flight and death (*op. cit.* p. 193).

CHAPTER IV

THE POSSESSION OF ANTIOCH

'He hath put forth his hands against such as be at peace with him: he hath broken his covenant.'   PSALMS LV, 20

The capture of Antioch was an achievement that gladdened Christian hearts. But when their triumphant frenzy died down and the Crusaders took stock of their position, they found themselves little better off than before. Great advantages had been gained. They had the city fortifications, undamaged in the battle, to protect them from Kerbogha's hosts; their civilian followers, numerous still in spite of disease and desertion, were sheltered and no longer the liability that they had been in the camp. The Turkish army that the city had contained was almost annihilated and no longer a steady threat. But the defence of the long line of the walls needed more men than they could now afford. The citadel was untaken and must be picketed. Though its garrison was too weak to take the offensive, from its summit every movement in the city could be watched; and it was impossible to prevent it from establishing a liaison with Kerbogha. In the city the Crusaders found none of the stores of food that they had hoped for, and themselves in their intoxication had destroyed most of its wealth. And though the Moslems were slain the native Christian population could not be trusted. The Syrians, in particular, had been treacherous in the past and had little sympathy for the Latins. Their treachery provided a far greater risk to an army defending the city than to one encamped outside. Moreover, the victory brought to a head a question that already showed signs of splitting the Crusade: to whom should the city be given?

At first there was no time to spare to debate the city's future.

Kerbogha was advancing; and it must be defended against this present attack. Bohemond, whatever he might be planning, had not the troops to man the walls without the help of his colleagues. All must share in the defences; and each of the princes took over a section of the fortifications. The army's immediate task was to clear up the city and to bury the dead quickly, before the decaying corpses started an epidemic. While the soldiers were thus engaged, the Bishop of Le Puy arranged for the Cathedral of St Peter and the other churches that the Turks had desecrated to be cleaned and restored to Christian worship. The Patriarch John was released from his prison and replaced on the Patriarchal throne. John was a Greek, who disliked the Latin rite; but he was the legitimate Patriarch of a see still in full communion with Rome. Adhemar was certainly not going to offend against legitimacy and local sentiment by ignoring his rights. Nor did any of the Crusaders, aware of John's sufferings for the Faith, resent his restoration; except, perhaps, Bohemond, who may have foreseen its inconvenience to himself.[1]

The Crusaders were barely able to instal themselves in the city before Kerbogha came up. On 5 June he reached the Orontes at the Iron Bridge; and two days later he encamped before the walls, on the very positions that the Franks had recently occupied. Shams ad-Daula at once sent envoys from the citadel to ask for his help. But Kerbogha insisted that the citadel should be taken over by his own troops. Shams begged to be allowed to retain command till the city should be retaken, but in vain. He was obliged to hand over the fortress and all its stores to Kerbogha's trusted lieutenant, Ahmed ibn Merwan.[2]

Kerbogha's first plan was to penetrate into the city from the citadel. Foreseeing the danger, Bohemond and Raymond had constructed a rough wall to cut it off from the city fortifications. As it was the most vulnerable sector of the defence, it seems that the princes took turns to man it. After a little reconnoitring Ahmed

---

[1] Albert of Aix, IV, 3, p. 433. He calls John 'virum Christianissimum'.
[2] Kemal ad-Din, *op. cit.* pp. 582–3; *Gesta Francorum*, IX, 21, p. 112.

ibn Merwan launched an assault on this sector, probably early on 9 June. Hugh of Vermandois, the Count of Flanders and the Duke of Normandy were in charge of its defence, and were almost over-powered; but in the end they drove him back with heavy loss. After this Kerbogha decided that it would be less costly to blockade the Franks more closely and attack them later when they were weakened by starvation. On the 10th he moved in to encircle the city completely. The Crusaders sought to hinder him and made a fierce sortie but were soon forced to retreat again to the safety of the walls.[1]

The failure of their effort cast the Crusaders into gloom. Their morale, raised for a while a week before by the capture of the city, sank now to its lowest depths. Food was again short. A small loaf cost a bezant, an egg two bezants and a chicken fifteen. Many men lived only on the leaves of trees or on dried hides. Adhemar of Le Puy vainly tried to organize relief for the poorer pilgrims. Amongst the knights there were many who thought that Stephen of Blois had chosen the wisest course. During the night of the 10th a company led by William and Aubrey of Grant-Mesnil and Lambert, Count of Clermont, managed to pass through the enemy lines and hurried down to the sea at St Symeon. There were Frankish ships in the harbour, probably some Genoese and some belonging to Guynemer's fleet. When the fugitives arrived and announced that the Crusading army was inevitably doomed, they hastily weighed anchor and set out for a safer port. The fugitives sailed with them for Tarsus. There they joined forces with Stephen of Blois, who had planned to return to Antioch when he heard of its capture but had been deterred by a distant view of Kerbogha's army. William of Grant-Mesnil had married Bohemond's sister Mabilla; and the defection of so close a relative of the Norman chief could not fail to impress the army.[2]

---

[1] Kemal ad-Din, *loc. cit.*; *Gesta Francorum*, XI, 21, p. 114; letter of princes to Urban II, in Hagenmeyer, *op. cit.* p. 162; William of Tyre, VI, 4, 1, p. 240.
[2] Raymond of Aguilers, XI, pp. 256–8; *Gesta Francorum*, IX, 23, pp. 126–8; letter of clergy of Lucca, in Hagenmeyer, *op. cit.* p. 166, where William of

It seemed now to the men inside Antioch that their only chance
of salvation would be the arrival of the Emperor and his forces. It
was already known that Alexius had started out from Constantinople. During the spring John Ducas had advanced from Lydia
into Phrygia as far as the main road down which the Crusaders had
travelled and at some time had reopened the road to Attalia.
Alexius therefore judged it safe to take his main army on into the
heart of Asia Minor in order to bring help to the Crusade, though
many of his advisers disliked an expedition that would take him
so far from his capital through country that was not yet cleared of
the enemy. By the middle of June he was at Philomelium. While
he was preparing to march on, Stephen and William appeared at
the camp. They had sailed from Tarsus together, and on their
journey, probably at Attalia, they heard of the Emperor's where-
abouts. Leaving their men to go on by sea they hurried northward
to Philomelium to tell him that the Turks by now were certainly
in Antioch and the Crusader army annihilated. About the same
time he was joined by Peter of Aulps, who had deserted his post
at Comana, east of Caesarea, to report that a Turkish army was
advancing to strike at Alexius before he could reach Antioch.
Alexius had no reason to doubt their stories. Stephen had been
a loyal and reliable friend in the past; and such a disaster was by no
means improbable. The news forced him to reconsider his plans.
If Antioch was taken and the Franks had perished, the Turks
would certainly continue their offensive. The Seldjuks would undoubtedly attempt to regain what they had lost and they would
have the whole victorious Turkish world behind them. Under such
circumstances it would be madness to proceed with the expedition.
As it was, his left flank was dangerously exposed to Turkish attacks.
To lengthen his communications at this juncture, for a cause that

Grant-Mesnil is called 'cognatus Boemundi'. Ducange, in his notes on Anna
Comnena, in *Recueil des Historiens des Croisades, Historiens Grecs*, vol. II, p. 27,
gives references about his wife Mabilla, though he assumes that her marriage
was of recent date. Orderic Vitalis, VIII, 28, vol. II, p. 455, tells us that they
were married in Apulia before the Crusade.

was already lost, was unthinkable. Even had he been an adventurer such as the princes of the Crusade, the risk would hardly have been worth while. But he was responsible for the welfare of a great and vulnerable Empire; and his first duty was to his subjects. He summoned his council and told them that it was necessary to retire. There was a Norman prince on his staff, Bohemond's half-brother Guy, who had been for many years in his service. Guy was moved by the thought of the Crusaders' plight and begged the Emperor to march on, on the chance that they could still be saved. But no one supported his plea. The great Byzantine army retreated northward, leaving a cordon of waste land to protect the newly-won territory from the Turks.[1]

It would have been well for the Empire and for the peace of eastern Christendom had Alexius listened to Guy's pleading; though he could not have reached Antioch before the decisive battle had been fought. For when the rumour came to the Crusaders that the imperial army had turned back, their bitterness was intense. They saw themselves as the warriors of Christ against the infidel. To refuse to hurry to their aid, however hopeless it might seem, was an act of treason towards the Faith. They could not appreciate the Emperor's other duties. Instead, his neglect seemed to justify all the suspicion and dislike that they already felt for the Greeks. Byzantium was never forgiven; and Bohemond found it all to the profit of his ambition.[2]

The Crusaders realized that Stephen of Blois was also to be blamed. Their chroniclers talked angrily of his cowardice; and the story soon reached Europe. He himself returned by easy

---

[1] *Gesta Francorum*, IX, 27, pp. 140–6, telling of the intervention of Bohemond's brother Guy; Anna Comnena, XI, vi, 1–2, vol. III, pp. 27–8. Anna says that Peter of Aulps came with the other fugitives from Antioch. But he had been left as governor of Placentia, from whence he must have come, bringing news of the Turkish army approaching from the east to cut Alexius off if he advanced. Anna makes it clear that it was this news that made Alexius turn back. If the Franks had been already defeated at Antioch, it would have been madness for him to continue his march.

[2] The news of the Emperor's retreat cannot have reached Antioch till well after Kerbogha's defeat. See below, pp. 250, 256.

stages home, to a wife who was furiously ashamed of him and who never rested till she had sent him out again to the East, to make atonement.[1]

Meanwhile Kerbogha continued to press on Antioch. On 12 June a sudden attack almost gave him the possession of one of the towers on the south-west wall; which was preserved only by the bravery of three knights from Malines. To avoid the recurrence of such risks, Bohemond burnt down whole streets of the city near to the walls, thus enabling the troops to manoeuvre with greater ease.[2]

At this juncture the spirits of the Christians were raised by a series of events which seemed to them to show God's special favour. The soldiers were hungry and anxious; the faith that had hitherto sustained them was wavering, but it was not broken. It was an atmosphere in which dreams and visions thrived. To the men of the Middle Ages the supernatural was not considered impossible nor even very rare. Modern ideas of the power of the subconscious were unknown. Dreams and visions came from God, or, in some cases, from the devil. Scepticism was confined to a flat disbelief in the word of the dreamer. This attitude must be remembered in considering the episode that follows.

On 10 June 1098, a poorly dressed peasant came to Count Raymond's tent and demanded to see him and the Bishop of Le Puy. His name was Peter Bartholomew, and he had come on the Crusade as the servant of a Provençal pilgrim called William-Peter. He was not entirely illiterate, despite his humble origin, but he was known to his fellows as a rather disreputable character, interested only in the grosser pleasures of life. His story was that during the last months he had been tormented by visions in which Saint Andrew had revealed to him where one of the holiest relics in Christendom could be found, the Lance that had pierced the side

---

[1] Orderic Vitalis, x, 19, vol. IV, p. 118, tells of Adela's shame, till she could induce Stephen to go again on a Crusade.

[2] *Gesta Francorum*, IX, 26, p. 136; Radulph of Caen, LXXVI, pp. 660-1, who says that Robert of Flanders had the quarter burnt; Albert of Aix, IV, 35, p. 413, telling of the knights from Malines.

of Christ. The first vision had occurred at the time of the earth-quake of 30 December. He had been praying in terror when suddenly there appeared an old man with silver hair, accompanied by a tall and wonderfully beautiful youth. The old man, saying that he was Saint Andrew, bade him go at once to see the Bishop of Le Puy and Count Raymond. The Bishop was to be reproved for his neglect of his duties as a preacher; while to the Count was to be revealed the hiding-place of the Lance, which the saint now proposed to show to Peter Bartholomew. Peter then found himself borne, dressed as he was only in his shirt, to the interior of the city to the Cathedral of St Peter, which the Turks were keeping as a mosque. Saint Andrew led him in through the south entrance to the southern chapel. There he vanished into the ground to reappear carrying the Lance. Peter wished to take it at once but was told to return with twelve companions after the city was taken and to search for it in the same place. He was then wafted back to the camp.

Peter disregarded the saint's commands; for he feared that no one would listen to so poor a man. Instead, he went off on a foraging expedition to Edessa. At cock-crow on 10 February, when he was staying in a castle near Edessa, Saint Andrew and his companion appeared to him again, to reprove him for his dis-obedience, for which he was punished with a temporary malady of the eyes. Saint Andrew also lectured him about God's special protection of the Crusaders, adding that all the saints longed to resume their bodies to fight by their side. Peter Bartholomew admitted his guilt and returned to Antioch; but there his courage failed again. He did not dare accost the great princes, and was relieved when in March his master, William-Peter, took him on a journey to buy food in Cyprus. On the eve of Palm Sunday, 20 March, he was sleeping with William-Peter in a tent at St Symeon, when the vision occurred once more. Peter repeated his excuses; and Saint Andrew, after telling him not to be afraid, gave instructions which Count Raymond was to follow when he came to the river Jordan. William-Peter heard the conversation but saw nothing. Peter Bartholomew then returned to the camp at Antioch but was unable to obtain an audience with the Count. He therefore left for Mamistra in order to continue his journey to Cyprus. Saint Andrew came to him there and angrily ordered him back. Peter wished to obey; but his master made him embark to cross the sea. Three times the boat was driven back and at last went ashore on an island near St Symeon; where the journey was abandoned. Peter was ill for a while; when he recovered Antioch had been captured; and he entered the city. He took part in the battle on 10 June and he narrowly escaped death from being crushed between two horses; whereupon Saint Andrew made another appearance and spoke to him so sternly that he could no longer disobey. He first told the story to his comrades. Despite the scepticism with which it was received, he came now to repeat it to Count Raymond and the Bishop of Le Puy.[1]

Adhemar was not impressed. He considered Peter Bartholomew to be a disreputable and unreliable character. Possibly he resented the criticism of his own zeal as a preacher. Possibly he remembered having seen at Constantinople a Holy Lance whose claim of authenticity was longer established. As an experienced churchman he distrusted the visions of the ignorant. But Raymond, whose piety was simpler and more enthusiastic, was ready to be convinced. He arranged to attend at a solemn search for the Lance in five days' time. In the meantime he confided Peter Bartholomew to the care of his chaplain.[2]

Visions breed rapidly. That evening all the princes were gathered in the upper city, by the wall guarding the citadel, when a priest

---

[1] Peter Bartholomew's story is given fully by Raymond of Aguilers, x, pp. 253–5, who believed in him entirely. The short account in the *Gesta Francorum*, IX, 35, pp. 132–4, written probably at the time, shows belief. So does the letter of the princes to Urban II, in Hagenmeyer, *op. cit.* p. 163, which was drafted by Bohemond.

[2] Raymond of Aguilers, *ibid.* p. 255. For the Lance kept at Constantinople, see Ebersolt, *Les Sanctuaires de Byzance*, pp. 9, 24, 116. See also Runciman, 'The Holy Lance found at Antioch', in *Analecta Bollandiana*, vol. LXVIII. Peter Bartholomew's bad reputation, as reported by Bohemond, is given in Radulph of Caen, CII, p. 678.

from Valence called Stephen demanded to see them. He told them that on the previous evening, believing that the Turks had taken the city, he had gone with a group of clerics to the Church of Our Lady to hold a service of intercession. At the end of it the others had fallen asleep; but as he lay wakeful there, he beheld before him a figure of marvellous beauty, who asked him who were these men and who seemed glad to learn that they were good Christians and not heretics. The visitor then asked Stephen if he recognized him. Stephen began to say No, but noticed a cruciform halo surrounding his head, as in the picture of Christ. The visitor admitted that he was Christ and next asked who was in command of the army. Stephen replied that there was no one commander but that the chief authority was given to a bishop. Christ then told Stephen to inform the bishop that his people had done evil with their lusts and fornication, but if they returned to a Christian way of life he would send them protection in five days' time. A lady with a brilliant countenance then appeared, saying to Christ that these were the people for whom she had so often interceded; and Saint Peter also joined them. Stephen tried to waken one of his comrades to bear witness to the vision; but before he succeeded the figures were gone.

Adhemar was prepared to accept this vision as genuine. Stephen was a reputable cleric and moreover swore on the Gospel that he had told the truth. Seeing that the princes were impressed with the story, Adhemar at once induced them to swear by the Holy Sacrament that none of them would henceforward leave Antioch without the consent of all the others. Bohemond swore the first, then Raymond, then Robert of Normandy, Godfrey and Robert of Flanders, followed by the lesser princes. The news of the oath raised the spirits of the army. Moreover Stephen's mention of a sign of divine favour due to come after five days gave support to Peter Bartholomew's claim. Expectation ran high in the camp.[1]

On 14 June a meteor was seen which seemed to fall on to the Turkish camp. Next morning Peter Bartholomew was conducted

[1] Raymond of Aguilers, XI, pp. 255–6; *Gesta Francorum*, IX, 24, pp. 128-32.

to St Peter's Cathedral by a party of twelve, which included
Count Raymond, the Bishop of Orange and the historian, Raymond of Aguilers. All day long workmen dug into the floor and
found nothing. The Count went away in disappointment. At last
Peter himself, clad only in a shirt, leapt into the trench. Bidding
all present to pray, he triumphantly produced a piece of iron.
Raymond of Aguilers declared that he himself embraced it while
it was still embedded in the ground. The story of its discovery
soon spread round the army and was received with excitement
and with joy.[1]

It is useless to attempt now to judge what really happened. The
cathedral had recently been cleaned on its reconsecration. Peter
Bartholomew may have worked on the job after his return to
Antioch, the date of which he never revealed, and would thus have
had the chance of burying a piece of iron below the floor. Or he
may have had the diviner's gift that can tell the presence of metal.
It is remarkable that even in that age when miracles were universally
considered to be possible, Adhemar clearly kept to the view that
Peter was a charlatan; and, as the sequel was to show, this distrust
was shared by many others. But it was not yet voiced. The finding of
the relic had so heartened the Christians, even including the Greeks
and Armenians, that no one wished to spoil its effect. Peter Bartholomew himself, however, somewhat shook his supporters two
days later, when he announced another visit from Saint Andrew.
Jealous, perhaps, of Stephen's direct conversation with Christ, he
was pleased to hear from the saint that the silent companion in his
visions was indeed Christ. Saint Andrew then gave him careful
instructions of the services to be held in celebration of the discovery
and on its anniversaries. The Bishop of Orange, made suspicious
by all the liturgical detail, asked Peter if he could read. In reply
Peter thought it wiser to declare that he was illiterate. This was

[1] Raymond of Aguilers, xi, p. 257. All the authorities mention the finding of
the Lance, including Anna Comnena, xi, vi, 7, vol. iii, p. 30, who calls it a
nail not a lance, and attributes its discovery to Peter the Hermit, and Matthew
of Edessa, ii, clv, p. 223. Ibn al-Athir frankly says that Peter buried a lance
himself, *op. cit.* p. 195. See Runciman, *op. cit.*

shown to be a lie; but his friends were soon reassured; for thenceforward he was no longer able to read. Saint Andrew soon reappeared, to announce a forthcoming battle with the Turks that should not be long delayed, as the Crusaders were menaced with starvation. The saint recommended five fast-days, as a penance for the people's sins; then the army should attack the Turks, and it would be given the victory. There was to be no pillaging of the enemy's tents.[1]

Bohemond, now in supreme command as Count Raymond was ill, had already decided that the only course was to launch a full assault on Kerbogha's camp; and it was possible that Saint Andrew had been inspired from earthly sources in his latest advice. While the Crusaders' morale was improving, Kerbogha was finding increasing difficulty in keeping together his coalition. Ridwan of Aleppo still held aloof from the expedition; but Kerbogha now felt the need for his help. He began to negotiate with him, and thus offended Duqaq of Damascus. Duqaq was nervous about Egyptian aggression in Palestine and was anxious to return to the south. The Emir of Homs had a family feud with the Emir of Menbij and would not co-operate with him. There was friction between the Turks and the Arabs in Kerbogha's own forces. Kerbogha himself attempted to maintain order by the use of autocratic authority which all the Emirs, who knew him to be a mere *atabeg*, resented. As the month went on there were more and more desertions from his camp. Large numbers of Turks and Arabs alike returned to their homes.[2]

Kerbogha's difficulties were undoubtedly known to the Crusading leaders, who made an attempt to persuade him to abandon the siege. On 27 June they sent an embassy composed of Peter the Hermit and a Frank called Herluin, who spoke both Arabic and Persian, to his camp. The choice of Peter indicates that he had recovered from the disrepute caused by his attempted

[1] Raymond of Aguilers, *ibid.* pp. 257-9.
[2] Kemal ad-Din, *op. cit.* 583; Abu'l Feda, *Moslem Annals*, p. 4; Ibn al-Athir, *op. cit.* p. 194.

flight five months before. It was probably because they feared that the envoys' immunity would not be respected that none of the leaders could be allowed to go on the mission; and Peter was chosen as the best-known non-combatant with the army. His acceptance of the task showed courage and did much to restore his prestige. We do not know what terms Peter was empowered to offer; for the speeches put into his and Kerbogha's mouth by later chroniclers are clearly fictional. Possibly, as some of the chroniclers say, it was suggested that a series of single combats might decide the issue. Kerbogha, despite his growing weakness, still demanded unconditional surrender; and the embassy returned empty-handed. But in the course of it Herluin may have acquired some useful information about the state of affairs in the Turkish camp.

After the failure of the embassy there could be no alternative to battle. Early on Monday morning, 28 June, Bohemond drew up the Crusading troops for action. They were divided into six armies. The first was composed of the French and Flemish, led by Hugh of Vermandois and Robert of Flanders; the second of the Lotharingians, led by Godfrey; the third of the Normans of Normandy, under Duke Robert; the fourth of the Toulousans and the Provençals, under the Bishop of Le Puy, as Raymond was seriously ill; and the fifth and sixth of the Normans of Italy, under Bohemond and Tancred. To keep watch on the citadel, two hundred men were left in the city, for Raymond to command from his sickbed. While some of the priests and chaplains of the army held a service of intercession on the walls, others marched with the troops. To the historian Raymond of Aguilers was given the honour of carrying the Holy Lance into the battle. Each prince could be distinguished by his banner; but the panoply of the knights was a little tarnished. Many had lost their horses and had to go on foot or ride inferior beasts of burden. But, strengthened by the recent signs of divine favour, the soldiers' courage was high as they marched out, one after the other, across the fortified bridge.[1]

[1] *Gesta Francorum*, IX, 28, pp. 146–50; Fulcher of Chartres, I, xxi, 1–2, pp. 247–9; Raymond of Aguilers, XI, p. 259; Albert of Aix, IV, 44–6, pp. 420–1.

As they emerged out of the gate, Kerbogha's Arab commander, Watthab ibn Mahmud, urged him to attack at once. But Kerbogha feared that to strike too soon would only destroy the Crusaders' advance-guard, whereas if he waited he might dispose of their whole forces in one stroke. In view of the temper of his troops he could not afford that the weary siege should go on. But when he saw the full array of the Franks he hesitated and sent a herald to announce, too late, that he would now discuss terms for a truce. Ignoring his messenger, the Franks advanced; and Kerbogha adopted the usual Turkish technique of retiring and luring them on into rougher ground, where suddenly his archers poured arrows into their ranks. Meanwhile he sent a detachment round to out-flank them on the left, where they were unprotected by the river. But Bohemond was ready for this, and composed a seventh army, under Rainald of Toul, to hold this attack. On the main front the fighting was hard; among the slain was Adhemar's own standard bearer. But the Turkish archers could not stop the Crusaders' advance; and the Turkish line began to waver. The Christians pressed on, encouraged by a vision on the hill-side of a company of knights on white horses, waving white banners, whose leaders they recognized as Saint George, Saint Mercury and Saint Demetrius. More practical aid was given them by the decision of many of Kerbogha's Emirs to desert his cause. They feared that victory would make him too powerful and they would be the first to pay for it. With Duqaq of Damascus at their head they began to leave the field; and their going spread panic. Kerbogha set fire to the dry grass in front of his line, in a vain attempt to delay the Franks while he restored order. Soqman the Ortoqid and the Emir of Homs were the last to remain faithful to him. When they too fled he saw that the game was up and abandoned the battle. The whole Turkish army broke up in panic. The Crusaders, following Saint Andrew's advice not to delay to sack the enemy camp, followed the fugitives as far as the Iron Bridge, slaying vast numbers of them. Others who tried to seek shelter in the castle of Tancred were rounded up and perished. Many of the survivors of the battle were massacred in their flight by the Syrians and Armenians of the countryside. Kerbogha himself reached Mosul with a remnant of his forces; but his power and prestige were lost for ever.

Ahmed ibn Merwan, the commander of the citadel, had watched the battle from his mountain-top. When he saw that it was lost, he sent a herald to the city to announce his surrender. The herald was taken to Raymond's tent; and Raymond dispatched one of his own banners to be raised over the citadel-tower. But when Ahmed learnt that the banner was not Bohemond's, he refused to display it; for he had, it seems, already made a secret arrangement with Bohemond to be carried out in event of a Christian victory. He did not open his gates till Bohemond himself appeared, when the garrison was allowed to march out unharmed. Some of them, including Ahmed himself, became converts to Christianity and joined Bohemond's army.[1]

The Crusaders' victory was unexpected but complete. It decided that Antioch should remain in the possession of the Christians. But it did not decide to which of the Christians its possession would pass. The oath that all the princes except Raymond had sworn to the Emperor clearly demanded that the city should be handed over to him. But Bohemond had already shown his intention to retain it; and his colleagues, with the exception of Raymond, were ready to consent, as it was he who had planned the capture of the city and he to whom the citadel had surrendered. They were a little uncomfortable at flouting their oaths. But the Emperor was far away. He had not come to their aid. Even his representative had left them; and they had taken the city and defeated Kerbogha without his help. It seemed to them impracticable to keep a garrison there till Alexius should deign to appear himself or send a lieutenant; and it seemed impolitic to waste time and to risk the enmity and perhaps the desertion of their most eminent soldier in

---

[1] *Gesta Francorum*, IX, 29, pp. 150–8 (the most vivid account); Raymond of Aguilers, XII, pp. 259–61; Fulcher of Chartres, XXII–XXIII, pp. 251–8; Albert of Aix, IV, 47–56, pp. 421–9; Anselm of Ribemont, letter in Hagenmeyer, *op. cit.* p. 160; Kemal ad-Din, *loc. cit.*; Ibn al-Athir, *op. cit.* pp. 195–6.

defending the rights of an absentee. Godfrey of Lorraine clearly
thought it foolish to stand in the way of Bohemond's ambitions.
Raymond, however, was always bitterly jealous of Bohemond.
And it would be unfair to regard his jealousy as his only motive
in supporting the claims of Alexius. He had made friends with
Alexius before he left Constantinople; and he was shrewd enough
to see that by failing to restore Antioch to the Empire the Crusaders
would forfeit the Emperor's goodwill, which was necessary for
them if their communications were to be adequately maintained
and if the inevitable Moslem counter-action was to be kept in
check. The Crusade would no longer be an effort of united
Christendom. Adhemar of Le Puy shared Raymond's point of
view. He was determined to co-operate with the eastern Christians,
as his master, Pope Urban, undoubtedly wished, and he saw the
danger of offending Byzantium.[1]

It was probably due to Adhemar's influence that Hugh of Vermandois was sent to explain the situation to Alexius. Now that
Antioch was secure, Hugh wished to return home and to travel by
way of Constantinople. The Crusaders still believed that Alexius
was on his way across Asia Minor. News of his retreat after his
interview with Stephen of Blois had not yet reached them. Adhemar
and Raymond hoped that Hugh's mission would cause Alexius
to hurry on to them. At the same time it was resolved that
the Crusade should wait at Antioch till 1 November, before it
attempted to march on to Jerusalem. It was a natural decision;
for the army was tired, and to advance in the full heat of the
Syrian summer, along little-known roads where water might be
scarce, would be an act of folly. Moreover the question of Antioch
must first be settled; and Adhemar doubtless hoped that the
Emperor would have come by then. Hugh set out early in July,
accompanied by Baldwin of Hainault. On the road through Asia
Minor his party was attacked and severely mauled by the Turks.
The Count of Hainault disappeared and his fate was never known.
It was already autumn before Hugh arrived at Constantinople and

[1] Albert of Aix, v, 2, pp. 433–4. Adhemar's role is conjectural.

could see the Emperor to tell him the full story of Antioch. By then the season was too late for a campaign across the Anatolian mountains. It was not feasible for Alexius to reach Antioch before the coming spring.[1]

Meanwhile in Antioch tempers grew frayed. At first the citadel had been occupied jointly by Bohemond, Raymond, Godfrey and Robert of Flanders, but Bohemond retained the chief towers in his control. Now he succeeded in ejecting his colleagues' troops, probably with the consent of Godfrey and Robert, so that Raymond's objections were overruled. Raymond was furious, and in reply kept sole control of the fortified bridge and the palace of Yaghi-Siyan. But Raymond was still too ill to be active; and now Adhemar fell ill. With their two leaders in retirement, the southern French found themselves maltreated by the other troops, particularly by the Normans; and many of them longed for Raymond to be reconciled with Bohemond. Bohemond behaved as though he were already master of the city. Many Genoese had hastened to Antioch as soon as Kerbogha's defeat was known, eager to be the first to capture its trade. On 14 July Bohemond gave them a charter, allowing them a market, a church and thirty houses. Henceforward the Genoese would advocate his claims; and he could count on their assistance to keep open his communications with Italy. They agreed to support him in Antioch against all comers, except only the Count of Toulouse. In such a combat they would remain neutral.[2]

While Raymond and Bohemond warily watched each other, the lesser nobles rode off to join Baldwin at Edessa or made expeditions to capture plunder or even to set up fiefs in the country around. The most ambitious of these raids was conducted by a Limousin in Raymond's army, called Raymond Pilet, who set out on 17 July across the Orontes to the east, and three days later occupied the town of Tel-Mannas, whose Syrian population received him gladly.

[1] *Gesta Francorum*, X, 30, pp. 161–2; Albert of Aix, V, 3, pp. 434–5.
[2] Raymond of Aguilers, XIII, pp. 261–2; charter of Genoese with Bohemond, in Hagenmeyer, *op. cit.* pp. 155–6.

After capturing a Turkish castle in the neighbourhood he moved on to attack the larger town of Maarat an-Numan, with an army composed mainly of native Christians. But they were unused to bearing arms; and when they met the troops sent by Ridwan of Aleppo to save the town they turned and fled. But Ridwan was unable to eject Raymond Pilet from Tel-Mannas.[1]

In the course of July a serious epidemic broke out in Antioch. We cannot tell its precise nature, but it was probably typhoid, due to the effect of the sieges and battles of the last month and the Crusaders' ignorance of the sanitary precautions necessary in the East. Adhemar of Le Puy, whose health had for some time been failing, was its first distinguished victim. He died on 1 August.[2]

Adhemar's death was one of the greatest tragedies of the Crusade. In the chroniclers' pages he is rather a shadowy figure; but they show him to have wielded greater personal influence than any other Crusader. He commanded respect as the Pope's representative; and his own character won him the affection of the whole army. He was charitable and cared for the poor and the sick. He was modest and never aggressive; but he was always ready to give wise advice, even on military matters; as a general he was both courageous and shrewd. The victory at Dorylaeum had been largely due to his strategy; and he presided over many of the army councils during the siege of Antioch. Politically he worked for a good understanding with the Christians of the East, both with Byzantium and with the Orthodox churches of Syria. He had been in Pope Urban's confidence and knew his views. While he lived, the racial and religious intolerance of the Franks could be kept in check, and the selfish ambitions and quarrels of the princes restrained from doing irreparable harm to the Crusade. Though he had been careful never to attempt to dominate the movement, he was considered, as the priest Stephen reported to Christ in his vision, to be the leader

---

[1] *Gesta Francorum*, x, 30, pp. 162–4; Kemal ad-Din, *op. cit.* p. 584.
[2] *Gesta Francorum*, x, 30, p. 166; Raymond of Aguilers, xiii, p. 262; Fulcher of Chartres, i, xxiii, 8, p. 258; letter of the princes to Urban II, in Hagenmeyer, *op. cit.* p. 164.

of the Crusade. After his death there was no one that possessed any overriding authority. The Count of Toulouse, who had also long ago discussed Crusading policy with Pope Urban, inherited his views. But Raymond was not so able a man, and he could only argue with Bohemond as an equal, not as the spokesman of the Church. And none of the princes, in his absence, had sufficient breadth of outlook to see to the preservation of the unity of Christendom. Adhemar's charity, his wisdom and his integrity were never questioned by his comrades, even by those whose ambitions he opposed. Bohemond's followers mourned his loss as sincerely as did his own men from France; and Bohemond himself swore to carry his body to Jerusalem. The whole army was moved and disquieted by his death.

There was, however, one man that felt no sorrow. Peter Bartholomew had never forgiven the legate for showing disbelief in his visions. Two days later he took his revenge. He announced that he had been visited again by Saint Andrew who was on this occasion accompanied by Adhemar. Adhemar announced that, as punishment for his incredulity, he had spent the intervening hours since his death in hell, from which he had only been rescued by the prayers of his colleagues and especially of Bohemond, and by his gift of a few coins for the upkeep of the Lance. He was forgiven now, and asked that his body should remain in St Peter's Cathedral at Antioch. Then Saint Andrew delivered himself of advice to Count Raymond. Antioch, he said, should be given to its present claimant, if he were proved to be a righteous man. A Patriarch of the Latin rite should be elected to decide on his righteousness. The Crusaders should repent of their sins and march on to Jerusalem, which was only at ten days' distance; but the journey would take ten years if they did not return to godlier habits. That is to say, Peter Bartholomew and his friends among the Provençals considered that Bohemond should be allowed to have Antioch, so long as he undertook to help the Crusade further; that the army should set out soon for Jerusalem; and that there should be no truck with the Byzantines and the local Orthodox churches.

These revelations were embarrassing to Raymond. He honestly believed in the Holy Lance; and its possession by his troops gave him prestige. For though many might say that the battle against Kerbogha was won by Bohemond's strategy, many others gave the credit of the victory to the relic, and so indirectly to Raymond. But Raymond's other main source of authority sprang from his long association with Adhemar. If the divine messenger who had revealed the position of the Lance were now to question Adhemar's judgement and to repudiate the policy which Raymond had inherited from him and which fitted with Raymond's own views, one or other of Raymond's props must be discarded. He temporized. While remaining loyal to his belief in the Lance, he indicated that he doubted whether Peter Bartholomew's visions continued to be genuine. For, in spite of Saint Andrew's words, he, and others with him, still maintained that Antioch should be given to the Emperor. He found himself in consequence in opposition to most of his troops.

Among the army in general the posthumous attack on Adhemar made a bad impression. Publicizing as it did the legate's disbelief in the relic, it revived the doubt that many had originally felt. In particular, the Normans and the northern French, who had always disliked the Provençals, began to decry the relic and to use the scandal of the forgery to discredit Count Raymond and his plans. In defending Adhemar's reputation they were thus enabled to work against the policy that he had advocated. We may assume that Bohemond enjoyed the situation.[1]

As the epidemic spread through Antioch, the leading Crusaders sought refuge in the country. Bohemond crossed the Amanus mountains into Cilicia, where he strengthened the garrisons left there by Tancred the previous autumn and received their homage. He intended that his principality of Antioch should include the Cilician province. Godfrey went northward, to the towns of

---

[1] Raymond of Aguilers, xiii, pp. 262–4. It seems to have been about now that Bohemond began to cast doubts on the authenticity of the Lance (Radulph of Caen, *loc. cit.*).

Turbessel and Ravendel, which his brother Baldwin handed over to him. Godfrey was jealous of his brother's success; and, as all the princes were seeking territory near Antioch, he wished to have his share. He probably undertook to return the towns to Baldwin, if the army marched on to Palestine. Raymond's movements are uncertain; while Robert of Normandy went to Lattakieh.[1]

Before the Turkish invasions Lattakieh had been the southernmost port of the Byzantine Empire. It had been taken by the Turks about the year 1084 but had later passed under the suzerainty of the Arab Emir of Shaizar. In the autumn of 1097 Guynemer of Boulogne descended upon the port and captured it. His garrison remained in possession over the winter; but in March the fleet commanded by Edgar Atheling, after unloading supplies for the Crusaders at St Symeon, sailed on to Lattakieh. Guynemer's men were driven out and the town taken over in the name of the Emperor. But Edgar could only leave a small detachment to guard the town; so an appeal was made to the Crusading army to supplement the defence. Soon after the victory over Kerbogha Robert of Normandy came in answer to the appeal; and Lattakieh was handed over to him in trust for the Emperor. But Robert's only idea of government was to extract as much money as possible from the governed. So unpopular was his rule that after a few weeks he was forced to retire from the town, which was now given a garrison by the Byzantine governor of Cyprus, Eustathius Philocales.[2]

[1] Raymond of Aguilers, XIII, p. 262; Albert of Aix, v, 4, p. 435, 13, pp. 440–1.

[2] For the question of Lattakieh, see Chalandon, *Essai sur le Règne d'Alexis Comnène*, pp. 205–12, and David, *Robert Curthose*, pp. 230 ff. Albert of Aix, VI, 45, pp. 500–1, says that Guynemer took Lattakieh from the Turks in the autumn of 1097 and held it under Raymond of Toulouse. Orderic Vitalis says that Edgar Atheling and the English took it from the Emperor, some time early in 1098, and placed it under Robert of Normandy (*loc. cit.* on p. 228 n. 1). David, *loc. cit.*, disbelieves Albert's story and says that the English must have taken it direct from the Turks and that Robert was there during the winter of 1097–8. Raymond of Aguilers tells us that Robert was absent from Antioch at the time of the expedition

In September the epidemic abated, and the princes returned to Antioch. On the 11th they met together to draft a letter to Pope Urban to give him the details of the capture of Antioch and to announce the death of his legate. Feeling the need of a supreme authority to overrule the quarrelling factions, they urged him to come in person to the East. Antioch, they pointed out, was a see founded by Saint Peter, and he as Saint Peter's heir should be enthroned there; and he should visit the Holy City itself. They were ready to wait his arrival before marching on into Palestine.[1] Bohemond's name headed the list of princes; and the letter was probably written in his secretariat. The effect of Adhemar's absence was shown by the implied rejection of the rights of the Patriarch John and by a note of hostility towards the native Christian sects, which were denounced as heretical. The Crusaders can hardly have expected that the Pope would be able to journey to the East; but the appeal enabled them to postpone once more the need to decide upon the fate of Antioch; while the Pope would no doubt send a legate who could be given the responsibility for the decision. It was clear by now that the Emperor would not penetrate into Syria this season. Possibly his retreat from Philomelium was already known.

Among the soldiers and pilgrims of the army conditions were very bad. Owing to the fighting no crops had been harvested in the plain of Antioch; and food was still short. Largely to secure supplies Raymond began to organize a raid into Moslem territory. Before he had decided upon his objective he was invited by Godfrey to come on a joint campaign to the town of Azaz, on the main road from Edessa and Turbessel to Antioch. The Emir of

in December 1097. But it is doubtful if the English arrived off the Syrian coast before March. Radulph of Caen says that Robert went to Lattakieh, which was under the Emperor's rule, at the time of Stephen of Blois's flight (LVIII, p. 649). But he took part in the battle against Kerbogha, a few days later, where all the sources admit his presence. Guibert of Nogent (XXXVII, p. 254) says that at one time Robert had governed Lattakieh but had been ejected because of his financial oppression. I have given the version that I think most convincing.

[1] Letter of the princes to Urban II, in Hagenmeyer, *op. cit.* pp. 161-5.

Azaz, Omar, was in revolt against his overlord, Ridwan of Aleppo, who was marching to punish him. One of Omar's generals had captured and fallen in love with a Frankish lady, the widow of a Lorrainer knight; and it was on her suggestion that Omar appealed for help to Godfrey. Godfrey responded gladly; for it was inconvenient for him that Azaz should be in Ridwan's hands. Raymond accepted Godfrey's invitation though he insisted that Omar's son should be handed over as a hostage; and Baldwin sent troops from Edessa. At the approach of the Christian army Ridwan retired from Azaz; and Omar was confirmed by Godfrey in its possession, and paid him homage. Raymond was able to collect provisions in the neighbourhood, but suffered heavy losses from Turkish ambushes on the return journey. The episode showed that not only were the Moslem princes prepared now to use Frankish help in their own quarrels, but that the Franks, modifying their militant faith, were prepared to accept Moslem vassals.[1]

In October, in spite of Peter Bartholomew's report that Saint Andrew had again demanded an early departure for Jerusalem, Raymond set out on another raid to secure provisions. He had already occupied Rugia on the Orontes, some thirty miles from Antioch. From there he attacked the town of Albara, a little to the south-east. The inhabitants, who were all Moslem, capitulated, but were either massacred or sold as slaves in Antioch; and the town was repeopled with Christians. The mosque was converted into a church. To the delight of his army Raymond then appointed one of his priests, Peter of Narbonne, to be its bishop. The appointment was only made because there was no Orthodox bishopric already established in the town. No one yet conceived of a schism between the Greek and Latin churches that would involve a duplication of bishoprics. The new bishop, Latin though he was, was consecrated by the Greek Patriarch, John of Antioch. But Peter of Narbonne's elevation marked the beginning of a Latin church resident in the East, and encouraged those of the Crusaders who,

[1] Raymond of Aguilers, XIII, pp. 264–5; Albert of Aix, v, 5–12, p. 435–40; Kemal ad-Din, *op. cit.* p. 586.

like Peter Bartholomew, were now anxious to see the local Greek ecclesiastics replaced by Latins.[1]

In the debates that followed Kerbogha's defeat, the princes had vowed to start for Jerusalem in November. On 1 November they began to assemble at Antioch to discuss their plans. Raymond came from Albara, where he had left most of his troops. Godfrey rode in from Turbessel, bringing with him the heads of all the Turkish prisoners that he had made in a series of small raids in the district. The Count of Flanders and the Duke of Normandy were already at Antioch; and Bohemond, who had been ill in Cilicia, arrived two days later. On the 5th the princes and their advisers met together in the Cathedral of St Peter. It appeared at once that there was no agreement between them. Bohemond's friends opened by claiming Antioch for him. The Emperor was not coming; and Bohemond was an able man and the Crusader of whom the enemy was most afraid. Raymond retorted by sharply reminding the assembly of the oath to the Emperor that all except himself had sworn. Godfrey and Robert of Flanders were known to favour Bohemond's claim, but dared not speak up for it for fear of the accusation of perjury. The argument continued for several days. Meanwhile the soldiers and pilgrims waiting outside for a declaration grew impatient. Their one desire was to carry out their vows and to reach Jerusalem. They longed to leave Antioch where they had delayed so long and suffered so much. Spurred on by Peter Bartholomew and his visions, they presented an ultimatum to their chiefs. With an equal contempt for both Bohemond's and Raymond's ambitions, let those, they said, that wished to enjoy the revenues of Antioch do so, and let those that were eager for gifts from the Emperor await his coming; for themselves they would march on to Jerusalem; and if their leaders continued to haggle over the possession of Antioch they would raze its walls before they left. Faced with this and fearing that Raymond and Bohemond would soon resort to arms, the more moderate leaders

---

[1] Raymond of Aguilers, XIV, p. 266; *Gesta Francorum*, X, 31, pp. 36–8, saying that the bishop was brought to Antioch to be consecrated.

suggested a more intimate discussion which only the chief princes would attend. There, after further angry scenes, a temporary arrangement was made. Raymond would agree to the decisions that the council might ultimately make about Antioch, so long as Bohemond swore to accompany the Crusade on to Jerusalem; while Bohemond took an oath before the bishops not to delay nor harm the Crusade to suit his personal ambitions. The question of Antioch was not settled; but Bohemond was confirmed in his possession of the citadel and three-quarters of the town, while Raymond remained in control of the fortified bridge and the palace of Yaghi-Siyan, which he placed under William Ermingar. The date for the departure for Jerusalem was still unfixed; but, to occupy the troops meanwhile, it was decided to attack the fortress of Maarat an-Numan, whose reduction was advisable to protect the army's left flank when it should advance southward towards Palestine.[1]

On 23 November Raymond and the Count of Flanders set out for Rugia and Albara and on the 27th they reached the walls of Maarat an-Numan. Their attempted assault on the town next morning was a failure; and when Bohemond and his troops arrived that afternoon and a second assault also failed, it was decided to conduct a regular siege. But, though the town was completely invested, for a fortnight no progress was made. The countryside had to be scoured for wood to make siege machines. Food was short; and detachments of the army would desert their posts in order to search for corn and for vegetables. At last on 11 December, after Peter Bartholomew had announced that success was imminent, a huge wooden castle on wheels, built by Raymond's men and commanded by William of Montpelier, was pushed against one of the city towers. An attempt to scale the tower from it was repulsed; but protection given by the castle enabled the wall on one side of the tower to be mined. In the evening the wall collapsed and a number of humble soldiers forced their way into the town

[1] Raymond of Aguilers, xiv, pp. 267–8; *Gesta Francorum*, x, 3, pp. 168–70; *Historia Belli Sacri*, xcii, p. 208.

and began to pillage. Meanwhile Bohemond, jealous of Raymond's success and eager to repeat his coup at Antioch, announced by a herald that if the town surrendered to him he would protect the lives of all the defenders that took refuge in a hall near to the main gate. During the night the fighting died down. Many of the citizens, seeing that the defences were pierced, fortified their houses and cisterns but offered to pay a tax if they were spared. Others fled to the hall that Bohemond had indicated. But when the battle reopened next morning no one was spared. The Crusaders poured into the town, massacring everyone that they met and forcing an entrance into the houses, which they looted and burnt. As for the refugees who relied on Bohemond's protection, the men were slaughtered and the women and children sold as slaves.

During the siege Bohemond's and Raymond's troops had co-operated with difficulty. Now, when Bohemond by his treachery had secured the greater part of the loot though it was Raymond's army that had taken the town, the enmity between the southern French and the Normans flared up again. Raymond claimed the town and wished to place it under the Bishop of Albara. But Bohemond would not evacuate his troops unless Raymond abandoned his area of Antioch and, as a counter-attack, he began openly to question the authenticity of visions reported by Peter Bartholomew.

Meanwhile disaffection increased in the whole army. Raymond's troops in particular demanded the resumption of the march on Jerusalem. About Christmas Day representatives of the soldiers indicated to Raymond that if he would organize its departure the army would recognize him as leader of the whole Crusade. Raymond felt that he could not refuse, and a few days later he left Maarat an-Numan for Rugia, announcing that the expedition was about to leave for Palestine. Bohemond thereupon returned to Antioch; and Maarat an-Numan was put into the hands of the Bishop of Albara.[1]

[1] Raymond of Aguilers, xiv, pp. 267–70; *Gesta Francorum*, x, 33, pp. 172–8; Ibn al-Qalānisī, *Damascus Chronicle*, pp. 46–7; Ibn al-Athir, *op. cit.* pp. 196–7.

But even after his announcement Raymond delayed. He could not bring himself to leave for the south with Antioch in Bohemond's hands. Bohemond, seeing, perhaps, that the more Raymond hesitated the more mutinous grew his troops, and knowing that the Emperor would not come down across Asia Minor during the winter months, suggested a postponement of the expedition till Easter. To bring matters to a head, Raymond summoned all the princes to meet him at Rugia. There he attempted to buy them to accept his leadership. The sums that he offered presumably corresponded to the strength that each now possessed. To Godfrey he proposed to give ten thousand sous and the same to Robert of Normandy, to Robert of Flanders six thousand, five thousand to Tancred and lesser sums to the lesser chiefs. Bohemond was offered nothing. He had hoped that he would thus be established as unquestioned head of the Crusade and could thus keep Bohemond in check. But his overtures were received very coldly.[1]

While the princes conferred at Rugia, the army at Maarat an-Numan took direct action. It was suffering from starvation. All the supplies of the neighbourhood were exhausted; and cannibalism seemed the only solution. Even the Turks were impressed by its tenacity in such conditions, though, as the chronicler Raymond of Aguilers sadly remarks: 'We knew of this too late to profit by it.' The Bishop of Orange, who had some influence over the Provençals, died from these hardships. At last, despite the protests of the Bishop of Albara, the men determined to force Raymond to move by destroying the walls of Maarat an-Numan. At the news, Raymond hurried back to the town but realized that there could be no more postponement.[2]

On 13 January 1099, Raymond and his troops marched out of Maarat an-Numan to continue the Crusade. The Count walked barefoot, as befitted the leader of a pilgrimage. To show that there would be no turning back the town was left in flames. With

[1] Raymond of Aguilers, XIV, p. 271; *Gesta Francorum*, X, 34, p. 178. See Appendix II.
[2] Raymond of Aguilers, XIV, pp. 270-2; *Gesta Francorum*, X, 33-4, pp. 176-8.

Raymond were all his vassals. The Bishop of Albara and Raymond Pilet, lord of Tel-Mannas, deserted their towns to travel with him. The garrison that he had kept at Antioch under William Ermingar could not hold out against Bohemond and hastened after him. Of his colleagues among the princes, Robert of Normandy at once set out to join him, accompanied by Tancred, whom Bohemond doubtless wished to watch over Norman-Italian interests in the Crusade. Godfrey of Lorraine and Robert of Flanders hesitated for nearly a month before public opinion forced them to follow. But Baldwin and Bohemond remained in the lands that they had captured.[1]

Thus the quarrel between the two great princes seemed to have found a solution. Raymond was now unchallenged leader of the Crusade; but Bohemond was in possession of Antioch.

[1] Raymond of Aguilers, xiv, p. 272; *Gesta Francorum*, x, 34, p. 180. The author of the *Gesta* accompanied Tancred's contingent.

BOOK V

THE PROMISED LAND

CHAPTER I

THE ROAD TO JERUSALEM

*'Therefore now go, lead the people unto the place of which
I have spoken unto thee.'*   EXODUS XXXII, 34

When Stephen of Blois, writing to his wife from Nicaea, had
expressed the fear that the Crusade might be held up at Antioch,
he never dreamed how long the delay would last. Fifteen months
had passed since the army had reached the city walls. During this
period there had been important changes in the Moslem world.
The Fatimids of Egypt, like the Byzantines, had, before the Crusade
began, recovered from the first shock of the Turkish onslaught,
and, like the Byzantines, they hoped to use the Crusade to consolidate their recovery. The real ruler of Egypt was Shah-an-Shah
al-Afdal, who had succeeded his father, the Armenian renegade
Badr al-Jamali, as vizier to the boy Caliph, al-Mustali. Al-Afdal's
embassy to the Crusader camp at Antioch had not produced any
results. Frankish ambassadors had returned with his envoys to
Cairo; but it soon was clear that they were not authorized to
negotiate an alliance and that the Crusaders, far from being willing
to aid the Egyptians to recover Palestine, had every intention of
themselves marching on Jerusalem. Al-Afdal therefore determined
to profit by the war in northern Syria. As soon as he heard of
Kerbogha's defeat at Antioch and realized that the Turks throughout Asia were in no position to resist a new attack, he invaded
Palestine. The province was still in the hands of the sons of Ortoq,
Soqman and Ilghazi, who admitted the suzerainty of Duqaq of
Damascus. As al-Afdal advanced they retired behind the walls of
Jerusalem. They knew that Duqaq could not at once come to their
aid; but they hoped that the great fortifications of Jerusalem and

Syria at the time of the First Crusade

the fighting ability of their Turcoman troops would enable them to hold out till rescue came. Al-Afdal's army was equipped with the latest siege machines, including forty mangonels; but the Ortoqids resisted for forty days, till at last the walls were so battered that they were forced to capitulate. They were allowed to retire with their men to Damascus, whence they went on to join their cousins in the district round Diarbekir. The Egyptians then occupied the whole of Palestine and by the autumn had fixed their frontier at the pass of the Dog River, on the coast just north of Beirut. In the meantime they repaired the defences of Jerusalem.[1]

In northern Syria the local Arab dynasties were equally delighted by the collapse of Turkish power and were ready to make terms with the Franks. Even the Emir of Hama, Ridwan's father-in-law, and the Emir of Homs, who had fought well for Kerbogha, abandoned any idea of opposing them. More important to the Crusaders was the attitude of the two leading Arab families, the Munqidhites of Shaizar and the Banū 'Ammār of Tripoli. The former controlled the country immediately ahead of the Crusaders, from the Orontes to the coast, and the latter the coast line from the middle Lebanon to the Fatimid frontier. Their friendship, or at least their neutrality, was essential if the Crusade was to advance.[2]

From Maarat an-Numan Raymond marched on to Kafartab, some twelve miles to the south. There he waited till 16 January, collecting provisions to revictual his troops; and there Tancred and Robert of Normandy joined him. Thither, too, came ambassadors from the Emir of Shaizar, offering to provide guides and cheap provisions for the Crusaders if they would pass peaceably through his land. Raymond accepted the offer; and on the 17th the Emir's guides conducted the army across the Orontes, between Shaizar

---

[1] Ibn al-Athir, *op. cit.* pp. 197-8. See Buhl's article 'Al Kuds', and Zetter-steen's article 'Sukman ibn Ortok', in the *Encyclopaedia of Islam*.

[2] Honigmann's article 'Shaizar', and Sobernheim's article 'Ibn Ammar', in the *Encyclopaedia of Islam*.

and Hama, and led it up the valley of the Sarout. All the flocks and herds of the district had been driven for safety into a valley adjoining the Sarout; into which, by error, one of the guides introduced the Franks. The herdsmen and the local villagers were not strong enough to prevent the Franks from systematically taking over the beasts. The commander of the castle that dominated the valley thought it best to buy immunity for himself. So rich was the booty that several of the knights went off to sell their surplus in Shaizar and in Hama, in return for pack-horses, of which they bought a thousand. The Arab authorities freely allowed them to enter their towns and make their purchases.[1]

While these supplies were being collected, Raymond and his commanders met to discuss what route should now be taken. Raymond himself favoured the view that the army should strike due west across the Nosairi range in order to reach the coast as soon as possible. Lattakieh was already in Christian hands; and so long as he kept to the coast he would be in touch with Antioch and could obtain supplies from the Byzantine authorities in Cyprus, with whom he was on good terms. But Tancred pointed out that to be sure of the coast road it would be necessary to capture all the great fortresses that lay on the way. The fighting strength of the army was now only a thousand knights and five thousand infantrymen. How could such a force indulge in siege warfare? They ought, he argued, to march straight on to Jerusalem, avoiding the necessity of capturing the coastal fortresses. If they could take Jerusalem, not only would the news bring more soldiers out from Europe, but cities like Tripoli, Tyre and Acre would no longer attempt to hold out against them. The argument against his view was that all the country between the Lebanon and the desert was held by Duqaq of Damascus, who, unlike the Arab princelings, would undoubtedly oppose the Crusaders' progress. It was eventually decided to strike the coast further to the south, through the Buqaia, the plain between the Nosairi range and the Lebanon, which provides the only easy access from inner Syria to the sea,

[1] Raymond of Aguilers, XIV, pp. 272–3; *Gesta Francorum*, X, 34, pp. 180–2.

and to waste as little time as possible on attempts to reduce enemy fortresses.[1]

On 22 January the Crusaders reached the town of Masyaf, whose lord hastened to conclude a treaty with them. From there they turned south-south-east, to avoid the massif of the Jebel Helou. Next day they came to the town of Rafaniya, which they found deserted by its inhabitants but full of supplies of every kind. They remained there for three days, then descended into the Buqaia. The plain was commanded by the huge fortress of Hosn al-Akrad, the Castle of the Kurds, built on the height where the ruins of Krak des Chevaliers now stand. The local inhabitants had driven all their herds to shelter within its walls; and, for the purpose of revictualment rather than for strategic reasons, the Crusaders decided that it must be taken. On 28 January they attacked the fortifications. But the defence, aware of their habits, opened a gate and let out some of their beasts. So intent were the Franks on rounding up all this booty that they scattered; and a sortie from the castle not only prevented them from reassembling but also nearly succeeded in capturing Count Raymond himself, who had been deserted by his bodyguard. Next day the Franks, ashamed of having been tricked, planned a serious assault; but when they reached the walls they found that the castle had been abandoned during the night. There was still considerable booty left within; and the army settled down to spend three weeks there, while further discussions about strategy were held. The Feast of the Purification was celebrated within the castle.[2]

While Raymond was at Hosn al-Akrad, envoys reached him from the Emir of Hama, offering him gifts and promising not to attack his men. They were followed by envoys from the Emir of Tripoli. This Emir, Jalal al-Mulk Abu'l Hasan, of the dynasty of the Banū 'Ammār, a family noted more for its learning than for its warlike qualities, had maintained the independence of his emirate by playing off the Seldjuks against the Fatimids. With the Turkish

---

[1] Raymond of Aguilers, XIV, p. 273.
[2] Raymond of Aguilers, XIV, pp. 273-5; *Gesta Francorum*, X, 34, p. 182.

power in decline, he was ready to encourage the Franks against the renascent Egyptians. Raymond was invited to send representatives to Tripoli to discuss arrangements for the passage of the Crusade and to bring the banners of Toulouse, which the Emir would unfurl over the city. The prosperity of Tripoli and the surrounding country greatly impressed the Frankish ambassadors; who on their return to the camp advised Raymond that if he made a show of force against one of the fortresses of the emirate, the Emir would certainly pay a large sum to buy immunity for the rest of his dominions. Raymond, who was in need of money, took their advice and ordered his army to attack the town of Arqa, situated some fifteen miles from Tripoli, where the Buqaia opens out to the coast. He arrived before its walls on 14 February.[1]

Meanwhile, anxious as he was to establish communications with the garrison at Lattakieh and the sea, Raymond encouraged Raymond Pilet and Raymond, Viscount of Turenne, to attempt a surprise attack on Tortosa, the one good harbour on the coast between Lattakieh and Tripoli. The two Raymonds, with a small detachment, hurried westward and arrived before the town after dark on 16 February. They lit a series of camp fires all round the walls, to suggest the presence of a far larger army than they possessed. The ruse was successful. The governor of Tortosa, who was subject to the Emir of Tripoli, was so seriously alarmed that he evacuated himself and his garrison by sea during the night. Next morning the gates of the town were opened to the Franks. At the news of their conquest the governor of Marqiye, ten miles to the north, hastened to recognize Raymond's suzerainty. The capture of Tortosa greatly strengthened the Crusade. It opened up easy communications by sea with Antioch and Cyprus and with Europe.[2]

This success roused jealousy among the Crusaders still at Antioch and decided them to follow Raymond southward. About the end of February Godfrey of Lorraine, Bohemond and Robert of

[1] Raymond of Aguilers, XIV–XV, p. 275; *Gesta Francorum*, X, 34, p. 184.
[2] Raymond of Aguilers, XV, p. 276; *Gesta Francorum*, X, 34, pp. 184–6.

Flanders set out from Antioch to Lattakieh. There Bohemond turned back. He thought that after all it would be wiser to consolidate himself in Antioch lest the Emperor might march towards Syria in the spring. Godfrey and Robert moved on to besiege the small sea-port of Jabala. While they lay there, the Bishop of Albara reached them from Raymond, begging them to join him at Arqa.[1]

The siege of Arqa was not going well. The town was well fortified and courageously defended; and Raymond's army was not large enough to invest it completely. Tancred's warning that the army was in no condition to attempt to storm fortresses was fully justified. But once Raymond had begun the siege he could not abandon it for fear that the Emir of Tripoli, seeing his weakness, would become openly hostile. It is possible that the soldiers made no great effort. Life was comfortable in the camp. The countryside was fertile and further supplies began to arrive through Tortosa. After all that they had endured the men were pleased to relax themselves a while. Early in March there was a rumour that a Moslem army was assembling to relieve Arqa, led in person by the Caliph of Baghdad. The rumour was false, but it alarmed Raymond into summoning Godfrey and Robert of Flanders. On the receipt of the message Godfrey and Robert made a truce with the Emir of Jabala, who accepted their suzerainty, and hurried southward to Arqa. They celebrated their arrival by an attack on the suburbs of Tripoli and by several successful raids to round up beasts of all sorts, including camels, in the Buqaia.[2]

Raymond soon regretted the arrival of his colleagues. He had been for two months the accepted leader of the Crusade. Even Tancred had acknowledged his authority in return for five thousand sous. But now he had been obliged to call on his rivals for help. Tancred, whose advice he had ignored, moved over to Godfrey's camp, saying that Raymond had not paid him sufficiently. The two Roberts showed little inclination to admit Raymond's

[1] *Gesta Francorum*, x, 35, p. 186; Albert of Aix, v, 33, p. 453.
[2] *Gesta Francorum, loc. cit.*; Raymond of Aguilers, xvi, pp. 277-8.

hegemony. In his attempt to assert his rights he aroused resentment; and quarrels began. The men of each army, seeing their leaders at loggerheads, followed suit and would not co-operate with each other.

The controversy was worsened by the arrival in early April of letters from the Emperor. Alexius informed the Crusaders that he was now ready to start out for Syria. If they would wait for him till the end of June, he would be with them by St John's Day and would lead them on into Palestine. Raymond wished to accept the offer. As the Emperor's faithful ally he could count on imperial backing to help him to reassert his supremacy over the Frankish army. Amongst his own men, there were many, like Raymond of Aguilers, who, much as they disliked the Byzantines, felt that the Emperor's arrival would at least provide the Crusade with a leader whom all the princes would admit. But the bulk of the army was impatient to move on to Jerusalem; and none of the other princes wished to find himself under imperial suzerainty. Against such strong public opinion, Raymond's policy could not prevail. It is probable that Alexius never expected that the Crusaders would wait for him. Disgusted by their behaviour at Antioch he had already decided upon an attitude of neutrality. This to a Byzantine diplomat was not a passive attitude but meant the establishment of relations with both sides in order that benefits might be reaped whichever should be victorious. He was in communication with the Egyptians, who had probably written to him when the Crusade advanced towards their territory to ask if it was acting on his account. In answer Alexius repudiated the movement. He had reason for so doing. Bohemond's actions taught him that he could not count upon the loyalty of the Franks; nor was he particularly interested in Palestine. It lay outside the lands that he had hoped to recover for the Empire. His only obligation there was towards the Orthodox Christians, whose protector he was. He may well have considered that they would fare better under the tolerant rule of the Fatimids than under the Franks who were already showing at Antioch a marked hostility towards native Christianity. At the same time he did not wish to sever his connection with the Crusade, which might still be of use to the Empire. His correspondence with Egypt later fell into the hands of the Crusaders, who were genuinely shocked by the evidence of his treachery to them, though their treachery to him seemed to them perfectly reasonable and right. They blamed it on him that the ambassadors they had sent to Cairo from Antioch had been detained there for so long.[1]

These ambassadors returned to the army at Arqa a few days later, bearing the Fatimids' final offer for a settlement. If the Crusade would abandon any attempt to force its way into Fatimid territory, its pilgrims would be allowed free access to the holy places and everything would be done to facilitate the pilgrimage. The suggestion was at once rejected.[2]

In spite of the desire of the other princes to resume the march, Raymond refused to leave Arqa untaken. To bring matters to a head, Peter Bartholomew announced that on 5 April Christ, Saint Peter and Saint Andrew had all appeared to him to announce that an immediate assault on Arqa must be made. The bulk of the army was growing tired of Peter's revelations, which they regarded as a political device of Count Raymond's. A section of the northern French, led by Robert of Normandy's chaplain, Arnulf of Rohes, now openly declared their disbelief and even questioned the authenticity of the Holy Lance, remarking that Adhemar of Le Puy had never been convinced of it. The Provençals rallied to Peter's support. Stephen of Valence reminded the army of his vision at Antioch. Raymond of Aguilers told how he had kissed the Lance while it was still embedded in the ground. Another priest, Peter Desiderius, reported that Adhemar had appeared to him after his death and had described the hell-fire to which his doubts had led him. Another, Everard, said that when he was visiting Tripoli on business during the Turkish siege of Antioch

[1] Raymond of Aguilers, xvi, p. 277, xviii, p. 286.
[2] Raymond of Aguilers, xvi, p. 277; William of Tyre, vii, 19, vol. i, pt i, pp. 305–6.

a Syrian there had told him of a vision in which Saint Mark had spoken of the Lance. The Bishop of Apt, who had been a sceptic, mentioned a vision that had caused him to change his mind. One of Adhemar's own entourage, Bertrand of Le Puy, announced that the bishop and his standard-bearer had both come to him in a vision to admit that the Lance was genuine. Faced by this impressive evidence, Arnulf publicly confessed that he was convinced; but his friends continued to cast doubt on the whole story; till at last Peter Bartholomew in a fury demanded to be allowed to defend himself by the ordeal of fire. Whatever the truth may have been, he clearly by now believed firmly in his divine inspiration.

The ordeal took place on Good Friday, 8 April. Two piles of logs, blessed by the bishops, were erected in a narrow passage and set alight. Peter Bartholomew, clad only in a tunic, with the Lance in his hand, leapt quickly through the flames. He emerged horribly burnt and would have collapsed back into the fire had not Raymond Pilet caught hold of him. For twelve days he lingered on in agony, then died of his wounds. As a result of the ordeal the Lance was utterly discredited, save only by the Provençals, who maintained that Peter had passed safely through the flames but had been pushed back by the enthusiastic crowd in their eagerness to touch his sacred tunic. Count Raymond still kept the Lance with all reverence in his chapel.[1]

The army lingered on for a month outside Arqa before Raymond could be induced to abandon the siege. The fighting there had cost many lives, including that of Anselm of Ribemont, whose letters to his liege lord, the Archbishop of Reims, had given a vivid account of the Crusade.[2] On 13 May Raymond yielded to his colleagues' persuasion and, with tears in his eyes, ordered the camp

---

[1] Raymond of Aguilers, XVII–XVIII, pp. 279–88, in support of Peter Bartholomew; Fulcher of Chartres, I, xviii, 4–5, pp. 238–41; Albert of Aix, V, 13, p. 452; Radulph of Caen, CVIII, p. 682. Both Fulcher and Albert are sceptical but non-committal. Radulph is frankly hostile to Peter. The author of the *Gesta* omits the episode.

[2] Raymond of Aguilers, XVI, pp. 276–7; *Gesta Francorum*, X, 35, p. 188; Fulcher of Chartres, I, xxv, 8, p. 270, who tell us that he was killed by a stone.

to be struck; and the whole host moved down to Tripoli. There had been further discussions about the route to be followed. The Syrians informed Raymond that there was an easy road passing through Damascus, but though food was plentiful there, water was short. The road over the Lebanon was well watered, but it was difficult for beasts of burden. The third alternative was the coast road; but there were many places where it could be blocked by a handful of the enemy. However, local prophecies declared that the deliverers of Jerusalem would travel along the coast. This was the road that was chosen, less for its prophetic reputation than for the contact that it provided with the English and Genoese fleets that were now cruising in Levantine waters.[1]

As the Crusaders approached, the Emir of Tripoli hastened to buy immunity for his capital and its suburbs by releasing some three hundred Christian captives that were in the town. He compensated them with fifteen thousand bezants and fifteen fine horses; and he provided pack-animals and provender for the whole army. He was further reported to have offered to embrace Christianity if the Franks defeated the Fatimids.[2]

On Monday, 16 May, the Crusaders left Tripoli, accompanied by guides provided by the Emir; who led them safely along the dangerous road that rounded the cape of Ras Shaqqa. Passing peacefully through the Emir's towns of Batrun and Jebail, they reached the Fatimid frontier on the Dog River on 19 May. The Fatimids kept no troops in their northern territory, except for small garrisons in the towns on the coast, but they possessed a considerable navy, which could provide additional defence for these towns. Thus, though the Crusaders did not meet with any opposition on the road, they could not hope to capture any of the ports that they passed; and the Christian fleet could no longer keep in touch with them. Fear of running short of supplies obliged them thenceforward to hurry on as quickly as possible to their final objective.

---

[1] Raymond of Aguilers, xviii, pp. 288, 290–1.
[2] *Ibid.* p. 291; *Gesta Francorum*, x, 35–6, pp. 188–90.

As they drew near to Beirut the local inhabitants, dreading the destruction of the rich gardens and orchards that surrounded the city, hastened to offer them gifts and a free passage through their lands on condition that the fruit trees, the vines and the crops were unharmed. The princes accepted the terms and led the army quickly on to Sidon, which was reached on 20 May. The garrison of Sidon was of sterner stuff and made a sortie against the Crusaders as they were encamped on the banks of the Nahr al-Awali. The sortie was repulsed; and the Crusaders retorted by ravaging the gardens in the suburbs. But they moved on as soon as possible to the neighbourhood of Tyre, where they waited two days to allow Baldwin of Le Bourg and a number of knights from Antioch and from Edessa to catch them up. The streams and greenery of the neighbourhood made it a delightful halting-place. The garrison of Tyre stayed behind its walls and did not molest them. Tyre was left on the 23rd; and the army crossed without difficulty over the pass called the Ladder of Tyre and over the heights of Naqoura, and arrived outside Acre on the 24th. The governor, following the example of Beirut, secured immunity for the fertile farms around the town by the gift of ample provisions. From Acre the army marched to Haifa and along the coast under Mount Carmel to Caesarea, where four days were spent, from the 26th to the 30th, in order that Whitsun might be properly celebrated. While it was encamped there a pigeon was killed by a hawk overhead and fell near the tent of the Bishop of Apt. It was found to be a carrier, with a message from the governor of Acre to rouse the Moslems of Palestine against the invaders.[1]

When the march was resumed, the coast was followed only as far as Arsuf, where the army turned inland, arriving before Ramleh on 3 June. Ramleh, unlike most of the towns of Palestine, was a Moslem town. Before the Turkish invasions it had been the administrative capital of the province, but had declined in recent years. The approach of the Crusaders alarmed the inhabitants; the

---

[1] Raymond of Aguilers, XVIII–XIX, p. 291; *Gesta Francorum*, X, 36, pp. 190–2; Fulcher of Chartres, I, xxv, 10–12, pp. 271–6.

garrison was small and they were too far from the sea for the Egyptian navy to help them. They fled in a body from their homes, away toward the south-west, having first, as an act of defiance, destroyed the great Church of St George that stood in the ruined village of Lydda, a mile from Ramleh. When Robert of Flanders and Gaston of Béarn rode up in the van of the Crusading army they found the streets deserted and the houses empty.

The occupation of a Moslem town in the heart of the Holy Land elated the Crusaders. They vowed at once to rebuild the sanctuary of St George and to erect Ramleh and Lydda into a lordship to be his patrimony, and to create a new diocese whose bishop should be its lord. A Norman priest, Robert of Rouen, was appointed to the see. As at Albara this did not mean the displacement of a Greek bishop in favour of a Latin, but the establishment of a bishopric in conquered Moslem country. The appointment showed that public opinion amongst the Crusaders considered that conquered territory should be given to the Church. Robert was left in charge of Ramleh with a small garrison to protect him.[1] Meanwhile the princes debated what next should be done; for some considered that it would be foolish to attack Jerusalem in the height of summer. It would be better, they argued, to advance against the real enemy, Egypt. After some discussion their advice was rejected and the march to Jerusalem was resumed on 6 June.[2]

From Ramleh the army took the old road that winds up into the Judaean hills to the north of the present thoroughfare. As it passed through the village of Emmaus envoys came to the princes from the city of Bethlehem, whose entirely Christian population begged to be delivered from the yoke of the Moslems. Tancred and Baldwin of Le Bourg at once rode off with a small detachment of knights over the hills to Bethlehem. They arrived in the middle of the night, and the frightened citizens at first believed them to be part of an Egyptian army come to reinforce the defence of Jerusalem. When

---

[1] Raymond of Aguilers, XIX, pp. 291–2; *Gesta Francorum, loc. cit.*; William of Tyre, VII, 22, vol. I, pt I, p. 313, who gives us the name of the bishop.

[2] Raymond of Aguilers, XIX, p. 292.

dawn broke and the knights were recognized as Christians, the whole city came out in procession, with all the relics and the crosses from the Church of the Nativity, to welcome their rescuers and to kiss their hands.[1]

While the birthplace of Christ was being restored to Christian rule, the main Christian army pressed on all day and through the night towards Jerusalem. It was heartened by an eclipse of the moon, foreboding the eclipse of the Crescent. Next morning a hundred of Tancred's knights from Bethlehem rejoined their comrades. Later in the morning, the Crusaders reached the summit of the road, at the Mosque of the prophet Samuel, on the hill-top that the pilgrims called Montjoie; and Jerusalem with its walls and towers rose in the distance before them. By that evening of Tuesday, 7 June 1099, the Christian army was encamped before the Holy City.[2]

[1] Fulcher of Chartres, I, xxv, 13-17, pp. 277-81; Albert of Aix, v, 44-5, pp. 461-3.
[2] *Gesta Francorum*, x, 37, p. 194; Raymond of Aguilers, xx, p. 292; Albert of Aix, v, 45, p. 463.

CHAPTER II

THE TRIUMPH OF THE CROSS

*'Shout unto God with the voice of triumph. For the Lord
most high is terrible.'*   PSALMS XLVII, I, 2

The city of Jerusalem was one of the great fortresses of the medieval
world. Since the days of the Jebusites its site had been famed for
its strength, which the skill of men had improved down the
centuries. The walls beneath which the Crusaders found themselves followed the same line as the walls built later by the Ottoman
Sultan, Suleiman the Magnificent, which surround the old city
to-day. They had been laid out when Hadrian rebuilt the city; and
the Byzantines, the Ommayads and the Fatimids in turn had added
to them and repaired them. On the east the wall was protected by
the steep slopes of the ravine of the Kedron. On the south-east the
ground fell to the Vale of Gehenna. A third valley that was only
slightly less deep skirted the western wall. It was only on the south-
west, where the wall cut across Mount Sion, and along the length
of the northern wall that the terrain favoured an attack on the
fortifications. The citadel, the Tower of David, was placed half-
way down the western wall, commanding the road that slanted up
the hill-side to the Jaffa Gate. Though there were no springs within
the city, its ample cisterns secured the water supply. The Roman
drainage system, still in use in the twentieth century, kept it from
disease.

The defence of the city was in the hands of the Fatimid governor,
Iftikhar ad-Dawla. The walls were in good condition; and he had
a strong garrison of Arab and Sudanese troops. On the news of
the Franks' approach he took the precaution of blocking or
poisoning the wells outside the city, and driving the flocks and

herds from the pastures round the city into places of safety. Next, he ordered all the Christian population of the city, Orthodox and heretic alike, to retire outside the city walls. The Jews, however, were permitted to remain within. It was a wise move. In the tenth century the Christians outnumbered the Moslems in Jerusalem; and though the Caliph Hakim's persecutions had reduced their numbers, and though many more, including most of the Orthodox clergy, had departed with the Patriarch during the uneasy times that followed Ortoq's death, there were still thousands left, useless as fighting men as they were forbidden to carry arms, and unreliable in a battle against fellow-Christians. Moreover their exile meant that there would be fewer mouths to feed in the beleaguered city. At the same time Iftikhar sent urgently to Egypt for armed aid.[1]

Even had the lie of the land permitted it, the Crusaders had insufficient forces to invest the whole city. They concentrated their strength on the sectors where they could come near to the walls. Robert of Normandy took up his station along the northern wall opposite to the Gate of Flowers (Herod's Gate), with Robert of Flanders on his right, opposite to the Gate of the Column (St Stephen's or the Damascus Gate). Godfrey of Lorraine took over the area covering the north-west angle of the city, as far down as the Jaffa Gate. He was joined here by Tancred, who rode up when the army was already in position, bringing flocks that he had taken on his way from Bethlehem. To his south was Raymond of Toulouse, who, finding that the valley kept him too far from the walls, moved up after two or three days on to Mount Sion. The eastern and south-eastern sectors were left unguarded.[2]

The siege began on 7 June, the very day that the Crusade arrived

---

[1] Fulcher of Chartres (I, xxvii, 12, p. 300) mentions 'Aethiopian' troops. Raymond of Aguilers (xx, pp. 293-4) and the *Gesta Francorum* (x, 37, p. 198) mention the poisoning of the wells. The Armenian Catholicus Vahram was in Jerusalem at the time but it seems that he was able to escape out of the city (Matthew of Edessa, II, clvii, p. 225).

[2] Raymond of Aguilers, xx, p. 293; *Gesta Francorum*, x, 37, p. 194; Albert of Aix, v, 46, pp. 463-4.

at the walls. But it was soon clear that time was on the side of the besieged. Iftikhar was well supplied with food and water. His armaments were better than the Franks'; and he was able to strengthen his towers with sacks full of cotton and of hay, which enabled them to withstand the shock of the bombardment by the Frankish mangonels. If he could hold out till the relieving army from Egypt appeared, all would be over with the Crusade. But, large though the garrison was, it was barely sufficient to man all the walls. The Crusaders on their part soon were in difficulties over their water supply. Iftikhar's measures had been effective. The only source of pure water available to the besiegers came from the pool of Siloam, below the south walls, which was dangerously exposed to missiles from the city. To supplement their supplies of water, they had to travel six miles or more. Knowing this, the garrison would send out small companies to ambush the paths to the springs. Many soldiers and pilgrims perished from such surprise attacks. Food also began to run short; for little could be obtained near the city. Heat and dust and lack of shade added to the discomfort of the Crusaders, coming as they did from cooler climates and wearing, many of them, armour ill-suited to the Judaean summer. It was clear to them all that they could not afford a long siege but must quickly take the city by assault.[1]

On 12 June the princes made a pilgrimage to the Mount of Olives. There an aged hermit addressed them, bidding them attack the walls on the morrow. They protested that they lacked the machines for a successful assault; but the hermit would have none of that. If they had faith, God, he said, would give them the victory. Emboldened by his words, they ordered a general attack to be made next morning. But the hermit was mistaken or else their faith was too weak. The Crusaders went to the attack with great fervour and soon overran the outer defences of the north wall. But they had too few ladders to be able to scale the walls simultaneously in a sufficient number of places. After several hours

[1] Raymond of Aguilers, xx, pp. 293–4; *Gesta Francorum*, x, 37, pp. 194–8.

of desperate fighting they saw that their attempts were useless and withdrew.[1]

The failure of the assault caused bitter disappointment; but it made clear to the princes the need for building more siege machines. At a council on 15 June they decided to withhold further attacks till they were better supplied with mangonels and ladders. But they lacked the material with which to build them. As at Antioch, they were now saved by the timely arrival of help from the sea. On 17 June six Christian vessels put into the harbour of Jaffa, which they found deserted by the Moslems. The squadron consisted of two Genoese galleys, under the brothers Embriaco, and four ships probably from the English fleet. They were carrying food supplies and armaments, including the ropes, nails and bolts required for making siege machines. Hearing of their arrival the Crusaders at once sent a small detachment to establish contact with them. Near Ramleh these troops were ambushed by a Moslem company, operating from Ascalon, and were only rescued by the coming of Raymond Pilet and his men close on their heels. Meanwhile an Egyptian fleet appeared off the coast and blockaded Jaffa. One of the English ships slipped through the blockade and sailed back to Lattakieh. The other ships were abandoned by their crews as soon as the cargo was landed; and the sailors marched up under Raymond Pilet's escort to the camp outside Jerusalem. They themselves and the goods that they brought were very welcome. But it was still necessary to find wood with which to build the machines. Little was to be obtained on the bare hills round Jerusalem; and the Crusaders were obliged to send expeditions for many miles to collect what was required. It was only when Tancred and Robert of Flanders penetrated with their followers as far as the forests round Samaria and came back laden with logs and planks carried on camel-back or by captive Moslems, that work could start upon the machines. Scaling-ladders were made; and Raymond and Godfrey each began to construct a wooden castle fitted with catapults and set on wheels. Gaston of Béarn was responsible for

[1] Raymond of Aguilers, xx, p. 293; *Gesta Francorum*, x, 37, p. 196.

the construction of Godfrey's castle, and William Ricou of Raymond's.[1]

But the work went slowly; and meanwhile the Franks suffered terribly from the heat. For many days the sirocco blew, with its deadly effect on the nerves of men unused to it. The provision of water grew increasingly difficult. Numbers of the pack-animals and the herds that the army had collected died daily from thirst. Detachments would go as far as the Jordan to find water. The native Christians were well-disposed and acted as guides to the springs and the forests of the neighbourhood; but it was impossible to prevent forays and ambushes from Moslem soldiers, either of the garrison or of companies that were wandering freely round the country. Quarrels arose again among the princes, concerning, first, the possession of Bethlehem. Tancred had liberated the town and had left his banner waving over the Church of the Nativity. But the clergy and the rival princes felt it to be wrong that so holy a building should be in the power of one secular lord. Tancred defended his claims to Bethlehem; and, though public opinion was against him, the matter was deferred. Next, discussions were begun about the future status of Jerusalem. Some of the knights suggested that a king should be appointed; but the clergy unanimously opposed this, saying that no Christian could call himself king in the city where Christ was crowned and suffered. Here again public opinion was on the side of the clergy; and further discussions were postponed. Their physical miseries, combined with disappointment at the failure of the attempted assault and the renewed quarrels of the princes, induced many of the Crusaders even now to desert the Crusade. A company of them went down to the Jordan to undergo rebaptism in the holy river; then, after gathering palm branches from the river bank, they journeyed straight down to Jaffa, hoping to find boats to carry them back to Europe.[2]

Early in July it was learnt in the camp that a great army had set out from Egypt to relieve Jerusalem. The princes realized that

[1] Raymond of Aguilers, xx, pp. 294-7; *Gesta Francorum*, x, 37, pp. 196-200.
[2] Raymond of Aguilers, xx, pp. 295-6.

there was no time for delay. But the morale of their men was low. Once more a vision came to their support. On the morning of 6 July the priest Peter Desiderius, who had already testified that he had seen Bishop Adhemar after his death, came to Adhemar's brother, William Hugh of Monteil and to his own lord, Isoard of Gap, to say that the bishop had again appeared to him. After ordering the Crusaders to give up their selfish schemes, Adhemar ordered them to hold a fast and to walk in procession barefoot round the walls of Jerusalem. If they did so with repentant hearts, within nine days they would capture Jerusalem. When Peter Desiderius had claimed to see Adhemar suffering hell-fire for his doubting of the Holy Lance, he had been widely disbelieved; but now, perhaps because the beloved bishop was shown in a nobler light, and because the family of Monteil gave their support, the vision was at once accepted as genuine by all the army. Adhemar's instructions were eagerly obeyed. A fast was commanded and steadfastly observed during the next three days. On Friday, 8 July, a solemn procession wound around the path that surrounded the city. The bishops and priests of the Crusade came first, bearing crosses and their holy relics. The princes and the knights followed, then the foot soldiers and the pilgrims. All were barefoot. The Moslems gathered on the walls to mock them; but they gloried in such mockery, and having completed the circuit ascended the Mount of Olives. There Peter the Hermit preached to them and after him Raymond's chaplain, Raymond of Aguilers, and Robert of Normandy's chaplain, Arnulf of Rohes, who was now considered the finest preacher with the army. Their eloquence moved and excited the host. Even Raymond and Tancred forgot their quarrels and vowed to fight together for the Cross.[1]

The enthusiasm lasted on. During the next two days, in spite of their sufferings from thirst, the men of the army worked hard to complete the great siege towers. The skill of the Genoese, under William Embriaco, was of great assistance; and even the old men

---

[1] Raymond of Aguilers, **xx**, pp. 296–7; letter of Daimbert to the Pope, in Hagenmeyer, *op. cit.* pp. 170–1; *Gesta Francorum*, **x**, 38, pp. 200–2.

and the women did their part in sewing ox-hide and camel-hide and nailing it on the exposed parts of the woodwork, as a protection against the Greek fire used by the Saracens. On the 10th the wooden structures were ready and were wheeled up to their stations, the one against the north wall and the other on Mount Sion. A third, slightly smaller, was built to go against the north-west corner of the defences. The work of construction had been carefully carried on out of sight of the soldiers of the garrison; who were astounded and alarmed to find such castles opposing them. The governor, Iftikhar, hastened to reinforce the weaker sections of the defences; and the siege towers were steadily bombarded with stones and with liquid fire to prevent them from closing in against the walls.[1]

It was decided that the assault should begin during the night of 13-14 July. The main attack would be launched simultaneously from Mount Sion and on the eastern sector of the northern wall, with a feint attack on the north-west angle. According to Raymond of Aguilers, whose figures need not be doubted, the effective fighting strength of the army was now twelve thousand foot-soldiers and twelve or thirteen hundred knights. There were in addition many pilgrims, whose numbers he does not try to assess, men too old or too sick to fight, and women and children. The first task of the assailants was to bring their wooden castles right up to the walls; which involved the filling up of the ditch that ran round their feet. All night long and during the day of the 14th the Crusaders concentrated on their task, suffering heavily from the stones and the liquid fire of the defence, and answering with a heavy bombardment from their own mangonels. By the evening of the 14th Raymond's men had succeeded in wheeling their tower over the ditch against the wall. But the defence was fierce; for it seems that Iftikhar himself commanded in this sector. Raymond could not establish a foothold on the wall itself. Next morning Godfrey's tower closed in on the north wall, close to the present Gate of Flowers. Godfrey and his brother, Eustace of Boulogne, commanded from the upper storey. About midday they succeeded in

[1] Raymond of Aguilers, **xx**, p. 298; *Gesta Francorum*, **x**, 38, p. 200.

making a bridge from the tower to the top of the wall; and two Flemish knights, Litold and Gilbert of Tournai, led the pick of the Lotharingian army across, followed soon by Godfrey himself. Once a sector of the wall was captured, scaling ladders enabled many more of the assailants to climb into the city. While Godfrey remained on the wall encouraging the newcomers and sending men to open the Gate of the Column to the main forces of the Crusade, Tancred and his men, who had been close behind the Lorrainers, penetrated deep into the city streets. The Moslems, seeing their defences broken, fled towards the Haram es-Sherif, the Temple area, where the Dome of the Rock and the Mosque of al-Aqsa stood, intending to use the latter as their last fortress. But they had no time to put it into a state of defence. As they crowded in and up on the roof, Tancred was upon them. Hastily they surrendered to him, promising a heavy ransom, and took his banner to display it over the mosque. He had already desecrated and pillaged the Dome of the Rock. Meanwhile the inhabitants of the city fled back in confusion towards the southern quarters, where Iftikhar was still holding out against Raymond. Early in the afternoon he realized that all was lost. He withdrew into the Tower of David, which he offered to hand over to Raymond with a great sum of treasure in return for his life and the lives of his bodyguard. Raymond accepted the terms and occupied the Tower. Iftikhar and his men were safely escorted out of the city and permitted to join the Moslem garrison of Ascalon.[1]

They were the only Moslems in Jerusalem to save their lives. The Crusaders, maddened by so great a victory after such suffering, rushed through the streets and into the houses and mosques killing all that they met, men, women and children alike. All that afternoon and all through the night the massacre continued. Tancred's

[1] Raymond of Aguilers, xx, pp. 293–300; *Gesta Francorum*, x, 38, pp. 202–4. These two eyewitness accounts agree with each other. Fulcher of Chartres, I, xxvii, 5–13, pp. 295–301. Fulcher and Raymond agree in placing the entry into the city at midday. The *Gesta* says that it took place at the hour of the death of Christ. Albert of Aix (VI, 19–28, pp. 477–83) gives a long but less reliable account.

banner was no protection to the refugees in the mosque of al-Aqsa. Early next morning a band of Crusaders forced an entry into the mosque and slew everyone. When Raymond of Aguilers later that morning went to visit the Temple area he had to pick his way through corpses and blood that reached up to his knees.[1]

The Jews of Jerusalem fled in a body to their chief synagogue. But they were held to have aided the Moslems; and no mercy was shown to them. The building was set on fire and they were all burnt within.[2]

The massacre at Jerusalem profoundly impressed all the world. No one can say how many victims it involved; but it emptied Jerusalem of its Moslem and Jewish inhabitants. Many even of the Christians were horrified by what had been done; and amongst the Moslems, who had been ready hitherto to accept the Franks as another factor in the tangled politics of the time, there was henceforward a clear determination that the Franks must be driven out. It was this bloodthirsty proof of Christian fanaticism that recreated the fanaticism of Islam. When, later, wiser Latins in the East sought to find some basis on which Christian and Moslem could work together, the memory of the massacre stood always in their way.

When there were no more Moslems left to be slain, the princes of the Crusade went in solemn state through the desolate Christian quarter, deserted since Iftikhar had exiled its inhabitants, to give thanks to God in the Church of the Holy Sepulchre. Then, on 17 July, they met together to appoint a ruler for the conquered city.[3]

The ruler whom most would have welcomed was dead. The

[1] Raymond of Aguilers, xx, p. 300; *Gesta Francorum*, x, 38, pp. 204–6; letter of Daimbert in Hagenmeyer, *op. cit.* p. 171; Abu'l Feda, *op. cit.* p. 4, and Ibn al-Athir, *op. cit.* pp. 198–9, describe the massacres. The latter gives Raymond the credit of having kept his word. See also Ibn al-Qalānisī, *Damascus Chronicle*, p. 48.
[2] Ibn al-Qalānisī, *loc. cit.*
[3] Raymond of Aguilers, xx, p. 300; *Gesta Francorum*, x, 38, p. 206; Fulcher of Chartres, I, xxix, 1–4, pp. 304–6.

whole army grieved that Bishop Adhemar of Le Puy should not be living to see the triumph of the cause that he had served. It was not to be believed that he had not really seen it. Soldier after soldier testified that there had been a warrior fighting in the forefront of the assault, in whom they had recognized the features of the Bishop.[1] Others too, who would have rejoiced in the victory, did not survive to hear of it. Symeon, Patriarch of Jerusalem, had died a few days earlier in exile in Cyprus.[2] Far away in Italy the founder of the Crusade was lying sick. On 29 July 1099, a fortnight after his soldiers had entered the Holy City, but before any news of it could reach him, Pope Urban II died at Rome.[3]

[1] Raymond of Aguilers, *loc. cit.*
[2] Albert of Aix, VI, 39, p. 489.
[3] *Vita Urbani II*, in *Liber Pontificalis*, II, p. 293.

CHAPTER III

'ADVOCATUS SANCTI SEPULCHRI'

'In those days there was no king in Israel.' JUDGES XVIII, 1

The goal had been reached. Jerusalem was recovered to Christendom. But how was it to be preserved? What was to be its government? The question over which every Crusader must have pondered in private could not now be deferred. It seems that public opinion, remembering that the Crusade had been planned by the Church for the glory of Christ, felt that the Church should have the ultimate authority. Had Adhemar of Le Puy still been alive there is no doubt that he would have been expected to plan the constitution and to name its officers. He was beloved and respected, and he knew Pope Urban's wishes. Probably he envisaged an ecclesiastical state under the Patriarch Symeon, with himself as papal legate to act as his adviser, and with Raymond of Toulouse as lay protector and commander of its armies. But we cannot claim to describe his intentions; for they had perished with him. Pope Urban had, indeed, unknown as yet to the Crusade, appointed a legate to succeed him, Daimbert of Pisa.[1] But Daimbert proved to be personally so ambitious and at the same time so easily influenced that he cannot be regarded as an interpreter of papal policy. There was no one left with the Crusade whose advice would be unquestionably obeyed.

On 17 July the leaders met together to deal with immediate matters of administration. The streets and houses had to be cleared of corpses, whose disposal must be arranged. Quarters within the city had to be allotted to the soldiers and the pilgrims. Preparations

[1] Daimbert reached Lattakieh by September 1099. He must therefore have left Italy well before the capture of Jerusalem. See below, pp. 299–300.

must be made to meet the coming Egyptian counter-attack. It was also discussed whether Tancred should be allowed to keep all the treasure, which included eight huge silver lamps, that he had taken from the Dome of the Rock.[1] Then someone raised the question of the election of a king. The clergy at once protested. Spiritual needs came first. Before a king could be elected a Patriarch must be appointed, who would preside over the election. William of Tyre, writing nearly a century later when the monarchy was fully accepted, regarded this, archbishop though he was, as a scandalous attempt of the Church to go beyond its rights. But it was only resented at the time because its promoters were unworthy churchmen. A Patriarch was needed. Had Symeon still been living, his rights would have been respected. Adhemar had approved of him; and the Crusaders remembered gratefully the gifts that he had sent to them to Antioch. But no other Greek or Syrian ecclesiastic would have been acceptable. None, indeed, was there to put in a claim; for the higher Orthodox clergy of Jerusalem had followed the Patriarch into exile. A Latin must be elevated to the see; but amongst the Latin clergy there was now no one outstanding. After Adhemar's death, William of Orange had been the most respected of the bishops. But he had died at Maarat an-Numan. The most active ecclesiastic now was a Norman-Italian, Arnulf, Bishop of Marturana. He proposed that his friend Arnulf Malecorne of Rohes, Robert of Normandy's chaplain, should become Patriarch and he himself would be rewarded by the archbishopric of Bethlehem. Arnulf of Rohes was not undistinguished. He had been tutor to William the Conqueror's daughter, the nun Cecilia, and she had induced her brother Robert to engage him and to promise him a bishopric. He was an excellent preacher and a man of letters but he was considered to be very worldly, and he was remembered as the enemy of Peter Bartholomew. Moreover the whole transaction looked like a Norman plot. The southern French clergy, supported, no doubt, by Raymond of Toulouse, would not co-

[1] Raymond of Aguilers, xx, pp. 300–1; *Gesta Francorum*, x, 39, p. 206; Fulcher of Chartres, I, xxviii, 1–2, pp. 301–3.

operate; and the proposal to elect the Patriarch before the king was abandoned. The episode was not as important as William of Tyre believed. As the sequel showed, public opinion still backed the Church against the secular power.[1]

The next days were spent in intrigues about the appointment to the throne. Of the great princes that had set out from Constantinople, only four now were left with the Crusade; Raymond of Toulouse, Godfrey of Lorraine, Robert of Flanders and Robert of Normandy. Eustace of Boulogne had always played a shadowy role behind his brother Godfrey; and Tancred, for all his prowess, had few followers and was considered to be little more than Bohemond's poor relation. Of these, Raymond was the most formidable candidate. His age, his wealth, his experience and his long association with Adhemar were assets that no one else commanded. But he was unpopular with his colleagues. He had shown too often and too arrogantly that he regarded himself as the secular leader of the Crusade. His policy of friendship with the Emperor was greatly disliked, even by many of his own following. His few months as unquestioned commander had not been successful; the fiasco at Arqa and the disavowal of the Holy Lance had damaged his prestige; and, though his personal courage and energy were not doubted, he had not brought off any great victory as a soldier. As a king, he would be overbearing and autocratic but would not inspire confidence in his generalship nor in his politics. Of the others, Robert of Flanders was the ablest. But he was known to wish to return to his home as soon as Jerusalem was secure. Robert of Normandy was well liked and commanded prestige as the head of the Norman race. But he was not a formidable character; and he too was inclined to return to Europe. There remained Godfrey. As Duke of Lower Lorraine he had in the past

[1] Raymond of Aguilers, xx–xxi, pp. 301–2; William of Tyre, IX, 1, vol. I, pt I, pp. 364–6. Fulcher of Chartres (I, xxx, 2, p. 308) says that no Patriarch was elected till the Pope's advice should be obtained. He is probably alluding to this first debate. For Arnulf's early career, see David, *Robert Curthose*, pp. 217–20. David calls him Arnulf of Choques and considers that the name 'of Rohes' is incorrect.

filled a higher post than any of his colleagues. He had not been a very efficient duke; and his behaviour at Constantinople had shown him to possess the suspicious obstinacy of a weak and unintelligent man. But his failings as a statesman and an administrator were unknown to the Crusaders, who saw him to be a gallant and godly man and a devoted servant of their cause. It was said that when the electors made inquiries about the private lives of each leader, Godfrey's entourage had no fault in him to report save for an excessive fondness for pious exercises.[1]

Who constituted the electors is unknown. Probably they were the higher clergy and such knights as were tenants-in-chief to the princes of the Crusade. The crown was first offered to Raymond; but he refused it. His refusal has surprised historians, so obvious was his ambition to lead the Crusade. But he realized that the offer did not have the sincere support of the majority of the Crusaders and that his colleagues would never in fact submit to his authority. Even his own soldiers, anxious to return to Europe, declared themselves to be against his acceptance. He therefore announced that he would not wish to be king in Christ's holy city, hoping thus to make it impossible for anyone else to become king. The electors then turned with relief to Godfrey, who was known to be favoured by Robert of Flanders and Robert of Normandy. Godfrey, after some show of unwillingness, accepted the power but asked to be excused from wearing the title of a king. He would be called *Advocatus Sancti Sepulchri*, the dedicated defender of the Holy Sepulchre.[2]

Raymond considered that he had been tricked. But Godfrey was certainly sincere when he declined to wear a crown in the city

---

[1] William of Tyre, IX, I, vol. I, pt I, pp. 365–6.
[2] Raymond of Aguilers, XX, p. 301, reporting Raymond's refusal of the crown; *Gesta Francorum*, X, 39, pp. 206–8, saying that Godfrey was elected 'princeps civitatis' for the purpose of fighting against the Saracens; Fulcher of Chartres, I, XXX, I, using the title of 'princeps'; Albert of Aix, VI, 33, pp. 485–6, also mentioning Raymond's refusal; William of Tyre, IX, 2, vol. I, pt I, pp. 366–7. For Godfrey's title, see Moeller, 'Godefroid de Bouillon et l'Avouerie du Saint-Sépulcre', *passim*.

where Christ had worn a crown of thorns. His chief asset was that his piety corresponded with the piety of the average Crusader. He never rid himself of the conviction that the Church of Christ should be the ultimate ruler of the Holy Land. It was only after his death and after the bulk of the pilgrims had gone home, leaving behind a colony mainly made up of adventurers and practical men of affairs, that a king could be crowned in Jerusalem.[1]

Raymond took Godfrey's victory very badly. He possessed the Tower of David, and he refused to yield it to the new ruler, saying that he intended to remain in Jerusalem to celebrate the following Easter there, and meantime the Tower would be his residence. After Robert of Flanders and Robert of Normandy had both remonstrated with him, he agreed to leave it in the care of the Bishop of Albara till a general council of the Crusade should settle the case. But soon after he had moved out, the bishop, without waiting for a judicial decision, handed it over to Godfrey. The bishop excused himself before Raymond, saying that he was defenceless and obliged to give way; but Raymond of Aguilers himself saw the great stacks of arms that the faithless prelate took with him when he moved to a house near the Holy Sepulchre. He may have been encouraged in his action by those of Raymond's men who were anxious to induce their master to return to France. In his rage Raymond at first announced that he would at once return home. He left Jerusalem, but went down with all his troops to the valley of the Jordan. Obedient to the instructions given him by Peter Bartholomew at Antioch, he led his men, each carrying a palm-leaf, from Jericho to the river. When he returned the whole company, reciting prayers and psalms, bathed in the holy stream and dressed themselves in clean garments; 'though why the holy man told us to do all this', remarked Raymond of Aguilers, 'we do not yet know'. Unwilling to return to the scene of his humiliation at Jerusalem, Raymond then set up his camp at Jericho.[2]

---

[1] See Chalandon, *Histoire de la première Croisade*, pp. 290-2.
[2] Raymond of Aguilers, xx, pp. 301-2; William of Tyre, IX, 3, vol. I, pt I, pp. 367-8.

Raymond's failure to secure the crown weakened his followers. When the clergy assembled on 1 August to elect a Patriarch the opposition of the Provençals to Arnulf of Rohes was ineffectual. Secure in the support of the Lorrainers and the Normans of France and Italy, the Bishop of Marturano was able to persuade the majority in the assembly to appoint Arnulf. In vain Raymond of Aguilers and his friends pointed out that the election was un-canonical, as Arnulf was not even a subdeacon, and that his morals were such that rhymes had been made about them in the army. The general public welcomed his enthronement.[1] As a politician Arnulf was moderate. If the clergy had expected him to dictate to Godfrey, they were disappointed. Conscious, perhaps, that he did not carry the weight to be the ruler of Jerusalem, he restricted his activities to ecclesiastical affairs. There his aim was to latinize the see. With Godfrey's approval he installed twenty canons to hold daily services at the Holy Sepulchre, and he provided the church with bells to call the people to prayer—the Moslems had never permitted the Christians to use them. Next, he banished the priests of the eastern rites who had held services in the church. For then, as now, it contained altars belonging to all the sects of oriental Christendom, not only Orthodox Greeks and Georgians but also Armenians, Jacobites and Copts. The local Christian population had eagerly returned to Jerusalem on the morrow of the Latin conquest; but now they began to regret the change of masters. When they had been ejected from the city by Iftikhar, certain of the Orthodox priests had taken with them the holiest relic of the Church of Jerusalem, the major portion of the true Cross. They were unwilling to hand it over now to a pontiff who ignored their rights. It was only by the use of torture that Arnulf forced its guardians to reveal where they had hidden it. But, though their resentment was growing, the native Orthodox Christians had no choice but to accept the Latin hierarchy. Their own higher

---

[1] Raymond of Aguilers, **XXI**, p. 30; *Gesta Francorum*, X, 39, p. 208, calling Arnulf 'sapientissimum et honorabilem virum'; William of Tyre, IX, 4, vol. I, pt I, p. 369.

clergy were scattered; and it never occurred to them to appoint their own bishops and Patriarch in opposition to the Latins. There was as yet no schism between eastern and western Orthodoxy in Palestine, though Arnulf had taken the first steps towards making it inevitable. The heretic churches, who had enjoyed tolerance under the Moslems, found that the Latin conquest began for them a period of eclipse.[1]

Godfrey's relations with the colleagues that had hitherto supported him deteriorated after his elevation. For some reason he soon offended Robert of Normandy; and Robert of Flanders grew cooler towards him. Tancred had gone off meanwhile to Nablus, whose inhabitants had sent to Jerusalem surrendering themselves into the Crusaders' hands. Possibly in order to prevent his usual practice of taking all the booty for himself, he was accompanied by Godfrey's brother, Eustace of Boulogne. They were well received there; but it seems that they obtained no loot.[2]

Soon after their departure an Egyptian embassy reached Jerusalem, to reproach the Franks for their breach of faith and to order them to leave Palestine. It was followed by the news that the Egyptian army, under the command of the vizier, al-Afdal himself, had crossed into Palestine and was advancing on Ascalon. Godfrey therefore sent to Tancred and to Eustace, telling them to descend into the maritime plain and report on the movements of the enemy. They hastened down towards Caesarea, then turned southward to Ramleh. On their way they captured several scouts sent ahead by the Egyptians; and from them they extracted information about the numbers and the disposition of the vizier's forces. Gathering that al-Afdal was waiting for his fleet to join him with additional supplies and that he did not expect the Franks to attack him, they sent to Godfrey to urge that the Crusaders should take him by surprise. Godfrey at once mustered his army and called upon his colleagues to join him. Robert of Flanders responded to

---

[1] Raymond of Aguilers, *loc. cit.*; Fulcher of Chartres, I, xxx, 4, pp. 309-10; William of Tyre, *loc. cit.*

[2] *Gesta Francorum*, x, 39, pp. 208-10.

the summons; but Robert of Normandy and Raymond, who was still in the Jordan valley, answered that they would wait till the news was confirmed. It was only after their own scouts had been sent to discover what was happening that they consented to move.[1]

On 9 August Godfrey set out from Jerusalem with Robert of Flanders and all their men. The Patriarch Arnulf accompanied them. When they arrived at Ramleh and met with Tancred and Eustace, the Bishop of Marturano was hastily ordered back to Jerusalem to announce how dangerous was the situation and to urge every fighting man to join the army. Robert of Normandy and Raymond were convinced by now, and left Jerusalem on the 10th. Only a tiny garrison remained behind in the city, where Peter the Hermit was instructed to hold services and processions of intercession, at which Greeks and Latins alike should pray for the victory of Christendom. Early on the 11th the whole host of the Crusaders assembled at Ibelin, a few miles beyond Ramleh. They advanced at once into the plain of Ashdod, where at dusk they discovered and rounded up the herds that the Egyptians had brought to feed their troops. After a brief night's rest they emerged into the green and fertile plain of al-Majdal, just to the north of Ascalon, where the vizier's army was encamped. They formed their battle-array in the dim light of dawn, with Raymond on the right, by the sea, the two Roberts and Tancred in the centre and Godfrey on the left; and as soon as the ranks were ordered they charged into the Egyptian army. Al-Afdal was taken entirely by surprise. His scouting was at fault; and he had not expected the Franks to be so near. His men put up hardly any resistance. In a few minutes they were fleeing in panic. A large company took refuge in a sycamore grove, where they were burnt to death. On their left flank Raymond drove great numbers into the sea. In the centre Robert of Normandy and Tancred penetrated into the heart of their camp; and Robert's bodyguard captured the vizier's standard and many of his personal belongings. The vizier himself, with a handful of officers, managed to escape into Ascalon and

[1] *Ibid.* pp. 209–10.

there took a ship to return to Egypt. In a few hours the victory was complete; and the Crusaders' possession of Jerusalem was assured.[1]

The booty taken by the victors was immense. Robert of Normandy bought the vizier's standard for twenty silver marks from the Norman that had captured it, and presented it to the Patriarch Arnulf. The vizier's sword was sold to another prince for sixty bezants. Bullion and precious stones were found in huge quantities amongst the Egyptian luggage; and a vast amount of armaments and of beasts fell into the Crusaders' hands. On Saturday, 13 August, a triumphal procession returned to Jerusalem laden with spoil. All that could not be carried with them was burnt.[2]

The significance of the victory was fully realized. But while it ensured that the Egyptians could not recover the territory that they had lost, it did not mean that at once all Palestine would be occupied by the Franks. The Egyptian navy still commanded the coasts and offered protection to the seaports. Godfrey had hoped to follow up the battle by the capture of Ascalon; whose garrison knew that it could not be held against the united forces of the Crusade. But the massacre at Jerusalem had not been forgotten. The Moslems in Ascalon had no wish to suffer a similar fate. They knew that the only survivors at Jerusalem had been those that had surrendered to Raymond of Toulouse, whose reputation for chivalry therefore stood high. They sent now to the Crusader camp, saying that they would give up the city to him alone. Godfrey, deeply suspicious of Raymond since the affair of the Tower of David, refused to recognize any terms of surrender that did not give himself the town. Raymond was angry and humiliated, and at once began to move northward with all his men; and Robert of Normandy and Robert of Flanders were so shocked by

[1] *Ibid.* pp. 210–16; Raymond of Aguilers, XXI, pp. 302–4; Fulcher of Chartres, I, xxxi, 1–11, pp. 311–18; Albert of Aix, VI, 44–50, pp. 493–7; Ibn al-Athir, *op. cit.* p. 202.

[2] *Gesta Francorum*, X, 39, pp. 216–18; Raymond of Aguilers, XXI, pp. 304–5; Albert of Aix, VI, 47, p. 495; Fulcher of Chartres, I, xxxi, 10, pp. 316–17. Both Raymond and the *Gesta* end their histories with the battle of Ascalon.

Godfrey's pettiness that they too deserted him. Without their help Godfrey could not venture to attack Ascalon, which was thus lost to the Franks for more than half a century.[1]

The little town of Arsuf next offered to surrender to Raymond. But again Godfrey refused to honour any such agreement; and again Raymond moved angrily away. Godfrey's friends declared that Raymond even encouraged the garrison of Arsuf to hold out against Godfrey, whose weakness he carefully emphasized to them.[2]

By the end of August Raymond and the two Roberts had decided to leave Palestine. Both the Duke of Normandy and the Count of Flanders were now eager to return home. They had done their Christian duty and could consider that their vows had been fulfilled. In spite of the recent quarrels Godfrey's heart sank to see them go. At their farewell interview with him he besought them when they reached Europe to do everything possible to urge soldiers to come out east to fight for the Cross, reminding them how precarious was the position of those that were staying in the Holy Land. Early in September they began their journey northward up the coast.[3] Raymond accompanied them. But in his case the departure was not so definite; for he had sworn to remain in the East. He had lost Jerusalem; but there was no reason why he should not now copy the examples of Bohemond and of Baldwin and found his own principality. The territory that could offer him most scope was central Syria, safely distant from both the Turks and the Egyptians, and mainly in the hands of the unwarlike Banū 'Ammār. He could hope, too, to have the support of Byzantium.[4]

With Raymond and the Roberts marched most of their men. A few stayed behind from each army, to settle in Palestine. But, to balance them, a number of Godfrey's men, including Baldwin of Le Bourg, returned northward under the banner of the

---

[1] Radulph of Caen, cxxxviii, p. 703; Albert of Aix, vi, 51, pp. 497–8.

[2] Albert of Aix, *loc. cit.*

[3] Albert of Aix, vi, 53, p. 499; Fulcher of Chartres, i, xxxii, 1, pp. 318–20; Orderic Vitalis, x, 11, vol. iv, p. 69.

[4] Albert of Aix, *loc. cit.* It is uncertain when Raymond decided upon a principality in central Syria.

Count of Flanders. Tancred and his small following remained in Palestine.[1]

The journey northward was achieved without difficulty. The Moslem governors of the coastal cities hastened to supply the army with provisions as it passed by. In mid-September it reached Tortosa, which was still held by a garrison of Raymond's men, and moved on to Jabala. There the leaders heard news that greatly shocked and disquieted them.[2]

Shortly before his death Pope Urban had appointed a legate to take the place of Adhemar in Palestine. His choice fell upon Daimbert, Archbishop of Pisa. Urban knew his fellow-Frenchmen well, but with the Italians he made mistakes. Daimbert had been an energetic archbishop and was known to be interested in the holy war. The Pope had therefore sent him in 1098 to be his legate at the court of King Alfonso VI of Castile. There Daimbert had shown himself full of zeal and competent in his efforts to organize the Church in the lands conquered from the Moors. But there were rumours that his administration had not been free of corruption, and in particular he had kept for himself a large proportion of the treasure sent by King Alfonso to the Pope. In spite of his vigour it was clear that he was vain, ambitious and dishonest. In appointing him legate in the East Urban went far to undo his own policy.[3]

Daimbert set out from Italy before the end of 1098. He was accompanied by a Pisan fleet, equipped by the municipality of Pisa. No doubt he hoped, by his influence over the Pisans, to use them to establish his own position, while they on their side saw how useful his help would be to obtain them concessions. They formed a lawless company. On their way eastward they indulged in profitable raids on the islands of the Heptannese, Corfu, Leucas, Cephalonia and Zante. News of their outrages soon reached Constantinople; and the Emperor sent out against them a fleet

[1] *Ibid.* VI, 54, pp. 499–500.   [2] *Ibid. loc. cit.*
[3] A hostile account of Daimbert's past life is given by Albert of Aix, VII, 7, pp. 51–2. See also *Annales Pisani* (ed. Tronci), vol. I, pp. 178 ff. It is possible that he set out before Urban knew of Adhemar's death and was either appointed legate while on his journey or assumed the authority as senior ecclesiastic in the East.

commanded by Taticius, who had not been back for many months from Antioch, and the Italian-born sailor, Landulf. The Byzantines attempted to intercept the Pisans as they sailed past Samos, but arrived too late, and failed also to catch them up off Cos. Eventually the fleets came into sight of each other off Rhodes. The Byzantines tried to force an action, and captured a Pisan ship, with a kinsman of Bohemond on board; but a sudden storm blew up and enabled the Pisans to slip away. Next, the Pisans tried to make a landing on the Cypriot coast, but were driven off with some loss by the Byzantine governor, Philocales. They then sailed across to the Syrian coast, while the Byzantine fleet put into Cyprus.[1]

Since the departure of his colleagues to Jerusalem, Bohemond had been occupied in consolidating himself in Antioch. He had little to fear from the Turks at present. His main occupation was with the Byzantines. The Emperor, he knew, would never forgive him; and so long as the Emperor possessed the best fleet in eastern waters and the port of Lattakieh, just to the south of his territory, he could not feel secure. About the end of August he decided to bring matters to a head and marched to attack Lattakieh. But without sea-power he could do nothing. The fortifications were strong; and the garrison could be supplied and reinforced from Cyprus. The arrival off the coast of a Pisan fleet which had no cause to like the Byzantines was therefore very timely; and he hastened to come to terms with Daimbert and the Pisan captains, who promised him every assistance.[2]

The Emperor had ordered his admiral to punish acts of piracy committed by the Latins, but he wished to avoid an open breach. Taticius was uncertain how he should deal with this new development. After consulting with the governor of Cyprus, he asked the Byzantine general Butumites, who was in Cyprus, probably in order that he might act as an ambassador-at-large in the East, to cross to Antioch and interview Bohemond. But Bohemond was intransigent; and the embassy achieved nothing. Butumites returned

[1] Anna Comnena, XI, x, 1–6, vol. III, pp. 41–4.
[2] Albert of Aix, VI, 45, pp. 500–1.

to Cyprus and set sail with Taticius and the main fleet for Constantinople, to report on the situation and receive further instructions. Off Syce, on the west Cilician coast, many of the Byzantine ships were wrecked in a fierce tempest; but the admiral's own squadron was able to proceed on the voyage. The Pisan ships then moved into position to blockade Lattakieh from the sea.[1]

At this point Raymond and the two Roberts arrived at Jabala. That Raymond should be horrified by the events at Lattakieh was natural. He disliked anything that Bohemond might do; and his policy was one of alliance with Byzantium. But his colleagues were equally distressed. However much they had deplored some of the Emperor's actions, they realized the necessity for some collaboration between eastern and western Christians; and they were faced with the problem of conveying their armies back to Europe, a task that would be almost impossible without Byzantine help. It was also particularly unsuitable that the new papal legate to the East should start his legature by an action that the bulk of the eastern Christians would bitterly resent. Daimbert was summoned to the camp at Jabala. Faced by the angry remonstrances of the leaders, he saw his mistake and called off the Pisan fleet. Without its help and with his colleagues angry against him, Bohemond was forced to abandon the siege. Raymond then entered Lattakieh, accompanied by the two Roberts, with the full consent of the inhabitants, and hoisted his standard on the citadel, side by side with that of the Emperor. The governor of Cyprus, informed of these developments, announced his approval and offered to provide free transport to take Robert of Flanders and Robert of Normandy to Constantinople, on the first stage of their homeward voyage. The offer was gratefully accepted. The two Roberts sailed safely to Constantinople, where they were well received by the Emperor. They refused his suggestion that they should stay on in the East in his service; and after a short visit they continued their journey to the West. We do not know how many of their men

[1] Anna Comnena, XI, x, 7–8, vol. III, p. 45; Albert of Aix, *loc. cit.*

sailed with them. Some may have taken passages in Genoese ships direct for Italy. Raymond remained at Lattakieh.[1]

Meanwhile Daimbert had rejoined Bohemond at Antioch. Bohemond knew his man and very soon recovered his influence over him. The legate was anxious to move on to Jerusalem; and Bohemond decided to accompany him. Along with the other Crusaders, Bohemond had taken the vow to worship at the Holy Sepulchre; and his failure to fulfil it was damaging his prestige. The opportunity to make the pilgrimage with Daimbert and thus to ensure his alliance was too good to be missed. There was also the future of Jerusalem to consider. Godfrey was without a natural heir and his health was poor. The papal legate might well control the succession; and it would anyhow be wise to have some personal knowledge of the situation there. It was announced that Daimbert and Bohemond would leave Antioch in the late autumn, in order to be at the Holy City for Christmas.[2]

On hearing the news, Baldwin sent from Edessa to say that he would accompany the pilgrimage. He too needed to fulfil his vow; he felt that he could leave Edessa for a while; and it was obviously in the general interest that the party should be as strong as possible. But he, too, was interested in the succession. He was Godfrey's brother and next of kin in the East—for Eustace of Boulogne had probably left Palestine in the wake of Robert of Flanders—and he was as ambitious as Bohemond. Bohemond may later have regretted his company. With Bohemond and Baldwin came all their men that could be spared from the defence of their territories and a great number of women. According to Fulcher of Chartres they numbered twenty-five thousand.[3]

The pilgrims set out early in November. Bohemond and Daimbert followed the coast road, with the Pisan fleet guarding their

[1] Albert of Aix, VI, 56–60, pp. 501–5; Orderic Vitalis, vol. IV, pp. 70–2; Guibert of Nogent, p. 232.

[2] Fulcher of Chartres, I, xxxiii, 1–6, pp. 322–6; Albert of Aix, VII, 6, p. 511.

[3] Fulcher of Chartres (*loc. cit.*) says that Bohemond invited Baldwin to accompany him, because greater numbers would give greater safety. Fulcher gives the number of pilgrims, which is doubtless exaggerated (*ibid.* 8, p. 328).

flank. As they passed by Lattakieh, Raymond refused to help them with provisions. At Bulunyas, a little to the south, they paused to enable Baldwin to catch them up; he had only arrived at Antioch after Bohemond's departure, but he had been better received by Raymond at Lattakieh. The inhabitants of Bulunyas, Greek Christians who apparently acknowledged the Emperor's authority, did not welcome the pilgrims' arrival and were apparently very unhelpful over supplies. When the pilgrims moved on they soon suffered from hunger. Tortosa, which they passed at the end of the month, had reverted into Moslem hands; and the garrison attacked and massacred the stragglers in the rear of the pilgrimage. No food was to be obtained there, nor much at Tripoli, where bread was sold at so dear a price that only the rich could afford it. Some nourishment was extracted from the sugar-cane growing in the neighbourhood of Tripoli; but though it interested the pilgrims as a novelty it was insufficient for their needs. December was unexpectedly cold; and the rain fell ceaselessly. Mortality was high among the aged and the more delicate, and most of the pack-animals perished. But they struggled on, stopping nowhere longer than was essential. In mid-December they reached Caesarea, where they were able to buy food; and on 21 December they arrived at Jerusalem.[1]

Godfrey was glad to see them come. His need for man-power was pressing; and he hoped to persuade many of them to remain in Palestine and occupy the estates that he was now able to offer them. In this he had some success. When Bohemond and Baldwin returned to the north, several knights and their men stayed behind with him. The defeat of the Egyptians at Ascalon had meant that, though the coastal cities, with the exception of Jaffa, were still held by Fatimid governors, protected by the Egyptian fleet, the uplands of Judaea and Samaria had passed right out of their control. The villages there were mainly occupied by Christians, a passive population of small cultivators, forbidden for generations to carry arms and exploited by their Moslem lords whenever the central

[1] Fulcher of Chartres, *ibid.* 7-18, pp. 326-32.

government was weak. They welcomed at first the change of masters; and by the end of the summer Godfrey's authority stretched up to the plain of Jezreel on the north and beyond Hebron into the Negeb in the south; though there, in southern Judaea, his control was less complete; for the natives were mainly Moslems, and there was a continuous infiltration of Bedouins from the desert. Hebron, which the Crusaders called St Abraham, was strongly fortified in order to control the district.[1]

Meanwhile Tancred, with a small company of twenty-four knights and their men, had penetrated into Galilee. Galilee had been recently disputed between the Fatimids and Duqaq of Damascus; but Duqaq had not had time to occupy the province since the Fatimid defeat at Ascalon. The local Moslems therefore made no resistance to Tancred. As his small army approached Tiberias, their capital, they fled into Damascene territory. The Christians, who had been in a minority in the town, received him gladly. The Jews, who had a numerous colony there, were more sullen, remembering the fate of their brethren at Jerusalem. Tancred fortified Tiberias, then moved on to the Christian town of Nazareth and to Mount Tabor, and rounded off his conquest by the capture and fortification of Beisan (Scythopolis), which commands the pass from the plain of Jezreel to the Jordan. The Moslems in Galilee hastened to leave the province; and Tancred followed up their departure with a series of brilliant and swift raids, in the style of the Arabs, on the Moslem lands around. These not only brought him and his followers copious booty but they confirmed him in the possession of Galilee. The Christian state was thus enlarged into a solid block of territory cutting off entirely the Fatimid cities of the coast from the hinterland of Transjordan and the Hauran. With the Egyptians unready as yet to take their revenge for Ascalon and with Duqaq of Damascus too deeply involved in family quarrels to risk an aggressive war, Godfrey had no immediate danger to face. It was as well; for with a fighting

[1] According to William of Tyre, Godfrey had only 300 cavalry and 2000 infantry (IX, 19, vol. I, pt I, p. 393).

force that William of Tyre, using the records of the time, estimated at three hundred knights and two thousand infantrymen, he would not have been able to withstand a serious counter-attack. It was, above all, the disunion of the Arabs that permitted the small intrusive state to be established within their lands.[1]

Daimbert and Bohemond as they travelled southward together planned their future policy. Godfrey needed their help. He needed the sea-power provided by the Pisan ships, whose allegiance Daimbert commanded, and he needed as many knights as Bohemond could spare for him. The pilgrims spent Christmas at Bethlehem. As soon as the festivities were over, the newcomers showed their hand. The Patriarch Arnulf, who had many enemies, and whose patron, the Duke of Normandy, was now far away, was deposed on the grounds that his election had been uncanonical; and, on Bohemond's instigation, Daimbert was elected Patriarch of Jerusalem in his place. There were rumours that gifts made both to Bohemond and to Godfrey had helped on the transaction. Immediately after his enthronization both Godfrey and Bohemond knelt before him and received from him the investiture of the territories of Jerusalem and Antioch.[2]

The ceremony was significant; and its meaning was clear. Public opinion amongst the pilgrims had always considered that the Holy Land should be the patrimony of the Church. But Arnulf had not possessed the authority nor the personality to establish any supremacy over the lay powers. Daimbert came out as papal legate, with a prestige derived from his appointment by Pope Urban; and he brought with him the practical asset of a squadron of ships and the vigorous backing of Bohemond. The average Crusader would not deny his claims; and Godfrey, who in spite of his fits of obstinacy was a weak man and felt himself insecure, shared this genuine respect for the Church. He hoped

---

[1] Radulph of Caen, cxxxix, pp. 703–4; William of Tyre, ix, 13, vol. i, pt i, p. 394.
[2] Albert of Aix, vii, 7, pp. 511–12; William of Tyre, ix, 15, vol. i, pt i, p. 387.

that by acknowledging its suzerainty he put his own position on a proper moral basis and would command its full support in the lay government of the land. He did not as yet know Daimbert. Bohemond's motives were subtler. The recognition of Daimbert's suzerainty cost him nothing; for Daimbert would be too far away to interfere in Antiochene affairs. He was glad to ignore the rights of the Patriarch of Antioch, a Greek, whom he suspected as an agent of Byzantium. By formally basing his authority on the chief Latin ecclesiastic in the East he gave an answer that all the Latins would welcome to the claims put forward by the Emperor and could hope for their whole-hearted aid should the Emperor seek to attack him. It was probably on this occasion that he took the title of Prince of Antioch. The title of prince (*princeps*), attached to a territory, was little known in the West, except in southern Italy, where it was used by certain Norman rulers who had taken over Lombard lands and who admitted no lay overlord other than the see of St Peter. It therefore suited Bohemond perfectly. At the same time his nephew Tancred took the title of Prince of Galilee, probably to show that his suzerain was not Godfrey but the Patriarch. Daimbert was delighted with the homage paid to him.[1] Urban II had probably intended that the Holy Land should become an ecclesiastical patrimony, though he had not wished to upset the existing ecclesiastical arrangements. Doubtless he would have welcomed the succession of a Latin to each of the eastern Patriarchates, if it could be brought about lawfully and peaceably. But we may question whether he would have approved of an action in which the Patriarchate of Jerusalem arrogated to itself authority over the older and historically senior Patriarchate of Antioch. Daimbert was asking for the Patriarchate claims to religious and secular sovereignty in the East as high as any that Pope Gregory VII himself had put forward for the Papacy in the West. The moment was well chosen; for Urban II was dead. News of the accession of Paschal II, who was raised to the pontificate on 13 August, must have reached Jerusalem by the winter.

[1] See Grousset, *Histoire des Croisades*, vol. 1, pp. 194–6, and Moeller, *op. cit.*

Daimbert was probably acquainted with Paschal, who had preceded him as papal legate in Spain, and knew him to be a man of mediocre ability and little force of character. He was unlikely to make trouble so long as his nominal supremacy was recognized.[1]

Baldwin of Edessa did not pay homage to the Patriarch. Whether he was asked to do so and refused or whether the question was not raised is unknown; but it seems that his relations with Daimbert were not cordial.[2]

When the ceremony was over, Bohemond and Baldwin set off together on New Year's Day, 1100, to their territories. Most of their followers returned with them; but a number stayed behind and were presented by Godfrey with fiefs in Palestine. Godfrey and Daimbert accompanied the pilgrims to Jericho and the Jordan, where they passed the Feast of the Epiphany, to celebrate the Blessing of the Waters. Then Bohemond and Baldwin turned northward up the valley to Beisan and on to Tiberias. There they decided not to take the coastal road home, but to go straight on, past Baniyas and the Litani valley into Coele-Syria. They met with no opposition till they were well into Coele-Syria, close to the ruins of Baalbek. The district owed allegiance to Duqaq of Damascus, who planned to intercept them there. The column was marching with Bohemond at its head and Baldwin in the rear when the Damascene forces attacked. But Duqaq was more concerned to hurry them out of his territory than to destroy them; and his onslaught was not very vigorous. It was easily driven off; and the Franks continued on their way, coming down to the sea through the Buqaia, and thence taking the coastal road past Tortosa and Lattakieh to Antioch. Before the end of February Baldwin was back in Edessa.[3]

The additions to his armed strength enabled Godfrey to extend his rule over the maritime plains of Palestine. His territory had

[1] For Paschal II, see article 'Pascal II' by Amann in Vacant and Mangenot, *Dictionnaire de Théologie Catholique*.
[2] There is no evidence that Baldwin ever did homage to Daimbert for Edessa. It is clear from later events that Daimbert distrusted him.
[3] Fulcher of Chartres, I, xxxiii, 19–21, pp. 332–4.

been cut off from the sea, except for a corridor leading to Jaffa. During the autumn he had attempted to widen this corridor by the capture of the small port of Arsuf to the north of Jaffa. The men of Arsuf, after their offer to surrender to Raymond of Toulouse had been rejected through Godfrey's interference, thought it wise when Raymond left Palestine to come to terms with Godfrey, to whom they sent hostages. In return they admitted into their town, partly as a resident and partly as a hostage, a knight from Hainault, Gerard of Avesnes. But Godfrey wished for a more direct control; and in the late autumn he marched with a small force to attack the town. His first victim was his friend, Gerard of Avesnes, whom the men of Arsuf promptly bound and hung over the walls fully exposed to the arrows of the assailants. In vain Gerard shouted down to Godfrey begging him to spare him; but Godfrey replied that were it his own brother Eustace hanging there he would still press the assault. Gerard was soon hauled back into the town, transfixed by twelve of his compatriot's arrows. But his martyrdom was in vain. Godfrey's men could make no impression against the walls of the town; and the two towers on wheels that he constructed were, one after the other, destroyed by the garrison's Greek fire. On 15 December he raised the siege. But he left half of his army at Ramleh, with orders to ravage the country round Arsuf and to make it impossible for the citizens to till their fields.[1]

With the arrival of reinforcements Godfrey continued this policy on a larger scale. His men began to raid the hinterland of all the Fatimid cities of the coast, Ascalon, Caesarea and Acre as well as Arsuf, till none of them could obtain any supplies from the countryside. At the same time, with the help of the Pisan sailors, he refortified Jaffa and improved its harbour. Ships from all the Italian and Provençal ports, attracted by the prospect of trade with the new state, came there to join the Pisans and to share in their opportunities. With their help, Godfrey was able to blockade the Palestinian coast. It was increasingly difficult for Fatimid ships to bring supplies by sea to the Moslem ports. There was piracy on

[1] Albert of Aix, VII, 1–6, pp. 507–11.

both sides; but on the whole it was the citizens of these ports that suffered the most.[1]

In mid-March the Egyptians, in answer to an urgent appeal, sent by sea a small detachment to supplement the garrison of Arsuf. Emboldened by this, the men of Arsuf organized a counter-raid against the Franks only to fall into an ambush, in which the greater part of their army was slain. In despair the town now sent an embassy to Godfrey, which arrived at Jerusalem on 25 March, bringing to him the symbolical gift of the keys of their towers and offering to pay an annual tribute. Godfrey accepted their submission and gave the right to receive the tribute to one of his foremost knights, Robert of Apulia. A few days later Godfrey was surprised and delighted when Gerard of Avesnes suddenly appeared at Jerusalem. He had recovered from his wounds and was now sent back by the authorities in Arsuf as a token of their goodwill. Godfrey, whose conscience had been uneasy about him, presented him with the fief of St Abraham, that is to say, Hebron.[2]

Ascalon, Caesarea and Acre were not long in following the example of Arsuf. Early in April their Emirs came together and sent envoys to Godfrey, laden with presents of corn and fruit and oil and Arab horses. They offered him a monthly tribute of five thousand bezants if they might be allowed to cultivate their lands in peace. Godfrey accepted their overtures; and soon cordial relations were established between the Moslem cities and their Christian overlord. Various petty Moslem sheikhs of the foothills had already made their submission. While Godfrey was encamped before Arsuf a delegation of them had visited him with gifts of food and had been touched and pleased by the simplicity in which he lived— a simplicity dictated as much by his poverty as his tastes. It fitted with their conceptions of a great but modest warrior, and made their friendship easier to obtain.[3]

The sheikhs of Transjordan were the next to seek an understanding with him. They had been used to sending their surplus

[1] *Ibid.* vii, 12, 14, pp. 515–16. [2] *Ibid.* vii, 13, 15, pp. 515–16.
[3] *Ibid. loc. cit.*; William of Tyre, ix, 20, vol. 1, pt 1, pp. 395–6.

produce to the cities of the coast; and the Frankish state cut across their routes. They asked to be enabled to send their caravans across Judaea once more. Godfrey gave his permission, but tried to divert the trade as much as possible to the Christian port of Jaffa. At the same time the Italians were encouraged to intercept, whenever they could, any trade between the Moslem coastal cities and Egypt, to make them dependent on their trade with the Christians. Thus the whole of Palestine began to be integrated into an economic whole, with its overseas connections with Europe. The Frankish policy brought a quick return in wealth and prosperity for the Crusader state.[1]

His growing influence amongst his Moslem neighbours encouraged Godfrey to attempt to extend his rule over lands beyond the Jordan. In the land of Suwat, on the east of the Sea of Galilee, there lived an Emir whom the Crusaders called the Fat Peasant. Tancred had raided his land and had induced him to recognize Frankish suzerainty; but the Fat Peasant had shaken off the vassalage as soon as Tancred had departed and had appealed for help to his overlord, Duqaq of Damascus. Tancred therefore appealed to Godfrey. A foothold there might enable the Franks to divert the rich trade of the Jaulan and the Hauran to the ports of Palestine; while the district of Suwat was itself famed for its fertility. Godfrey was eager to join in its conquest. He brought up troops early in May, to combine with Tancred's in a raid that led them through the Fat Peasant's territory right into the heart of the Jaulan. As they were returning, laden with booty, Duqaq fell on the rearguard, which Tancred commanded. Godfrey in the van moved on, ignorant of what was happening; and Tancred only extricated himself after losing many of his men and all his share of the loot. But Duqaq did not feel himself strong enough to pursue the Franks. Having made sure that they had left his lands he returned to Damascus. Godfrey went on with his booty to Jerusalem; but Tancred burned for revenge. As soon as he had rested his army at Tiberias and had collected reinforcements he conducted another

[1] Albert of Aix, VII, 14, p. 516.

raid into Damascene territory which was so fierce that Duqaq sent to suggest a truce. In return Tancred dispatched six knights to Damascus with a message that he must either become a Christian or leave Damascus. Furious at the insult, Duqaq retorted to the envoys that they must become Moslems or die. Only one renounced his faith; the five others were slaughtered. Tancred at once asked Godfrey to help him avenge their martyrdom; and Godfrey set off again to join him in a raid more formidable than their first. For a fortnight they devastated the Jaulan, while the Moslems cowered behind the walls of their towns. Duqaq, nervous as ever of committing himself to a campaign, made no attempt to oppose them. The Fat Peasant saw himself deserted by his suzerain and impoverished by the Franks, and agreed once more to accept Tancred as his overlord and to pay him a regular tribute.[1]

Though Godfrey was gaining amongst his Moslem neighbours, within his own dominions his power was declining. With Tancred, the greatest of his vassals, his relations were cordial; but it seems that Tancred, for all his requests for Godfrey's help, shaped his policy according to his own desires. But, while the Prince of Galilee acted as an independent monarch, Godfrey found his own independence more and more restricted by the suzerain that he had rashly accepted, the Patriarch Daimbert. Daimbert was not content that his lordship should be nominal and theoretical; he wished it to be based on positive power. Godfrey, always diffident before the Church and fearful of losing the aid of the Pisans, did not like to refuse his requests. At Candlemas, 2 February 1100, he handed over to the see of Jerusalem one quarter of the city of Jaffa. Next, Daimbert demanded that he should be given control not only of the whole city of Jaffa but of Jerusalem itself and its citadel, the Tower of David. Godfrey yielded again but, urged perhaps by his outraged knights, he insisted on delay. At a solemn ceremony on Easter Day, 1 April, he endowed the Patriarchate with the two cities, but announced that he would remain in

[1] *Ibid.* VII, 16–17, pp. 517–18.

possession of them till his death, or till he should conquer two great cities from the infidel. It was an unsatisfactory solution; for it was not easy to build an organized kingdom round a temporary capital. Godfrey seems to have had no governmental body apart from his own household; nor could he hope to found one now at Jerusalem. Had Daimbert been a great administrator or, like Adhemar, a wise statesman, it is just possible that the hierarchical rule that he envisaged might have endured; but his short-sighted attempt to drive the lay defenders on whom the security of the Christian state was bound to depend out of the capital city would have been disastrous. Even the respite that Godfrey gained only added to the uncertainty of the future. But Providence showed mercy to Jerusalem.[1]

When he returned to Galilee, about 18 June, from his raid in the Jaulan, Godfrey learnt that a strong Venetian squadron had put into Jaffa. Knowing how useful it would be for the control of the coasts, he hurried down to greet it. From Tiberias he travelled past Acre and Haifa to Caesarea. The Emir, anxious to show respect to his suzerain, invited him to a banquet where he was treated with the utmost honour. From the banquet Godfrey went straight on to Jaffa. He was feeling ill when he arrived, and collapsed when he reached the hostel that he had himself constructed for distinguished visitors. His friends remembered all the fruit that he had eaten at the Emir's table and whispered of poison. In truth his illness was probably typhoid. Next day he had recovered his strength sufficiently to receive the commander of the Venetian fleet and a bishop that accompanied him, and to discuss the terms on which they would aid the Crusaders. But the effort was too much for him; and he asked his household to convey him up to Jerusalem. In the cooler air of the capital he rallied a little; but he was too weak to conduct business.[2]

---

[1] William of Tyre, IX, 16–17, vol. I, pt I, pp. 388–90.
[2] Albert of Aix, VII, 18, p. 519. Matthew of Edessa, presumably relying on local Christian gossip, says roundly that Godfrey was poisoned by the Emir (II, clxv, p. 229).

Round his sick-bed the politicians wrangled. Daimbert waited impatiently for the moment when he should take over the city. The Venetians were eager to fix up their arrangements. They came in two parties up to Jerusalem to worship at the holy places, the first on 21 June and the second on the 24th; but their commander and their bishop probably remained longer to carry on the negotiations. Hearing of their coming, and of Godfrey's illness, Tancred hastened south from Galilee. From his sick-room Godfrey deputed his cousin, the Burgundian count, Warner of Gray, to act for him; and he gave his approval to the terms that the Venetians put forward. They were to be allowed to trade freely throughout the Frankish state; they were to receive a church and a market in every town of the state; they were to receive a third of every town that they helped to capture, and the whole of the city of Tripoli, for which they would pay Godfrey a tribute. In return they would give their aid to the Crusaders up to 15 August.[1] Discussions then were held to decide which towns should be attacked that summer. It was agreed that, in spite of the Emir's treaty with Godfrey, Acre should be the main objective, and Haifa should also be taken. Tancred hoped to secure Acre for his principality; but Godfrey personally promised Haifa to his friend Geldemar Carpenel.[2]

During the first fortnight of July Godfrey seemed a little stronger; and it was thought that he might recover. Plans for the expedition against Acre were pushed ahead. Tancred's troops joined him at the capital; and Warner of Gray was put in command of Godfrey's troops. The Patriarch Daimbert then determined to accompany the expedition, in order to show himself as the chief authority in the land and to have a say in any distribution of territory. He distrusted Warner, and he thought it safe to leave Jerusalem when Godfrey was too ill to take any action and all his men were away on the campaign. He never made a worse calculation.

---

[1] *Translatio Sancti Nicolai in Venetiam, R.H.C.Occ.*, vol. v, pt I, pp. 272–3; Albert of Aix, VII, 19, p. 519.
[2] *Translatio Sancti Nicolai, loc. cit.*; Albert of Aix, VII, 20, p. 520.

The Patriarch, Tancred and Warner and all their men left Jerusalem on 13 July and marched down to Jaffa to establish liaison with the Venetians. As they approached Jaffa Warner fell suddenly ill. He was clearly in no state to continue on the campaign; so he remained for four days at Jaffa and then was carried back in a litter to Jerusalem. Meanwhile the army marched swiftly northward along the coast; and the Venetian ships prepared to sail up on its flank. But the north wind held them back, and they made little progress.[1]

Warner had hardly arrived in Jerusalem when Godfrey's weary heart gave out. On Wednesday, 18 July, strengthened by the last rites of the Church, Godfrey, Duke of Lorraine and Advocate of the Holy Sepulchre, sank quietly to his rest. He had been a weak and unwise ruler; but men of every nation had respected him for his courage, his modesty and his faith. In Jerusalem the news of his death was greeted with mourning. For five days he lay in state; then they buried him in the Church of the Holy Sepulchre.[2]

[1] *Translatio Sancti Nicolai, loc. cit.*
[2] Albert of Aix, vii, 21, pp. 520–1; William of Tyre, ix, 23, vol. i, pt i, p. 399.

CHAPTER IV

THE KINGDOM OF JERUSALEM

'Nay; but we will have a king over us.'   I SAMUEL VIII, 19

As he lay ill Godfrey of Lorraine had made a will in which, faithful to his promise at Easter, he bequeathed the city of Jerusalem to the Patriarch. When he died there was no one of any authority left in Jerusalem, except for Warner of Gray. The Patriarch and the leading knights were all away on the campaign against Acre. Warner himself was a dying man, but he saw what must be done. Rising from his sick-bed he at once occupied the Tower of David and manned it with Godfrey's personal guard. Then, after consulting with the officers of Godfrey's household, Matthew the Seneschal and Godfrey the Chamberlain, and with Robert, Bishop of Ramleh, and the ex-Patriarch Arnulf, he sent the Bishop of Ramleh with two knights post-haste to Edessa, to tell Baldwin of his brother's death and to summon him to take over the heritage; for they would only obey one of his kin. The move had been planned beforehand; for the invitation to Baldwin ran in the names also of knights at present with the army, such as Geldemar Carpenel and Wicher the Aleman. The group consisted of Lorrainers and northern French, who had come to the Crusade with Godfrey or who had attached themselves to him, and who were bitterly opposed to the Normans and the Italians, under whose influence Godfrey had fallen. But their secret was well kept; and they thought it wise still to keep it. News of the Duke's death was not sent to the army.[1]

[1] Albert of Aix, VII, 30, p. 526; William of Tyre, X, 3, vol. I, pt I, pp. 403–4. It is clear that the army leaders were only informed of Godfrey's death by the Venetians.

But while the Venetian ships were still close to Jaffa waiting for the north wind to drop, a messenger came through to them from Jerusalem to tell them that Godfrey was dead. Their commander, wondering how this would affect the campaign, at once dispatched his three swiftest galleys up the coast to overtake Tancred and the Patriarch and ask what their plans would now be. The news came as a shock to the army, by whom Godfrey was well liked. Daimbert seems to have hesitated. He was anxious about his inheritance. But he had confidence in Godfrey's will, and he believed the Lorrainers to be leaderless. When Tancred, who was determined not to waste this opportunity of Venetian aid, suggested that the attack on Acre might be postponed but that Haifa at least should be taken, he concurred. But he sent an envoy to Jerusalem to take over the Tower of David in his name.[1]

The army moved on to Haifa and encamped on the slopes of Mount Carmel; and soon afterwards the Venetian squadron sailed into the bay. Haifa was inhabited mostly by Jews, with a small Egyptian garrison. The Jews, remembering how their colonies in Jerusalem and Galilee had fared, were ready to defend themselves to the end. The Moslems provided them with arms; and they fought with all the tenacity of their race. The Venetians after losing a ship in a battle in the harbour moved out discouraged into the bay; while Tancred, furious on learning suddenly that Godfrey had promised Haifa to Geldemar Carpenel, called off his men and retired to sulk in his tent. Daimbert needed all his tact to persuade him to resume the attack. He pointed out that the Venetians were already preparing to sail away, and he promised to see to it that the best man should be given Haifa. When Tancred agreed to co-operate once more, a fresh assault was launched. After a desperate struggle the chief tower in the defences was stormed and an entrance was forced. Those of the Moslems and Jews that could escape from the town fled to Acre or to Caesarea; but the majority were massacred.[2]

[1] *Translatio Sancti Nicolai in Venetiam*, pp. 275–6; William of Tyre, *loc. cit.*
[2] Albert of Aix, VII, 22–5, pp. 521–3; *Translatio Sancti Nicolai*, pp. 276–8.

Haifa fell on about 25 July. Immediately afterwards the leaders of the army held a conference to decide to whom it should be allotted. Tancred had the larger forces and Daimbert's support. Geldemar Carpenel could do nothing against him and was driven out of the town. He retired, accompanied by the Lorrainers in the army, and made his way to the south of Palestine, where he established himself in Hebron; whose former lord, Gerard of Avesnes, was probably still at Haifa with Tancred.[1] Next, Daimbert and Tancred came together to discuss the greater question, the future of the government of Jerusalem. Daimbert had by now heard from Jerusalem. His envoy had found Warner of Gray in possession of the Tower of David, which he refused to hand over to the Patriarch's representatives; and he learnt that Baldwin had been summoned south. Warner himself died on 23 July, worn out by his last exertions; but though the Patriarch's friends saw in his death the hand of God, punishing him for his impiety, it did them no good; for the tower was safely in the possession of the Lorrainers.[2] Daimbert could not hope to realize his claims unaided. Tancred's alliance was essential; for his principality now stretched from the east of the Sea of Galilee to the Mediterranean, cutting off Jerusalem from the north. Tancred, for his part, had loathed Baldwin ever since their quarrels in Cilicia, three years before. With Tancred's full approval, Daimbert decided that the government of Palestine should be offered to Bohemond. His own secretary, Morellus, was ordered to set off at once for Antioch with a letter for the prince.

Daimbert did not intend Bohemond to hold any illusions about the nature of his future sovereignty. He opened his letter by recalling that Bohemond had helped to elect him to the Patriarchate of the see which he described, with a superb disregard of the claims of Rome, as the mother of all Churches and the mistress of the nations. He next told of the concessions that he

---

[1] Albert of Aix, vii, 6, pp. 523–4. There is no record of Gerard having protested against Geldemar's action.
[2] William of Tyre, *loc. cit.*

had extracted from Godfrey and complained of the attempts of the Duke's entourage to prevent them. He repeated the terms of the endowment made on Easter Day and emphasized that by it Jerusalem should have passed to him on Godfrey's death. But Warner of Gray had wrongfully seized the Tower of David and had offered the inheritance to Baldwin. Daimbert therefore summoned Bohemond to come to his assistance, just as Bohemond's father had come to the assistance of Pope Gregory VII when the German emperors oppressed him—a memory that was not so propitious for the Church as Daimbert seems to have thought. Bohemond was to write to Baldwin to forbid him to come to Palestine without the permission of the Patriarch; and if Baldwin disobeyed then Bohemond must use force to restrain him. That is to say, in order that the Patriarch might rule over Palestine in defiance of the wishes of the knights on whom the defence of the country rested, the Christian Prince of Antioch was to declare war on the Christian Count of Edessa.[1]

What answer Bohemond would have given to the letter cannot be known. It is unlikely that he would have been rash enough to risk a conflict with Baldwin; nor, had he come to Palestine, would he have long remained subservient to the Patriarch. But the invitation never reached him. Daimbert's luck was out.

During the last few months there had been changes in the situation in northern Syria. Raymond of Toulouse had spent the winter months at Lattakieh, governing it in condominium with the representatives of the Emperor. He was on excellent terms with the governor of Cyprus, from whom he could receive supplies. Some time in the spring he received a letter from Alexius, thanking him for his help and asking him to hand over Lattakieh to the Byzantine authorities. An invitation to visit the imperial court was included. It is probable that the letter was conveyed from Constantinople by the eunuch Eustathius, recently elevated to be admiral of the imperial fleet, who came out with

[1] Albert of Aix, VII, 27, p. 524. The text of Daimbert's letter is given in William of Tyre, X, 4, 1, pp. 405–6.

a strong squadron and at once set about the recapture of the ports of western Cilicia, Seleucia and Corycus, and then extended his power over Bohemond's Cilician territory further east, occupying Tarsus, Adana and Mamistra. Raymond accepted the invitation and sailed for Constantinople at the beginning of June. At Cyprus he met the Venetian squadron that was on its way to Jaffa, and he arrived at the imperial capital about the end of the month. His countess, Elvira of Aragon, who had stayed by his side throughout all his travels, remained at Lattakieh, under the protection of the Byzantine authorities, together with what was left of the armies of Toulouse and Provence.[1]

Daimbert's secretary Morellus arrived at Lattakieh at the end of July on his way to Antioch. The authorities detained him to examine his papers and discovered the letter to Bohemond. Raymond's men, to whom it was sent for translation, were so shocked by it that they suppressed it and arrested Morellus.[2]

Had Bohemond received the letter, his whole future would have been happier. At the beginning of August, still ignorant of events in Palestine, he marched from Antioch up the Euphrates, in answer to an appeal from the Armenians of Melitene. In the early summer he had been able to consolidate his south-eastern frontier beyond the Orontes, defeating a counter-attack from Ridwan of Aleppo, who was driven to ask for help from the Emir of Homs.[3] Relations between Homs and Aleppo were too uncertain to cause Bohemond any alarm, even though the Moslems were able to recapture Tel-Mannas, which had been left without an adequate garrison when Raymond Pilet had left it to travel south with the Count of Toulouse. Bohemond felt able to extend his dominions towards the north. Owing to lack of sea-power he had not been able to prevent the Byzantine reconquest of Cilicia; but he was anxious to

---

[1] Anna Comnena, XI, vii, 4, x, 9–10, vol. III, pp. 345–6; Fulcher of Chartres, I, xxxii, 1, pp. 320–1; *Translatio Sancti Nicolai*, p. 271. Anna's chronological sequence is not clear, but the date can be confirmed from the western sources.
[2] Albert of Aix, *loc. cit.*
[3] Kemal ad-Din, *Chronicle of Aleppo*, pp. 588–9.

control the passes of the Anti-Taurus, through which any Byzantine expedition against Antioch itself would probably travel. In consequence, when Gabriel of Melitene, in expectation of an attack from Malik Ghazi Gümüshtekin, the Danishmend Emir of Sebastea, begged for his help, Bohemond gladly responded. For three summers the Danishmend Emir had raided Gabriel's territory; and it was feared now that he would march on the town itself. After the experience of his son-in-law Thoros of Edessa, Gabriel was unwilling to appeal to Baldwin, although he was nearer at hand. But Bohemond showed consideration towards the Armenians. Amongst his friends were the Armenian bishop of Antioch, Cyprian, and Gregory, Bishop of Marash. Using their mediation Gabriel offered to yield his city to Bohemond, if only the Turkish menace could be ended.[1]

Before he left Antioch to answer the appeal, Bohemond took an action which marked once for all his breach with the Greeks and which in its consequences caused the first irreparable schism between the Greek and Latin Churches. John IV, who had been reinstalled as Patriarch of Antioch by Adhemar, had hitherto continued in his office. But he was a Greek; and Bohemond suspected him of Byzantine sympathies and of encouraging the Orthodox of his Patriarchate to hope for deliverance by the Emperor. Bohemond now expelled him from the city, and appointed in his place a Latin, Bernard of Valence, who had been a chaplain of Adhemar's and whom Bohemond had recently made Bishop of Artah, taking him to Jerusalem for his consecration. Later Latins, such as William of Tyre, anxious to establish the legality of the Latin line of Patriarchs of Antioch, declared that John had already resigned his see; but in fact John only resigned after he reached Constantinople, to make way for a Greek successor. He settled in a monastery at Oxia, where he wrote a treatise denouncing Latin usages, in which he spoke bitterly of Latin oppression; and his rights were taken over by the Patriarch elected by his exiled clergy. Thus two rival lines

[1] Albert of Aix, *loc. cit.*; Matthew of Edessa, II, clxvii, pp. 230–1; Michael the Syrian (ed. Chabot), III, iii, p. 187; Ibn al-Athir, *op. cit.* pp. 203–4.

of Patriarchs, Greek and Latin, were instituted; and neither would yield to the other. In Antioch, thanks to Bohemond, the schism between the Churches was now made definite; and the Emperor added to his ambition to restore Antioch to his Empire the determination to replace the rightful line on the Patriarchal throne.[1]

Having thus eliminated the main possible source of treason in Antioch, Bohemond set out for Melitene. Not liking to leave his capital insufficiently garrisoned, he only took with him his cousin, Richard of Salerno, and three hundred knights, with a complement of infantry. The Armenian bishops of Antioch and Marash accompanied him; and some of his knights may have been Armenian. Confident that with even so small a force he could conquer the Turks, he marched carelessly up into the hills that separated Melitene from the valley of the Aksu. There the Danishmend Emir was waiting in ambush, and suddenly fell on him. The Franks were taken by surprise and surrounded. After a short and bitter contest their army was annihilated. The Armenian bishops were slain; and along with Richard of Salerno, Bohemond, so long the terror of the infidel, was dragged off into an ignominious captivity.[2]

It was Baldwin that saved northern Syria for Christendom. When he saw that he was captured, Bohemond cut off a mesh of his yellow hair and entrusted it to a soldier who managed to slip through the encircling Turks and hurried to Edessa. There, showing the hair to prove his authenticity, he gave Baldwin Bohemond's message. Bohemond begged to be rescued before the Turks

---

[1] William of Tyre, VI, 23, vol. I, pt I, pp. 273–5; Orderic Vitalis, vol. IV, p. 141, who illogically assumes that the change was made during Bohemond's captivity, yet Bohemond appointed the successor; Radulph of Caen, CXI, p. 704. See Leib, *Deux Inédits Byzantins*, pp. 59–69. John's act of abdication, dated October 1100, exists in a MS. at Sinai, given in Benechewitch, *Catalogus Codicum Manuscriptorum Graecorum*, p. 279. See Grumel, 'Les Patriarches d'Antioche du nom de Jean', in *Echos d'Orient*, vol. XXXII, pp. 286–98.

[2] Albert of Aix, VII, 27–8, pp. 524–5; Fulcher of Chartres, I, XXXV, 1–4, pp. 343–7; Radulph of Caen, CXLI, pp. 704–5; Matthew of Edessa, *loc. cit.*; Michael the Syrian (ed. Chabot), III, iii, pp. 188–9 (talking of Armenian treachery); Ibn al-Qalānisī, *Damascus Chronicle*, pp. 49–50; Ibn al-Athir, *op. cit.* p. 203; Kemal ad-Din, *op. cit.* p. 589.

would have time to carry him away into the depths of Anatolia. But Baldwin was more concerned with the safety of the Frankish states than with the person of his old friend and rival. He set out at once with a small force that contained only one hundred and forty knights; but his scouting was excellent; and rumour preceded him greatly increasing the size of his army. Malik Ghazi Gümüsh-tekin had on the morrow of his victory marched up to the walls of Melitene to display to the garrison the heads of his Frankish and Armenian victims. But when he heard of Baldwin's approach he thought it best to retire with his booty and his captives into his own territory. Baldwin followed him into the mountains; but he feared to advance far into the country where he could easily be ambushed, nor did he trust the local inhabitants. After three days he returned to Melitene. Bohemond and Richard of Salerno travelled on laden with chains to a long imprisonment in the bleak castle of Niksar (Neocaesarea) away in the mountains of Pontus.[1]

Gabriel of Melitene welcomed Baldwin as his deliverer and hastened to place himself beneath his suzerainty. In return Baldwin left him fifty knights to see to the defence of the town. Thanks to them Gabriel was able to repel a Danishmend attack a few months later, when news had reached the Turks that Baldwin had left the north.[2]

It was only on his return to Edessa after this campaign, about the end of August, that Baldwin received the envoys from Jerusalem who had come to tell him of his brother's death. He spent the month of September in making arrangements for his journey and for the government of Edessa. His cousin Baldwin of Le Bourg was at Antioch, where he seems to have acted as Bohemond's deputy and perhaps as a liaison between the two great leaders. He was summoned to Edessa, where Baldwin invested him with the county, under his suzerainty. On 2 October, Baldwin started out with his household and a bodyguard of two hundred knights and seven hundred infantrymen for Jerusalem, grieving a little, so

[1] Albert of Aix, vii, 29, pp. 525-6, and references in previous notes.
[2] Albert of Aix, *loc. cit.*

his chaplain Fulcher tells us, for the death of his brother, but rejoicing more at his inheritance.[1]

Daimbert's hopes that Bohemond might stop him were in vain. Bohemond was lost in captivity; and the Franks of Antioch were delighted to welcome the man whose intervention had saved them from the consequences of the disaster. From Antioch, where he remained for three days, he sent his wife and her ladies to travel by sea to Jaffa; for he feared to meet with trouble on his journey. At Lattakieh, where he was well received by the authorities and spent two nights, many other soldiers came to join him. But their enthusiasm was short-lived; for it was soon learnt that the Turks of Damascus were determined to destroy him as he marched down the coast. By the time that he reached Jabala his force had dwindled to a hundred and sixty knights and five hundred infantrymen. Forced marches brought him safely to Tripoli. The new Emir of Tripoli, Fakhr al-Mulk, was on the worst possible terms with Duqaq of Damascus, who was trying to encroach on to the Lebanese littoral. He therefore took pleasure in supplying Baldwin not only with all the foodstuffs that he needed but also with information about Duqaq's movements and plans.

As the coast road from Tripoli approaches Beirut, at the passage of the Nahr el-Kelb, the Dog River, it runs along a narrow ledge between the mountains and the sea. The pass was famed from the days of antiquity; and every conqueror that forced it, from Pharaoh Rameses onwards, celebrated his victory by an inscription on the face of the cliff. Here the Damascenes were waiting for Baldwin. Warned by the Emir of Tripoli, he advanced very cautiously, to find himself faced by Duqaq's whole army, together with the army of the Emir of Homs, while an Arab squadron from Beirut lay off the shore, ready to cut his retreat. His attempt to cross the river against such superior forces was a failure; and he was grateful when night fell and enabled him to retire. The Emir of Homs urged the Damascenes to attack him in the darkness; but Duqaq's generals preferred to wait for the dawn, when the Moslem fleet

[1] Fulcher of Chartres, II, i, 1, pp. 352–4; Albert of Aix, VII, 31, p. 527.

could work with them. Through the night they contented themselves with pouring arrows into the Frankish lines. 'How I wished I was back at home at Chartres or Orléans', wrote Fulcher when he described the battle, 'and others felt the same.' But Baldwin was not discouraged. Early next morning he feigned a further retreat; but he took care to place all his best-armed men in the rear. The Damascenes followed on in eager pursuit; but where the road narrows again, beyond Juniye, some five miles to the north, Baldwin suddenly turned and flung the full weight of his armour against his pursuers. They were taken by surprise and fell back upon the troops crowding behind them. Soon all was confusion on the narrow road; and Baldwin pressed home his attacks. The Arab ships were not able to come in close to the shore to help their allies, amongst whom panic now spread. By nightfall the whole Moslem army had fled into the mountains or behind the walls of Beirut. Baldwin encamped for the night at Juniye; and next morning, laden with booty, his army crossed the Dog River without opposition.

Thenceforward his journey was uninterrupted by the Moslems. He passed safely by Beirut and Sidon; and at Tyre the Egyptian governor willingly sent him supplies. On the last day of October he reached the Christian port of Haifa. Haifa belonged to Tancred; but Tancred was in Jerusalem where he was aiding Daimbert in a vain attempt to gain possession of the Tower of David from the Lorrainers before Baldwin should arrive. In his absence the Franks of Haifa offered to open their gates to Baldwin; but he was suspicious and preferred to camp outside the walls. When his troops had rested there for several days, he continued down the coast to Jaffa. On the news of his approach Tancred hastened to Jaffa to try to hold the town against him; but its citizens drove him out. Baldwin entered Jaffa amid the enthusiasm of the populace; but he did not delay there. On 9 November he marched up into the hills and entered Jerusalem.[1]

[1] Fulcher of Chartres, II, i, 2–iii, 9, pp. 354–66, a vivid eyewitness account of the journey; Albert of Aix, VII, 32–5, pp. 527–31.

As he drew near to the city the inhabitants came out to welcome him with tremendous manifestations of joy. Not only all the Franks but Greeks, Syrians and Armenians were in the throng which met him outside the walls and conveyed him in honour to the Holy Sepulchre. His enemies were scattered. Daimbert retired from the Patriarchal palace to a monastery on Mount Sion, where he spent his time in prayer and pious exercises. Tancred moved northward to his lands in Galilee. The anarchy which had lasted in Palestine since Godfrey's death was ended. On St Martin's Day, Sunday, 11 November, with general approval and rejoicing, Baldwin assumed the title of King of Jerusalem.[1]

Baldwin was too wise to be vindictive. Daimbert's enemies, such as the ex-Patriarch Arnulf, had hoped to see his immediate disgrace. But Baldwin took no action against him. He left him in the full possession of his rights while he went off himself on a campaign against the Arabs; and Daimbert came to realize that he would do well to accept his defeat and make the best of it. When Baldwin returned to Jerusalem in mid-December, Daimbert was ready to make peace with him. His hopes of establishing an active theocracy were ended; but he might still retain his nominal suzerainty and still wield a great influence on the kingdom. Baldwin, who had not lost sight of Daimbert's command of Pisan assistance, gladly forgave him and confirmed him in his see.[2] Tancred was more truculent. Baldwin summoned him to Jerusalem to answer for his disobedience to Godfrey's known wishes over the disposal of Haifa. Twice Tancred disobeyed the summons, before he agreed at last to meet Baldwin on the banks of the little river Auja, between Jaffa and Arsuf. But when the time came he would not appear but asked for an interview at Haifa instead. An easier solution was found. The Franks of Antioch were leaderless since Bohemond's captivity and Baldwin of Le Bourg's departure to govern Edessa. They suggested that Tancred should come to

[1] Fulcher of Chartres, II, iii, 13–14, pp. 368–9; Albert of Aix, VII, 36, pp. 531–2; William of Tyre, X, 7, 1, pp. 410–11.
[2] Fulcher of Chartres, II, iii, 15, pp. 369–70; William of Tyre, X, 9, 1, p. 413.

them as regent in his uncle's place. To Tancred the suggestion offered a fresh and wider field, where Baldwin would not over-shadow him; while Baldwin was happy to be rid with so little trouble of a vassal whom he distrusted and disliked. The interview at Haifa took place early in March 1101, in an atmosphere of cordiality. Tancred handed back his fief of Galilee to Baldwin and departed with his good wishes to Antioch.[1]

Already on Christmas Day, 1100, in the Church of the Nativity at Bethlehem, Baldwin had paid homage to the Patriarch Daimbert and had been crowned by him as King.[2]

Thus, more than four years after the princes of western Europe had left their homes for the Crusade, the kingdom of Jerusalem was founded. Of all the great leaders it was Baldwin, the penniless younger son of the Count of Boulogne, that had triumphed. One by one his rivals had been eliminated. Many of them had returned to the West, Robert of Normandy, Robert of Flanders, Hugh of Vermandois and Stephen of Blois. His own brother Eustace of Boulogne, who might have hoped for Godfrey's heritage, had preferred his lands by the English Channel. Of his chief competitors in the East, Bohemond lay helpless in his Turkish prison, and Raymond, landless still, was away in Constantinople as the client of the Emperor. But Baldwin had bided his time and had snatched at his opportunities. Of them all he had proved himself the ablest, the most patient and the most far-sighted. He had won his reward; and the future was to show that he deserved it. His coronation was a glorious one and a hopeful ending to the story of the First Crusade.

---

[1] Fulcher of Chartres, II, vii, 1, pp. 390–3; Albert of Aix, VII, 44–5, pp. 537–8.
[2] Fulcher of Chartres, II, vi, 1, pp. 384–5; Albert of Aix, VII, 43, pp. 536–7; William of Tyre, *loc. cit.*

PRINCIPAL SOURCES FOR THE HISTORY OF THE FIRST CRUSADE

The story of the First Crusade is almost entirely covered by contemporary or almost contemporary sources. In the footnotes I discuss points arising from minor and secondary sources; but the chief primary sources on which we are continuously dependent and which do not always agree among themselves need a general critical appreciation in order to assess their relative value.

1. GREEK

The only Greek source of prime importance is the *Alexiad* of ANNA COMNENA, which is the life of the Emperor Alexius by his favourite daughter. Anna wrote her book some forty years after the events of the First Crusade, when she was an old woman. Her memory may at times have played her false; in particular, her chronology is occasionally somewhat muddled. Moreover, she wrote in the light of later developments. She was also a devoted daughter and wished to show that Alexius had been invariably wise, scrupulous and kindly. She therefore tended to suppress anything that might in her opinion be interpreted to his discredit, or to the discredit of his friends. She is frankly not reliable when she deals with events that occurred outside the boundaries of the Empire, where she allows her prejudices full rein, as in her account of the career of Pope Gregory VII. But modern historians are too ready to belittle her. She was an intelligent and very well-educated woman; and she was a conscientious historian, who tried to verify her sources. Though she wrote in old age, she had long intended to be her father's biographer and must have collected most of her material during his lifetime, when she had full access to his official papers. Where she depends on a reliable informant, as in her account of the Crusaders' march across Anatolia, for which she clearly used Taticius's reports, she controls her prejudices; and though she undoubtedly committed sins of omission, she cannot be proved guilty of any sins of commission in describing events that took place at Constantinople or within the Empire. She enjoyed her father's confidence and herself had personal knowledge of many of the characters and incidents that she described. It is easy to make allowances for her piety and prejudices; but when that is done, her testimony on all affairs directly concerning Byzantium must be preferred to that of any other.[1]

The chroniclers ZONARAS and GLYCAS[2] and the brief popular work known as the *Synopsis Sathas*[3] add very little to our knowledge. No official Byzantine documents concerning the Crusade have survived except for letters written by Alexius to western princes and hierarchs, which exist only in Latin translations that are certainly not accurate. The letters of THEOPHYLACT, Archbishop of Bulgaria, as yet inadequately edited, provide a little additional information.[4]

2. LATIN

The Latin sources are more numerous and supply us with most of our information.

RAYMOND OF AGUILERS (or Aighuilhe, in the Department of Haute-Loire) joined the Crusade in the company of Adhemar of Le Puy, and soon became chaplain to Raymond of Toulouse. He began to write his chronicle, the *Historia Francorum qui ceperunt Jerusalem*, during the siege of Antioch and finished it at the end of 1099. He concentrated on the history of Count Raymond's expedition; but, though he was a loyal southern Frenchman, he was by no means uncritical of his chief, disapproving of the Count's delay in marching on from Antioch and unsympathetic with his pro-Byzantine policy. Only on one occasion (see above, p. 272) does he mention the Greeks without an unfriendly comment. His part in the episode of the Holy Lance has caused critics to doubt his veracity; but within his limits he was obviously sincere and

---

[1] The latest edition of Anna Comnena is published in the *Collection Budé* and edited by Leib, with a full introduction and notes. *Anna Comnena*, by Mrs Buckler, gives a detailed critical study of the *Alexiad*. There is an English translation of the *Alexiad*, by E. A. S. Dawes (London, 1928).

[2] Both edited in the Bonn *Corpus Scriptorum Historiae Byzantinae*.

[3] Ed. in Sathas, *Bibliotheca Graeca Medii Aevi*, vol. VII.

[4] Theophylact's letters are given in *M.P.G.* vol. CXXVI.

well informed. His work soon achieved a wide circulation; but though some early MSS. contain interpolations it was never re-edited.[1]

FULCHER OF CHARTRES attended the Council of Clermont, then went to the East in the company of his overlord, Stephen of Blois. In June, 1097, he became chaplain to Baldwin of Boulogne, in whose entourage he thenceforward remained. His *Gesta Francorum Iherusalem Peregrinantium* was written in three instalments, in 1101, 1106 and 1124–7. He was the best educated of the Latin chroniclers and the most reliable. Though devoted to Baldwin, his outlook was remarkably objective. It is only in his third instalment that any animosity against the Byzantines appears; and his general outlook towards the eastern Christians is fair and friendly. His work was much used by subsequent chroniclers.[2] BARTOLF OF NANGIS, writing probably in Syria, published in about 1108 an edition of the earlier chapters, with a few additions, mainly topographical.[3] A brief résumé of the later chapters is attributed to LISIARD OF TOURS.[4] WILLIAM OF MALMESBURY, RICHARD OF POITIERS and SICARD OF CREMONA all used the whole chronicle as their chief source when they wrote of the Crusade.[5]

The most popular of the contemporary accounts of the Crusade was the anonymous work known as the *Gesta Francorum et Aliorum Hierosolimitorum*. This was written, probably as a diary, by one of Bohemond's followers who went on to Jerusalem with Tancred. It ends with the story of the battle of Ascalon in 1099 and was first published in 1100 or early in 1101; Ekkehard read it in Jerusalem in 1101. But the oldest extant MSS. already contain interpolations, such as a 'literary' description of Antioch, and a passage falsifying the account of Bohemond's transactions at Constantinople (see above, p. 159 n. 1), inspired by Bohemond himself about the year 1105, as well as a passage borrowed from Raymond of Aguilers. The author was a simple soldier, honest according to his lights but credulous and prejudiced and a strong admirer of Bohemond. The wide success of the *Gesta* was mainly due

[1] Ed. in the *Recueil des Historiens des Croisades*. There is room for a good critical edition.
[2] The edition by Hagenmeyer, which is fully annotated, has superseded that in the *Recueil*.
[3] Ed. in the *Recueil*. See Cahen, *La Syrie du Nord*, p. 11 n. 1.
[4] Ed. in the *Recueil*.
[5] See Cahen, *loc. cit.* Sicard's chronicle no longer exists.

to Bohemond's own efforts. He regarded it as his *apologia* and himself hawked it round northern France during his visit there in 1106.[1] At an early date it was republished, almost word for word, by a Poitevin priest, himself a Crusader, called TUDEBOD. His version, the *De Hierosolymitano Itinere*, contains a few additional personal reminiscences.[2] About 1130 there appeared a *Historia Belli Sacri*, a clumsy compilation made by a monk of Monte Cassino, based on the *Gesta* but with a few passages taken from Radulph of Caen, from some source now lost and from current legendary traditions.[3] The *Gesta* was several times rewritten; in about 1109 by GUIBERT OF NOGENT, who added personal information and borrowed from Fulcher and who aimed at a more critical and moral tone;[4] in about 1110 by BAUDRI OF BOURGUEIL, Archbishop of Dol, who sought to improve its literary style;[5] and by ROBERT OF REIMS, whose popular and somewhat romantic version, the *Historia Hierosolymitana*, appeared in about 1122.[6] It also inspired a short anonymous *Expeditio contra Turcos*, and the chapters on the Crusades in the chronicles of HUGH OF FLEURY and HENRY OF HUNTINGDON.[7]

Three important chroniclers of the First Crusade did not themselves take part in it. EKKEHARD, Abbot of Aura, came to Palestine with the German Crusaders of 1101. On his return to Germany, in about the year 1115, he composed a work called the *Hierosolymita*, intended to be part of a world chronicle that he contemplated. It is made up of a few personal reminiscences and of stories told to him or to his friend, Frutholf of St Michelsberg, by actual members of the Crusade, supplemented by information taken from already published chronicles. He often gives his sources, but was a credulous man.[8]

---

[1] The latest edition is Bréhier's, under the title of *Histoire Anonyme de la Première Croisade*. The notes in Hagenmeyer's edition, *Anonymi Gesta Francorum* (Heidelberg, 1890) are still useful.

[2] Ed. in the *Recueil*. See Cahen, *op. cit.* pp. 8–9.

[3] Ed. in the *Recueil*. See Cahen, *loc. cit.*

[4] Ed. in the *Recueil*. See Cahen, *loc. cit.*

[5] Ed. in the *Recueil*. See Cahen, *loc. cit.*

[6] Ed. in the *Recueil*. See Cahen, *loc. cit.*

[7] Extracts of Hugh and Henry are published in the fifth volume of the *Recueil*. The *Expeditio Contra Turcos* is published with Tudebod in the third volume.

[8] The edition in the fifth volume of the *Recueil* is far better than that of Hagenmeyer (*Ekkehard von Aura*, Leipzig, 1888).

Appendix I

RADULPH OF CAEN came to Syria in 1108. He had already served with Bohemond in the Epirot campaign of 1107 and then attached himself to Tancred. After Tancred's death, in about 1113, he wrote the *Gesta Tancredi Siciliae Regis in Expeditione Hierosolymitana*. The book, which only exists in one MS., was never finished. Its style is that of an ignorant but very pretentious man. It contains a few exclusive scraps of information about its hero, but otherwise follows already published work; however, the author does not seem to have read the *Gesta Francorum*.[1]

The fullest contemporary account of the First Crusade is given in the *Liber Christianae Expeditionis pro Ereptione, Emundatione et Restitutione Sanctae Hierosolymitanae Ecclesiae* of ALBERT OF AIX (Aachen), written some time about the year 1130. We know nothing of Albert except that he never visited the East. Till the middle of the last century he was regarded as the most authoritative source for the history of the Crusade, and historians such as Gibbon trusted him absolutely. But since von Sybel's destructive criticism it has been the fashion to discredit him rather more than is fair. His work is a compilation of legends and eyewitness accounts, put together with very little critical sense and without citing the sources. His account of Peter the Hermit's earlier life is obviously unreliable; but the narrative of Peter's expedition was certainly supplied by someone who took part in it. Details such as the time taken to traverse stages in the march are wholly convincing. For the story of Godfrey's journey to Constantinople and the march across Anatolia he certainly relied on an account given him by a soldier in Godfrey's army. He had probably been in the habit of noting down information given him by returning soldiers and pilgrims long before he began to compile his book. It is fairly easy to identify the legendary material; but his narrative of the events of the Crusade itself should be treated with respect.[2]

WILLIAM OF TYRE, the greatest of the Crusader historians, wrote some seventy years after the Crusade. For his narrative up to the

[1] Ed. in the *Recueil*.

[2] Ed. in the *Recueil*. There is a large literature about Albert, of which the most important works are those of Krebs, Kügler, Kühne and Beaumont (see Bibliography). See also von Sybel, *Geschichte des ersten Kreuzzuges*, 2nd ed. (preface), and Hagenmeyer, *Le Vrai et le Faux sur Pierre l'Hermite*, especially pp. 9 ff.

establishment of the Crusaders in Palestine he used Albert of Aix almost exclusively; but after the capture of Jerusalem his story is also based on records and traditions surviving in the Crusader kingdom. But his tremendous *Historia Rerum in Partibus Transmarinis Gestarum* only becomes an important source after the accession of Baldwin. I hope to discuss it more fully in a later volume.[1]

A slightly different point of view is given by the Genoese CAFFARO, the author of the Annals of Genoa, covering the years between 1100 and 1163, and of a *De Liberatione Civitatum Orientis*, written in 1155, but discovered among some old papers a century later and possibly altered slightly before it was published. Caffaro belonged to a Genoese family that came to Palestine in 1100. His account is patriotic, but sober and reliable.[2]

The contemporary chroniclers of western Europe all mention the Crusade, but depend entirely on one or other of the sources that we have mentioned, with the exception of the *Chronicle* of ZIMMERN, which provides information about the German Crusaders.[3]

The Crusade produced its epics, both in Latin and in the *langue d'oil* and the *langue d'oc*. They are, however, more important for their literary interest than for their historical worth. The Latin poets, GEOFFREY THE LOMBARD, JOSEPH OF EXETER and GUNTHER OF BASLE, are historically valueless. The Provençal *Chanson d'Antioche*, attributed to GREGORY BECHADA, is more interesting and deserves further study. In the *langue d'oil* there exists, besides a version in verse of Baudri, a *Chanson d'Antioche* by GRAINDOR OF DOUAI, which is based partly on Robert the Monk and partly on an earlier *Chanson* composed by RICHARD THE PILGRIM, who apparently took part in the Crusade in Robert of Flanders' army. He was a simple, rather ignorant man, but with his own point of view. For instance, though he wishes that the Crusaders had taken Constantinople, he is friendly towards Taticius. There is also a poem in French by GILON with interpolations by a certain FULCHER, based on the same material, and a Spanish *Gran Conquista d'Ultramar*, late in date, which uses Bechada and Graindor and William of Tyre. The cycle with

---

[1] Ed. in the *Recueil*. See Prutz, *Wilhelm von Tyrus*, and Cahen, *op. cit.* pp. 17–18.

[2] Ed. in the fifth volume of the *Recueil*.

[3] Extracts are published by Hagenmayer in vol. II of the *Archives de l'Orient Latin*.

Godfrey of Lorraine as its hero, such as the *Chevalier au Cygne*, contains only legendary history.[1]

Very little contemporary correspondence has survived; but what remains is of great importance. There are a few letters to and from the Popes Urban II and Paschal II; two appeals from ecclesiastics in the East; two interesting, though not entirely disingenuous, dispatches from the Crusading leaders; and, most valuable, two letters each from two prominent Crusaders, STEPHEN OF BLOIS, and ANSELM, Bishop of Ribemont. Stephen wrote three letters home to his wife. The first, written on his arrival at Constantinople, has been lost. The second was sent from the camp at Nicaea and the third from the camp at Antioch. Stephen, though a weak man, was honest and enthusiastic; and his letters are the most human of the documents regarding the Crusade. Anselm's letters were both written from Antioch and were addressed to his superior, Manasses, Archbishop of Reims. They provide useful information but lack the personal quality of Stephen's.[2]

The few papal decrees regulating the Crusade and the charters concerned with the establishment of the Crusading kingdom are inevitably important. The archives of Genoa and Venice contain material of increasing value as the Italian towns took an increasing interest in the affairs of the Crusaders.

3. ARABIC

Arabic sources, though numerous and highly important for the later Crusades, give us very little assistance over the first. No official charters or documents of the period have survived. The great encyclopaedias and geographies, so popular with the Arabs, are barely concerned with these years, with one exception. The works of the chroniclers known to have lived at the time have only come down to us in sparse, short quotations in later writers. There are only three works of real value.

IBN AL-QALĀNISĪ of Damascus wrote, in the years 1140–60, a history of his native city from the time of the Turkish invasions to his own day. The title of the work, the *Mudhayyal Tarikh Dimashq* (the 'Continuation

---

[1] For the epics, see Hatem, *Les Poèmes Epiques des Croisades*, defending a Syrian origin for the poems, and the summary in Cahen, *op. cit.* pp. 12–16.

[2] The best edition of these letters is in Hagenmeyer, *Die Kreuzzugsbriefe*. A fuller collection is to be found in Riant, *Inventaire des Lettres historiques*.

of the Chronicle of Damascus') shows that it was intended as a sequel to the chronicle of the historian Hilal. But whereas Hilal aimed at giving the history of the world, Ibn al-Qalānisī was only interested in Damascus and its rulers. He spent his life in the chancery of the Damascene court, rising to be its chief official. He was therefore well-informed; and except when the reputations of his masters were at stake he seems to have been accurate and objective.[1]

IBN AL-ATHIR of Mosul wrote his *Kamil at-Tawarikh* ('Sum of World History') at the beginning of the thirteenth century. But his careful and critical use of earlier sources makes him an authority of primary importance, though his entries are usually very brief.[2]

KEMAL AD-DIN of Aleppo wrote his unfinished chronicle of Aleppo and his Encyclopaedia half a century later still. But he too made full use of earlier sources, and in his Encyclopaedia he cites them by name. Of these lost sources the most to be regretted is the history of the Frankish invasion by HAMDĀN IBN ABD AR-RAHĪM of Maaratha, of which even in Kemal ad-Din's time only a few pages survived. IBN ZURAIQ of Maarat an-Numan, who was born in 1051 and played a part in the events of the Crusade, left a history of his times also only known from a few extracts; and AL-AZIMI of Aleppo, born in 1090, left an account of northern Syrian history at the time of the Crusade, of which a slightly larger number of extracts still exist.[3]

4. ARMENIAN

There is one invaluable Armenian source covering the period of the First Crusade, the *Chronicle* of MATTHEW OF EDESSA. The work deals with the history of Syria from 952 to 1136 and must have been written before 1140. Matthew was a naïve man with a hatred for the Greeks and no great love for those of his compatriots who were Orthodox in religion. Much of his information about the Crusade must have been

---

[1] For Ibn al-Qalānisī, see the preface to Gibb's translation of the passages of the *Damascus Chronicle* that refer to the Crusades (see Bibliography). The full text in Arabic is published by Amedroz (Leyden, 1908).

[2] The full text of Ibn al-Athir's works is published in Arabic in 14 volumes by Tornberg (Leyden, 1851–76). Relevant passages are published in *R.H.C. Occ.*

[3] There is no good edition of Kemal ad-Din. Passages relative to the Crusades, from 1097 to 1146, are fully given in the *Recueil.*

deriyed from some ignorant Frankish soldier; but about events in his native city and its neighbourhood he was very fully informed.[1]

Later Armenian chroniclers, such as SAMUEL OF ANI and MEKHITAR OF AIRAVANQ, writing at the end of the twelfth century, and KIRAKOS OF GANTZAG and VARTAN THE GREAT, in the thirteenth century, treat only briefly of the First Crusade. They seem to have made use of Matthew and of a lost history written by a certain JOHN THE DEACON, whom Samuel praises highly and who showed special animosity not only against the Emperor Alexius but also against his mother, Anna Dalassena.[2]

5. SYRIAC

The only surviving Syriac work to treat of the First Crusade is the chronicle of MICHAEL THE SYRIAN, Jacobite Patriarch of Antioch from 1166 to 1199, who passes very briefly over the period before 1107. He made use of earlier Syriac chronicles that are now lost as well as of Arabic sources. His information is of little value till he reaches his own lifetime.[3]

Though some of the primary histories of the Crusade have been individually edited, the only collection of sources is the great *Recueil des Historiens des Croisades*, published in Paris from 1844 onwards. This includes Latin and Old French, Arabic, Greek and Armenian texts, with translations into French of the Greek and eastern writers. Unfortunately except for the last (fifth) volume of the Latin texts, published some years after the rest of the *Recueil*, the editing of the manuscripts has been careless. There are also many arbitrary lacunae; and the translations are not always accurate. Nevertheless the collection remains indispensable for the student of the Crusades.

[1] A French translation was published from the MSS. by Dulaurier in 1858 and extracts of the Armenian text with French translation in *R.H.C.Arm.* The full Armenian text was published in Jerusalem in 1868. I have not been able to obtain it, and have therefore used the translation by Dulaurier, checking it where possible with the extracts in Armenian in the *Recueil*.
[2] Extracts of these historians are published in the *Recueil*.
[3] Trans. and publ. by Chabot.

THE NUMERICAL STRENGTH OF
THE CRUSADERS

Every medieval historian, whatever his race, invariably indulges in wild
and picturesque exaggeration whenever he has to estimate numbers that
cannot easily be counted. It is therefore impossible for us to-day to
establish the actual size of the Crusading armies. When Fulcher of
Chartres and Albert of Aix tell us that the fighting men of the First
Crusade numbered 600,000, while Ekkehard gives 300,000 and Raymond
of Aguilers a modest 100,000, or when Anna Comnena declares that
Godfrey of Lorraine brought with him 10,000 knights and 70,000
infantrymen, it is clear that the figures are only meant to denote a very
large number indeed.[1] But when they are dealing with smaller numbers
the chroniclers need not be entirely distrusted, though they like to give
a round figure that can only be approximate. From their evidence we
can make certain deductions.

The proportion of non-combatants in the armies cannot be estimated.
It was certainly high. A large number of knights brought their ladies
with them. Raymond of Toulouse was accompanied by his wife, and
Baldwin of Boulogne by his wife and children. Bohemond had at least
one sister with him. We know the names of several ladies that took part
in Robert of Normandy's expedition; and occasionally other ladies
appear in the story. All these ladies brought attendants; and there was
certainly a large number of humbler women, respectable and the reverse,
with the army. We continually hear of male non-combatants, such as
Peter Bartholomew and his employer. The clergy with the army was
numerous. But it is probable that most of the male non-combatants
would be pressed into service in times of danger. The proportion of

---

[1] Anna Comnena, x, ix, 1, vol. II, p. 220; Fulcher of Chartres, I, x, 4, p. 183;
Ekkehard, *Hierosolymita*, XIII, p. 21; Raymond of Aguilers, v, p. 242. The
Chronicle of Zimmern, p. 27, gives Godfrey an army of 300,000.

permanent non-combatants, women, old men and children, cannot have been more than a quarter of the whole force.

It is probable also that the rate of mortality was particularly high amongst these non-combatants, especially the old men and children. Among the combatants the infantry must have died off from disease and hardships in greater proportion than the knights and ladies, who were better tended and better able to buy food. In battle the cavalry played a more exposed role than the infantry and therefore suffered as heavily.

The proportion of cavalry to infantry seems to have been about one to seven when every possible combatant was enrolled into the latter. Anna's estimate of the relative strength in Godfrey's forces, though her figures should be divided at least by ten, is probably correct. At the battle of Ascalon, when every available man in Palestine was employed, there were 1200 cavalry and 9000 infantry, a proportion of one to seven and a half.[1] At the siege of Jerusalem there were, according to Raymond of Aguilers, 1200 to 1300 knights out of an army of 12,000; which, however, included Genoese and English engineers and marines.[2] The term 'knights' must be used to mean armed horsemen, and not in any chivalrous sense; while many of the infantrymen were not fully armed. The archers and pikemen were probably only a fairly small proportion of the whole.

Of the individual armies it is almost certain that Raymond's was the largest; but we have only one indication of its size. When he heard at Coxon the false rumour that the Turks had evacuated Antioch he sent a cavalry force of 500, including some of his leading knights, to occupy the city.[3] The number 500 occurs with suspicious frequency; but it may well have been considered the proper unit for a large raid or expedition of this type. It is unlikely that Raymond would have spared half his cavalry strength at this stage. If we accept this figure of 500 as approximately correct, his whole cavalry strength must have been 1200 or more, and his total force about 10,000, apart from old men, women and children.[4]

---

[1] William of Tyre, IX, 12, vol. I, pt. I, p. 380.
[2] Raymond of Aguilers, XIX, p. 292.
[3] See above, p. 191.
[4] Raymond's army was still clearly of formidable dimensions when he left Palestine, as his subsequent campaigns show.

The Chronicle of Lucca tells us that Bohemond went to the East with 500 knights.[1] Anna Comnena notes that he did not have a particularly large army; so this figure may well be correct.[2] He allowed Tancred 100 knights and 200 infantrymen for his Cilician expedition, though he sent another 300 infantrymen after him. These numbers fit together reasonably.[3]

The only indication that we have of the proportionate size of the other armies is given by Raymond's action at Rugia, when he attempted to bribe his rivals to accept his leadership. He offered Godfrey and Robert of Normandy each 10,000 sous, Robert of Flanders 6000, and Tancred 5000, and lesser sums to the lesser chiefs. The sums must have been fixed in relation to the strength that each prince could now supply, though Tancred was probably offered a disproportionately high sum in order to detach him and as many Normans as possible from Bohemond.[4]

Our only evidence for the size of Godfrey's army, apart from Anna's fantastic figure, is provided by his willingness to spare 500 cavalry and 2000 infantry to his brother Baldwin for his Cilician expedition. It is most unlikely that he would have parted with more than half his cavalry strength, even though he intended this force to rejoin him before reaching Antioch. It is tempting to assume that Raymond's offer at Rugia was made on the basis of ten sous for each head of cavalry. If at the same time we divide Anna's figures by ten, we may credit Godfrey with some 1000 cavalry and 7000 infantry at the time of his arrival at Constantinople. He must have suffered considerable losses before the date of the conference at Rugia, quite apart from the knights that accompanied Baldwin to Edessa; but he had been joined by survivors from Peter the Hermit's Crusade and the abortive German Crusades, as well as by some of Guynemer's marines; who, as their master was a Boulonnais, would naturally associate themselves with the Count of Boulogne and his brothers.[5]

Robert of Normandy ranked equal to Godfrey at Rugia. If Godfrey commanded 1000 head of cavalry, he must have been equally strong.

---

[1] Quoted by Chalandon, *Histoire de la première Croisade*, p. 133. I have not been able to discover to what chronicle he refers.

[2] Anna Comnena, x, ix, 1, vol. II, p. 230: 'Bohemond...did not have large forces because he was short of money...'.

[3] See above, p. 197. [4] See above, p. 261.

[5] See above, pp. 149-50, 201.

A century later Normandy was obliged to provide its duke with slightly under 600 knights.[1] For the Crusade Robert might well have been able to raise a rather larger number of horsemen, perhaps 650. He was joined by soldiers from Brittany and across the Channel; which may have given him another 100 or 150 horsemen. Moreover, after the return to Europe of Stephen of Blois and Hugh of Vermandois, he had assumed command of such of their forces as remained behind. Stephen, whose territories were not large but were rich, may have provided 250 or 300 horsemen. Hugh probably did not bring with him many more than 100. In all Robert may well have had close on 1000 under his command at the time of Rugia.

On the same basis Robert of Flanders must be credited with 600 cavalrymen, some of whom came from the territory of his neighbour, the Count of Hainault. Robert legally owed his liege, the king of France, only twenty fully armed knights; but in 1103 he offered in a treaty to provide Henry I of England with 1000 cavalrymen.[2] He could therefore easily raise 600 for the Crusade.

Bohemond's force of 500 cavalrymen, mentioned by the Chronicle of Lucca, fits in with these figures. If we assume that the armies of the lesser lords are to be counted in with the greater armies, and that the sums offered to them by Raymond at Rugia were purely personal, we reach a total for the whole expedition of roughly 4200 to 4500 cavalry and 30,000 infantry, including civilians that could be pressed into service. The letter written by Daimbert to the Pope numbers the army of Crusaders at 5000 cavalry and 15,000 infantry. By the latter armed combatants alone were probably included. The former figure is a permissible exaggeration from 4000.[3]

This seems a small enough army. Yet when we come to the figures given by the chroniclers for individual battles, the numbers are smaller still. At the battle of the Lake of Antioch, when, we are told, all the available knights were used, there were only 700 of them. But many of

---

[1] *Milites Regni Franciae*, in Bouquet, *R.H.F.* vol. XXII, pp. 684–5. This gives 60 bannerets for Normandy in the time of Philip Augustus. Each banneret probably had approximately ten horsemen. See also list *ibid.* vol. XXIII, p. 698, giving the duchy of Normandy 581 knights.

[2] *Actes des Comtes de Flandres*, ed. by Vercauteren, nos. 30, 41, quoted with comments by Lot, *L'Art Militaire et les Armées du Moyen Age*, vol. I, p. 130 n. 2.

[3] Letter in Hagenmeyer, *Die Kreuzzugsbriefe*, p. 172.

the knights were sick at the time; and it appears from a letter of Anselm of Ribemont that the real shortage was of horses. He estimates that only about 700 were available for use at the time of the siege of Antioch, so many had perished from hunger and from cold. He declares that there was no shortage of men.[1] Moreover, on this occasion, it is probable that Raymond's cavalry remained with him to guard the camp. The raiding expedition led by Bohemond and Robert of Flanders the following month was said to have been composed of 2000 cavalry and 15,000 infantry; and this definitely excluded Raymond's army.[2] But again, only 1200 or 1300 cavalry were present at the siege of Jerusalem, and a little over 10,000 infantry; and the strength of the army at Ascalon was very similar.[3] Though many soldiers had died or been killed and many had returned home, it is impossible that the strength of the army should have declined by two-thirds between the time of the conference at Rugia and the siege of Jerusalem.

We can only therefore repeat that any estimate must be taken with reserve. I believe that the whole army at the time that it left Constantinople roughly reached the total that I have suggested above. In the course of the next two years it was very much reduced; and at Rugia Raymond was using an out-of-date and highly optimistic calculation on which to base his offers. The comparatively small figures given in the chronicles of Baldwin's exploits can, I think, be accepted as roughly accurate.

The size of Peter the Hermit's original expedition is equally impossible to calculate. The figure of 40,000 given by Albert of Aix is clearly excessive; but his followers may have numbered as many as 20,000. Of these non-combatants formed the vast majority.[4]

For purposes of comparison it may be noted that the whole Byzantine army in the ninth century has been calculated to have numbered 120,000. The loss of the Anatolian provinces must have resulted in a reduction of available forces by the end of the eleventh century; but Alexius could probably dispose of about 70,000 men, most of which

[1] See above, p. 222.   [2] See above, p. 220.
[3] See above, p. 337 nn. 1 and 2.
[4] Chalandon, *op. cit.* p. 59, estimates that 15,000 persons left France with Peter. It is impossible to check the number, which seems plausible. The *Chronicle of Zimmern*, pp. 27–8, says that Peter had 29,000 persons with him at Civetot, after 3200 Germans had been killed (at Xerigordon).

were needed to garrison his far-flung frontiers; while a large proportion was probably disbanded every winter for purposes of economy. It is improbable that the largest army led into battle by the Byzantines at this period numbered more than 20,000 men, well equipped and well trained. It is impossible to estimate the size of the Moslem armies. Kerbogha's army probably numbered about 30,000; but no actual evidence exists. It was able to undertake a more effective blockade of Antioch than the Crusader army could manage. The Egyptian army at Ascalon was certainly larger than the Crusaders'; but its actual size can only be guessed. It is doubtful if the Turkish army at Dorylaeum was as large as the Crusaders'. The Turks relied on their sudden attack and their mobility to compensate for any disadvantage in numbers.

BIBLIOGRAPHY

I. ORIGINAL SOURCES

1. COLLECTIONS OF SOURCES

[Note. The abbreviations at the end of certain items are used to refer to these items in the footnotes and the following sections of the bibliography.]

ACHÉRY, L. D'. *Spicilegium sive Collectio veterum aliquot Scriptorum*, 13 vols. Paris, 1655–77. 2nd ed. (ed. L. F. J. de la Barre), 3 vols. Paris, 1723.

Acta Sanctorum (Bollandiana). Antwerp-Paris-Rome-Brussels, 1643– (in progress). [*Aa. Ss.*]

Acta Sanctorum Ordinis Sancti Benedicti (ed. J. Mabillon and L. d'Achéry), 9 vols. Paris, 1668–1701.

AMEDROZ, H. F. and MARGOLIOUTH, D. S. *The Eclipse of the Abbasid Caliphate: Original Chronicles of the Fourth Islamic Century*, 6 vols. and Index. Oxford, 1920–1.

Archives de l'Orient Latin, pub. Société de l'Orient Latin, 2 vols. Paris, 1881–4.

ASSEMANI, J. S. *Bibliotheca Orientalis*, 3 vols. Rome, 1719–28.

BENECHEWITCH, V. *Catalogus Codicum Manuscriptorum Graecorum qui in Monasterio Sanctae Catharinae in Monte Sinai Asservantur*. St Petersburg, 1911.

BOUQUET, M. and others. *Recueil des Historiens des Gaules et de la France*, 23 vols. Paris, 1738–1876. New series, Paris, 1899– (in progress). [*R.H.F.*]

BROSSET, M. F. *Collection d'Historiens Arméniens*, 2 vols. St Petersburg, 1874–6.

CAETANI, L. See Bibliography, p. 352.

Corpus Scriptorum Christianorum Orientalium (ed. J. B. Chabot and others). Paris, 1903– (in progress). [*C.S.C.O.*]

Corpus Scriptorum Ecclesiasticorum Latinorum. Vienna, 1866– (in progress).

Corpus Scriptorum Historiae Byzantinae. Bonn, 1828–97. [*C.S.H.B.*]

DÖLGER, F. *Regesten der Kaiserurkunden des Oströmischen Reiches*, 3 vols. Munich-Berlin, 1924–32.

Fonti per la Storia d'Italia, Istituto Storico Italiano. Rome, 1887– (in progress).

HAGENMEYER, H. *Die Kreuzzugsbriefe aus den Jahren 1088–1100*. Innsbruck, 1902.

HOLTZMANN, W. See Bibliography, p. 355.

JAFFÉ, P. *Bibliotheca Rerum Germanicarum*, 6 vols. Berlin, 1864–73.

JAFFÉ, P. *Regesta Pontificum Romanorum*, 2nd ed. (ed. W. Wattenbach, S. Loewenfeld, and others), 2 vols. Leipzig, 1885–8.

LEIB, B. *Deux Inédits Byzantins sur les Azymites au début du XIIme Siècle*. Rome, n.d. (1924).

Bibliography

Liber Pontificalis (ed. L. Duchesne), 2 vols. Paris, 1884–92.

MABILLON, J. *Annales Ordinis Sancti Benedicti*, 6 vols. Paris, 1703–39.

MABILLON, J. *De Re Diplomatica Libri VI*. Paris, 1681.

MANSI, J. D. *Sacrorum Conciliorum Amplissima Collectio*, 31 vols. Florence, Venice, 1759–98. *Continuation* (ed. J. B. Martin and L. Petit). Paris, 190– (in progress).

MIGNE, J. P. *Patrologiae Cursus Completus.*
    I, *Patrologia Latina*, 221 vols. Paris, 1844–55. [*M.P.L.*]
    II, *Patrologia Graeco-Latina*, 161 vols. in 166. Paris, 1857–66. [*M.P.G.*]

MONTFAUCON, B. DE. *Bibliotheca Coisliniana*. Paris, 1715.

Monumenta Germaniae Historica (ed. G. H. Pertz, T. Mommsen, and others). Hanover, 1826– (in progress). [*M.G.H.*]

MURATORI, L. A. *Rerum Italicarum Scriptores*, 25 vols. Milan, 1723–51. [*R.I.Ss.*]

NEUBAUER, A. and STERN, M. *Quellen zur Geschichte der Juden in Deutschland*, 2 vols. Berlin, 1892.

Palestine Pilgrims' Text Society, 13 vols. and Index. London, 1896–7. [*P.P.T.S.*]

Patrologia Orientalis (ed. R. Graffin and F. Nau). Paris, 1907– (in progress). [*P.O.*]

Recueil des Historiens des Croisades. Publ. Académie des Inscriptions et Belles Lettres. Paris, 1841–1906.
    Documents Arméniens, 2 vols. 1869–1906. [*R.H.C.Arm.*]
    Historiens Grecs, 2 vols. 1875–81. [*R.H.C.G.*]
    Historiens Occidentaux, 5 vols. 1844–95. [*R.H.C.Occ.*]
    Historiens Orientaux, 5 vols. 1872–1906. [*R.H.C.Or.*]

RIANT, P. *Inventaire critique des Lettres historiques des Croisades, Archives de l'Orient Latin*, vol. I. Paris, 1881.

RÖHRICHT, R. *Regesta Regni Hierosolymitani*, 2 vols. Innsbrück, 1893–1904.

ROZIÈRE, E. DE. *Recueil général des Formules usitées dans l'Empire des Francs du Vme au Xme Siècle*, 2 vols. Paris, 1859.

SATHAS, K. N. Μεσαιωνικὴ Βιβλιοθήκη, *Bibliotheca Graeca Medii Aevi*, 7 vols. Venice-Paris, 1872–9.

TOBLER, T. and MOLINIER, A. *Itinera Hierosolymitana et Descriptiones Terrae Sanctae*, 2 vols. Geneva, 1879.

UGHELLI, F. *Italia Sacra*, 9 vols. Rome, 1644–62.

VAISSÈTE, DOM. See Bibliography, p. 359.

2. WESTERN SOURCES, LATIN, OLD FRENCH AND GERMAN

Adamnan. *Arculf's Narrative about the Holy Places* (trans. J. R. Macpherson). *P.P.T.S.* vol. III.

Aetheria. See *Pilgrimage of Saint Silvia.*

Bibliography

Aimé of Monte Cassino. *Chronicon, L'Ystoire de li Normant* (ed. O. Delarcq). Rouen, 1892.

Albert of Aix (Albertus Aquensis). *Liber Christianae Expeditionis pro Ereptione, Emundatione et Restitutione Sanctae Hierosolymitanae Ecclesiae*, in *R.H.C.Occ.* vol. IV.

Alexius I Comnenus. Letters nos. I, V and XI, in Hagenmeyer, *Die Kreuzzugsbriefe*.

Ambrose, St, Archbishop of Milan. *Epistolae*, in *M.P.L.* vol. XVI.

Annales Altahenses Majores, in *M.G.H. Scriptores*, vol. XX.

Annales Pisani (ed. P. Tronci), 4 vols. Pisa, 1828–9.

Anonymi Gesta Francorum et Aliorum Hierosolimitorum (ed. L. Bréhier as *Histoire Anonyme de la Première Croisade*). Paris, 1924. (Also ed. H. Hagenmeyer. Heidelberg, 1890.)

Anselm of Ribemont. Letters nos. VIII and XV, in Hagenmeyer, *Die Kreuzzugsbriefe*.

Augustine, St, of Hippo. *Contra Faustum*, in *M.P.L.* vol. XLII.

Augustine, St, of Hippo. *De Civitate Dei*, in *M.P.L.* vol. XLI.

Augustine, St, of Hippo. *Epistolae*, in *M.P.L.* vol. XXXIII.

Bartolf of Nangis. *Gesta Francorum Iherusalem Expugnantium*, in *R.H.C.Occ.* vol. III.

Baudri of Dol. *Historia Jerosolimitana*, in *R.H.C.Occ.* vol. IV.

Baudri of Dol. *Vita di Roberti de Arbrisello*, in *Aa. Ss.* (23 February), vol. III.

Bechada, Gregory. *Chanson d'Antioche en provençal* (ed. P. Meyer) in 'Fragment d'une Chanson d'Antioche en provençal', in *Archives de l'Orient Latin*, vol. II.

Benedict of Accolti. *Historia Gotefridi*, in *R.H.C.Occ.* vol. V, pt. II.

Berno. *Libellus de Officio Missae*, in *M.P.L.* vol. CXLII.

Bernold of Constance (Saint-Blaise). *Chronicon*, in *M.G.H. Scriptores*, vol. V.

Bohemond. Charter no. X, and letters (with other princes) nos. XII and XVI, in Hagenmeyer, *Die Kreuzzugsbriefe*.

Caffaro de Caschifelone. *Annales Ianuenses*, in *Fonti per la Storia d'Italia*, vols. I and II.

Caffaro de Caschifelone. *De Liberatione Civitatum Orientis Liber*, in *R.H.C.Occ.* vol. V, pt. I.

Cartulaire de Saint-Chaffre (ed. U. Chevalier). Paris, 1881.

Chanson du Chevalier au Cygne (Belgian version, ed. Reiffenberg and Borgnet), 3 vols. Brussels, 1846–59.

Chanson du Chevalier au Cygne (ed. Hippeau), 2 vols. Paris, 1874–7.

Chronicon Barense, in Muratori, *Rerum Italicarum Scriptores*, vol. V.

Chronique de Zimmern (German text with French trans., ed. Hagenmeyer), in *Archives de l'Orient Latin*, vol. II.

Clementia, Countess of Flanders. Charter no. VII, in Hagenmeyer, *Die Kreuzzugsbriefe*.

Clergy of Lucca. Letter no. XVII, in Hagenmeyer, *Die Kreuzzugsbriefe*.

Bibliography

Commemoratorium de Casis Dei vel Monasteriis, in Tobler and Molinier, *Itinera Hierosolymitana*, vol. I.

Cosmas of Prague. *Chronicon*, in *M.G.H. Scriptores*, vol. VII.

Daimbert (Dagobert), Archbishop of Pisa and Patriarch of Jerusalem. Letters nos. XVIII and XXI, in Hagenmeyer, *Die Kreuzzugsbriefe*.

De Sancto Wlphlagio, in *Aa. Ss.* (7 June), June, vol. II.

Ekkehard of Aura. *Chronicon Universale*, in *M.G.H. Scriptores*, vol. VI.

Ekkehard of Aura. *Hierosolymita*, in *R.H.C.Occ.* vol. V, pt. I.

Ennodius. *Libellum pro Synodo*, in *Corpus Scriptorum Ecclesiasticorum Latinorum*, vol. VI. Vienna, 1882.

Expeditio Contra Turcos (ed. at base of Tudebod), in *R.H.C.Occ.* vol. III.

Fulbert of Chartres. *Epistolae*, in *R.H.F.* vol. X.

Fulcher of Chartres. *Gesta Francorum Iherusalem Peregrinantium* (ed. H. Hagenmeyer). Heidelberg, 1913.

Genoese citizens. Pact with Bohemond no. XIV, in Hagenmeyer, *Die Kreuzzugsbriefe*.

Gesta Adhemari Episcopi Podiensis Hierosolymitana, in *R.H.C.Occ.* vol. V, pt. II.

Gesta Francorum. See *Anonymi Gesta Francorum*.

Gilon. *De Via Hierosolymitana*, in *R.H.C.Occ.* vol. V, pt. II.

Glaber. See Radulph.

Graindor of Douai. See Richard the Pilgrim.

Gregory VII, Pope. *Epistolae*, in *Monumenta Gregoriana*, vol. II of Jaffé, *Bibliotheca Rerum Germanicarum*.

Gregory VII, Pope. *Registra* (ed. E. Caspar), in *M.G.H. Epistolae*, vol. II.

Gregory of Tours. *De Gloria Martyrum*, in *M.P.L.* vol. LXXI.

Guibert of Nogent. *Historia Hierosolymitana*, in *R.H.C.Occ.* vol. IV.

Gunther of Basle. *Solymarius*, in *Archives de l'Orient Latin*, vol. I.

Henry of Huntingdon. *De Captione Antiochiae*, in *R.H.C.Occ.* vol. V, pt. II.

Historia Belli Sacri (*Tudebodus Continuatus*), in *R.H.C.Occ.* vol. III.

Historia et Gesta Ducis Gotfridi, in *R.H.C.Occ.* vol. V, pt. II.

Hugh of Fleury. *Itineris Hierosolymitani Compendium*, in *R.H.C.Occ.* vol. V, pt. II.

Hugh of Lerchenfeld. *Breviarium Passagii in Terram Sanctam*, in *R.H.C.Occ.* vol. V, pt. II.

Itinerary of Bernard the Wise (trans. J. H. Bernard), in *P.P.T.S.* vol. III.

Itinerary of the Bordeaux Pilgrim (trans. A. Stewart), in *P.P.T.S.* vol. I.

Jerome, St. *De Viris Illustribus*, in *M.P.L.* vol. XXIII.

Jerome, St. *Epistolae*, in *M.P.L.* vol. XXII.

Jerome, St. *Liber Paralipumenon*, in *M.P.L.* vol. XXVIII.

John VIII, Pope. *Epistolae*, in *M.P.L.* vol. CXXVI.

Joseph of Exeter. *Poemata* (ed. J. Jusserand), *De Josepho Exoniensi*. Paris, 1877.

Joseph the Historiographer. *Tractatus de Exordio Sacrae Domus Hospitalis Jerosolimitani*, in *R.H.C.Occ.* vol. V, pt. II.

345

Lambert of Arras. Canons of the Council of Clermont, in Mansi, *Concilia*, vol. xx.

Leo IX, Pope. *Epistolae*, in *M.P.L.* vol. CXLIII.

Leo of Ostia. *Chronicon Monasterii Casinensis*, in *M.G.H. Scriptores*, vol. VII.

Lisiard of Tours. *Historiae Hierosolimitanae Secunda Pars*, in *R.H.C.Occ.* vol. III.

Liudprand of Cremona. *Opera* (ed. J. Becker). Hanover-Leipzig, 1925.

Malaterra, Gaufredus. *Historia Sicula*, in *M.P.L.* vol. CXLIX.

Martin I, Pope. *Epistolae*, in *M.P.L.* vol. LXXXVII.

Milites Regni Franciae, in *R.H.F.* vol. XXII.

Miracles de Saint-Benoît (ed. E. de Certain). Paris, 1856.

Miracula Sancti Wolframni Senonensis, in *Acta Sanctorum Ordinis Sancti Benedicti*, ser. III, pt. II.

Monitum in Balduini III Historiae Nicenae vel Antiochenae Prologum, in *R.H.C.Occ.* vol. V, pt. I.

Nicholas I, Pope. *Epistolae*, in *M.G.H. Epistolae*, vol. VI.

Notitiae Duae Lemovicenses de Praedicatione Crucis in Aquitania, in *R.H.C.Occ.* vol. V, pt. II.

Orderic Vitalis. *Historia Ecclesiastica* (ed. A. Le Prevost and L. Delisle) in Société de l'Histoire de France, 5 vols. Paris, 1838–55.

Paschal II, Pope. Letters nos. XIX and XXII, in Hagenmeyer, *Die Kreuzzugsbriefe*.

Peregrinatio Frotmundi, in *Aa. Ss.* (24 October), Oct., vol. X.

Pilgrimage of Saint Silvia of Aquitaine (trans. A. Stewart), in *P.P.T.S.* vol. I.

Prudentius. *Carmina* (ed. J. Bergman), in *Corpus Scriptorum Ecclesiasticorum Latinorum*, vol. LXI.

Radulph of Caen. *Gesta Tancredi Siciliae Regis in Expeditione Hierosolymitana.* in *R.H.C.Occ.* vol. III.

Radulph Glaber. *Historiarum Sui Temporis Libri V*, in *R.H.F.* vol. X.

Raymond of Aguilers. *Historia Francorum qui ceperunt Jerusalem*, in *R.H.C.Occ.* vol. III.

Richard the Pilgrim. *La Chanson d'Antioche*, in *Roman des Douze Pairs: La Chanson d'Antioche composée au Commencement du XIIme Siècle par le Pélérin Richard, renouvelée sous le Règne de Philippe Auguste par Graindor de Douai et publiée pour la première fois par Paulin Paris*, 2 vols. Paris, 1848.

Robert the Monk. *Historia Hierosolymitana*, in *R.H.C.Occ.* vol. III.

Sigebert of Gembloux. *Chronicon*, in *M.G.H. Scriptores*, vol. VI.

Stephen of Blois. Letters nos. IV and X, in Hagenmeyer, *Die Kreuzzugsbriefe*.

Symeon, Patriarch of Jerusalem (with others). Letters nos. VI and IX, in Hagenmeyer, *Die Kreuzzugsbriefe*.

Tolomeo. *Annales Lucchenses*, in *M.G.H. Scriptores* (new ser.), vol. VIII.

Translatio Sancti Nicolai in Venetiam, in *R.H.C.Occ.* vol. V, pt. I.

Tudebod. *De Hierosolymitano Itinere*, in *R.H.C.Occ.* vol. III.

Urban II, Pope. Letters nos. II and III, in Hagenmeyer, *Die Kreuzzugsbriefe*.

Bibliography

Victor II, Pope. Letter no. 1 (wrongly attributed to Victor III), in *M.P.L.* vol. CXLIX.

Victricius, St. *Liber de Laude Sanctorum*, in *M.P.L.* vol. XX.

Vita Genovefae Virginis Parisiensis, in *M.G.H. Scriptores Rerum Merovingiarum*, vol. III.

Vita Lietberti, in d'Achéry, *Spicilegium*, vol. IX.

Vita Urbani II, in *Liber Pontificalis*, vol. II.

William of Malmesbury. *Gesta Regum* (ed. W. Stubbs), Rolls Series, 2 vols. London, 1887–9.

William of Tyre. *Historia Rerum in Partibus Transmarinis Gestarum*, in *R.H.C. Occ.* vol. I, pts. I and II. Old French version, *L'Estoire de Eracles, Empereur, et la Conqueste de la Terre d'Outremer, ibid.*

Willibald. *Hodoeporicon* (trans. W. R. Brownlow), in *P.P.T.S.* vol. III.

3. GREEK SOURCES

Anna Comnena. *Alexiad* (ed. B. Leib), in *Collection Byzantine de l'Association Guillaume Budé*, 3 vols. Paris, 1937–45. (Also ed. Ducange, in *R.H.C.G.* vol. I.)

Attaliates, Michael. *Historia* (ed. I. Bekker), in *C.S.H.B.* Bonn, 1853.

Basil, St. *Opera*, in *M.P.G.* vols. XXIX–XXXII.

Bryennius, Nicephorus. *Historia* (ed. A. Meineke), in *C.S.H.B.* Bonn, 1836.

Cedrenus, Georgius. *Synopsis Historiarum* (ed. I. Bekker), in *C.S.H.B.* 2 vols. Bonn, 1839.

Cerularius, Michael, Patriarch. *Epistolae*, in *M.P.G.* vol. CXX.

Chronicon Paschale (ed. L. Dindorf), in *C.S.H.B.* 2 vols. Bonn, 1832.

Constantine Porphyrogennetus. *De Ceremoniis Aulae Byzantinae* (ed. J. J. Rieske), in *C.S.H.B.* 2 vols. Bonn, 1829–30. (Also ed. A. Vogt, in *Collection Byzantine de l'Association Guillaume Budé*, 4 vols. Paris, 1935–40.)

Doctrina Jacobi nuper Baptizati (ed. N. Bonwetsch), in *Abhandlungen der Königlichen Gesellschaft der Wissenschaft zu Göttingen, Phil.-Hist. Klasse*, Neue Folge, vol. XII, no. 3. Berlin, 1910.

Eastern Patriarchs. Letter to Theophilus, in *M.P.G.* vol. XCV.

Eusebius of Caesarea. *Ecclesiastical History* (trans. H. J. Lawlor and J. E. L. Oughton), 2 vols. London, 1928.

Glycas, Michael. *Chronicon* (ed. I. Bekker), in *C.S.H.B.* Bonn, 1836.

Gregory Nazianzene, St. *Epistolae*, in *M.P.G.* vol. XLVI.

John VI Cantacuzenus. *Historia* (ed. L. Schopen), in *C.S.H.B.* 3 vols. Bonn, 1828–32.

John Chrysostom, St. *Opera*, in *M.P.G.* vols. XLVII–LXIV.

John the Oxite, Patriarch of Antioch. Περὶ τῶν 'Αζύμων, in Leib, *Deux Inédits Byzantins*.

Nicephorus Callistus. *Historia Ecclesiastica*, in *M.P.G.* vol. CXLVI.

Nicephorus, Patriarch. *Opuscula Historica* (ed. C. de Boor), in *Bibliotheca Teubneriana*. Leipzig, 1880.

Origen. *In Joannem*, in *M.P.G.* vol. XIV.

Passio LX Martyrum et Legenda Sancti Floriani (ed. H. Delehaye), in *Analecta Bollandiana*, vol. XXIII. Brussels, 1903.

Peter, Patriarch of Antioch. Letter to Michael Cerularius, in *M.P.G.* vol. CXX.

Synopsis Chronicon, in Sathas, Μεσαιωνική Βιβλιοθήκη, vol. VII.

Theodosius, Patriarch of Jerusalem. Letter to Ignatius of Constantinople, in Mansi, *Concilia*, vol. XVI.

Theophanes Confessor. *Chronographia* (ed. C. de Boor), 2 vols. Leipzig, 1883–5.

Theophylact, Archbishop of Bulgaria. *Epistolae*, in *M.P.G.* vol. CXXVI.

Zonaras, Joannes. *Epitome Historiarum*, vol. III (ed. T. Büttner-Wörst), in *C.S.H.B.* Bonn, 1897.

4. ARABIC AND PERSIAN SOURCES

[*Note.* The titles of the works are translated into English.]

Abu'l Feda. *Moslem Annals* (selection, with French trans.), in *R.H.C.Or.* vol. I. (Full text with Latin trans. ed. J. Reiske. Copenhagen, 1789–94.)

Abu'l Mahāsin. MS. passages quoted with Russian trans. in Rosen, *Emperor Basil the Bulgar-slayer*.

Agapius of Maboug. *Universal Chronicle* (ed. with French trans. by A. A. Vasiliev), in *P.O.* vols. V, VII and VIII.

Antiochus the Stratege. *Capture of Jerusalem by the Persians*, Arabic version (ed. with French trans. by A. Couret), in *Revue de l'Orient Chrétien*. Paris, 1897. See Bibliography, p. 350.

Balādhurī. *The Conquest of the Nations*, Arabic text. Cairo, A.H. 1319. (English trans. by P. K. Hitti and F. C. Murgotten, 2 vols. New York, 1916–24.)

Chronicle of Seert (ed. with French trans. by A. Scher), in *P.O.* vols. IV, V, VII and XIII.

Eutychius, Patriarch of Alexandria. *Annals* (Latin trans. in *M.P.G.* vol. CXI).

Ibn al-Athir. *History of Atabegs of Mosul* (selection, with French trans.), in *R.H.C.Or.* vol. II, pt. II.

Ibn al-Athir. *Sum of World History* (selection, with French trans.), in *R.H.C.Occ.* vol. I. (Full Arabic text ed. C. J. Tornberg, 14 vols. Leyden-Upsala, 1851–76.)

Ibn Khaldūn. *Universal History*, Arabic text, 7 vols. Bulaq, A.H. 1287. (Partial Latin trans. by C. J. Tornberg. Upsala, 1840.)

Bibliography

Ibn al-Qalānisī. *Continuation of the Chronicle of Damascus: The Damascus Chronicle of the Crusades* (selected and trans. into English by H. A. R. Gibb). London, 1932. (Full Arabic text ed. H. F. Amedroz. Leyden, 1908.)

al-Jahiz. *Three Essays* (ed. J. Finkel). Cairo, 1926.

Kemal ad-Din. *Chronicle of Aleppo* (selection, with French trans.), in *R.H.C.Or.* vol. III.

Miskawaihi. *The Experiences of the Nations* (concluding portions with English trans. by D. S. Margoliouth), in Amedroz and Margoliouth, *Eclipse of the Abbasid Caliphate*, vols. I and II (Arabic text); vols. IV and V (English text).

Mukaddasi. *Description of Syria* (English trans. by G. Le Strange), in *P.P.T.S.* vol. III.

Nasir-i-Khusrau. *Diary of a Journey through Syria and Palestine* (English trans. from the Persian by G. Le Strange), in *P.P.T.S.* vol. IV.

Severus of Aschmounein. *History of the Patriarchs of Alexandria* (ed. with English trans. by B. Evetts), in *P.O.* vols. I and V.

5. ARMENIAN SOURCES

Aristaces of Lastivert. *History* (Armenian text). Venice, 1844.

Kirakos of Gantzag (Guiragos of Kantzak). *History* (extracts with French trans.), in *R.H.C.Arm.* vol. I.

Matthew of Edessa. *Chronicle* (French trans. by E. Dulaurier). Paris, 1858. (Extracts with French trans., in *R.H.C.Arm.* vol. I.)

Mekhitar of Airavanq. *History* (Armenian text). St Petersburg, 1867.

Samuel of Ani. *Chronological Tables* (French trans.), in Brosset, *Collection d'Historiens Arméniens*, vol. II.

Sebeos. *History of Heraclius* (Armenian text). Constantinople, 1851.

Sembat, Constable of Armenia. *Chronicle* (Armenian text). Paris, 1859.

Vahram Rabuni. *History of the Rupenian Dynasty* (rhyming chronicle, Armenian text with French trans.), in *R.H.C.Arm.* vol. I.

Vartan the Great. *History* (extracts with French trans.), in *R.H.C.Arm.* vol. I.

6. SYRIAC SOURCES

Anonymous Chronicle (ed. A. S. Tritton with English trans.) in 'First and Second Crusades from an anonymous Syriac chronicle', in *Journal of the Royal Asiatic Society*. London, 1933.

Anonymous Chronicle. (ed. with Latin trans. by I. Guidi), in *C.S.C.O. Scriptores Syri*, ser. III, vol. IV. (Quoted as *Anon. Guidi*.)

Bar Hebraeus, Gregory, called Abu'l Faraj. *Chronography*. Part I, *Political History* (ed. with English trans. by E. A. W. Budge), 2 vols. Oxford, 1932. Parts II and III, *Ecclesiastical History* (ed. with Latin trans. by

Bibliography

J. B. Abbeloos and T. J. Lamy), 2 vols. Louvain, 1872–7. (Extracts in
Assemani, *Bibliotheca Orientalis*, vol. II.)

Elias of Nisibin. *Chronicle* (ed. with French trans. by E. W. Brooks and J. B.
Chabot), in *C.S.C.O. Scriptores Syri*, ser. III, vols. VII and VIII.

Michael the Syrian. *Chronicle* (ed. with French trans. by J. B. Chabot), 4 vols.
Paris, 1899–1910.

'Thomas the Priest.' *Book of the Caliphs* (ed. as *Chronicon Miscellaneum ad
annum Domini 724 pertinens* with Latin trans. by E. W. Brooks), in
C.S.C.O. Scriptores Syri, ser. III, vol. IV.

7. Hebrew Sources

Anonymous of Mainz-Darmstadt. *Memorial* (ed. with German trans.), in
Neubauer and Stern, *Quellen zur Geschichte der Juden*, vol. II.

Eliezer bar Nathan. *Relation* (ed. with German trans.), in Neubauer and Stern,
Quellen zur Geschichte der Juden, vol. II.

Ephraim bar Jacob. *Relation* (ed. with German trans.), in Neubauer and Stern,
Quellen zur Geschichte der Juden, vol. II.

Martyrology of Nuremberg, Das Martyrologium des Nürnberger Memorbuches (ed.
with German trans.), in Safeld, *Quellen zur Geschichte der Juden*, vol. III.
Berlin, 1898.

Salomon bar Simeon. *Relation* (ed. with German trans.), in Neubauer and
Stern, *Quellen zur Geschichte der Juden*, vol. II.

8. Various Sources

Antiochus the Stratege. *Capture of Jerusalem by the Persians*, in Georgian (ed.
with Russian trans. by A. Marr), in *Textes et Recherches rélatifs à la Philologie
Arménienne*, vol. IX. St Petersburg, 1909. (This work was probably
originally written in Greek. The Georgian version is derived from a lost
Arabic version, of which the work mentioned in Bibliography, p. 348,
is an abridgement. A second Georgian and a slightly fuller Arabic version
have since been discovered. See P. Peeters in *Analecta Bollandiana*, vols.
XXXI and XXXVIII.)

John of Nikiu. *Chronicle* (trans. from the Ethiopic by R. H. Charles). London,
1916. (This work was originally written in Greek and translated into Arabic
and from Arabic into Ethiopic. Both the Greek and Arabic versions are
lost.)

II. MODERN WORKS

AMANN, E. and DUMAS, A. *L'Eglise au pouvoir des Laïques*, vol. VII of A. Fliche
and V. Martin, *Histoire de l'Eglise*. Paris, 1940.

AMANTOS, K. Ἱστορία τοῦ Βυζαντινοῦ Κράτους, 2 vols. Athens, 1939–48.

AMARI, M. *Storia dei Musulmani di Sicilia*, 9 vols. Florence, 1854–72.

350

Bibliography

AMÉLINEAU, E. 'La Conquête de l'Egypte par les Arabes', in *Revue Historique*, vol. CXIX. Paris, 1915.

ANDERSON, J. G. C. 'The Road-System of Eastern Asia Minor', in *Journal of Hellenic Studies*, vol. XVII. London, 1897.

ARCHER, T. A. and KINGSFORD, C. L. *The Crusades.* London, 1894.

ARNOLD, T. and GUILLAUME, A. *The Legacy of Islam.* Oxford, 1931.

BALLESTEROS Y BERETTA, A. *Historia de España*, vol. II. Barcelona, 1908.

BARKER, E. Article 'The Crusades', in *Encyclopaedia Britannica*, 11th ed.

BARTHOLD, W. Article 'Turks', in *Encyclopaedia of Islam*.

BARTHOLD, W. *Turkestan down to the Mongol Invasion.* Gibb Memorial Series. Oxford, 1928.

BAUDRILLART, A., VOGT, A. and ROUZIÈS, M. *Dictionnaire d'Histoire et de Géographie Ecclésiastique.* Paris, 1912– (in progress).

BEAUMONT, A. A. 'Albert of Aachen and the County of Edessa', in *The Crusades and other Historical Essays presented to D. C. Munro.* New York, 1928.

BECKER, C. H. Article 'Djizya', in *Encyclopaedia of Islam*.

BERCHEM, M. VAN. 'The Mosaics of the Dome of the Rock at Jerusalem and of the Great Mosque at Damascus', ch. V in Creswell, *Early Muslim Architecture*.

BLEYE, A. *Manual de Historia de España*, 2 vols. Bilbao, 1927–8.

BOGIATZIDES, I. Ἱστορικαὶ Μελέται. Thessalonica, 1932.

BOISSONNADE, P. 'Cluny, la Papauté et la première grande Croisade internationale contre les Sarrasins d'Espagne', in *Revue des Questions Historiques*, vol. CXVII. Paris, 1932.

BOISSONNADE, P. *Du nouveau sur la Chanson de Roland.* Paris, 1923.

BRÉHIER, L. *L'Eglise et l'Orient au Moyen Age: Les Croisades.* Paris, 1928.

BRÉHIER, L. and AIGRAN, A. *Grégoire le Grand, les Etats barbares et la Conquête Arabe*, vol. V of Fliche and Martin, *Histoire de l'Eglise*.

BREYSIG, T. 'Gottfried von Bouillon vor dem Kreuzzuge', in *Westdeutsche Zeitschrift für Geschichte*, vol. XVII. Trier, 1898.

BROWNE, L. E. *The Eclipse of Christianity in Asia.* Cambridge, 1933.

BUCKLER, G. *Anna Comnena.* Oxford, 1929.

BUHL, F. Articles 'Al Kuds' and 'Muhammed', in *Encyclopaedia of Islam*.

BURKITT, F. C. *Early Eastern Christianity.* London, 1904.

BURY, J. B. *History of the later Roman Empire from Arcadius to Irene*, 2 vols. London, 1889.

BURY, J. B. *Selected Essays* (ed. Temperley). Cambridge, 1930.

BURY, J. B. 'The Ceremonial Book of Constantine Porphyrogennetos', in *English Historical Review*, vol. XXII. London, 1907.

BUTLER, A. J. *The Arab Conquest of Egypt.* Oxford, 1902.

BYRNE, E. H. 'Genoese Colonies in Syria', in *The Crusades and other Historical Essays presented to D. C. Munro.* New York, 1928.

CABROL, F. and LECLERCQ, H. *Dictionnaire d'Archéologie chrétienne et de Liturgie.* Paris, 1907– (in progress).

CAETANI, L. C. *Annali dell' Islam,* 7 vols. Milan, 1905–14.

CAHEN, C. 'Diyar Bakr au temps des premiers Artuqides', in *Journal Asiatique,* vol. CCXXVII. Paris, 1935.

CAHEN, C. 'La Campagne de Mantzikert d'après les Sources Mussulmanes', in *Byzantion,* vol. IX. Brussels, 1934.

CAHEN, C. 'La première Pénétration turque en Asie Mineure', in *Byzantion,* vol. XVIII. Brussels, 1948.

CAHEN, C. *La Syrie du Nord à l'Epoque des Croisades.* Paris, 1940.

CAHEN, C. 'La Tughra Seldjucide', in *Journal Asiatique,* vol. CCXXXIV. Paris, 1943–5.

Cambridge Medieval History (planned by J. B. Bury), 8 vols. Cambridge, 1911–36.

CAUWENBERGH, E. VAN. *Les Pèlerinages expiatoires et judiciaires dans le droit communal de la Belgique au Moyen Age.* Louvain, 1922.

CAVAIGNAC, E. *Histoire du Monde.* See Gaudefroy-Demombynes.

CHALANDON, F. *Essai sur le Règne d'Alexis Comnène Ier.* Paris, 1900.

CHALANDON, F. *Histoire de la Domination normande en Italie et en Sicile,* 2 vols. Paris, 1907.

CHALANDON, F. *Histoire de la première Croisade.* Paris, 1925.

CHALANDON, F. *Les Comnènes,* t. II: *Jean II Comnène et Manuel Comnène.* Paris, 1913.

CHAMICH, M. *History of Armenia* (trans. J. Avdall), 2 vols. Calcutta, 1827.

CHEVALIER, U. *Cartulaire de Saint-Chaffre.* See Bibliography, p. 344.

CHRISTENSEN, A. *L'Iran sous les Sassanides.* Paris-Copenhagen, 1936.

COGNASSO, F. *La Genesi delle Crociate.* Turin, 1934.

COURET, A. *La Palestine sous les Empereurs grecs.* Grenoble, 1869.

COURET, A. *La Prise de Jérusalem par les Perses en 614.* Orléans, 1896.

CRESWELL, K. A. C. *Early Muslim Architecture,* 2 vols. Oxford, 1932–40.

CROZET, R. 'Le Voyage d'Urbain II et ses arrangements avec le Clergé de France', in *Revue Historique,* vol. CLXXIX. Paris, 1937.

DAVID, C. W. *Robert Curthose.* Cambridge, Mass., 1920.

DELBRÜCK, H. *Geschichte der Kriegskunst im Rahmen der politischen Geschichte,* 3 vols. Berlin, 1907.

DELEHAYE, H. *Les Origines du Culte des Martyres,* in *Analecta Bollandiana,* vol. XLIV. Brussels, 1925.

DELEHAYE, H. *Sanctus: Essai sur le Culte des Saints.* Brussels, 1927.

DER NERSESSIAN, S. *Armenia and the Byzantine Empire.* Cambridge, Mass., 1945.

DESCHAMPS, P. *Les Châteaux des Croisés en Terre Sainte:* vol. I, *Le Crac des Chevaliers.* Paris, 1934; vol. II, *La Défense du Royaume de Jérusalem.* Paris, 1939.

Bibliography

DEVREESSE, R. *Le Patriarchat d'Antioche*. Paris, 1945.

DIEHL, G. and MARÇAIS, G. *Le Monde Oriental de 395 à 1081*, vol. III of *Histoire Générale*, fondée par G. Gloetz, *Histoire du Moyen Age*. Paris, 1936.

DIEHL, C., MARÇAIS, G., OECONOMOS, L., GUILLAUD, R. and GROUSSET, R. *L'Europe Orientale de 1081 à 1453, ibid.* vol. IX. Paris, 1945.

DODU, G. *Histoire des Institutions Monarchiques dans le Royaume Latin de Jérusalem*. Paris, 1894.

DÖLGER, F. *Regesten der Kaiserurkunden des Oströmischen Reiches*, vol. II. Munich-Berlin, 1925.

DOZY, R. *Histoire des Musulmans d'Espagne* (new ed.), 3 vols. Leyden, 1932.

DUCANGE, C. DU F. *Les Familles d'Outremer* (ed. E. G. Rey). Paris, 1869.

DUCHESNE, L. *Les Premiers Temps de l'Etat Pontifical*. Paris, 1898.

DUNCALF, F. 'The Pope's Plan for the First Crusade', in *The Crusades and other Historical Essays presented to D. C. Munro*. New York, 1928.

DUVAL, R. *Histoire politique, religieuse et littéraire d'Edesse*. Paris, 1892.

DUSSAND, R. *Topographie historique de la Syrie antique et médiévale*. Paris, 1927.

DVORNIK, F. *The Photian Schism*. Cambridge, 1948.

EBERSOLT, J. *Les Sanctuaires de Byzance*. Paris, 1921.

EBERSOLT, J. *Orient et Occident*, 2 vols. Paris, 1928–9.

Encyclopaedia of Islam, 4 vols. Leyden-London, 1908–34.

ENLART, C. *Les Monuments des Croisés*, 2 vols. (with albums). Paris, 1925–8.

ERDMANN, C. *Die Entstehung des Kreuzzugsgedankens*. Stuttgart, 1935.

EVERY, G. *The Byzantine Patriarchate*. London, 1947.

FLICHE, A. *Le Règne de Philippe Ier, Roi de France*. Paris, 1912.

FLICHE, A. *L'Europe Occidentale de 888 à 1125*, vol. II of *Histoire Générale*, fondée par G. Gloetz, *Histoire du Moyen Age*. Paris, 1930.

FLICHE, A. 'Urbain II et la Croisade', in *Revue de l'Histoire de l'Eglise de France*, vol. XIII. Paris, 1927.

FLICHE, A. and MARTIN, E. V. *Histoire de l'Eglise*. See Amann and Bréhier.

FRITSCHE, E. *Islam und Christentum im Mittelalter*. Breslau, 1930.

FRYE, R. and SAYILI, A. 'Selcuklardan evvel Ontasarkta Türkler', in *Belleten*, vol. VII. Istanbul, 1946.

GAUDEFROY-DEMOMBYNES, J. and PLATONOV, S. F. *Le Monde Musulman et Byzantin jusqu'aux Croisades*, in E. Cavaignac, *Histoire de Monde*, vol. VII^1. Paris, 1931.

GAY, J. *L'Italie Méridionale et l'Empire Byzantin*. Paris, 1904.

GAY, J. *Les Papes du XIe siècle et la Chrétienté*. Paris, 1926.

GIBBON, E. *Decline and Fall of the Roman Empire* (ed. J. B. Bury), 7 vols. London, 1896.

GINDLER, P. *Graf Balduin I von Edessa*. Halle, 1901.

GOEJE, M. J. DE. *Mémoire sur la Conquête de la Syrie par les Arabes*. Leyden, 1900.

GORDLEVSKY, A. *Seldjuk Empire in Asia Minor* (in Russian). Moscow, 1941.

Bibliography

GRAEFE, E. Article 'Hakim', in *Encyclopaedia of Islam*.

GRAETZ, H. *Geschichte der Juden*, 11 vols. Leipzig, 1866–78.

GRAF, G. *Geschichte der Christlichen Arabischen Litteratur*, 2 vols. Vatican City, 1944–7.

GRANDCLAUDE, M. *Etude Critique sur les Livres des Assises de Jérusalem*. Paris, 1930.

GRÉGOIRE, H. 'Mahomet et le Monophysisme', in *Mélanges Charles Diehl*, vol. I. Paris, 1930.

GRÉGOIRE, H. 'Notes sur Anne Comnène', in *Byzantion*, vol. III. Brussels, 1926.

GROUSSET, R. *Histoire de l'Arménie des Origines à 1071*. Paris, 1947.

GROUSSET, R. *Histoire des Croisades et du Royaume Franc de Jérusalem*, 3 vols. Paris, 1934–6.

GROUSSET, R. *L'Empire du Levant*. Paris, 1946.

GRUMEL, V. 'Jérusalem entre Rome et Byzance', in *Echos d'Orient*, vol. XXXVIII. Paris, 1939.

GRUMEL, V. 'Les Patriarches d'Antioche du nom de Jean', in *Echos d'Orient*, vol. XXXII. Paris, 1933.

GRUNEBAUM, G. E. V. *Medieval Islam* (2nd imp.). Chicago, 1947.

GÜTERBOCK, C. *Der Islam im Lichte der byzantinischen Polemik*. Berlin, 1912.

HAGENMEYER, H. *Chronologie de la Première Croisade*. Paris, 1902.

HAGENMEYER, H. *Die Kreuzzugsbriefe*. See Bibliography, p. 342.

HAGENMEYER, H. *Peter der Eremite*. Leipzig, 1879. French trans. (without appendices) by Furcy Raynaud, *Le Vrai et le Faux sur Pierre l'Hermite*. Paris, 1883.

HALPHEN, L. *L'Essor de l'Europe*, vol. VI of *Peuples et Civilisations* (ed. I. Halphen and P. Sagnac), 2nd ed. Paris, 1940.

HANSEN, W. *Das Problem des Kirchenstaates in Jerusalem*. Fribourg, 1928.

HATEM, A. *Les Poèmes Epiques des Croisades*. Paris, 1932.

HEERMANN, O. *Die Gefechtsführung der abendländischen Heere im Orient in der Epoche des ersten Kreuzzuges*. Marburg, 1887.

HEFELE, C. J. *Histoire des Conciles* (trans. and ed. H. Leclercq). Paris, 1907– (in progress).

HERGENRÖTHER, J. *Photius, Patriarch von Konstantinopel*, 3 vols. Regensburg, 1887–9.

HEYD, W. *Histoire du Commerce du Levant* (trans. Furcy Raynaud; 2nd reimp.), 2 vols. Leipzig, 1936.

HILL, G. *A History of Cyprus*, vol. I. Cambridge, 1940.

HOGARTH, D. G. and MUNRO, J. A. R. *Modern and Ancient Roads in Eastern Asia Minor*. Royal Geographical Society, Supplementary Papers (new ser.), vol. III. London, 1893.

Bibliography

HOLTZMANN, W. 'Die Unionsverhandlungen zwischen Kaiser Alexios I und Papst Urban II im Jahre 1089', in *Byzantinische Zeitschrift*, vol. XXVIII. Leipzig, 1928.

HONIGMANN, E. *Die Ostgrenze des byzantinischen Reiches von 363 bis 1071*, in *Corpus Bruxellense Historiae Byzantinae*, vol. III. Brussels, 1935.

HONIGMANN, E. Articles 'al Lâdhiqiya', 'Izniq', 'Macarrat al Numan', 'Malatya', 'Marash', 'Missis', 'Orfa', 'Ortoqids' and 'Shaizar', in *Encyclopaedia of Islam*.

HOUTSMA, M. T. Article 'Seljuks', in *Encyclopaedia Britannica*, 11th ed.; articles 'Menguchek' and 'Tutush', in *Encyclopaedia of Islam*.

HUART, C. *Histoire des Arabes*, 2 vols. Paris, 1911–12.

HUBERTI, L. *Studien zur Rechtsgeschichte der Gottesfrieden und Landfrieden*. Ansbach, 1892.

HUSSEY, J. M. *Church and Learning in the Byzantine Empire*. Oxford, 1937.

IORGA, N. *Histoire de la Vie Byzantine*, 3 vols. Paris, 1934.

IORGA, N. *Histoire des Croisades*. Paris, 1924.

IORGA, N. *Les Narrateurs de la Première Croisade*. Paris, 1928.

Islam Ansiklopedisi. Istanbul, 1940–   (in progress).

JIREČEK, C. *Die Heerstrasse von Belgrad nach Constantinopel und die Balkanpässe*. Prague, 1877.

JORANSON, E. 'The Great German Pilgrimage of 1064–65', in *The Crusades and other Historical Essays presented to D. C. Munro*. New York, 1928.

JUGIE, M. *Le Schisme Byzantin*. Paris, 1941.

JUGIE, M. 'Le Schisme de Michel Cérulaire', in *Echos d'Orient*, vol. XXXV. Paris, 1937.

JUYNBOLL, T. W. Article 'Kharadj', in *Encyclopaedia of Islam*.

KLEIN, C. *Raimund von Aguilers: Quellenstudie zur Geschichte des ersten Kreuzzuges*. Berlin, 1892.

KNAPPEN, M. M. 'Robert II of Flanders in the First Crusade', in *The Crusades and other Historical Essays presented to D. C. Munro*. New York, 1928.

KÖPRÜLÜ, M. F. 'Anadolun Selcuklarî Tarihi'nin Yerli Kaynaklari', in *Belleten*, vol. VII. Istanbul, 1943.

KÖPRÜLÜ, M. F. *Les Origines de l'Empire Ottoman*. Paris, 1935.

KRAUSS, S. *Studien zur byzantinisch-jüdischen Geschichten*. Leipzig, 1914.

KREBS, F. *Zur Kritik Alberts von Aachen*. Münster, 1881.

KREY, A. C. 'A Neglected Passage in the *Gesta*', in *The Crusades and other Historical Essays presented to D. C. Munro*. New York, 1928.

KREY, A. C. 'Urban's Crusade, Success or Failure?', in *American Historical Review*, vol. LIII. New York, 1918.

KRUMBACHER, K. *Geschichte der byzantinischen Litteratur*. Munich, 1897.

KÜGLER, B. *Albert von Aachen*. Stuttgart, 1885.

KÜGLER, B. *Bohemund und Tankred*. Tübingen, 1862.

Bibliography

KÜGLER, B. *Geschichte der Kreuzzüge.* Berlin, 1891.

KÜGLER, B. 'Peter der Eremite und Albert von Aachen', in *Historische Zeitschrift*, vol. XLIV. Berlin-Munich, 1880.

KÜHNE, E. *Zur Geschichte des Fürstentums Antiochien, 1098–1130.* Berlin, 1897.

KULAKOVSKY, Y. 'Criticism of evidence in Theophanes' (in Russian), in *Vizantiiski Vremennik*, vol. XXI. St Petersburg, 1915.

KULAKOVSKY, Y. *History of Byzantium* (in Russian), 3 vols. Kiev, 1913–15.

KURAT, A. N. *Peçenek Tarihi.* Istanbul, 1937.

Kuseir Amra. Published by Kaiserliche Akademie der Wissenschaften, 2 vols. Vienna, 1907.

LABOURT, J. *De Timotheo I, Nestorianorum Patriarcha.* Paris, 1904.

LABOURT, J. *Le Christianisme dans l'Empire Perse.* Paris, 1904.

LAMMENS, H. *Etudes sur le Siècle des Ommayades.* Beirut, 1930.

LAMMENS, H. *L'Arabie Occidentale avant l'Hégire.* Beirut, 1928.

LAMMENS, H. *La Syrie: Précis Historique*, 2 vols. Beirut, 1921.

LA MONTE, J. L. *Feudal Monarchy in the Latin Kingdom of Jerusalem.* Cambridge, Mass., 1932.

LANE POOLE, S. *A History of Egypt in the Middle Ages.* London, 1925.

LANE POOLE, S. *The Mohammedan Dynasties.* Paris, 1925.

LANGLOIS, V. *Numismatique de l'Arménie au Moyen Age.* Paris, 1855.

LAURENT, J. *Byzance et les Turcs Seldjoucides jusqu'en 1081.* Nancy, 1913.

LAURENT, J. 'Byzance et les Origines du Sùltanat de Roum', in *Mélanges Charles Diehl*, vol. I. Paris, 1930.

LAURENT, J. 'Des Grecs aux Croisés: Etude sur l'histoire d'Edesse', in *Byzantion*, vol. I. Brussels, 1924.

LAURENT, J. *L'Arménie entre Byzance et l'Islam.* Paris, 1919.

LAURENT, J. 'Le Duc d'Antioche Katchatour', in *Byzantinische Zeitschrift*, vol. XXX. Leipzig, 1929–30.

LAURENT, J. 'Les Arméniens de Cilicie', in *Mélanges Schlumberger*, vol. I. Paris, 1924.

LEIB, B. *Deux Inédits Byzantins sur les Azymites.* See Bibliography, p. 343.

LEIB, B. *Rome, Kiev et Byzance à la fin du XIème siècle.* Paris, 1924.

LE STRANGE, G. *Lands of the Eastern Caliphate.* Cambridge, 1905.

LE STRANGE, G. *Palestine under the Moslems.* London, 1890.

LOEWE, H. M. J. 'The Seljuks', in *Cambridge Medieval History*, vol. IV, ch. X, B. Cambridge, 1923.

LONGNON, J. *Les Français d'Outremer au Moyen Age.* Paris, 1929.

LOT, F. *L'Art Militaire et les Armées du Moyen Age*, 2 vols. Paris, 1946.

LUCHAIRE, A. 'Les premiers Capétiens', in E. Lavisse, *Histoire de France*, vol. II, 2. Paris, 1901.

MANSELLI, R. 'Normanni d'Italia alla Prima Crociata: Boemondo d'Altavilla', in *Japigia*, vol. IX. Naples, 1940.

Bibliography

MANTEYER, G. DE. *La Provence du Ier au XIIe Siècle.* Paris, 1908.

MARICQ, A. 'Un "Comte de Brabant" et des "Brabançons" dans deux textes byzantins', in *Académie Royale de Belgique, Bulletin de la Classe des Lettres*, 5ème série, vol. XXXIV. Brussels, 1948.

MÉLY, F. DE. 'La Croix des premiers Croisés', in supplementary vol. to Riant, *Exuviae Sacrae Constantinopolitanae.* Paris, 1904.

MICHAUD, J. F. *Histoire des Croisades*, 5 vols. Paris, 1817-22.

MICHEL, A. *Amalfi und Jerusalem im griechischen Kirchenstreit. Orientalia Christiana Analecta*, no. 121. Rome, 1939.

MICHEL, A. *Humbert und Kerularios*, 2 vols. Paderborn, 1924-30.

MOELLER, C. 'Godefroid de Bouillon et l'Avouerie du Saint-Sépulcre', in *Mélanges Godfried Kurth*, vol. I. Liège, 1908.

MORAVCSIK, G. *Byzantinoturcica*, 2 vols. Budapest, 1942-3.

MORDTMANN, J. H. Articles 'Izmir' and 'Eskişehir', in *Encyclopaedia of Islam.*

MUIR, W. *The Caliphate, its Rise, Decline and Fall* (rev. ed.). Edinburgh, 1915.

MUKRIMIN HALIL (YINANÇ). Article 'Danismend', in *Islam Ansiklopedisi.*

MUKRIMIN HALIL (YINANÇ). *Türkiye Tarihi, Selcuklu Dairi*, vol. I, *Anadolun Fethi.* Istanbul, 1934.

MUNRO, D. C. 'Did the Emperor Alexius I ask for aid at the Council of Piacenza?', in *American Historical Review*, vol. XXVII. New York, 1922.

MUNRO, D. C. *The Kingdom of the Crusaders.* New York, 1936.

MUNRO, D. C. 'The Speech of Pope Urban II at Clermont', in *American Historical Review*, vol. XI. New York, 1906.

NAU, F. *Les Arabes Chrétiens de Mésopotamie et de Syrie du VIIème au VIIIème siècle.* Paris, 1933.

NICHOLSON, R. H. *Tancred.* Chicago, 1940.

NORDEN, W. *Das Papsttum und Byzanz.* Berlin, 1903.

OECONOMOS, L. *La Vie Religieuse dans l'Empire Byzantin.* Paris, 1918.

O'LEARY, DE L. *Arabia before Mohammed.* London, 1927.

O'LEARY, DE L. *A short History of the Fatimid Khaliphate.* London, 1923.

O'LEARY, DE L. *How Greek Science passed to the Arabs.* London, 1948.

OMAN, C. W. C. *A History of the Art of War in the Middle Ages* (2nd ed.), 2 vols. London, 1924.

ORMANIAN, M. *L'Eglise Arménienne.* Paris, 1910.

OSTROGORSKY, G. 'Agrarian Conditions in the Byzantine Empire', in *Cambridge Economic History of Europe*, vol. I. Cambridge, 1942.

OSTROGORSKY, G. *Geschichte des byzantinischen Staates.* Munich, 1940.

PARIS, G. 'La Chanson d'Antioche provençale et la Grande Conquista de Ultramar', in *Romania*, vols. XVII, XIX and XXII. Paris, 1888, 1890, 1893.

PAULOT, L. *Un Pape Français: Urbain II.* Paris, 1903.

PERNICE, A. *L'Imperatore Eraclio.* Florence, 1905.

PFISTER, C. *Etudes sur le Règne de Robert le Pieux.* Paris, 1885.

357

Bibliography

PIGEONNEAU, H. *Le Cycle de la Croisade et la Famille du Bouillon.* Saint-Cloud, 1877.

PIGNOT, J. H. *Histoire de l'Ordre de Cluny,* 3 vols. Autun, 1868.

PIGULEVSKAYA, N. V. *Byzantium and Iran in the Sixth and Seventh Centuries* (in Russian). Moscow, 1946.

PONTIERI, E. *Tra i Normanni nell' Italia meridionale.* Naples, 1948.

POUPARDIN, R. *Le Royaume de Bourgogne.* Paris, 1907.

PRUTZ, H. G. *Wilhelm von Tyrus.* Munich, 1883.

RAMSAY, W. M. *The Historical Geography of Asia Minor. Royal Geographical Society, Supplementary Papers,* vol. IV. London, 1890.

RAMSAY, W. M. 'The Intermixture of Races in Asia Minor', in *Proceedings of the British Academy,* vol. VII. London, 1917.

RASOVSKY, D. 'The Polovtsians' (in Russian), in *Seminarium Kondakovianum,* vols. VI–X. Prague-Belgrade, 1935–9.

REY, E. G. *Les Colonies Franques de Syrie.* Paris, 1883.

REY, E. G. 'Les Dignitaires de la Principauté d'Antioche', in *Revue de l'Orient Latin,* vol. VIII. Paris, 1900–1.

RIANT, P. *Donation de Hugues, Marquis de Toscane. Académie d'Inscriptions et de Lettres, Histoires et Mémoires,* vol. XXXI. Paris, 1884.

RIANT, P. *Expéditions et Pèlerinages des Scandinaves en Terre Sainte.* Paris, 1865.

RIANT, P. *Exuviae Sacrae Constantinopolitanae,* 2 vols. Geneva, 1877–8.

RIANT, P. *Inventaire critique des Lettres historiques des Croisades.* See Bibliography, p. 343.

RICHMOND, E. T. *The Dome of the Rock in Jerusalem.* Oxford, 1924.

RÖHRICHT, R. 'Die Pilgerfahrten nach dem Heiligen Lande vor den Kreuzzügen', in Raumer, *Historisches Taschenbuch,* vol. V, Folge 5. Leipzig, 1875.

RÖHRICHT, R. *Geschichte des ersten Kreuzzuges.* Innsbruck, 1901.

RÖHRICHT, R. *Geschichte des Königreichs Jerusalem.* Innsbruck, 1898.

RÖHRICHT, R. *Regesta Regni Hierosolymitani.* See Bibliography, p. 343.

ROSEN, V. R. *Emperor Basil the Bulgar-slayer* (in Russian). St Petersburg, 1883.

ROUSSET, P. *Les Origines et les Caractères de la première Croisade.* Neuchâtel, 1945.

RUNCIMAN, S. 'Charlemagne and Palestine', in *English Historical Review,* vol. L. London, 1935.

RUNCIMAN, S. 'The Byzantine "Protectorate" in the Holy Land', in *Byzantion,* vol. XVIII. Brussels, 1948.

RUNCIMAN, S. *The Emperor Romanus Lecapenus.* Cambridge, 1929.

RUNCIMAN, S. 'The Holy Lance found at Antioch', in *Analecta Bollandiana,* vol. LXVIII. Brussels, 1950.

SACKUR, E. *Die Cluniacenser,* 2 vols. Halle, 1892–4.

SCHLUMBERGER, G. 'Deux Chefs normands des Armées byzantines', in *Revue Historique,* vol. XVI. Paris, 1881.

Bibliography

SCHLUMBERGER, G. *L'Epopée Byzantine*, 3 vols. Paris, 1896–1905.

SCHLUMBERGER, G. *Numismatique de l'Orient Latin*, 2 vols. Paris, 1878–82.

SCHLUMBERGER, G. *Récits de Byzance et des Croisades*, 2 vols. Paris, 1917–22.

SCHLUMBERGER, G. *Sigillographie de l'Empire Byzantin*. Paris, 1884.

SCHLUMBERGER, G. *Sigillographie de l'Orient Latin* (continued by F. Chalandon and completed by A. Blanchard). Paris, 1943.

SCHLUMBERGER, G. *Un Empereur Byzantin, Nicéphore Phocas*. Paris, 1890.

SIMON, G. *Der Islam und die Christliche Verkündigung*. Gütersloh, 1920.

SOBERNHEIM, M. Article 'Ibn Ammar', in *Encyclopaedia of Islam*.

STARR, J. 'Byzantine Jewry on the eve of the Arab Conquest', in *Journal of the Palestine Oriental Society*, vol. XV. Jerusalem, 1935.

STARR, J. *The Jews in the Byzantine Empire, 641–1204*. Athens, 1939.

STEVENSON, W. B. 'Islam in Syria and Egypt' and 'The First Crusade', in *Cambridge Medieval History*, vol. V, chs. VI and VII. Cambridge, 1926.

STEVENSON, W. B. *The Crusaders in the East*. Cambridge, 1907.

SYBEL, H. VON. *Geschichte des ersten Kreuzzuges* (2nd ed.). Leipzig, 1881.

TER MIKELIAN, A. *Die Armenische Kirche in ihren Beziehungen zur Byzantinischen Kirche*. Leipzig, 1892.

TER MINASSIANTZ, A. *Die Armenische Kirche in ihren Beziehungen zu den Syrischen Kirchen*. Leipzig, 1904.

THIBAUDET, A. *Cluny*. Paris, 1928.

THUROT, C. 'Etudes Critiques sur les Historiens de la Première Croisade', in *Revue Historique*, vol. I. Paris, 1876.

TOMASCHEK, W. *Zur historischen Topographie von Kleinasien im Mittelalter. Sitzungsberichte der Kaiserlichen Akademie der Wissenschaften, Philos.-hist. Classe*, vol. CXXIV. Vienna, 1891.

TOURNEBIZE, F. *Histoire politique et religieuse de l'Arménie*. Paris, 1910.

TRITTON, A. S. *The Caliphs and their non-Muslim Subjects*. Oxford, 1930.

USENER, H. *Der Heilige Tychon, Sonderbare Heilige*, no. 1. Leipzig-Berlin, 1907.

USPENSKY, F. I. *History of the Crusades* (in Russian). St Petersburg, 1900.

VACANT, A. and MANGENOT, E. *Dictionnaire de Théologie Catholique*. Paris, 1899– (in progress).

VAILHÉ, S. 'La Prise de Jérusalem par les Perses en 614', in *Revue de l'Orient Chrétien*, vol. VI. Paris, 1901.

VAILHÉ, S. 'Les Juifs et la Prise de Jérusalem en 614', in *Echos d'Orient*, vol. XII. Paris, 1907.

VAISSÈTE, DOM. *Histoire de Languedoc* (ed. A. Molinier), 10 vols. Toulouse, 1874.

VASILIEV, A. A. *Byzantium and the Arabs* (in Russian), 2 vols. St Petersburg, 1900–2. Vol. I trans. H. Grégoire and E. M. Canard as *Byzance et les Arabes*, in *Corpus Bruxellense Historiae Byzantinae*, vol. I. Brussels, 1935.

Bibliography

VASILIEV, A. A. *Histoire de l'Empire Byzantin*, 2 vols. Paris, 1932.

VASILIEV, A. A. 'The Opening Stages of the Anglo-Saxon Immigration to Byzantium in the Eleventh Century', in *Seminarium Kondakovianum*, vol. IX. Prague-Belgrade, 1937.

VASILIEVSKY, V. G. *Works* (in Russian), vol. I, containing *Byzantium and the Petchenegs*, and *The Varango-Russian and the Varango-English Company in Constantinople*. St Petersburg, 1908.

VERLINDEN, C. 'Robert Ier, Le Frison, Comte de Flandre', in *Werken mitgegeven door de Faculteit der Wijsbegeerde en Letteren te Gent*. Ghent, 1935.

VILLEY, M. *La Croisade: Essai sur la Formation d'une Théorie juridique*, vol. VI of H. X. Aquillière, *L'Eglise et l'Etat au Moyen Age*. Paris, 1942.

VINCENT, H. and ABEL, R. *Jérusalem*, vol. II, *Jérusalem Nouvelle* (2 fasc.). Paris, 1914–26.

WELLHAUSEN, J. *Das Arabische Reich und sein Sturz*. Berlin, 1902.

WIET, G. *L'Egypte Arabe*, vol. IV of C. Hanataux, *Histoire de la Nation Egyptienne*. Paris, 1937.

WILKEN, F. *Geschichte der Kreuzzüge*, 7 vols. Leipzig, 1807–32.

WITTEK, P. 'Byzantinisch-seldschukische Beziehungen', in *Ostersche Genootschap in Nederland, Verlag van het achste Congress*. Leyden, 1936.

WITTEK, P. 'Deux Chapitres de l'Histoire des Turcs de Roum', in *Byzantion*, vol. XI. Brussels, 1936.

WITTEK, P. 'Le Sultan de Rum', in *Annuaire de l'Institut de Philologie et d'Histoire orientales et slaves*, vol. VI. Brussels, 1938.

WITTEK, P. *The Rise of the Ottoman Empire*. London, 1938.

WOLFF, T. *Die Bauernkreuzzüge des Jahres 1096: ein Beitrag zur Geschichte des ersten Kreuzzuges*. Tübingen, 1891.

YAKUBOVSKY, A. 'The Seldjuk Invasion and the Turcomans in the Eleventh Century' (in Russian), in *Proceedings of the Academy of Science of the U.S.S.R.* Moscow, 1936.

YEWDALE, R. B. *Bohemund the First*. New York, 1917.

YINANÇ. See Mukrimin Halil.

ZETTERSTEEN, K. V. Articles 'Sukman ibn Ortok' and 'Suleiman ben Qutulmush', in *Encyclopaedia of Islam*.

ZLATARSKY, V. N. *History of the Bulgarian Empire* (in Bulgarian), 3 vols. in 4. Sofia, 1918–40.

INDEX

Note. Names of peoples, such as Arabs, Greeks, Turks, Franks, Frenchmen, Italians, of states, such as Byzantium or the Caliphate, or of countries such as Syria, Palestine, Egypt or Asia Minor which appear very frequently in the text are not included in this index.

Index

Index

Flavigny, Abbot of, 45
Fleury, *see* Hugh
Flowers, Gate of, at Jerusalem, 280
Fontevrault, Order of, 113
Fostat, 19; *see* Cairo
France, 43, 46, 85, 88, 91–2, 101–2, 104–5,
106–12, 113, 122, 134, 163, 164–8, 169–70,
184; king of, 339
Francis-Lambert of Monteil, lord of
Peyrins, 160–1
Frederick of Zimmern, 132
Fréjus, 88
Frisians, 199
Fromond, pilgrim, 45 n.
Frutholf of St Michelsberg, 313.
Fulcher of Chartres, historian, 107–8,
147 n., 165, 170, 189, 201, 210, 302, 323,
324, 329, 330, 336
Fulcher, poet, 382
Fulk Nerra, Count of Anjou, 46
Fulk of Chartres, 210, 233, 235 n.
Fulk of Orléans, 131–2

Gabitha, 16
Gabriel, lord of Melitene, 75, 177, 195–6,
202, 206, 320–2
Gaeta, 55–6
Galilee, 31, 304, 306, 312, 313, 316, 325–6
Galilee, Sea of, 16, 310, 317
Gantzag, *see* Kirakos
Gap, *see* Isoard
Gargano, Monte, 44, 46, 56
Gargar, 205; *see also* Constantine
Garigliano, river, 88
Gascony, 89
Gaston of Béarn, 160, 208, 277, 282–3
Gaul, 5; Church of, 86
Gaza, 15
Gebze, 152 n.
Gehenna, Valley of, 279
Geldemar, *see* Carpenel
Geneviève, Saint, 42
Genèvre, Col de, 160
Genoa, Genoese, 112, 219, 238, 251, 275,
282, 284, 332, 333, 337
Geoffrey of Esch, 147, 150
Geoffrey of Rossignuolo, 155, 156
Geoffrey the Lombard, 332
Geoffrey, *see* Burel; Guerin
George, St, church of, at Lydda, 277;
Gate of, at Antioch, 216, 226, 228, 234

George, *see* Palaeologus
Georgia, 60, 294
Gerard of Avesnes, 308, 317
Gerard of Roussillon, 160
Germanicea, *see* Marash
Germany, 51, 57, 75, 95, 100–1, 114, 121–3
126, 128–31, 134–40, 318
Gethsemane, 38
Ghassan, Banū, Arab tribe, 14, 16, 28
Ghaznavid dynasty, 59–60
Ghent, 166; *see also* Baldwin of Alost
Ghuzz Turks, 60, 62, 124
Gibraltar, Straits of, 47
Gilbert of Tournai, 286
Gilon, poet, 332
Girard, Bishop of Ariano, 155
Gislebert, Bishop of Lisieux, 115 n.
Glaber, Radulph, chronicler, 46
Glycas, historian, 328
Godfrey II, Duke of Lower Lorraine, 145
Godfrey of Bouillon, Duke of Lower
Lorraine, 'Advocatus Sancti Sepulchri',
joins Crusade, 112, 145–7; blackmails
Jews, 136, 137; journey to Constan-
tinople, 147–9; at Constantinople,
149–54, 158–9; at Nicaea, 177–9; at
Dorylaeum, 184–6; in Anatolia, 189, 190;
at Antioch, 217, 220, 227, 233, 244, 247,
250–1; at Turbessel, 255–6; at Azaz, 257;
discussion about policy, 258, 261, 262;
moves towards south, 270–1; at siege of
Jerusalem, 280, 282–3, 285–6; 'Advocatus
Sancti Sepulchri', 291–314; death, 314–
16, 318. Other references, 140, 164 n.,
166, 175 n., 325, 326, 331, 336–40
Godfrey the Chamberlain, 315
Godvere (Godhild) of Tosni, wife of
Baldwin of Boulogne, 147, 192, 198,
200
Göksü, river, 197
Golden Horn, 149, 150–1
Gorizia, Count of, 45
Goslar, 88
Gottschalk, 114, 123, 137, 140–1
Grado, Patriarch of, *see* Dominicus
Grados, 90
Graindor of Douai, 332
Grant-Mesnil family, 165; *see also* Aubrey;
Hugh; William
Gray, *see* Warner
Greece, 74

367

Index

Index

Kedron, brook, 279
el-Kelb, Nahr, *see* Dog River
Kerbogha, atabeg of Mosul, 78, 203, 210, 213, 215, 229, 230–3, 235–8, 241, 246–9, 251, 254, 258, 265, 267, 341
Khazars, 59
Khorassan, 60, 130, 202
Kiev, *see* Anne; Praxedis
Kilij Arslan, Seldjuk Sultan, 77, 128, 177–82, 184–6, 189
Kirakos of Gantzag, 335
Kogh Vasil, Armenian prince, 195–7, 202, 204
Kolskeggr, pilgrim, 47
Konz-Saarburg, *see* Dudo
Koritsa, 156 n.
Krak des Chevaliers, 267
Kurds, 73, 78, 269

La Fère, *see* Thomas
Lagery, *see* Urban II
Lagman Gudrödsson, King of Man, 47
Lahore, 59
Lambert, Count of Clermont, 238
Lambert, pilgrim, 126
Lampron, 196
Lance, Holy, relic, 241–6, 247, 253–4, 273–4, 284, 291, 328
Langres, 41
Languedoc, 164 n.
Laodicea, 194
Lattakieh (Laodicea in Syria), 30, 49, 75, 216, 228 n., 255–6, 268, 270, 281, 289 n., 300–3, 307, 318–19, 323
Lebanon, Lebanese, 5, 13, 21, 36, 51, 267–8, 275, 324
Le Bourg, *see* Baldwin II
Le Forez, *see* Raymond
Leisingen, *see* Emich, Count of
Leitha, river, 147
Leo I, Pope, 8
Leo IX, Pope, 57, 58, 84, 96–7
Leon, 89
Le Puits, *see* Everard
Le Puy, 85, 106, 108, 110; *see also* Adhemar, Bishop of; Bertrand
Lesbos, 77, 194
Leucas, 299
Leuce, 184, 186 n.
Liège, 146
Lietbert, Bishop of Cambrai, 46, 49, 75

Limoges, 110, 111
Lisieux, *see* Gislebert, Bishop of
Litani, river, 307
Litold, Flemish knight, 286
Loire, river, 110
Lombardy, Lombards, 56, 96, 111, 306
Lorraine, 46, 94, 114, 146, 147, 184
Lower Lorraine, 145–6, 150; *see* Godfrey, Duke of
Lucca, 228 n.; Chronicle of, 338–9
Luke, Saint, 40, 49
Lydda, 277
Lyons, 106, 107

Maarat an-Numan, 252, 259–61, 267, 334
Maaratha, 334
Mabilla de Hauteville, 238–9
Macedonia, 74, 155
Macedonian dynasty, 54
Macrembolitissa, *see* Eudocia
Mahmud, Ghaznavid prince, 59–60
Mahomerie, la, castle, 228
Mahomet, Prophet, 3, 14–15
Mahomet ibn-Ali, *see* Almanzor
Main, river, 139
Mainz, 46, 136, 138–9; *see also* Rothard, Archbishop of
Maiolus, Saint, Abbot of Cluny, 106
al-Majdal, plain, 296
Malavilla, 124 n.
Malecorne, *see* Arnulf
Male Couronne, herald, 233
Malik Ghazi Gümüshtekin, Danishmend Emir, 320, 322
Malik Shah, Seldjuk Sultan, 64–5, 67, 75, 76, 77, 78, 213
Malines, 241
Malmesbury, *see* William
Malregard, castle, 219
Mamas, Saint, 41
Mamistra (Missis, Mopsuesta), 73, 199–201, 224 n., 319
Man, *see* Lagman Gudrödsson
Manasses, Archbishop of Reims, 274, 333
Mangjaloz, 148
Manuel, general, 19
Manuel, *see* Butumites
Manzikert, 60, 63, 64, 66, 75
Marash (Germanicea), 30, 190, 192–3, 195, 200, 202, 215; *see also* Gregory, Bishop of
Marata, 215

370

Index

Mardaites, 21
Maria of Alania, Empress, 68–70
Marianus, *see* Argyrus; Mavrocatacalon
Mark, Saint, 273–4
Marmora, Sea of, 76, 77, 128, 149, 152, 173
Marne, river, 168
Maronites, 13
Marqiye, 270
Martin I, Pope, 42
Martina, Empress, 17, 18
Marturano, *see* Arnulf, Bishop of
Mary, St, of the Latins, church at Jerusalem, 29
Mary, Virgin, 40, 49–50, 166, 244
Masyaf, 269
Matthew of Edessa, historian, 205, 334–5
Matthew, Saint, 166
Matthew, Seneschal, 315
Matilda, Countess of Tuscany, 101
Maurienne, 41
Mavrocatacalon, Marianus, 167
Mavrocatacalon, Nicholas, admiral, 117–18, 167
Maximus the Confessor, Saint, 13
Mecca, 13, 33, 36
Medina, 13, 19
Mekhitar of Airavanq, historian, 335
Melfi, 56; Councils of, 57, 102
Melissenus, Nicephorus, usurper, 69–70
Melitene, 61, 75, 177, 195, 202–3, 319, 321–2; *see also* Gabriel, lord of
Melk, 48
Melkites, 9
Melun, *see* William the Carpenter
Menbij, 246
Menguchek, Turkish Emir, 65, 72
Meram, 189
Mercury, Saint, 248
Mersin, 199
Meryem, Queen of Persia, 10
Mesopotamia, 7, 27, 31, 215, 230
Metz, 139
Meuse, river, 114, 146
Michael III, Emperor, 32 n.
Michael VI, Stratioticus, Emperor, 54
Michael VII, Ducas, Emperor, 61, 65–8, 73–4, 98–9
Michael, Jacobite Patriarch of Antioch, 20, 335
Michael, Saint, Archangel, 44, 46, 56; *see also* Gargano, Monte

Michael, *see* Cerularius
Milan, 96
Mirdasite dynasty, 34
Moabites, 24
Moawiya, Caliph, 25
Monoergism, 12
Monophysite heretics, 7–9, 11–12, 14; *see also* Jacobite Church
Monothelete heretics, 13
Montaigu, *see* Conon
Monteil family, 284; *see also* Adhemar; Francis-Lambert; William-Hugh
Montgomery, Count of, 165
Montier-en-Der, 43, 45
Montjoie, 278
Montpelier, *see* William
Montreuil, *see* William
Moors, 299
Morellus, secretary, 317–18
Mortagne, Count of, 165
Moschus, John, 4–5
Moselle, river, 139
Moson, *see* Wiesselburg
Mosul, 29, 30, 31, 78, 203, 249
Mosynopolis, 117
Moulins, 106
Munqidhite dynasty, 267
al-Mustali, Caliph, 229, 265

Nablus, 295
Nangis, *see* Bartolf of
Naples, 51, 55–6
Naqoura, 276
Narbonne, 87, 89; *see* Peter
Nasir-i-Khusrau, 37
Nativity, Church of the, at Bethlehem, 10, 278, 283, 326
Navarre, 89–90
Nazareth, 24, 31, 50, 304
Neckar, river, 122, 123
Negeb, 304
Nekhavend, battle, 18
Neocaesarea (Niksar), 61, 322
Nesle, *see* Drogo
Nestorian heretics, 7–11, 13–14, 20, 27, 28, 59
Nestorius, Patriarch of Constantinople, 7
Netherlands, 199
Neuss, 140
Nicaea, 68–9, 76, 77, 128, 130–1, 152 n., 169, 173–83, 184, 186 n., 194, 197, 218, 333

371

Index

Nicephorus II, Phocas, Emperor, 30–1, 32–3

Nicephorus III, Boteniates, Emperor, 68–9, 74, 99; *see* Bryennius; Melissenus

Nicetas, governor of Bulgaria, 122–6, 148

Nicholas I, Pope, 84

Nicholas II, Pope, 57

Nicholas III, Patriarch of Constantinople, 102; *see* Mavrocatacalon

Nicholas, Saint, 166

Nicomedia, 68, 76, 128, 152, 168, 183

Nicusus, Armenian, 203

Nile, river, 24

Nîmes, 111

Nineveh, 11

Nish, 117, 122–3, 125–6, 148

Nisibin, 31

Nitra, 140

Nogent, *see* Guibert

Norfolk, *see* Guader, Earl

Normandy, 56, 86, 90

Normandy, Duke of, 46; *see also* Richard; Robert; William I

Norsemen, 43, 47–8, 62, 114

Norway, Norwegians, 47

Nosairi mountains, 32, 268

Ochrida, 117, 170

Odilo, Abbot of Cluny, 89–90

Odo, Bishop of Bayeux, 112, 165

Odo, Count of Déols, 86; *see* Urban II

Odo, the Good Marquis, 155

Oedenburg, 123, 148

Olaf Tryggvason, King of Norway, 47

Olaf II, King of Norway, 47

Oliba, Bishop of Vich, 86

Olives, Mount of, 4, 38, 281, 284

Olivola, Bishop of, 45

Omar, Caliph, 3–4, 15

Omar, lord of Azaz, 256–7

Ommayad dynasty, 25–7, 279

Onopnicles, river, 216, 219

Orange, *see* Rambald, Count of; William, Bishop of

Orel, 114

Origen, 39 n.

Orléannais, 114

Orléans, 324

Orontes, river, 16, 30, 31, 192, 213, 215, 216, 220, 237, 251, 257, 267, 319

Ortoq, governor of Jerusalem, 76, 78, 222, 265, 280

Ortoqid family, 209, 230, 265; *see* Ilghazi, prince; Soqman, prince

Oshin, Armenian prince, 73, 196, 199

Ostia, 100

Otranto, Terra d', 154

Otto I, western emperor, 45

Otto II, western emperor, 85

Ouigour Turks, 59

Oxia, 320

Oxus, river, 18

Palaeologus, George, 182

Palli, Cape, 144

Paphlagonia, 55, 77

Paris, 88; *see also* Robert

Parma, *see* John, Bishop of

Partzapert, 196

Paschal II. Pope, 306–7

Paul, St, Gate of, at Antioch, 216, 217

Paulician heretics, 156, 192

Pazouni, 196 n.

Peasant, *see* 'Fat Peasant'

Peeldelau, Radulph, 149

Pelecanum, 152, 159, 173, 177, 181

Pella, 17

Pendik, 152 n.

Pentapolis, 18

Pera, 150–1

Persia, Persians, 5, 7, 9, 10–14, 16, 18, 20, 26, 59, 60, 213, 215, 230

Petchenegs, 63, 71, 77, 104, 124–5, 150–1, 156, 161, 162, 180

Peter III, Patriarch of Antioch, 97

Peter Bartholomew, discovers Holy Lance, 241–6; subsequent visions, 253–4, 257, 258, 259, 260, 273; dies in ordeal, 274. Other references, 290, 293, 336

Peter Desiderius, 273, 284

Peter of Aulps, 191, 239

Peter of Castillon, 191–2

Peter of Narbonne, Bishop of Albara, 257–8, 260, 261, 271, 293

Peter of Roaix, 192

Peter of Stenay, 147, 198

Peter, Saint, 8, 57, 213, 244, 256, 273, 306; Cathedral of, at Antioch, 214–5, 237, 242, 245, 253–8; church of, at Rome, 89

Peter the Hermit, preaches, 113–5; leads

372